ROSE

Portrait of Dame Rose Heilbron DBE by June Mendoza.
Reproduced by kind permission of the Masters of the Bench of the
Honourable Society of Gray's Inn.

About the Author

Hilary Heilbron is the only child of the late Rose Heilbron and herself a barrister and Queen's Counsel. Having practised as a commercial litigator for most of her career, she now focuses principally on international arbitration, sitting regularly as an international arbitrator all over the world and also acting as an advocate in both international arbitrations and court-related arbitration cases. She lives in London.

Rose QC

The Remarkable Story of Rose Heilbron: Trailblazer and Legal Icon

Hilary Heilbron

•HART•

OXFORD • LONDON • NEW YORK • NEW DELHI • SYDNEY

HART PUBLISHING

Bloomsbury Publishing Plc

Kemp House, Chawley Park, Cumnor Hill, Oxford, OX2 9PH, UK

HART PUBLISHING, the Hart/Stag logo, BLOOMSBURY and the Diana logo are
trademarks of Bloomsbury Publishing Plc

First published in Great Britain 2019

Copyright © Hilary Heilbron, 2019

First printed in 2012 (hardback) as *Rose Heilbron: The Story of England's
First Woman Queen's Counsel and Judge*

Hilary Heilbron has asserted her right under the Copyright, Designs and
Patents Act 1988 to be identified as Author of this work.

A catalogue record for this book is available from the British Library.

ISBN: 978-1-50993-363-1

Typeset by Compuscript Ltd, Shannon
Printed and bound in Great Britain by CPI Group (UK) Ltd, Croydon CR0 4YY

MIX
Paper from
responsible sources
FSC® C013604

With thanks to Carcanet Press Ltd
for permission to reproduce an extract
from work by Robert Graves, which first
appeared in the *Sunday Times*

To find out more about our authors and books visit www.hartpublishing.co.uk.
Here you will find extracts, author information, details of forthcoming events
and the option to sign up for our newsletters.

For my Mother and Father

Deeply loved and greatly missed

Foreword

by Cherie Blair QC

As a child growing up in my grandmother's house in Liverpool there was one name that always made my grandmother excited: Rose Heilbron QC. When Rose Heilbron was arguing a case before a jury at the Liverpool Assizes my grandmother would follow her cases avidly, sometimes even from the public gallery. "She is simply the best" she would say "and so beautiful too". So Rose Heilbron became a role model for me and an example of what a Liverpool girl could achieve in the law. That was only reinforced when in the late 1960s, in a TV series called 'Justice', the glamorous Margaret Lockwood played a female barrister loosely based on Rose. My grandmother and I watched religiously every week. So when the time came for me to decide what I was going to do with my life, it was no surprise that I reckoned the law was a good place for a girl from Liverpool.

However I was shocked to then discover that the reason Rose was so famous was that she was so rare, in 1949 the first woman ever to become a QC, and she remained the *only* practising woman QC even in the mid-1960s. When, in 1974, she was finally appointed to the High Court Bench at the age of 60 by a Labour Lord Chancellor, the overwhelming consensus was that had she been a man, she would have been appointed ten years earlier. This was important because when you are appointed a judge in the High Court it's like being the new girl at school and you have to work your way up over a number of years to get to the next level, a Court of Appeal judge. So it wasn't until 1988 that Elizabeth Butler-Sloss became the first woman to be appointed to the Court of Appeal, one of the few legal firsts Rose did not achieve. Even today when over 50% of the new entrants to the legal profession are women, there is still a glass ceiling in the judiciary with only around 29% of judges being women. But thanks to inspirational pioneers like Rose, the glass is slowly breaking.

But it wasn't her novelty that made Rose's career at the Bar such a glittering success. She broke the mould because she was a brilliant advocate and a master of her brief. There were other women advocates by the 1970s, but her melodious voice and charm belied those who, even when I was first a law student in 1972, would claim women were not suited to being advocates because their weak voices would not carry in Court! She also proved that you could not only be a great advocate but also a real woman, not just someone imitating a man, for at the same time she was a happy wife and mother of her daughter Hilary, who herself became only the 29th woman QC in 1987—not a great deal of progress for women in 38 years.

Rose's daughter gives us in this book a personal and warm insight into Rose, the advocate, with a comprehensive account of a glittering variety of her legal cases from the notorious to the more mundane. But above all she gives us Rose, the woman, the brilliant and attractive woman who rose above the petty rules of the profession that impeded her career, the working mum who always found time for her family and who was a caring and much-loved employer to both her domestic and professional staff, and the feminist—in the true sense of the word—who cared about equality and justice for other women and who, throughout her public life, spoke up for a woman's right to achieve what men take for granted—a fulfilling career and a wonderful family life.

Preface

Writing any biography is a difficult task: writing a biography of one's mother is a daunting one. I hope that any lack of objectivity caused by such a close relationship between writer and subject is offset by my familiarity with it.

I had always known that my Mother was famous, but the research for this book has been a revelation to me. In many ways the most interesting period of her life was before I was born and when I was a small child and thus too young to understand the implications of her career and fame. My memories of such times were until recently, therefore, largely the product of family anecdotes.

The phenomenal press coverage she received not only in England, but throughout the world, particularly in the early years of her career, would be envied by any celebrity of the modern age. Yet such publicity occurred at a time when professional rules debarred my Mother from even speaking to the press, let alone giving an interview. Her fame stemmed not only from the fact that she was a pioneer with an impressive list of firsts in the law; but also because of her brilliance as a lawyer and skill as an advocate in her many famous cases. She was contemporaneously described as a 'Modern Portia' or 'Portia' accompanied by a variety of different adjectives, after the character in Shakespeare's play 'The Merchant of Venice', reflecting the fact that it was as an inspiring female advocate of the modern era that she made her name.

She captured the public fascination with a professional working woman who was also a wife and mother, a rarity in the middle of the twentieth century. Her youth and beauty were intoxicating additives to the novelty of her position. Above all, the publicity she received was universally laudatory not only of her abilities, but also of her as a person.

It is as a person, of course, that I knew her best. In many ways she had an uncomplicated personality which belied her public persona. She was always smiling and with an infectious laugh. She loved her home and her family. Home was the bedrock of her life and particularly my Father, who with his common touch and wonderful sense of humour and fun, coupled with his enduring love and devotion, was able to keep her feet firmly on the ground. She was passionate about the things she did and showed great warmth towards people.

She was incredibly diffident, at least in the early years of her career, and equally modest and humble as to her achievements.

As an early product of a working mother, before this became commonplace, I felt no deprivation from the fact that my Mother went out to work and I gained much. I had no conception of a non-working mother. Yet I did not feel that I lost out because she was not there every minute of the day. There seemed to be plenty of times when she was there and, more particularly, she was there when I needed her—in the evenings, at weekends and in holiday time and I had a very normal childhood. In fact I saw more of her than I would have done had I gone to boarding school. Life as a barrister, because of the legal terms, gave her long holidays which tended to coincide with school holidays. She worked hard of an evening and weekends, but as I got older I had homework. In many ways it was a privileged childhood, because I met people and had opportunities I would not otherwise have had, had my Mother not been so famous. While from an early age I had sensed that my Mother was special because people wanted to meet her: to me she was special because she was my Mother.

I have been faced with the difficult judgement of how to do justice to such a remarkable career and life, of interest not just to lawyers, but to a wider audience as well. A litany of her cases, while they are interesting in themselves, only touches a part of this kaleidoscope. She was a barrister who happened to be a woman and not a woman who happened to be a barrister. She never set out to blaze a trail. She wanted to become a successful barrister. But it is undoubtedly true that it was because she achieved so much as a woman, which had never been achieved before, that she hit the headlines and became a household name, inspiring so many others to follow in her path.

I was prompted to write this biography in part by the fact that so few of the current generation, men and women, know of her accomplishments. Some will have known her, others will have heard of her, but many, especially those born towards the end of her professional life or after, may know little, if anything, about her.

Today the latest available statistics from the Bar Standards Board (2018) show just over a third of barristers practising at the independent Bar in England & Wales are women (4,617 women out of a total of 13,171) of which 275 are Queen's Counsel (approximately 16% of the total of 1,695). Just over half those called to the Bar in 2017–18 were women (694 out of 1,351). Particularly encouraging is the fact that 56% of tenancies given to young lawyers in Barristers chambers in 2017–8, the first step on the legal ladder for a Barrister, were given to women. As for the judiciary, the figures (April 2018) show that women represent 29% of court judges, including 24% of the Court of Appeal and the same percentage of the High Court Judges. Since then more women have been appointed to the senior bench. The Supreme Court now has three female Justices including its first female President, Baroness Hale.

Yet my Mother, as a renowned advocate, one of the two first women King's Counsel (later Queen's Counsel) in 1949, first woman Recorder in 1956 and second woman High Court Judge in 1974, was the one who first lit the torch which current and future female barristers and judges carry and will continue to carry in years to come. She paved the way, not in any strident feminist manner, but simply by getting on with the job and in so doing helping to promote the role of women. As one very distinguished female judge from a different part of the world wrote to me on reading an earlier edition of this biography: "*Your mother was a role model and inspiration to me and women practicing law all over the world.*"

Things which today we take for granted were struggles to be overcome in her day. Most of the reforms which she advocated in relation to legal and women's issues have, after many years, come to fruition and this would have given her great satisfaction. It was in many ways a life of a different era: a time of capital punishment, of rations, when women always wore hats and where deference was part of common courtesy.

I hope that this biography, set in its historical context, will be a testament to her remarkable life, enabling others to learn about her and to recognise the contribution she has made not only to the progress of women in the law, in particular at the Bar and on the Bench, but also indirectly to working and professional women generally. Above all, I sincerely hope that it will be of interest to both men and women and to lawyers and non-lawyers alike.

I have been lucky to have been able to tap into many valuable written sources. My Mother was a hoarder. She left me a vast assortment of material including diaries, press cuttings, letters and speeches as well as her own contemporaneous notes from which, together with my own knowledge and that of my late Father, I have been able to draw upon. It is only in relation to her childhood that there is limited material. Being a barrister myself has, of course, given me added insight. I have endeavoured to make the biography more digestible to the reader by writing it in the third person, even if simultaneously creating a rather strange experience for myself.

I had always hoped that my Mother would write her autobiography. She had been asked to do so many times. But even on retirement she seemed disinclined to do so, possibly by then due to her age. She was always a very private person and I have tried to respect that in this book. Nonetheless she had always indicated to me that there was a story to be written and wanted me to be the beneficiary of it. I hope and believe that she would have been pleased that I have written it and have done so entirely by myself and, more importantly, I hope that she would have been pleased with what I have written.

A POSTSCRIPT

2019 marks the centenary of the Sex Disqualification (Removal) Act 1919, legislation which entitled women to enter the professions for the first time in the United Kingdom, a reform long overdue.

My Mother was in the vanguard of the consequent progression towards female emancipation in the professional workplace, in her case the law, which such legislation enabled. She was also a very strong and vocal proponent of the enhanced role of women generally in society. The obstacles faced by such pioneers as my Mother over the last century are difficult to comprehend in today's environment. Moreover, the liberation of women from entrenched Victorian attitudes to enable them to achieve success in the professions has been a slow process.

It is fitting therefore that the relaunch of this biography of my Mother in paperback should coincide with the above centenary. Her own contribution as a trailblazer and legal icon has been recognised over the years in many ways, but most recently as the face of the 100 Years' Project, celebrating 100 years of women in the law.[1]

My Mother would undoubtedly have been delighted to have seen the progress and advances women have made in recent years, particularly in her own profession of the law. What were merely aspirations in her day have become expectations and entitlements, but I am confident that had she been alive today, she would not have been complacent as to women's accomplishments and would have recognised that the journey which was started 100 years ago still has some way to go.

---

[1] https://first100years.org.uk/

Acknowledgements

The gestation of this book over several years was a solitary exercise shared only with my Father, who gave me much-needed encouragement to undertake the task. But once it metamorphasised into a completed manuscript I received unstinting support and invaluable input from several friends, in particular Christopher and Judith Rose, Diana Kerr and Peter Butler, each with a different perspective and insight. I owe a great debt to Richard Hart who had the courage to take on this biography—and me—and to his wonderful team, including Jo Ledger, Mel Hamill and Jane Parker and more recently to Sinead Moloney. I am also much indebted to Cherie Blair QC for so kindly writing the Foreword to this book.

Any factual errors in this biography are entirely mine and the unintentional consequence of the historical nature of the material upon which I have relied.

Contents

1

Childhood

ROSIE HEILBRON WAS born in Liverpool on Wednesday, 19 August 1914. It was not the most auspicious of times to enter this world. Two weeks earlier England had declared war on Germany: a war which was to engulf large parts of the globe for the next four years. Her parents, Max and Nellie Heilbron, undoubtedly overjoyed at her birth must have wondered, like many other parents at that time, what the future held for their baby daughter in a world torn apart by conflict. Yet it was the experiences of this ghastly and bloody war, including the use of female labour in areas hitherto the exclusive domain of men, which laid the foundations for the transformation of Edwardian England into a more egalitarian, although still unequal, society for women and others alike and from which young Rosie ultimately benefitted. In the years to come Rosie Heilbron, later known as Rose, was to blaze a trail for women in the law and become an icon of her day.

At the time of her birth in 1914 no one could have predicted her success, for the stirrings towards female emancipation were in their infancy. Women still did not have the vote, despite an aggressive suffragette movement. This was not achieved, and then only for women over 30, until the Representation of the People Act 1918. The Act enfranchised over 8 million women in Britain giving them just under 40 per cent of the national vote, but full enfranchisement had to wait until 1928. It was only at the end of the nineteenth century that legislation had enabled a married woman to enter into a contract which bound her personally and to hold independent property.[1] A typical female employee received around one half of the wages of a man in both manual and non-manual occupations.

---

[1] In particular the Married Women's Property Act 1882 and subsequent legislation.

Women were still not able to enter many of the professions, including the law. In 1904 Christabel Pankhurst, one of the leading suffragettes, had been refused permission to apply to become a barrister. In 1913 the Court of Appeal[2] refused to allow a woman to take the Law Society's examination on the basis that women were, according to the common law of England, under a general disability by reason of their sex and so could not become attorneys or solicitors. It was not until the Sex Disqualification (Removal) Act 1919 that such prohibitions were abolished and thus made way for those, like Rosie Heilbron, who wanted to enter a profession. The experience and invaluable deployment of women in the two World Wars made them more assertive and self-confident and thereafter the gradual dismantling of barriers to their future progression was inevitable.

Although just over a century ago, the contrast between the England of Rosie Heilbron's birth and the England of today is remarkable. King George V had recently acceded to the throne. England, with a population of 40 million, possessed a vast Empire, spanning large swathes of the globe. The two main parties of politics were the Conservatives and the Liberals. The Labour Party was a small party and not a contender for office. There was no form of instant communication. Social intercourse was by letter or cable. Even radio broadcasting and telephones were not available to most ordinary households. Transportation was limited to trains, buses, tramcars, and a very few motor cars. International travel was by ship. Air travel was not available other than in a military context. Entertainment comprised reading, the music halls, the theatre and black and white movies. It was over a decade before the arrival of the 'talkies'. People, including many children, died of ailments which are readily curable today and there was still great poverty. In 1914 the compulsory school leaving age was 14 and some children worked part time at 12. Before the First World War men still wore top hats and women did not dare show their ankles in public. It was the stuff of period drama and aeons away from the modern world we know today with e-mail, internet, social media, flat-screen colour televisions, multi media home entertainment and space travel. This was the world into which young Rosie Heilbron was born.

Liverpool, or 'Lieurpul', a muddy pool, the town of her birth, is situated on the north western coast of England in the County

---

[2] *Bebb v Law Society* [1914] 1 Ch 286.

of Lancashire and bestrides the river Mersey. To the west lie the Irish Sea and Ireland: to the east lie the Pennines and the county of Yorkshire. A happy rivalry still exists between the neighbouring counties dating back to the far more combative War of the Roses between the Houses of Lancaster and York in the fifteenth century culminating in the Tudor dynasty: the red rose of Lancashire versus the white rose of Yorkshire. In 2007 Liverpool celebrated 800 years of existence and in 2008 was the European City of Culture.

In the early twentieth century Liverpool was a thriving port and business centre, the second city in the country with a population of nearly three quarters of a million people. It had built its reputation in the era of the steamship as the world's premier liner port. It had developed as a gateway importing raw materials and exporting the finished product, particularly grain and cotton, the latter of which on the eve of the Great War made up 30 per cent of the value of Liverpool's imports and over 40 per cent of its exports. In the nineteenth century Liverpool had also become an important transhipment port or staging post for emigrants from Europe to the New World. Its waterfront was dominated by its huge commercial docks, and later its overhead railway. In the early twentieth century a more recognisable landmark was built in the form of what has become known as the 'Three Graces': the three sea-facing buildings dominating the horizon, comprising the domed Mersey Docks and Harbour Building, the Royal Liver Building with its liver birds and the Italian Renaissance palazzo of the Cunard Building.

Liverpool's cosmopolitan origins, particularly its large Irish immigrant population (Ireland was still part of the UK until 1922), its vibrant and sometimes violent society, the early religious tensions between its Catholic and Protestant populations, the militancy of its unions and some of its labour force, the hardship and poverty suffered by many of its citizens, its very own Liverpudlian accent, and the renowned sense of humour and warmth of its people together made for a heady mix. This intoxicating city, in which Rosie Heilbron was to live for over 60 years, was to provide the backdrop and stimulus for many of her successes in life and for several of her famous and fascinating cases.

ROSIE'S FAMILY

Rosie Heilbron was born at home at 27 St James Road in the shadows of the emerging Anglican Cathedral, the magnificent monument designed by Giles Gilbert Scott, standing atop St James Mount, the highest point in Liverpool. Max and Nellie Heilbron already had a daughter, Annie (also known as Anne), who was two years old, and the birth of Rosie completed their family. Both Jewish, they had married on 27 December 1910 at the orthodox Princes Road Synagogue in Liverpool followed by a dinner, reception and ball at the Exchange Station Hotel. Max Heilbron was 28, his wife 22. Max Heilbron was the sixth of eight children. Rosie was probably called after Max Heilbron's late sister, Rose, who died tragically young, Rosie being a Yiddish derivation of Rose. The family ancestry is, as with many Jews, cosmopolitan. Max Heilbron's father was German, the name 'Heilbron' meaning 'well of good health'. His mother was American and four of his siblings were born in the United States. Nellie Heilbron, née Summers, was the youngest living child with four elder siblings. Nellie Heilbron's father had been born in Poland and her mother in Germany. Rosie's maternal grandparents lived to a good age and in the family were apparently renowned for having a wonderful old parrot which would sing 'after the ball was over' and dance round its cage to welcome guests.

Max Heilbron was what has been described as an emigration or shipping agent. Following in his father's footsteps, he worked for the Cunard Line Passenger Agency and ran an emigrant lodging house at 29 Great George's Square, Liverpool, where emigrants en route from Europe to North American would lodge pending transhipment.[3] By all accounts his business prospered and for the first years of Rosie's life, before the effects of the Depression struck, the family was very comfortably off. They had a car and the family could afford holidays in Europe. Soon after Rosie's birth the family moved to 4 Rutherford Road, Wavertree and in 1931 to 22 Menlove Gardens North, a five-bedroomed house in a prosperous suburb of Liverpool, which they named 'Anrose' after the two girls. This was to be Rosie's home for nearly 30 years. Max Heilbron was a dilettante inventor, in his spare time inventing, amongst other things, something called 'Max's Panstick', a beauty aid more redolent of the twenty-first century than the early twentieth. Its precise purpose, save that it had, or was intended to have, a concealing and/or depilatory effect on the female visage, is lost in the mists of time.

---

[3] There is an evocative picture available on the internet entitled "Heilbron's Cunard Hotel" dated 1908, depicting a scene outside the Emigrant House. Unfortunately, it is not possible to verify whether this was Max Heilbron's hotel or belonged to another member of the Heilbron family.

Nellie (also spelt 'Nelly') Heilbron, was for many years principally a homemaker. She was apparently a very good cook with a particular aptitude for delicious pastry, a trait her daughter, Rosie, was never able to emulate. Behind this domesticity lay a strong personality. Nellie Heilbron was the driving force of the family, ambitious for her children and innovative in their education. She had a particularly close relationship with her younger daughter: whereas her husband was closer to their elder child, Anne. In 1922 Nellie and Rosie Heilbron were awarded a certificate of merit in the *Weekly Dispatch*'s 'Mother and Child' Ideal Picture Competition for a photograph 'admirably representative of British Motherhood and Childhood'.

Rosie grew up in a happy family environment. Family social activity largely revolved round the extended family. Her parents were religious and Rosie was instilled with the Jewish culture. The family went to synagogue regularly and as a child she attended Hebrew lessons run by the Princes Road Synagogue. In June 1929, aged 14, she completed the prescribed course of instruction in the Jewish religion, following which she was confirmed. She was asked to make the vote of thanks on behalf of all the girls who had been confirmed along with her. She later herself taught at Bible Class.

EARLY EDUCATION

Rosie attended Miss Bell's primary school followed by a Montessori independent school, and in October 1924, at the age of 10, she joined her older sister at Belvedere Girls' Public Day Trust School. Little is recorded of her on-going scholastic achievements, but it is clear that she was academically clever as well as studious. She received for her efforts many prizes, invariably anthologies or similar books bound in leather and with the School motto 'Knowledge is no more a fountain sealed' emblazoned on the front. She was awarded a matriculation certificate in July 1930 at the age of 16 in seven subjects: English composition, English literature, history, French, Latin, chemistry and mathematics, achieving a credit in six subjects and a distinction in history.

In 2007, Belvedere honoured Rosie by setting up a scholarship in her name for girls who wanted to read law at University. The scholarship was inaugurated by Cherie Blair QC, herself a barrister and from Liverpool. The ceremony was also attended by Rosie's daughter, Hilary, who the following year in Liverpool Cathedral presented the first Rose Heilbron scholarship to the deserving recipient.

Nellie Heilbron also ensured that Rosie was given piano lessons. She took several music examinations and became an accomplished pianist, but it was her elder sister, Anne, who was the real musical talent of the family. Nonetheless, Rosie retained a love of music all her life, although she preferred jolly music, whether classical or otherwise. Her tastes were far from highbrow. Surprisingly she did not much like chamber music or Mozart. Beethoven was one of her favourite composers and she loved opera and, at the other end of the scale, Frank Sinatra.

Rosie's talents lay elsewhere. In particular from a very early age there were signs of her developing oratorical and acting skills. Her mother had arranged elocution lessons for her and her sister. Rosie took various elocution examinations set by the Guildhall School of Music, regularly receiving high grades and medals. At the age of seven she won the first prize in elocution at the Wallasey Festival. She followed this achievement two years later with a silver medal at the Guildhall School of Music and a gold medal at the Liverpool Festival where the local press report describes her as 'the youngest child elocutionist'. While at the Montessori school she apparently wrote a play about Charles I and the civil war which the school-children performed. In the same year she made a broadcast at a Liverpool studio. She also won many other prizes for elocution. On 22 October 1930, in a foretaste of her many appearances as a barrister there in later years, she gave a recitation at St George's Hall, the nineteenth-century neoclassical auditorium in the centre of Liverpool and the erstwhile venue of the city's assize courts.

In the summer of 1931, aged 16, she passed with merit the Licentiateship of the Guildhall School of Music in elocution earning the letters LGSM after her name and entitling her to teach the subject. She was believed at the time to have been the youngest candidate in England to have taken such a degree. Her notebooks survive and indicate the breadth of study required. They illustrate Rosie's learning relating to the scientific aspects of 'breathing, tone and articulation' to the more artistic aspects of 'conversation, reading aloud, reciting, acting and lecturing which are dependent on inflection, modulation, word painting, pause, gesture, climax etc' to the analysis and understanding of poetry and language. In a comment resonant of the times she wrote that one of the reasons elocution is necessary is 'to speak well in one's intercourse with men. A good manner and clear tone give an impression of efficiency'.

Her trained voice stood her in good stead in later life as an advocate. It enabled her to modulate the tone of her voice and to project it without raising its pitch. Thus the frequently used, but unmerited criticism, that women's high-pitched voices made them unsuitable to be barristers, was at least one of the many discouraging comments from male colleagues that she was able to dispel as her career progressed.

ROSIE AS A YOUNG GIRL

It is often said that barristers are actors manqués. The first record of Rosie's enthusiasm for the theatre, if not actually for acting, appears in an entry in her diary aged 11 in the joyous and innocent words of a young girl where she records: 'Tempest 2nd, 3rd February 1926. I danced in it'. It is likely that she acted in other school plays. In particular it is known that on 30 and 31 October 1931, then having just turned 17, she played Petruchio in The Belverdere School Dramatic Society's production of Shakespeare's 'Taming of the Shrew' at the Crane Hall in Liverpool. All the parts were played by women. The reviews from the local papers were flattering. 'Rosie Heilbron gave us a finely swaggering Petruchio' commented the *Liverpool Post*. The *Liverpool Echo* said that 'Rosie Heilbron as Petruchio was as vigorously masculine as any charming young lady could be expected to be'.

Rosie's love of the theatre took her to the London stage for six months after leaving school to try her hand at acting professionally, where she apparently took the stage name of Rose Bron. It was something which she had kept secret, save from her family, all of her life. She appeared in the mystery murder play 'Hokuspokus', and stayed in lodgings, but the show closed after six months. It had clearly not been the experience that she had expected and she returned to start her studies in law.

But what of Rosie the girl? She was always pretty with her long cascades of black curls, but as she developed into a young woman this youthful prettiness became a natural beauty enhanced by a wonderful smile. She possessed a remarkably small waist which complemented her slender figure. In January 1930, aged 15, she made the following record in her diary: 'Height 9[ft].5½; weight 9.4; size 6 boots'. She exhibited a curious trait of standing or posing with her left hand on her waist, something she retained throughout her life and ultimately captured in her seventies in her magnificent portrait by June Mendoza. She also seems to have acquired early in life, as one can see from the annotations to her copy of the Taming of the Shrew, the habit of marking up books with comments in her large handwriting and underlining—sacrilege to some, but pragmatic to others.

Rosie was an avid reader which drew the comment from her sister that she always had her nose in a book and even read in the bath! But she was by no means a blue stocking, enjoying the things teenage girls normally do from visiting her friends, to shopping, going to the cinema, and having crushes on boys.

Apart from the brief interlude on the stage, it appears that Rosie had decided to become a barrister by the time of her matriculation. It is not clear why she chose this career, but it provided an obvious, if difficult, avenue for her combination of talents. It is likely that her mother encouraged her. Consideration was given to her going to Cambridge, but this never materialised. Whether this was because she was not accepted by a woman's college at Cambridge or because of her home circumstances is not known. She went instead, aged 18, to Liverpool University to read law and so to take the first steps on the path to becoming a barrister.

2

Liverpool University and Gray's Inn

IN THE EARLY 1930s it was still relatively rare for girls to go to university. Rosie went to Liverpool University at the start of the academic year beginning in October 1932. There was only one other girl reading law in her class. Women had, after all, only been taking such degrees for 15 years. Liverpool University had been established in 1881 as University College, Liverpool, becoming a fully-fledged independent university with the power to confer degrees in 1903. It is what is known as a 'red brick' university. This description was first coined by a Liverpool professor to describe the six civic British universities that that had been built in the Victorian era and characterised by red brick buildings of the age. Liverpool University was regarded as having an excellent law school. The Dean of the Law School was at the time Professor Batt, a kindly man, who seems to have been very supportive of young Rosie.

One of her lecturers was Hartley Shawcross. He was then practising on the Northern Circuit as a barrister, lecturing part time. A handsome and brilliant man with an attractive voice, he was destined for greater things. He later became Attorney General in the post-Second World War Labour Government and chief prosecutor at the Nuremburg trials and was ultimately ennobled. As their respective careers developed their relationship changed from one of student and teacher to one of professional colleagues. Hartley Shawcross was to feature in Rosie's professional life on many occasions at strategic times in her career. Sixty years later when both had retired, she sat at his side at one of the celebrations for his 90th birthday, no doubt reminiscing about the times that their paths had crossed over the years.

Rosie lived at home during her undergraduate university days, but this did not stop her from entering into university life with a vengeance. She became involved in various student societies, being elected Treasurer of the Jewish Students' Society in her first year, and later Honorary Treasurer of the Legal Society. She was a skilled debater, participating in university debates. She joined in university social life and regularly attended dances. She made many life-long friends and acquired a number of admirers attracted to her striking looks and lively personality. Of these some were to support her in her early years at the Bar and more than one vied to be the person to give her her first brief. Nor was she immune to falling in love. Her diaries are full of the minutiae one would expect from a young girl. She wrote about her passing attraction to various students from time to time including references to one or two boyfriends, together with the trials and tribulations surrounding such relationships. Her diaries also related some snippets of daily life at university.

A rounded personality, she was clearly popular. Her work, however, dominated her time at university. She set herself high standards, noting the daily and sometimes weekly number of hours she worked. Thus on 3 May 1933 she notes in her diary: 'Got 3 x 1st classes and 1 x 2nd ... I am top now but will have to work like—to keep it up'. On another occasion on 22 January 1935 she wrote: 'Not quite 90 [per cent] mark yet, but 88 in tort and private international law ... is probably about 89 [per cent]'. She excelled in her subject from the outset, regularly achieving very high marks. On one occasion in May 1935 she reached a 90 per cent target by achieving 93 per cent for an examination in private international law. She allegedly used to work 14 hours a day prior to her finals, though this may have been a bit of an exaggeration. She was rewarded for her efforts with a First Class Honours Degree in June 1935 following upon her earlier first class intermediate LLB. It was a notable achievement and one she was very proud of. There were only three Class 1 degrees awarded in law that year out of 29 Bachelor of Laws degrees. She was the first woman to achieve such a distinction at Liverpool University and only the second woman in the country to have done so. Her degree was conferred on her on 6 July 1935 at St George's Hall, the venue for some of her great successes in the future. It was the crucial first step that she needed to propel her along the path to success.

Her legal education as an undergraduate was not exclusively academic. For example she took the opportunity to visit a Police Court. She was clearly thrilled to meet the two High Court Judges on Assize, Mr Justice Lawrence and Mr Justice Atkinson, at the Legal Society Dance in October 1934, where apparently she was partnered by the latter in several dances, a fact which appeared in the press. She noted some tips he had given her about the art of cross-examination, including a story about the famous English advocate Marshall Hall. He was encouraging and recommended that she went into politics, but nonetheless her diary notes that he recited the contemporaneous mantra that 'where women failed at the Bar was in the smallness of their voices', an accusation that he could not level against his dancing partner for the evening.

A high-pitched voice was not the only alleged obstacle to a woman's success at the Bar. Discouragement came from all quarters, including from her most supportive admirers. She records that in February 1936 she had tea with Edward Hemmerde KC, then the Recorder of Liverpool, who told her 'there was not much chance for a woman at the Bar as there was unreasoning prejudice among solicitors, but he was all in favour of them'. This was true. Hemmerde was a great supporter of Rosie, as contemporaneous documents clearly show.

Rosie's degree did not terminate her relationship with Liverpool University for she determined to take an LLM, a postgraduate degree, which she acquired in May 1937. In November 1935 she stood as the Conservative candidate in the mock elections at Liverpool University, although her political allegiances changed in later years. This was no doubt one of the reasons many years later that she cautioned her own daughter against joining any university political party when she, in turn, went to university. Her succinct election banner 'Don't vote Red: vote Rose' proved to be more than a match for her opponent's 'Plump for Jump'. She won by 406 votes to Mr Jump's 217 votes.

1935 was a memorable year in Rosie's life for other reasons too. On 19 August she celebrated her 21st birthday and, in December, her parents celebrated their silver wedding. She noted that on 31 December she went through the Mersey tunnel which had opened the previous year, joining Liverpool to its hinterland in Birkenhead for the first time. At around this time the family acquired a golden retriever called Prince with a penchant for mischief and adventurous wanderings.

GRAY'S INN

Perhaps the most significant event after her degree was the award in November 1935 of the Lord Justice Holker Scholarship by Gray's Inn in the sum of £300 per year. Rosie was the first woman to have received such an award. She had no private means and without the scholarship she probably would not have been able to become a barrister. She was then admitted as a student to Gray's Inn. She was on her way to becoming a barrister. £300 was a substantial sum in those days, equivalent to about £15,000 today.

Gray's Inn is one of the four Inns of Court which an intending barrister needs to join to be called to the English Bar as a barrister. (The other three are Lincoln's Inn, Middle Temple and Inner Temple). It is likely that Rosie chose Gray's Inn rather than one of the other Inns of Court, not only because of its scholarships, but also because it had, and still has, a close association with many barristers from the Northern Circuit ie the North West of England. Students had to attend a certain number of dinners in the Elizabethan panelled hall each legal term. Here young budding barristers met and dined together, sitting in 'Messes' of four. It provided an opportunity to mingle with qualified barristers and Benchers ie senior barristers and judges elected to run the Inn, and participate in the various traditions of Gray's Inn, such as toasting each other and the 'Upper' and 'Lower' Mess with the house wine or port. They were lively occasions and many firm and long-term friendships were made. The obligation to dine and the traditions exist to this day, although the number of dinners required is less and the evenings now also have an educational content.

On 22 November 1935, Rosie attended her first such dinner for which she records she had bought a new frock. Thus began a lifelong association with Gray's Inn which was to give her much pleasure and be the source of some of her achievements and ultimately, in the later years of her life, her home.

Rosie clearly relished her trips to London to complete her dinners. She seems to have had a busy social life in London. She had by now cut her hair short in the style of the times. The combination of her brilliant mind, her looks, her ebullience and the fact that women students were a rarity was clearly an aphrodisiac to her young male fellow students and friends. On one occasion in June 1936 she dined at Gray's Inn with Randolph Churchill, the only son of Sir Winston Churchill, the wartime Prime Minister, and later Conservative MP for Preston. She had apparently been asked to keep him company. Her dinners at Gray's Inn also gave her the opportunity to be introduced to some judges and other members of the Bar.

So much did young Rosie enjoy London that by the middle of July 1936 she was writing in her diary that she would like to settle in London, but this may well have been influenced by the fact that her then boyfriend lived in London. She even appears to have applied for a scholarship to the London School of Economics and Political Science (LSE) and reached the shortlist, but did not succeed. She nonetheless vowed to spend more time in London, particularly during term-time, which she appears to have done. It was, however, to be almost another 40 years before she did in fact move permanently to London.

In October that year, simultaneously with studying for her LLM, she started to read for the Bar and attended lectures in London at the Inns of Court School of Law. This is a vocational course which all aspiring barristers needed to complete (and still do) before being called to the Bar. Its emphasis is on the more practical aspects of legal practice such as procedure and evidence, rather than purely substantive and academic law. One of Rosie's lecturers was the great legal historian, Sir William Holdsworth, of whom she does not seem to have been greatly enamoured as a lecturer. Rosie was exempted from Part I of the course because of her degree in law and only had to take Part II.

Rosie's introduction to Gray's Inn also had another important consequence for her. For many years young Rosie had used her first name interchangeably with Rose. When she first joined Gray's Inn she was advised by the then Under Treasurer to use the shorter version of her name when she was a barrister. Thereafter professionally and otherwise she went as Rose Heilbron and in that name she shall be referred to hereafter. It was wise advice. However, she did not shed Rosie altogether which remained an affectionate nick-name.

THE GREAT DEPRESSION

Rose's university career and student days at Gray's Inn coincided with the Great Depression, that deep and dreadful global economic crisis precipitated by the Wall Street stock market crash of 29 October 1929 which blighted the 1930s. Its epicentre was the United States and accordingly the attraction of emigration to the New World receded. Liverpool lost its position as a human entrepôt for emigrants.

As the Great Depression took hold the family's relative affluence consequently receded. Max Heilbron's emigration business was severely hit and the family had to find an alternative means of livelihood. In 1935 they opened a small hotel, 'The Dorchester', at

1a Rodney Street, later to become the medical street of Liverpool. All the family, Rose included, despite her studies, had to help in the business simultaneously keeping the family home running. On occasions young Rose, as would any young girl of her age, resented this, but she nonetheless pulled her weight. At some point Rose set out a cleaning schedule and rota for the limited staff the family could afford to employ. Her mother worked exceptionally hard in the business from early morning until late into the night, cooking for guests and helping to run the hotel with a small staff. This was very tiring as her letters to her daughter portray. Her sacrifices remained imprinted on Rose's memory throughout Rose's life and she would often recall the hardships and hard work her own mother had had to endure when the Depression struck.

It was a struggle both physically and financially and a marked contrast with the life the family had led in earlier years. The family was not on the breadline, but they were at times finding it difficult to make ends meet: foreign holidays as a family, new clothes and other luxuries had to be put to one side, but the children's education was not jeopardised. However, it seems that it did not prevent Rose going on a Cunard White Star cruise round the Mediterranean on the SS *Lancastria* in the summer of 1935, about which she raved. This family retrenchment was the first adverse event in young Rose's life, but it was as nothing as compared with an event two years later.

Although Rose appeared to have had considerable fun and entertainment when in London, money was scarce. In addition to the monies she received from the Lord Justice Holker Scholarship, Rose lectured at Liverpool University to earn some extra money. There was also some discussion about her lecturing at the School of Commerce, but it is unclear if she ever did. Nonetheless, she did manage to be able to afford to go on another cruise in the summer of 1936 with her old school friend Muriel Young.

When staying in London Rose resided at various lodgings including at 69 Warwick Road Earls Court and later at 22 Thomas Street in Mayfair, most likely run by Jewish families. Throughout her time in London she kept in close touch with her family with telephone calls and letters, particularly from her mother or 'Mater'. Her mother often gave her motherly advice in these letters, including a regular encouragement to drink a glass of Ovaltine before she went to bed as it would 'see her right'. She also sent Rose food and tuck boxes.

OTHER ACCOMPLISHMENTS

When not in London Rose's life in Liverpool continued much as before. One of her very close friends was another old school friend, Rene Lester, with whom she continued a friendship long into later life. Rene Lester never married and had a career in the retail business. At one point in the 1960s she was in some way directly or indirectly in charge of running the hairdressing salon at George Henry Lees, a large department store in Liverpool and part of the John Lewis chain. Saturday visits to the hairdresser therefore provided an opportunity for old friends to catch up. Rose also took up skating which she appeared to enjoy such that she wrote in capital letters in her diary on 2 March 1936 'I can skate'. There seems to have been one particular boyfriend, who proposed to her, but he was not Jewish and her mother was against it. In any event it appears that the ardour eventually fizzled out of the relationship.

Rose was also beginning to be noticed more widely for her accomplishments, someone even putting her name forward for the English Debating Team which was to visit the United States. On Saturday 5 October 1936 she presented the awards at the Liverpool Centre of the Guildhall School of Music and Drama, the first of many such honours. She was becoming something of a local celebrity with several small articles in the *Liverpool Daily Post* and *Liverpool Echo* written as to her achievements, providing a foretaste of what was to come.

3

Becoming a Barrister

TRAGEDY STRIKES

T HE SUMMER OF 1937 augured well. Rose received her LLM, aged 22, ahead of time at the end of June. She returned home from London to a wonderfully warm welcome from her family. They were delighted about her degree and thrilled by the publicity it had attracted in the *News Chronicle* where the short article was headed: 'Her Ambition—Youngest Barrister'. She noted that her mother was very proud of her younger daughter. The family attended the degree ceremony on Saturday, 3 July, once again at St George's Hall. The next step was being called to the Bar, but this nearly never happened.

Ten days later young Rose's life was turned upside down. Her mother was diagnosed with breast cancer. Her poignant entries in her diary and the tone of the family correspondence at this time witness the heartache she and her Father and sister suffered. One can see the effect it had on Rose in a letter her Father sent her in the summer of 1937 when he expresses his gratitude to her for all she has done 'never thinking of herself at such a precious time, almost denouncing her career'. Her mother underwent treatment, hopes were raised and then dashed, the family did all they could, she had the best possible medical care, but in less than a year, on 10 May 1938, she died aged only 49.

The effect on young Rose was profound. She nearly gave up her career so upset and traumatised was she by the loss of her mother to whom she had been so close. Life seems to have gone into a sort of limbo for several months. It is said that before her mother died, Rose hired a wig and gown so that her mother could see what she looked like when called to the Bar. The tragedy of losing her mother at such a young age stayed with Rose all her life and there were only rare times when her mother was not in her thoughts. Rose would talk about her frequently and of the sacrifices she had made. It was a void that was never filled for they were clearly incredibly close. Her mother, her guiding spirit, never lived to see her success, but she must have known that her daughter would one day make her mark. As Rose herself once said: 'She it was who had been the guiding force—mainstay of my whole life. To her I owe a debt that can never be repaid'.

There is little record of what the next months brought. Her diaries stopped. The business effectively ceased and The Dorchester was ultimately requisitioned in the War. Rose took on the task of organising the household and supporting her father. This in itself was a daunting task for a young girl of 24.

THE BAR BECKONS

Yet in the end it was her career that sustained her both financially and otherwise. Her career was her only means of support and in April 1939 she took out a £100 overdraft from the Union Bank of Manchester, but had to do so jointly with a male relative, presumably because she was a woman. There is regular mention in her diaries of much needed cheques arriving, indicating the precariousness of her financial position, something exacerbated by the slow payment of fees associated with payment at the Bar, particularly in those days. On 21 March 1941 she notes: 'Just managed to wheedle £40 out of the bank—hope I won't need it—but fees are damned slow in coming in' and in June of that year 'Cheque for £14.10.6—rent safe now'.

In a letter of condolence of great prescience dated 3 November 1938, a Patrick Fergus wrote:

> I have an unwavering belief that you will succeed more resplendently than any woman has yet succeeded in this perilous trade. I hope that this avowal of my belief in you ... will sustain and encourage you through a rather trying experience. Believe me, if God is good, we shall yet see you as the first woman 'silk' [ie King's Counsel].

Rose eventually returned to her studies and took her Bar exams. A year later on 2 May 1939 she was called to the Bar at Gray's Inn. She was 25, fulfilling the prophecy that she would be the youngest woman barrister, but not the first. Dr Ivy Williams had been called to the Bar in 1921. Rose decided to join the Northern Circuit, one of then seven legal Circuits or regions in England and Wales (reduced to six in 1946). The instigation of Circuits dates back to the twelfth century and the time of King Henry II. The rationale was to send judges around the country to hear cases rather than having them all heard in London. The Northern Circuit is no backwater. It has an illustrious list of advocates who have been members of the Circuit including: FE Smith (later Lord Birkenhead); Lord Kilmuir; Lord Shawcross and many others. At that time there were 313 members of the Northern Circuit. Rose's presence would increase the female representation to 12.

THE FIRST SIGNS OF PREJUDICE

The idea of an attractive young woman wanting to pursue a career dominated by men caught the public imagination. Her call to the Bar attracted some national and local publicity. Her own contemporaneous views on such matters are expressed in an article in the *Daily Express*. The article read:

> Portia, 24, is no blue stocking ... But Portia has not yet met her Bassanio. She is quoted as saying 'I am no blue stocking. The general impression of a woman lawyer seems to be a sober old maid. I have not adopted the law as a hobby. I am serious about my career, but that does not mean I shall give up dancing, swimming, golf or tennis. Legal problems will not keep me from the other jobs I love—housework and gardening. When I marry I intend to continue as a barrister. I have many men friends. Some have possibly fallen in love with me, but I have no plans for marriage. I am not in love. This does not mean I am sacrificing my life for my career. I am a home lover. I have kept house for my father since my mother died, so the job of running my own home when I am married will not be a strange one'.

But encouragement from the press was matched by discouragement in the profession. Once called to the Bar the next step for a budding barrister is to secure a pupillage. This is a form of apprenticeship. For a total period of 12 months a newly qualified barrister sits with and learns from a more senior junior barrister of over five years' seniority called a pupil-master. For this privilege a sum of a hundred guineas (£105) in those days changed hands, although today it is the pupil who receives payment. But despite Rose's academic achievements, the path to pupillage was a very difficult one.

Rose had no legal connections at a time when such connections could affect an introduction and ease one's path into the profession. Today candidates are judged on merit and connections play no part. She was also a woman at a time when women barristers were a rarity. It was thus on her ability alone that she had to secure a pupillage. A letter dated 2 June 1939 from Professor Batt, the Dean of the Faculty of Law at Liverpool University, under whom she had studied, reflects contemporary attitudes when he wrote:

My Dear Miss Heilbron,

Further consideration on the matter of your reading in Chambers with me has led to considerable difficulties. Mr Fraser Harrison feels unable to make any offer to take you for the latter six months or offer [at] any time and I have a definite feeling that the other men in these chambers and the clerk would not welcome a woman pupil.

As you saw, our accommodation is somewhat cramped and it is essential that the best relations should exist between all of us in Chambers. It is not of course any personal feeling with regard to you but it is simply that Barristers have not got used to women practising at the Bar and sharing Chambers with them and feel some constraint and diffidence when a woman is in Chambers.

It is not of course that any of them has definitely objected to your becoming a pupil but rather that I have a feeling that they would not be happy about it. But there is in my opinion a graver matter in your own interests and it is this—It has been made clear to me that there would be no room for you to remain after your year of pupillage was over and you would therefore have to seek Chambers elsewhere. That you would find very difficult because naturally it is easier to be accommodated in those Chambers in which you have served your pupillage.

If you would care to come and see me again, I can explain matters perhaps more fully,

Yours very sincerely

It must have been a great disappointment to Rose, particularly since Professor Batt himself held an enlightened view of women at the Bar. This was probably not the only rejection she received, but it is the only one that survives, as she often indicated how difficult it had been for her to get pupillage. It was Richard (Dick) Trotter, later a Circuit Judge, who eventually offered her a pupillage in chambers at 43 Castle Street, Liverpool. Rose joined him as his pupil in September 1939. The Head of Chambers, until he took silk earlier that year, had been Hartley Shawcross, her former lecturer at Liverpool University.

PUPILLAGE

A set of Chambers is a group of barristers, often selected according to areas of expertise, but sometimes not, who share office accommodation and administrative expenses. Pivotal to the chambers is the clerk who is effectively each barrister's agent and whose primary role is to look after each barrister's practice, getting in work, fixing cases and fees. Barristers' clerks still exist today, although their roles have become more sophisticated, particularly given the current much larger size of some sets of chambers. However, barristers are self-employed and do not share the profits of their practice. They can thus appear against one another, and often do, something which outsiders find difficult to comprehend.

Rose's Liverpool chambers comprised exclusively junior barristers, because on becoming a King's Counsel ie taking silk, barristers were then obliged to obtain a seat in London chambers. This is no longer the case and many chambers now comprise both silks and juniors both in London and on Circuit. Becoming a barrister also affected social customs. Barristers only addressed themselves by their surname and were not supposed to shake each other's hands, rules not readily applied in the twenty-first century. In court they address each other as 'My Learned Friend'.

Just as Rose's entry into this world had coincided with the First World War, so her entry into the profession of a barrister coincided with the outbreak of the Second World War. Britain and France had declared war on Germany on 3 September 1939. She noted in her diary how 'in Liverpool there is sandbagging everywhere' and 'how scarce things are in the shops'. She commented a few months later how she 'got several priceless possessions together in case of air bombardment or invasion'. This included her book of family photographs, in particular of her late mother, which still exists. In January 1941 she became a firefighter. In March 1941 she recorded that Birkenhead, a town the other side of the River Mersey from Liverpool, had been very badly hit, as well as noting a seven and a half hour blitz on Liverpool. This was the sobering background against which she started her career at the Bar. However, it also brought her opportunities as the male barristers were away at war.

The first few days as a pupil barrister were obviously thrilling and exhilarating and her diary entries reflect her excitement and enthusiasm. Her diary entry for her first day in pupillage recounts that she:

> [I] sat behind a crowded, two rows of bewigged barristers and felt generally thrilled. In the afternoon I purchased my wig and gown. That was another big moment. If only Mum was here to see me—anyway thank God Dad can see it ... It is going to be grand fun.

The next day she wore her wig and gown for the first time, but 'forgot the bands', the white oblong pieces of cloth which hang from the vent of the wing collar then worn by all barristers. She had to borrow her pupil-master's.

Later that week she commented in her diary: 'A Barrister's life is the thing'. She often recalled how once when she sought Dick Trotter's advice about a case to which she did not know the answer, he reprimanded her by saying: 'Know your bloody facts first'. The importance of knowing the facts of a case was a lesson she carried with her throughout her career. She would in later years comment on his courage in taking her on as his pupil and recount the tale of a colleague who, in her presence when she was sitting in his room, mockingly accused Dick, a bachelor, of 'living in forensic sin'.

STARTING PRACTICE

After six months of pupillage she was offered a room in Dick Trotter's chambers at 43 Castle Street, Liverpool. Rose was now able to take cases in her own right as well as assisting her pupil-master and others in chambers (known as devilling). She notes in her diary for Monday, 1 April 1940: 'Start in Practice—Lovely room—am deeply thrilled—with 3 cases to start'. Her name was inscribed on the door of chambers and she bought a new costume, but thought 'the shoulders a bit narrow'.

She had her foot on the first rung of the ladder, but although able to take cases on her own, she remained a pupil for a further six months. She had been elected to the Northern Circuit on 2 February 1940. The Recorder of Liverpool, Edward Hemmerde KC, proposed her. The next stage was to try to build up a practice. In those days barristers were exclusively a referral profession. They could only carry out legal work if instructed by a solicitor who in turn had direct access to the lay client. Barristers were advocates: solicitors did not have rights of audience except in the Police (now named Magistrates') Courts or the County Courts. Thus she had to attract work from solicitors.

Friendships Rose had made at university among lawyers who became local solicitors helped, and Barney Berkson, for example, was an early provider of work. She also almost immediately started to acquire a variety of small cases from different and new firms of solicitors. She was chosen by a defendant for a 'dock brief' among a group of male barristers, the colloquialism for when an unrepresented defendant picks out a barrister standing in the well of the court as his 'brief'. A week into her second six months of pupillage

Dick Trotter had a car accident and was hospitalised. This meant that young Rose found herself with an additional workload as she also had to undertake some of Dick Trotter's work.

In the 1940s the practice of a young barrister would primarily include, for criminal cases, appearances at Police Courts before benches of magistrates, Juvenile Courts and Quarter Sessions at various towns on the Circuit where crimes of an intermediate gravity were heard and, for civil cases, at County Courts and the Court of Passage, a civil court peculiar to Liverpool, sitting a few times a year with a limited jurisdiction. The most serious criminal and civil cases would be tried by High Court Judges sitting on Assize at various towns on each of the Circuits for a few weeks each legal term (Michaelmas (autumn), Hilary (winter), Easter (spring) and Trinity (summer)).

At the start of her career as a barrister, apart from appearances in the lower courts, Rose would draft pleadings (the documents in which the claim or defence is summarised in civil claims) and write legal opinions, although there was less civil than criminal work available for a young barrister. In later years Rose would appear more frequently before High Court Judges at Assizes in the various towns on the Northern Circuit. She would also begin to undertake cases off the Northern Circuit, on one of the other Circuits around the country for which she would have to pay a sum of money in order to be admitted.

There was much less work available for young barristers, whether men or women, when Rose started at the Bar than in later years. Many barristers left the Bar because of the lack of opportunity. Fees were much lower than they are today and there were far fewer courts in which to practise. There was no unified state funding by way of the legal aid scheme until the early 1950s following the Legal Aid and Advice Act 1949. In criminal cases barristers would sometimes provide their services free for the very poor by way of what was termed the 'in forma pauperis' procedure. There was some legal aid in criminal cases, but not in civil cases. Even then a barrister would get three guineas for a legal aid case and seven guineas if it was of exceptional length and difficulty, without any extra daily fee or refresher. The comparative figures for silks were 10 and 15 guineas. Cases tended to be shorter than they are today and there were more pleas of guilty.

The availability of privately paid work was limited. Even when a young barrister obtained work, receiving payment could take an extremely long time and would have a deleterious effect on cash flow, because chambers' overheads and travelling expenses, as well as other expenses, still had to be paid. Prosecutions were attractive as they were paid for by the state. Additionally, at several Quarter Sessions fees for prosecution work were paid in cash on the day of the case thereby avoiding the normal long delays barristers often had to endure in getting paid for their work.

Despite these inauspicious times, Rose made an impression on judges, solicitors and the public right from the start. On 22 April 1940 she appeared for a petitioner in a divorce case. The President of the Probate, Admiralty and Divorce Division, the most senior family law judge in the country, congratulated her in open court on her pertinacity and obstinacy and later sent his usher to ask when she had been called to the Bar and at which Inn of Court.

Rose was also starting in small ways to break down barriers. On the previous day she had sat unrobed on the barristers' benches at Liverpool Assizes before Mr Justice Birkett without a hat. Women were not then allowed into court without a hat, but when an usher sought to evict her, Mr Justice Birkett exclaimed in open court that 'This rule does not apply to you, Miss Heilbron'. The occasion brought considerable publicity, including the following piece from the *Liverpool Daily Post*, which proclaimed that:

> History has just been made today at Liverpool law courts by a woman barrister who during a case in which she was not personally engaged, sat in the barristers' benches without wig or hat ... All other women appearing in court are strictly required to wear hats.

Rose also recalled another similar incident early in her career. Once again she was sitting in court at Liverpool Assizes waiting for her case to come on. The next case, which involved a somewhat unsavoury sexual offence, was called on and the usher, following the then normal practice, shouted: 'All Ladies must leave the Court'. Rose was nonplussed and did not know what to do. As she rose to her feet the trial Judge turned to her and said: 'That does not apply to you Miss Heilbron—you are a member of the Bar'.

Since some of these courts had never had a woman barrister appear in them previously, Rose's presence was something of a novelty. Her appearance, for instance, as the first woman to appear in St Helens Police Court and in a court in Wales attracted press attention.

For the tax year ending 31 March 1942 Rose had earned £210 in fees before tax of £72. Her professional expenses of rent, travel, clerk and other miscellaneous items amounted to £102.2s. Briefs would be 'marked' ie fees agreed and written on the brief before the barrister went into court.

A further compliment from magistrates in Birkenhead, following a hearing to commit her client to trial, had led to an earlier article which had appeared in the *Birkenhead News* on 11 May 1939. Although Rose had only been practising at this point for some five weeks, the article was placed sufficiently prominently to take precedence over the announcement of the resignation the previous day of Neville Chamberlain, the Prime Minister. It read:

> Portia—1940 version. Local history has been made this week when for the first time a woman barrister has pleaded in the Birkenhead Police Court. Only 24 years old, a dark vivacious Jewess, Miss Rose Heilbron has already attracted a good deal of attention in the legal world, and after listening to her the other day a well-known solicitor remarked to me, 'There's no doubt about it: to borrow a phrase from Hollywood, she will be a sensation in four or five years' time'.

> Yet it is only just over twelve months since Miss Heilbron was called to the Bar after taking her first class honours degree at Liverpool University where, incidentally, she had more than once distinguished herself in debate. Already she has a polished court manner which gives the impression that she has had a vast amount of experience, and for concise presentation of cases she has won compliments not merely from magistrates, but from the President of the Divorce Division of the High Court, before whom she appeared three weeks ago.

> When she first began to practise, Miss Heilbron made up her mind quite firmly that she would not wear a hat in court—and she has stuck to that decision ever since. It is generally accepted that women should not appear in courts of law bareheaded, and the question had been raised in Birkenhead. But, she had remained adamant, and incidentally, has the support of Mr E G Hemmerde, the Liverpool Recorder, who has said he knows no reason at all why women should be forced to wear hats in court.

> Certainly no one could accuse Miss Heilbron of looking anything but business-like, for in her black tailored costume and crisp white blouse, she looks the essence of cool efficiency. When someone remarked to her the other day that the arrangement of her hair—in rolls down the side of her face—was reminiscent of a barrister's wig, she gave an assurance that that was pure coincidence. The resemblance had never even struck her before ...

> Among the interesting views she holds about women in public life, and especially in her own profession, is the opinion that there is nothing to stand in the way of women judges. Who knows?

4

Developing a Practice at the Bar

THE REASONS FOR ROSE'S EARLY SUCCESS

WHAT WAS IT that enabled Rose to fulfil the predictions and become a sensational success in her chosen profession 4–5 years after being called to the Bar? The odds were certainly stacked against her. She was only 25 when she started practice; she was single; she had recently lost her mother and was catapulted into running the family household. She was a woman and she was Jewish—both perceived as disadvantages to be overcome. Women barristers were still relatively rare. The legal profession was not women friendly. Rose had no source of money apart from what she could earn and had to help support her family. Yet other than when her mother died, she never seems to have considered giving up practice at the Bar.

It has often been said that she succeeded because she was given a head start when all the male barristers were away at the War. When this was put to her, the answer was plain. She acknowledged that the absence of male barristers during the War had been an advantage in starting at the Bar, but commented that, unlike most of the other female barristers, she kept her practice when the men returned from the War. She had a fine legal brain and a clear, modulated and trained voice which carried well. She could be a very persuasive and eloquent advocate to both judge and jury alike. But there was more. She really loved her work and was ambitious to succeed. The law was not only her work but also her hobby. She approached her work with a real enthusiasm, was thrilled when, judged by her own high standards, she did well or received praise, but was continually trying to improve and hone her skills as a cross-examiner and advocate.

HOME LIFE

A year at the Bar and Rose had already started to build up a practice, but it also meant hard work. On Saturday 19 April 1941 she wrote in her diary: '5 divorces to prepare and 4 of them paid. 6 cases on Monday ... It means working all day today and tomorrow too'. Nonetheless, there were periods when work was slack. Her increasing workload meant that she was finding it difficult to combine it with the household chores and maintaining the garden. After some considerable resistance from her father with whom she still lived, Rose and her sister, who appears by this time to have been living away from home, eventually managed to persuade him to let her employ a cleaner/housekeeper, the cost of which she shared with her father.

The arrival of 'Mrs B', aka Mrs Brenton, was welcome and 'not having to bother about dishes is a tremendous relief'. Mrs B introduced her cat to the family: whether it was this intrusion into his doggie territory or just his adventurous nature, Rose's diary notes a few weeks later that 'Prince keeps wandering off'. However, Prince aside, her first employment of domestic help—assistance Rose needed all her working life—did ease her burden a little. Unfortunately Mrs B seems not to have been wholly satisfactory and in March the following year was replaced by 'Mrs A', who has remained anonymous. The employment of Mrs B also enabled her to do some more serious reading which she enjoyed, but hitherto had had little time for. Rose always loved reading, although in later years had less time for it, but in this period of her life she read voraciously and she methodically listed her accomplished reading by month at the back of her diary.

May 1941 brought devastating and relentless blitzes to Liverpool, the worst of the Second World War. But the 4 May blitz had a direct impact on Rose's career. Her diary entry records: 'Hell of a fire blitz last night. Ended at 4 with terrific explosions till 6. Most of the town was hit. The town a dreadful sight—ruins everywhere. Chambers burned out. Lewis's [a major department store] destroyed'. Members of chambers asked Glynn Blackledge (later King's Counsel and Stipendiary Magistrate in Liverpool), who was then head of chambers at 34 Castle Street, if they could join his chambers. Barristers had to double up and Rose shared a room with Dick Trotter, her former pupil-master. The upheaval caused a temporary halt to the work flow, but it soon picked up again.

Her income allowed Rose to indulge herself a little and to commit the occasional extravagance, such as the purchase of 'a silver cigarette case which I've wanted for well over ten years'. In later life she gave up smoking. In July 1941 she 'took the plunge and bought the shoes I've wanted (black suede sandals) ... and a rather smart cotton frock—sacrificing 10 coupons in the process'. Nonetheless, money was limited and Rose undertook private coaching in law in the summer legal vacation to bring in some additional income.

Around the same time she refers in her diary for the first time to an attempt to lose some weight 'by walking and a strict diet'. Such dieting was a lifelong preoccupation, as Rose loved her food and had a particularly sweet tooth. Over the years she acquired an enviable library of diet books, as well as articles about dieting torn out of magazines, and as a result, a certain familiarisation with almost every new diet around. Fruit diets were a particular favourite, but others included: Weight Watchers, the Scarsdale diet and some more bizarre food combinations produced by the dietary fad of the moment. These were all tried with enthusiasm, but usually with only temporary success. Instead in dietary extremis Rose would take to adding pieces of material to the waists of her dresses and skirts or using safety pins discreetly hidden. However, although at times she was a little overweight, she was never really fat or obese: it was more that the svelte figure to which she aspired was not always attainable or, at least, not attainable for very long!

ROSE'S PRACTICE STARTS TO TAKE OFF

By the beginning of the legal year in October 1941, Rose's practice had really started to take off. Professor Batt, her erstwhile Dean, told her that she was doing better than any other woman at the Bar, which clearly pleased her. In October she was offered a 30 guinea brief with another 10 guineas for a conference and opinion, a substantial sum in those days, 30 guineas probably being worth approximately £1,300 in today's money. At the beginning of November she received four new briefs on one day and by the end of that month she noted: 'I've had the best month since I began: £82 certain and £18 earned but not paid'.

As her early career progressed she became a hard taskmaster on herself, perennially seeking to improve her skills and self-criticising when she thought she could have done better. Examples from her diaries include a reference in December 1941 to a 'telling off from Cassels [Mr Justice] yesterday—it will do me good'; and a comment the following month 'prepare cross-examination. New method'. In the following years she noted: 'I think my speech went down well ... I missed a few things out though. I must make larger notes' and 'my fluency is increasing thanks to reading F.E. Smith's essays'. Simultaneously she drew pleasure from occasions when she felt she had performed well, such as in November 1941 when she commented in her diary that she 'had a splendid fight—delivered my best speech [to the jury] yet—slow, expressive with just the right emphasis with an opening prepared but only noted'. Her thrill at new work and new clients is also self-evident, as was her genuine pleasure and delight at the increasing number of compliments she was beginning to receive for her work.

In later years Rose recalled a story when appearing before Mr Justice Donovan (later Lord Donovan), whether true or an embellishment is not clear. She had, in her peroration to the jury, apparently said: 'Members of the jury, when you retire you should have the defendant's evidence ringing in your ears'. Mr Justice Donovan, when summing up to the jury said: 'Miss Heilbron has asked you to consider your verdict with the defendant's evidence ringing in your ears—I hope no such disability afflicts you!'

1942, her second year in practice, began well. At the end of January she was briefed in a case involving seven men, including a local Councillor, David Rowan, accused of conspiring to enable men to evade service in the Forces. The hearing took place at Liverpool Assizes before Mr Justice Oliver and attracted considerable publicity. Her client, one Bernard McHale, a bookmaker's clerk, was alleged by leading Prosecuting Counsel, Neville Laski KC (later Recorder of Liverpool), who was leading her former pupil-master, Dick Trotter, to be the 'King Pin of the Conspiracy'.

McHale pleaded not guilty to a variety of offences. He was the only accused to plead not guilty and hence was tried separately. Although the prosecution had employed leading counsel, ie King's Counsel, Rose conducted the case on her own without a leader. Her client was found guilty and sentenced to two years' imprisonment. However, she considered this lenient as she was expecting him to receive four years. By contrast, one of the other conspirators, David Rowan, got seven years' penal servitude. She was complimented by her professional colleagues and the judge on the way she had conducted the case.

The Rowan case helped to cement her early reputation and the work thereafter arrived on a regular basis. She remarked in her diary: 'I seem to be getting known since the Rowan case'. By the end of February she was commenting: 'It has been an excellent month for work' and by June she stated: 'Am as busy as could possibly be—made nearly £200 last month—not bad for a 3rd year woman [the date taken from call to the Bar]'.

This must have been well received by her then clerk, Robertson. Barristers were originally paid in guineas, a guinea being one pound and one shilling. The shilling, equivalent to five pence in today's coinage, went to the clerk. Barristers' clerks were the first port of call of the solicitor, who would ring up the chambers and often rely on the advice of the clerk as to whom to brief. Clerks had tremendous power and could make or break the career of a barrister. Robertson, however, seems to have been supportive, albeit to be approached with kid gloves. In fairness, at a time when women were relatively rare at the Bar, he seems to have been progressive in his outlook. When Rose became engaged she took her fiancé, Nat Burstein, to tea to meet Robertson one Sunday at his home. He often described the deference he was told to show as 'like meeting the Pope'. Robertson apparently lived to a ripe old age, and died in 1985 aged 89.

ROSE'S FIRST SOLO MURDER TRIAL—THE CASE OF *LARKIN*

In October 1942, Rose was briefed for the defence by John A Behn, Twyford & Reece in her first murder trial on her own. She is believed to be the first woman to have represented a defendant in a murder trial without a leader. She was still only 28. This was another of the litany of firsts that was to mark her professional career. Murder trials attracted keen interest in those days not least because convicted murderers faced capital punishment and the judge, when sentencing a defendant to death by hanging, would don a black cap.

Henry Larkin, a 50-year-old dock labourer, was accused of murdering Mrs Elizabeth Dutton with whom he had been cohabiting for 10 years. To his displeasure she had met a Belgian seaman, although the Belgian said, untruthfully, that he had never been intimate with her. Larkin, in a fit of jealousy, cut her throat with a razor.

The trial took place at Liverpool Assizes on 29 and 30 October 1942 before Mr Justice Oliver and a jury. He ran the defence of provocation and accident contending that the razor had been intended for the Belgian to give him a fright, but the deceased had fallen on to the razor. Rose spoke in her final speech for 45 minutes. Larkin was acquitted of murder, but given five years for manslaughter. It was regarded as a good result in the circumstances and attracted considerable local press publicity under such banner headlines as 'Man, Mistress and Sailor' and 'Story of Scream from a House'. The case clearly made an impression on Dr Williams, Senior Medical Officer at Warrington Remand Centre, who some

32 years later, when Rose became a High Court Judge, wrote to her out of the blue reminiscing about the case.

Later in the year Rose appeared before the Lord Chief Justice, Viscount Caldecote, Mr Justice Humphreys and Mr Justice Asquith in the Court of Criminal Appeal, to appeal the verdict of manslaughter and the five-year sentence. It became a leading case on two issues: when a judge can put questions to a jury as to the basis of their verdict and the need for recommendations of mercy to come spontaneously from the jury without any direction from a judge. It was the first time a case in which Rose had been involved reached the Law Reports.[1]

A BROAD RANGE OF WORK DURING 1941–42

The volume of Rose's work was now increasing rapidly. For instance on 14 June 1942 she refers to working on 14 divorce cases and on 16 June to doing seven 'running down' cases (motor accident cases). By the end of July and the legal vacation she comments that she had been in court every day for weeks and was feeling a bit weary. Come 1 September and the end of the vacation, 16 sets of papers awaited her. Thus she found herself working most nights and weekends.

Importantly, not only was she receiving some local press attention, but judges were regularly complimenting her, and her own more senior colleagues were saying praiseworthy things about her. She was attracting supporters from among her barrister colleagues, such as Edward Steel (later a County Court and Circuit Court Judge) who was in the same chambers, and Neville Laski KC (later Recorder of Liverpool), as well as from local solicitors. She was also starting to get the occasional case from outside her own Circuit, the Northern Circuit, in May being instructed by a firm of solicitors in Leicester.

Several of the cases in which she was involved in 1941 and 1942 attracted local press interest: some because of the inherent interest of the case, others because of the novel involvement of a woman barrister. Not all resulted in success.

Rose acted for the defence in a number of cases involving criminal prosecutions arising out of breaches of wartime regulations, such as obtaining lambs in excess of rations and selling tinned meat. These had allegedly been sold in breach of an embargo on purchases other

---

[1] *R v Larkin* [1943] KB 174.

than by catering and manufacturing establishments. Then there was the case of George Farquhar whom she defended on a charge of stealing 4½ lbs of sweetbreads and neck ends to the value of 3s from the lairages of his employer. His defence had been that he had worked there for 44 years and it had been accepted custom to take home certain offal and bits of meat, but that changed during the War. Unfortunately his story did not convince and he was fined £5.

Abortion was then a criminal offence and Rose represented Annie Neary at Liverpool Assizes before Mr Justice Hallett. Annie Neary had been accused of conspiring with three other women to procure an abortion. She pleaded guilty to using an instrument or some other means on herself.

At this stage in her career, cases involving various forms of dishonesty, such as theft and obtaining money or goods by false pretences, were the bread and butter of her criminal practice. There was during this period the case where Rose unsuccessfully defended a man for stealing over 22,000 cigarettes. He was found guilty, but given a 'light' sentence of six months. She also appeared, led by Noel Goldie KC, at Liverpool Assizes before Mr Justice Stable defending one of five men charged with conspiracy, false pretences and theft in connection with timber and fittings and wages.

Rose was also starting to develop the civil side of her practice. She represented plaintiffs in several personal injury cases arising from motor car accidents or accidents involving buses. The epithet 'Portia' was beginning to be used more regularly to describe her. Thus there was the case where 'Portia at the Bar' represented a Mrs Annie Levy who had injured herself on a flagstone. On another occasion she successfully appeared at Penrith County Court for a company, David Bell Ltd, recovering damages and costs for her client in a claim for damage to clover seed alleged to have arisen when a lorry carrying the seed was ripped open in a collision.

She also became the first woman to appear in a North Wales Court. The case was the result of the publicity of the *Larkin* appeal which had reached a firm of London solicitors. They instructed Rose to represent the Principal of a Jewish girls' school, Mansfield College, which had been evacuated from Hove to Pentrevoelas during the War. The case, heard at Llandudno County Court, concerned the refusal of an architect to pay £23.18.7d, the balance of a term's school fees for his daughter, based on an alleged verbal agreement. Rose obtained judgment for her client with costs. Press articles appeared under such headings as: 'Judge's Praise for

Woman Counsel', and 'Woman Barrister Congratulated'. They also recorded that the Judge, Sir Thomas Artemis Jones, commented on the able way in which she had presented the case.

Infrequently, Rose undertook briefs for the prosecution. She acted for the prosecution in an appeal from the Police Court at Liverpool Quarter Sessions before Recorder Hemmerde concerning five prominent Merseyside men. The men had been convicted of having aided and abetted an alien in failing to furnish the necessary particulars under the Aliens Order to the registration officer of the district.

Occasionally a divorce case would bring a little light relief, such as when she represented a wife petitioning for divorce in July 1942. The petitioner's husband had taken ill earlier in the year. His wife, the petitioner, had visited the doctor who had told her that her husband had something on his mind and if she could find out what it was he would get better. She did. It was that he had committed adultery with a woman with whom he had been pretending to be on Home Guard duties. Whether he got better, history does not relate: but he did get divorced.

Although some of Rose's cases, such as the examples above, attracted publicity, many did not. As they illustrate, her caseload was very varied. Many were criminal cases; others were civil, personal injury and family cases. Rose was building up what is termed a good junior general common law practice. She continued to appear at Police Courts and Inquests, but was attracting more cases at Quarter Sessions and even had cases at Assizes, where the most serious cases were heard. In some of her more difficult cases she was led by a King's Counsel (KC), colloquially known as 'silk' after the silk gown worn by KCs. Simultaneously, in her civil work, her appearances continued at the County Court and Court of Passage. However, Rose was by this time making a positive effort to gear her practice to appearances at the higher courts. She travelled considerably, undertaking cases in various towns on the Northern Circuit including Carlisle, Preston, Manchester, Warrington, as well as her home town of Liverpool. She was learning all the time. She commented in May: 'up in the morning early for another new experience—Preston Sessions'.

These achievements were made against the backdrop of the Second World War. Liverpool was a prime target for bombardment because of its thriving port and was badly blitzed in the War. 1942 was a particularly bad year for air raids and blitzes. Rose had bought a shelter, but in air raids seems to have taken cover under the stairs. She did occasionally have to evacuate the house, taking her father, her book of photographs, providing the only memory of her late mother, and Prince with her. Her father still lived with her and a housekeeper had become a permanent fixture, albeit a constantly changing one. One arrived 'complete with four trunks!'

There was a noticeable decline in her social life at this point: no doubt in part because many of her male friends and colleagues had been called up to the War, but also because she was extremely busy and anxious to make her mark and seize all opportunities that came her way. She saw her cousins: she was particularly close to her cousin Dora, the daughter of her late mother's eldest sister, and spent time with girlfriends. She nonetheless continued to indulge herself with the odd extravagance. She also did various domestic chores, such as painting and cleaning out the store room or 'doing the greenhouse—30 bunches of grapes'. Her diary entry for 7 June 1942 perhaps epitomizes the sort of rushed life she was leading at the time: 'Did 7 running down then went and bought the Bechstein grand [piano]. Quite thrilled about it. 2 conferences and then home to prepare a running down'.

Her own conclusion at the end of 1942 recorded in her diary:

> I think I had a quite successful year. I'm getting as many, if not more briefs than I can manage—though I must see that fees are more adequate— I've made two tremendously new good friends—Everyone is quite charming and my financial position is at any rate solvent—as is Dad's, which is a load off my mind.

1943

The start of 1943 saw one of the products of a successful practice at the Bar. Rose was offered the brief for both the defence and prosecution in a case in Lancaster. Having accepted the defence, she could not take the prosecution. Professionally new horizons were opening up. In May she received her first brief from the Director of Public Prosecutions, the chief prosecuting lawyer in the country. It was to prosecute an infanticide case. She appeared as a junior in two more reported cases, one concerning stevedores' negligence and the effect of the Docks Regulations 1934, where she was led by Noel Goldie KC at Liverpool Assizes.[2] The other was a case in the Court of Appeal where she was led by George Lynskey KC (later a High Court Judge) in which her client, the plaintiff, was successful,

---

[2] *Collins v AE Smith & Son Ltd* (1943) 75 Lloyds Rep184.

the issue on appeal concerning the liability to an invitee.[3] She also did a case on her own in the Divisional Court in London, which in those days principally heard appeals from Magistrates' Courts by way of Case Stated.

On 28 January she noted: 'Liverpool Quarter Sessions: 60 prisoners and 12 appeals of which I got 9—must be a record for sessions'. In March she appeared in her second murder trial defending Hung Leung, accused of murdering the warden of the Chinese Seamen's Welfare Centre with a knife. The defendant alleged the victim had killed his father and stolen his property four years earlier. The trial took place at Manchester Assizes before Mr Justice Hallett. Rose's client was found guilty and the sentence of death was pronounced.

On 9 June she represented Walter Cecil Bentick, found guilty but insane before Mr Justice Lawrence at Liverpool Assizes. He had gassed his wife in the oven, putting a pillow over her head for good measure, having already given her a blow on the head with a flat iron. Simultaneously he left a note saying he loved her and the children. The case caused interest because expert evidence had been given of the accused's state of mind using 'a brain machine' which recorded brain impulses compared with a normal brain.

The following week Rose defended John Elijah Povall, a ship's steward, aged 41, instructed by Silverman & Livermore, on a charge of murdering his wife. The case was heard at Liverpool Assizes before Mr Justice Lawrence. Povall's wife had been associating with a Dutchman and possibly with other men while he had been at sea. He discovered this when he received an anonymous letter. When confronted, his wife said she was going to leave him and he killed her in a crazed attack not knowing what he was doing. The jury acquitted him of murder on the grounds of provocation, but found him guilty of manslaughter. Povall was sentenced to 10 years' imprisonment. It seems to have been a rather sad case as the husband was a devoted husband and family man. The dying wife had told him that she still loved him and wanted to start afresh and he kissed her. It was clearly a difficult case for Rose as a defence advocate. This is evident from the intervention of the Judge when, most unusually, he commented on the jury's verdict of manslaughter saying that he had thought the accused was guilty of murder.

---

[3] *Lomas v M Jones & Son Ltd* [1944] KB 4.

In early November Rose unsuccessfully defended on a capital murder charge at Liverpool Assizes, this time before Mr Justice Wrottesley and a jury. The case lasted two days. Thomas James, a 26-year-old seaman, was charged with murdering one Gwendoline Sweeney, someone with whom he had been associating on the night of 17 August 1943. Her body had been found in the cellar of an empty bomb-damaged house. Unfortunately he did not have much of a defence. The evidence was pretty overwhelming, but like every citizen he was entitled to representation and Rose put up a good fight and 'had excellent results in cross-examination'. The Bar operates what has become known as the cab-rank principle. It means that every barrister has to take any case within his or her expertise on the basis of a reasonable fee and is founded on the basic principle that everyone is entitled to be represented, whether in criminal or civil cases, irrespective of the distastefulness of the case.

The evidence as to the cause of death was from a serious wound to the vagina giving rise to substantial loss of blood and caused by the insertion of a piece of wood coupled with asphyxiation from strangulation. When the Detective Inspector initially told the accused that he believed him to be responsible for the woman's death, he replied: 'Not me, I would not strangle anybody, I would knife them'. Such gruesome candour caused him a real problem. No one had mentioned to him that the woman had been strangled and the only way he would have known was if he had done so himself. Unfortunately for him too, his drinking mate also gave evidence that, the day after the murder, the accused told him that he had held the deceased 'by the throat until she could not move'. His defence was that the woman, who allegedly was a sexual pervert, had strangled herself or had been strangled during a perverted sexual act with the accused, such that an acquittal or manslaughter would be the right verdict. The accused did not give evidence, usually a sign that he would not improve his case if he did. Nor did he call any witnesses. The prosecution did not give a closing speech, but Rose did for the defence. The jury only took half an hour to convict him.

After the conclusion of the case Rose endorsed her brief: 'Plea: not guilty; Verdict: guilty; sentenced to death'. It was not a case that she enjoyed. But as a barrister she learnt to become case hardened and to do her professional job. Murder self-evidently is a horrible crime frequently involving grisly facts. She often recounted the story of once having had to examine a pickled human neck in the course of one of her murder cases. Not quite the same as Damien Hirst's formaldehyde cow!

On 18 June she prosecuted in the case of To Kin, a seaman, who was charged with wounding with intent to do grievous bodily harm and appeared at Liverpool Assizes before Mr Justice Lawrence. It was alleged that armed with knives and iron bars he had entered a house where some Chinese were playing dominoes and a fight occurred, but he alleged that he did not start the fight. He was acquitted.

These were perhaps the most notable of her cases in 1943, but represented only a small part of her workload and a small number of the professional clients she was by then beginning to acquire. The frenetic existence of a busy junior continued, for example on 19 May she noted: 'Over to Birkenhead County Court, then hoping to make a dash back to Liverpool for 5 matrimonials'.

1943 also saw Rose falling in love again, but the relationship was far from satisfactory, although it lingered on and off for the next two years until eventually she realised the man in question was not the man for her. It was also the year when her sister became engaged to Arthur Davies, a soldier. They married later that year and had three children. Ralph, the youngest and an engineer, has inherited his grandfather's aptitude for invention. In April 1943 Rose purchased the family home, 22 Menlove Gardens North, from her father. Her father was by then not a fit man and suffered from diabetes and Rose continued to keep house and care for him. Her lifelong love of nice clothes is also apparent from such comments as 'bought a stunning costume' and the fact that she had acquired a dressmaker.

It was, however, the following year, 1944, in which Rose was really to make her mark in some important cases. Although Rose enjoyed advocacy, she also had a real love for the law. 1944 provided an opportunity for Rose to exhibit her legal skills in three cases in particular.

THE CASE OF *DUNBELL*

The first case inauspiciously concerned soapflakes. Soapflakes were rationed during the War to approximately 3oz per week. The plaintiff, one Dunbell, was stopped while riding his bicycle one night by two police officers, Roberts and Rothwell, and found to be in possession of 12–14 lbs of soapflakes. He was arrested and charged with their unlawful possession in that they had either been stolen or unlawfully acquired. His case was disposed of before the city magistrates two days later and, following further police enquiries, he was given an absolute discharge. He brought a claim for false imprisonment against the arresting constables. The Judge found against him and he appealed to the Court of Appeal before Lord Justices Scott, Luxmore and Goddard.

Rose was instructed on the appeal by Silverman & Livermore and was led by John Maude KC, a Chancery silk, who was more used to dealing with trusts and land issues than crime and general common law. The issue in the appeal related to the basis on which Dunbell was arrested. The two police officers sought to justify Dunbell's arrest by relying on certain statutory provisions. However, these required them to ascertain the plaintiff's name and address which they had not done. Nor, given the nature of the alleged offence, could they have relied upon a common law arrest without first obtaining a warrant, which they had not done either.

It was and remains the practice in the Court of Appeal that when leading counsel sits down following his or her submissions the bench asks junior counsel whether or not he or she would like to follow. Unless there has been some pre-arranged division of labour, such opportunity is invariably declined with a nod. Following leading counsel in such circumstances is regarded as something of a criticism on the way the leader has performed. On this occasion, in January 1944, Rose, then aged 29, bit the bullet and realising that by lunchtime the appeal was almost lost, and that her leader had not really dealt with or understood the key points in the case, rose to her feet. She had no doubt obtained, out of courtesy, the last minute agreement of her leader to do so. She spoke for one and a half hours, turning the case around. She herself described it as 'the most amazing experience'.

It was a courageous decision, not least to take on a court of that calibre and one which was initially distinctly against her case. Such is the legal terror that the interventionist questioning of leading counsel by some appellate courts instils in juniors quietly sitting behind a silk, that one junior has in more recent times accompanied his nod to an enquiry as to whether he would like to follow his leader by the additional comment of 'not without a crash helmet, my Lords!' Her courage paid off and her client succeeded on his appeal with costs. A new trial on the issue of damages was ordered, although the case subsequently settled. It was an important case legally and was reported in the Law Reports.[4]

---

[4] *Dunbell v Roberts* [1944] 1 All ER 326.

Such was the impression that Rose had made on the court that 12 years later, when writing to congratulate her on becoming a Recorder, one of the Judges who had heard the appeal, Lord Goddard, known to be a fairly ferocious judge, and by then Lord Chief Justice, wrote:

> I have not forgotten—though you may have—a case in the CA when in an appeal—was it from Lewis J or was it the Court of Passage—though I think it was the former—we were about to dismiss it being misinformed by your leader—Maude who did not know the meaning of demurrable [meaning fails to show a good defence].You pulled it out of the fire!

THE CASE OF *ADAMS v NAYLOR*

In May 1944 Rose found herself instructed by Silverman & Livermore once more for a two-day case in the Court of Appeal appearing without a leader against the then Solicitor General (later Lord Chancellor), Sir David Maxwell Fyfe, who was leading a team of two further barristers. Young Robert Adams had been severely injured and his friend had been killed while playing on some sand dunes. They had come upon a minefield which had recently been laid by the Ministry of Defence on requisitioned land, but whose perimeter and warning notice had been obscured by the silting of sand in high winds. The claim was for damages for negligence. Rose had not been instructed in the court below where the trial had been heard before Mr Justice Cassels. Robert Adams' young brothers aged 12 and 14, who had been playing with him, had given evidence about the circumstances of the accident. Despite the tragic circumstances of the case, the claim failed in the court below on the ground that the boys were trespassers.

The Judge pithily summed it up thus:

> You are not of course to put dynamite on to your land for the express purpose of blowing up a trespasser. The mines were not put on to this land for the purpose of blowing up trespassers. They were put on to the land for the purpose of blowing up the enemy, and if the enemy had come over and go to this minefield, everyone would have rejoiced when they met with their deserts ... And therefore if these lads were trespassers—and I am very much inclined to think that they were ... they would not be entitled to recover.

The appeal to the Court of Appeal was not successful, although Lord Justice Scott dissented.[5] The case was ultimately to reach

[5] *Adams v Naylor* [1944] KB 750.

the House of Lords and in turn lead to legal history being made. It was an important case as evidenced by the fact that the Ministry's counsel was the Solicitor General, the second law officer in the Government. Rose's written brief on the appeal had endorsed the case's importance beginning with this paragraph:

> This is an extremely important appeal ... The principal point in the appeal which is one of the greatest public importance is as to the liability of those responsible for the laying and maintenance of mine fields for injuries caused by them to members of the public and whether the Personal Injuries Emergency Provisions Act 1939 affords the Respondent a conclusive defence. There are a number of subsidiary questions peculiar to this case but the general question is one of principle and the case is probably regarded by the authorities as a test case.

Rose's brief in the Court of Appeal was marked 40 guineas and 1 guinea for the consultation, although when the case reached the House of Lords the brief was marked 'in forma pauperis', ie free representation. There were no photocopiers in those days. Instead Rose had had typed the relevant extracts from all the 30 cases she was intending to cite before the Court of Appeal. Among her papers for the case was found her old university notes on the common law of trespass and negligence indicating the depth of research she had undertaken to find historical precedent in the days before on-line search facilities.

LEARY CONSTANTINE

To this day the name Leary Constantine retains legendary status in the cricketing world. Leary Constantine was born in Trinidad in 1902. His cricketing prowess earned him a place on the West Indies national cricket team with which he first toured England in 1928. He quickly acquired a reputation as a distinguished all-rounder: in 1928 taking 100 wickets and making 1,000 runs and in 1930 leading his team to its first Test victory. He moved to England with his wife and daughter and joined the Nelson team in the Lancashire cricket league. In later life, after retiring from cricket, he became a commentator for the BBC, was called to the Trinidad Bar and served as Trinidad and Tobago's High Commissioner. He was later knighted and then ennobled.

His fame as a cricketer did not, however, lessen the discrimination and hostility he and his family suffered as a result of being black, emphasising the contrast, as his friend CLR James put it, 'between his first class status as a cricketer and his third class status as a man'. Leary Constantine became Rose's client. In July 1943 Leary Constantine was to captain the West Indies side against England at Lords in a charity match. He was given leave from his then employment with the Ministry of Labour as Welfare Officer in charge of West Indian technicians and trainees on Merseyside to do so. He had booked hotel accommodation for himself and his wife for four nights at the Imperial Hotel London and had inquired whether there would be any objection to his staying on the grounds of his colour and was told that there was not. When he arrived it was made clear to him that he and his family were not welcome. The manageress explained this to them in the most offensive terms by saying: 'We don't have niggers in this hotel'. When asked why, she replied: 'Because of the Americans ... He can stop the night but if he does not go tomorrow morning, his luggage will be put outside and his door locked'. He was then found alternative accommodation at the Bedford Hotel.

He brought an action for damages. Rose, instructed by Sidney W Price, was led by Sir Patrick Hastings KC, one of the leading advocates of his generation. Rose herself commented on his advocacy: 'he's terrific'. She always remembered the lesson he had taught her only to run one's best points in a case. The case was tried in an improvised air-raid shelter in the Law Courts by Mr Justice Birkett. It was the time of the War when there were flying bombs in London. The Judge began the proceedings by saying: 'I think I am entitled to take judicial notice of the fact that Mr Constantine is a world famous cricketer'. Under cross-examination Leary Constantine was asked: 'Colour prejudice is particularly in evidence in the US?' To which he replied 'Yes'. He was then asked: 'If a hotel had a large number of American guests it would be justifiable to consider whether the prejudice would exist among the guests?' He responded: 'I don't know how to answer that because I booked for four nights and they knew I was coloured'. The Judge accepted Leary Constantine's evidence and found that the defendant, Imperial Hotels Ltd, refused to receive and lodge Leary Constantine 'without any just cause or excuse' and awarded him £5 nominal damages.

As a junior Rose appears to have pleaded the case initially claiming damages 'for refusing to receive and lodge the plaintiff in the defendant's inn, the Imperial Hotel'. It was not an easy case legally, particularly as it was not possible to prove any special or actual monetary damage, which is normally a necessary ingredient in most legal civil actions. The case was essentially a discrimination case, but there was no anti-discrimination legislation in place in those days on which Rose could rely.

The case was therefore brought on the basis of breach of a common law right, namely Leary Constantine's right to be provided the accommodation upon payment. The legal term was an 'an action on the case' and it was argued successfully therefore that in such a case damage is presumed. One of the main legal authorities relied upon by the plaintiff and followed by Mr Justice Birkett, was the famous eighteenth-century case of *Ashby v White*,[6] a case about the right to vote where the fundamental principle, established by Chief Justice Holt, was that:

> If the plaintiff has a right, he must of necessity have a means to vindicate and maintain it, and a remedy if he is injured in the exercise or enjoyment of it; and indeed it is a vain thing to imagine a right without a remedy; for want of right and want of remedy are reciprocal.

It was a landmark case and an early legal victory against racial prejudice at a time when such matters did not readily impinge on people's consciences and for which English law then provided no direct remedy.[7]

ROSE'S DEVELOPING JURY ADVOCACY

Rose was now acquiring a reputation both as an incisive cross-examiner and also as a persuasive and eloquent jury and court advocate. Little survives of her jury advocacy from this time, but in 1944 she represented Ralph Joseph Fay, a jobbing builder, at Chester Assizes in a case that lasted for seven days, which was a long time for cases in those days. He was charged with conspiracy to defraud the War Damage Commission by submitting untrue statements and accounts and obtaining cheques and money by false pretences. He was alleged to have charged for materials he had not used and overcharged for labour and conspired with others to do so. The following is an extract from her speech to the jury:

> [Do you, members of the jury,] think Fay had been a little careless. Was he, in company with many other builders in Birkenhead and district, a little overworked? Do you think, after hearing his answers for seven

---

[6] (1703) 92 ER 126.
[7] *Constantine v Imperial Hotels* Ltd [1944] KB 493.

hours in the witness-box, that he was a man who set out to defraud? In 1941 builders were not looking for work; work was looking for builders. What reason had Fay to pile on work which was not there? Fay was a man who started in a small way with four men and after ten years could enlarge his business so that he became the employer of 30–35 men. Although Fay was an employer he had not acquired the habit of keeping every document. Who would think when doing hasty repairs for Birkenhead Corporation that two years afterwards every hundredweight of mortar and every bill would be dissected in this way.

It is not known whether or not her oratory was successful on his behalf.

Rose's professional reputation, at least locally, was by now soaring. She was extremely busy, being instructed in a whole range of cases both criminal and civil, often doing cases on her own which would normally have had leading counsel and achieving excellent results for her clients. From murders, manslaughters, conspiracies, even a breach of promise of marriage case, to two cases in the Court of Appeal reported in the Law Reports, indicative of their legal importance. One of these reported cases concerned the issue of liability of a shipowner to an injured electrical apprentice and the other the issue of stevedores' statutory duty to an injured ship's painter. In some cases she was led: others she did on her own.

ROSE'S FIRST APPEARANCE IN THE HOUSE OF LORDS

Rose also made her first appearance in the House of Lords, the highest court in the land. William Clark Tomlinson had been employed for 24 years as an engine driver by London Midland and Scottish Railway Company. In 1942 he was summarily dismissed arising out of an incident involving an alleged assault. He claimed that his dismissal was in violation of procedures negotiated under the Railways Act 1921 between, on the one hand, the Associated Society of Locomotive Engineers and, on the other hand, the Firemen and the Railway Company. He alleged that such procedures entitled him to proper notice of the allegations and to a hearing. He denied he was guilty of any misconduct. It was accepted that the procedures had not been followed. Although no case had been pleaded by way of defence that his actions amounted to gross misconduct justifying summary dismissal, this did not stop the Judge, Mr Justice Cassels, from finding for the Railway Company on the ground that Tomlinson's actions amounted to gross misconduct.

An appeal was made to the Court of Appeal. It failed, the court indicating, among other things, that in the circumstances it had been open to the Judge to find that the dismissal was for very grave misconduct despite such a case not having been pleaded. The Court of Appeal also refused leave to appeal to the House of Lords, a prerequisite to seeking leave from the House of Lords itself. Rose then petitioned the House of Lords. The petition drew attention to the wider implications of the conditions of employment for railway servants generally. Such a plea was necessary to engage the attention of their Lordships as one of the grounds for an appeal to the House of Lords [now the Supreme Court] is that it should involve a matter of general public importance. Rose was summoned for the hearing of the petition at short notice on 25 July 1944. It took place in the Committee Room, where all cases have, until recently, traditionally been heard. She commented that after 'an interesting argument' we 'lost'.

Rose was by now also becoming a local household name. Her cases were being reported in the press, mostly locally. Such publicity for her cases, together with the novelty factor of her being a woman undoubtedly helped her practice, but equally had she not been good at what she did she would not have attracted the quality of work she was getting nor the favourable publicity.

5

The End of the War and Marriage

THE END OF THE WAR IN EUROPE

1945 WAS A watershed year for Rose. The year started well, her recording in her diary that she had '26 cases [at Quarter Sessions] which I think must be a record for one counsel'. After a spectacular win in a particular case, one of her regular instructing solicitors even discussed her taking silk, promising to support her with £1,000 worth of work if she did, for taking silk was—and still is—a risky step for any barrister. She had only been in practice six years and was aged 30. Taking silk at such a young age was unheard of for a man, let alone a woman, but it was not that long before she did, and in so doing made legal history.

Her portfolio of cases continued to increase in variety and importance and she continued to cross new boundaries. On 18 January 1945 she appeared in a murder trial at the Old Bailey. On 24–25 January she appeared in another reported case in the Court of Appeal in conjoined appeals.[1] The appeals concerned an employer's liability for his servant's negligence which occurred at a time when the servant was temporarily working for someone other than his normal employer. In one of them she was led by Edward Hemmerde KC, who, after opening the case, invited her to argue it, showing great faith in her abilities. Scott LJ was in her favour, but she 'had a thoroughly enjoyable time persuading Du Parcq and Morton', which she did, as the appeal succeeded. At some point in 1945 she appeared against her good friend and fellow female barrister, Eileen MacDonald, also of the Northern Circuit, in what was apparently the first case in which two women barristers had appeared on opposite sides of a case.

Yet despite her success she was not complacent about her abilities and continued to learn from her mistakes. For example, on losing

---

[1] *Dowd v WH Boase & Co Ltd; MacFarlane v Coggins & Griffiths (Liverpool) Ltd* [1945] KB 301.

one particular case she noted: 'Lost ... which I shouldn't. I was upset about it because I didn't do it well'. On another occasion she records: 'Did a good plea. I find a little thought to the words beforehand can turn a bald drivel into something with style and it's worth the effort'. Nor had she lost the thrill and excitement of it all and commented in her diary on getting work from a new client 'what a marvellous client to capture'. She also took her first and only pupil, John Edward Jones, for six months of his year's pupillage. He was to become a Circuit Judge (formerly County Court Judge) in later life.

1945 saw Rose's first serious forays into the world of speech-making. On 15 February she gave an address to the Rotary Club of Liverpool. Among the guests were the Lord Mayor, Lord Sefton and the Bishop of Liverpool. Her talk, entitled 'Some Defects of the Law', highlighted several legal issues in need of reform, some of which reforms have since been implemented: others 60 years later are still being debated. They were themes that Rose regularly re-visited in her speeches. Among them was the problem of inconsistent sentencing, particularly by magistrates. This followed a then recent case which had caused public dissatisfaction. She suggested that guidelines should be provided. She referred to the disadvantages of having all appeals in London which was beyond the means of most litigants. She criticised the delay in such appeals, which in criminal cases could mean that a defendant whose appeal succeeded could have already spent his sentence in prison. In a review of her speech the writer noted that 'she enhanced the part which women are destined to play in civil life'. This early speech was the first of many that she was to make in her life on a range of subjects, but particularly on the issue of women and, of course, on the law.

On Monday, 7 May, peace was declared in Europe. For the following week everyone was in holiday mood and there were many parties. After almost six years of war things were to change in every walk of life in England: not least at the Bar. Male colleagues who had been serving in the War would return to practice and compete for the work that was available. The fact that Rose's career continued to go from strength to strength after the War, as will be seen, was testimony to her real talent and skill and proved that her success was not merely a product of the lack of male competition during the war years.

Looking back over her practice, which up to this time had been built up exclusively during the war years, it is interesting to note that, apart from her original difficulty getting into chambers, she does not appear to have suffered any obvious discrimination in developing her practice, or at least any she commented about in her detailed diaries. She may not have been instructed by the grander firms or by firms in London, save occasionally, but on her Circuit she had a very large number of regular clients. Certain professional rules and regulations did discriminate against women, but these became more relevant in later years. Why was this? One suspects because during the war years her male colleagues were distracted by participating in the War recognising that, as in other fields of endeavour in wartime, women were called upon to fill the shoes of men. The problems would arise in society generally when the men returned to civilian life after the War: and the Bar was no exception.

MEETING NAT

Luck plays a part in everyone's life and so it was to do for Rose. Had it not been raining one Thursday in late April 1945, she might never have met her future husband. Nathaniel (Nat) Burstein was a General Medical Practitioner with a practice in Anfield, a working class district of Liverpool. He was Irish by birth, but had moved to Liverpool, aged 23, on 12 June 1929. He had qualified as a doctor at Trinity College, Dublin and spent a couple of years working as a junior doctor at Mercers Hospital in Dublin. He was the youngest of six children and had five elder sisters. His parents were both from Poland, having met in their early twenties in Leeds to where they had independently emigrated. His father, who had had a small antiques shop, had died when he was 12 and his mother when he was 18. Nat had then lived with his eldest married sister, Julia, and her family during his university days.

Nat moved to Liverpool shortly after he qualified as a doctor, borrowing £5 (now worth about £250) from one of his brothers-in-law. He excelled in sport and had played the equivalent of county cricket in Ireland when 16. Up until his death at the grand age of almost 105, he still retained a keen interest in and knowledge of all sports. Through sport, particularly golf and tennis, and the Jewish community, he soon established a large circle of friends in and around Liverpool, as he was a very sociable and popular person. He was a keen bridge and poker player and altogether what one might describe as 'an all-round bloke'.

Yet, approaching 40, he had still not met the girl of his dreams. Nonetheless, despite being somewhat coy about such matters, he seems to have had no shortage of female attention attracted by his debonair looks and sense of fun. He was over 6 ft tall, slim, dark haired, although balding, and sported the then fashionable moustache which he retained throughout his life. He had wanted desperately to sign up for the War, but was not allowed to do so, as his partner had gone to war and someone was needed to run his, as well as some of the neighbouring, medical practices. He took virtually no holiday for the whole of the five and a half years of the War. He lived for some time over the surgery where his favourite bachelor meal, cooked by the caretaker, was apparently smoked salmon and chips! He later moved to live with one of his other married sisters, Annie, who by then had also moved to Liverpool. Rose and Nat had several friends in common, but somehow they had never met, despite the Jewish community in Liverpool being relatively small.

Every Thursday afternoon, their half day, Nat and three of his medical colleagues, Basil Levy, Jack Chisnall and Bill Dove used to play golf, a tradition that continued until Nat moved from Liverpool many years later. The four doctors were very close friends and ultimately their wives became good friends too. Only bad weather would stop this weekly outing at the Woolton Golf Club.

One evening at the Woolton Golf Club, Nat was having a few drinks with another friend called Bass Simpson, who was a Member of the Liverpool Cotton Exchange. Bass Simpson had some interest in the prison board and so had some knowledge of the courts. The conversation turned to the law and Nat was asked whether he had ever been to court. An arrangement was reached that if there was a wet Thursday when he could not play golf he would accompany Bass Simpson to court.

The wet Thursday duly arrived and Nat went to St George's Hall where the Assizes were held. There from his seat in an area reserved for members of the prison board in one of its cavernous and famous courts he saw Rose for the first time. He had heard of Rose because of her local celebrity. She was apparently defending someone on a hopeless robbery case. Whether the story is apocryphal or not, the defendant was alleged to have been seen throwing a brick through a window. That night Nat arrived late to his poker game at the house of his close friend Harry Epstein (whose best man he had been), father of the late Brian Epstein, manager of the Beatles. Clearly he had a glint in his eye, for apparently when he mentioned having seen Rose Heilbron in court earlier that day the assembled poker table teased him about the relationship by standing up and wishing him 'mazeltov'—and he had not even met Rose at that stage. Rose recalled that she did notice a dark stranger in the visitors' gallery.

He was clearly captivated and Nat was never one to procrastinate. A few days later Stuart Rayner, a solicitor who was also a patient, visited his surgery. Chatting at the end of the consultation Nat mentioned to Stuart Rayner that he had been to court and had seen Rose Heilbron. Stuart Rayner replied that he knew her very well and that his offices were above her chambers. He then mentioned that he was having a small party with a few friends, including Rose, in a couple of days to which party he invited Nat. There Rose and Nat met for the first time. This encounter very nearly never happened, as Rose had been very tired and did not want to go out. However, she was persuaded by her then invalid father to go. He told her to have a bath and she would feel refreshed.

Thus began a whirlwind courtship. Rose recalled that at one of their early meetings Nat was rather the worse for wear—everyone was celebrating the end of the War—and he was to be seen juggling spoons! He soon sobered up, however, in the pursuit of his love and bombarded her with wonderful gifts, mostly of food which was then rationed, and flowers. He had met the girl he wanted to marry and he was not going to let her get away. They met regularly for lunch at a Spanish restaurant in Bold Street, the then Liverpool equivalent to Bond Street in London. Approximately two weeks later they were engaged. Rose, who had a tendency to exaggerate when telling a story, had always said it was three days after they met, but her diaries say otherwise.

They were to marry three months later on 9 August 1945 in Harrogate. Nat was just 40 and Rose 30 (she was 31 ten days later). They were to be married for over 60 years and would celebrate their diamond wedding in 2005, receiving a card from Her Majesty the Queen. Although the Second World War in Europe had ended, the War continued in other arenas in the world and rationing still existed. Rose and Nat were married at a small ceremony in Harrogate by a cousin of Rose's, Rabbi Samuel Daiches. Her father was by then too frail to travel to Harrogate for the wedding and she was given away by her cousin, Dora's husband, Mo. Rose wore a fashionable dress in dusty pink and a black tulle hat with veiling. They were driven to the ceremony by one of Nat's patients who then drove them to Torquay for their honeymoon, which in those days was a very long journey. Only one photograph of their wedding survives. Nat apparently forgot to organise a photographer, for which it is pretty certain that he was good humouredly reprimanded and, according to legend, they stopped at a local photographer who took the photograph.

On their return from honeymoon Nat moved into Rose's house in Menlove Gardens North where they lived for the next 15 years. Rose always loved her home life and a nice home. Rose was very house-proud and had been replacing carpets, curtains and other items over the previous years when she had had enough money to do so. The house had five bedrooms and a large-ish garden with a greenhouse housing a prolific grape vine. It was amply big enough at first to accommodate the newlyweds and later their daughter and a Nanny, but eventually Rose wanted to move.

Rose's father went temporarily to live with Rose's sister. His diabetes and general ill health had by now left him confined to a wheelchair and he was deaf and blind. Eventually he went to a nursing home not far from where Rose and Nat lived where he spent the rest of his life enjoying his pipe and having regular visits from his family.

Married life brought Rose emotional security and great happiness. Nat's wicked sense of fun and humour and his common sense approach to life kept her feet on the ground. It was a family joke that she would always—in the words of a well-known advert—turn a crisis into a drama and it was Nat who brought a perspective to such events. He made her laugh—and she had the most infectious of laughs. He introduced her to a new circle of friends largely unassociated with the law. They had a lively social life. Every Thursday, for instance, after the four doctors had played golf they and their wives would regularly go out to dinner followed by dancing at the Bowler Hat Club on the other side of the Mersey. Both Rose and Nat were good dancers. There was, however, one area in which they were not wholly compatible. Nat was a great sportsman, but Rose was never very keen on sport, her sporting prowess being limited to temporarily taking up golf in the glow of early married life and playing a little tennis with her daughter in later years.

Nat provided a charming escort when Rose was invited to the more prestigious events associated with her increasing fame, and became popular amongst her friends and colleagues. He was also there for her, supporting her in more simple and endearing ways. He always met her at the train station when she had been out of London for a case, however late the train or the hour. His Liverpool practice meant that he never had to travel for professional reasons and so in later life after their daughter was born and Rose had to travel, this meant that there was always one parent at home.

Marriage also brought other more practical advantages. It gave Rose financial security. Even successful barristers, particularly in those days, were financially insecure. There was no guarantee of work. There was no regular pay-packet as barristers are self-employed. Even if there was work, payment was notoriously slow. Nonetheless expenses were high, including rent for chambers, clerks' fees and travelling, all of which had to be paid up-front. Rose therefore needed to have an overdraft facility, but despite her success she was finding her then bank manager distinctly unwilling to oblige. One wonders whether this was because she was a woman. Nonetheless, Nat introduced her to his bank manager and thereafter she had no problem. Moreover, Nat had a regular income as a doctor.

Nat remained in the same practice for almost 40 years until he retired. He was never overtly ambitious and was content to remain as a General Medical Practitioner, a role in which, because of his good bedside manner and intuitive medical sense, he excelled. He was never jealous of his wife's success: on the contrary he was happy to act as her consort, a role which in those days was relatively unique and pre-dated that of Denis Thatcher as the consort of Margaret Thatcher, our first female Prime Minister. Nat's medical status was, however, invariably misrepresented in the press which insisted on referring to him as a surgeon.

Married life also brought another asset, not one normally necessary in marriage, namely anonymity. In the years to come Rose's fame meant that, particularly locally, she was unable to go anywhere unrecognised once she gave her name. She was less likely to be recognised in the street because television was in its infancy and she did not appear on television. Moreover, photographs often captured her in her wig and gown, disguising her appearance to some extent, but her name was well known. She kept her maiden name professionally and her separate passport, as that was the name she was known by, but she used her married name not only for family matters, but also if she wanted to do something without anyone knowing who she was. On one occasion this led to some amusement. Many years later the family were en route to their holiday destination on a Greek island and stayed for one night in an Athens hotel in the shadows of the Acropolis. At the hotel reception Rose produced three passports: one in the name of Heilbron for herself; one for Nat in the name of Burstein and one for her daughter. When the man at the reception desk then looked at her quizzically—this was 1973—in her embarrassment she tried to explain that she and Nat were married. At which point the man threw up his hands and pronounced 'I don't care: I don't care!' This became a well-rehearsed joke in future life. The epithet 'Ms' had not yet arrived.

Marriage also saw the end of Rose's diary writing.

THE HANGING BOY CASE

The following year, on 26 July 1946, Rose took over the tenancy of the first floor of 34 Castle Street from Midland Bank previously occupied by Glyn Blackledge for an annual rent of £200 and she became head of her own chambers, something she did once again many years later in her career.

Following her marriage her junior practice continued to flourish until she ultimately took silk. One notable case in 1946 became known as the Hanging Boy Case. She defended Charles Lawrenson, aged 31, on trial for murder together with three other men. The case was heard at Liverpool Assizes before Mr Justice Sellers and a jury. It lasted for six days beginning on 29 April 1946. She was the only junior against four King's Counsel.

How did 11-year-old Charles Greeney, whose sister coincidentally was a patient of Nat's, come to be hanged from a clothes rack in the kitchen of his home at 62 Edge Lane, Liverpool? The issue for the jury was whether it was an accident, suicide or murder. Greeney had been sitting in a chair by the fireside doing a crossword puzzle and listening to the wireless when his father and mother last saw him alive as they left the house for a Saturday night drink. Two hours later they returned to find him hanged. Lawrenson, who had a criminal record gained in his youth for minor offences relating to larceny and the like, admitted burgling the house with the co-accused, but said that they had never touched the kid. He knew that Mrs Greeney was a moneylender and had money in the house and always went out for a drink on Saturday evenings. He said that they had peeped into the kitchen on the way upstairs to find the safe and saw the boy standing on a chair looking through a mirror on the mantelpiece. Evidence was given that the deceased was interested in the sea scouts and experienced in knot tying.

One of the key issues was to establish the cause of death. There were some marks on the boy that could have been sustained by him hitting his head on the mantelpiece either before or after asphyxiation. Another question was whether or not it would have been feasible for the boy to hang himself. Professor Glaister, Professor of Forensic Medicine at Glasgow University, who was called for the defence, said that he had found nothing to indicate that this boy was murdered. Nor was there any evidence of any disorder in the kitchen that would have been consistent with murder. In her opening speech to the jury, Rose said: 'The case is full of coincidence. Perhaps that is why you are here today. But coincidence, however strange, is not proof; certainly when a man's life is on trial'. All four were found not guilty. Lawrenson was subsequently given three years' penal servitude for the burglary to which he pleaded guilty.

A FLOURISHING AND WIDE-RANGING CIVIL PRACTICE

Many people remember Rose for her criminal cases: these were the ones that caught the public and press's attention, but she had a thriving and wide-ranging civil practice too. Commercial work, which her daughter later took up when she became a barrister, was simply beyond the realms of possibility for a woman in those days. Rose had several civil cases which were reported in the law reports. These included four Court of Appeal cases, namely: a case concerning landlord and tenant;[2] a case about the duties of a licensor in relation to personal injury to a young girl injured by a swing;[3] a case relating to issues concerning the Pensions (Mercantile Marine) Act 1942;[4] and a case involving issues of practice, joinder and costs.[5] In the first she appeared on her own and in the last three was led by Edward Wooll KC, who was also a playwright and a character of the Northern Circuit.

However, just as only a small fraction of her criminal cases were reported in the press, the vast majority of her civil cases also went unnoticed. The civil practice of a busy junior involves settling numerous pleadings: statements of claims and defences in particular. Civil cases were no longer tried by juries, save for some limited exceptions. Many such cases would have settled: others went on to trial either in the High Court if the claims were substantial, or, if lesser in value, in the local County Courts or the Court of Passage, whose jurisdiction was limited. The Court of Passage was abolished in 1971.

Those of her pleadings which still exist represent a window on life in Liverpool in the war years and immediately thereafter with its docks, extensive war damage and derelict and dangerous buildings and considerable poverty. Rose acted mostly for plaintiffs, though sometimes for defendants. The former were usually individuals

---

[2] *Greenhalgh v Tilson* (1946) 147 EH 269.
[3] *Sutton v Bootle Corporation* [1947] KB 359.
[4] *Makin v Masson* (1947) 81 Lloyd's Rep 39 (CA).
[5] *Wong Kwok Hong and another v AB Brown Ltd and another* (1948) 81 Lloyds Rep 199.

who had been injured at work or on the highways: the latter were almost invariably companies. There was no civil legal aid until the early 1950s and legal costs were usually borne by the Unions, whereas defendants were covered by insurance and so this work was better paid. In drafting her pleadings Rose would first write everything out in longhand. The document was then typed using carbon copy to produce a purple-inked copy which Rose retained. Often there was more than one draft. She retained many of these pleadings as precedents for future use and filed them under legal categories wrapped up in pink brief tape. This organised approach to her work continued and expanded commensurately with her career.

The first category of such pleadings comprised a huge array of unfortunate accidents on the sidewalk caused by alleged negligence. Being a pedestrian in Liverpool has always been a hazardous business and to this day Liverpool is notorious for what is colloquially known as 'slippers and trippers'—accidents on the pavement. In the 1940s Liverpudlians managed to trip over everything from tree stumps to pieces of wire, spades, loose straw, a pile of bricks, uneven flagstones and sandbags in aptly named Sandstone Road. Then there were those who slipped on wet pavements from leaks in drainpipes or on icy pavements caused by escaping water from a drinking fountain. Some cases were more dramatic and people fell down holes, air-raid shelters and excavation holes. Other pedestrians seem to have had a particular penchant for falling through metal coal grids into coal cellars. Even if they managed to navigate the pathway, they were liable to be hit by bricks falling off chimney stacks, coping stones off walls or debris from demolished buildings, or be knocked over by collapsing walls or milk cans falling off lorries. Some of the injuries sustained were very serious and occasionally people were killed: others were relatively trivial. Claims were usually made against the occupier of the property or the employer of the negligent defendant and occasionally the corporation was sued.

Then there were the accidents at the docks, where employees were injured all too frequently and the stevedores or ship-owner were sued. Although there were Docks Regulations, there was no Health and Safety Act, and the systems of work were often dangerous and inadequate and the employers negligent. Thus Rose regularly drafted claims for dockworkers and seamen, usually injured loading and unloading ships. Accidents, often producing very serious and permanent injury, occurred with slings and ropes breaking when hoisting bags of cement, bags of sugar, heavy sheets of armour plating and sheep's carcasses, to name but a few types of cargo.

Other accidents happened when people fell down hatches or holds on vessels, or were knocked over by cargo or hit by derricks or other parts of cranes or were struck by bogies or trains on the dockside.

Rose also drafted claims against employers in other places of work, particularly factories which were governed by the Factories Act 1937. Many of these were young boys and girls of 15 or 16. Any plaintiff under 21 was described as an infant and had to bring the claim by a parent and/or next friend. There were many cases where individuals fell off ladders or scaffolding collapsed. Others involved people slipping at work or falling down staircases, shutes and lift shafts. Machinery too collapsed, particularly lifting gear, causing injury. Serious hand injuries occurred with unguarded saws or bacon-cutting machines, or eye injuries when goggles were not worn and sharp metal objects flew into people's eyes. People were hit by barrels of beer, burned by caustic soda, died from burns from an ignited boiler, or were gassed by poisonous fumes or even contracted anthrax. Others fell into vats of boiling water or vats of boiling toffee and death or very serious injury resulted from explosions which occurred at munitions factories or in gas cylinders.

Injury claims were also drafted by Rose for many motor accident injuries, or to use the more colloquial description, 'running down' cases. In addition she drafted medical negligence claims, an area of law in which she undertook a considerable number of cases in later life. In this period claims against hospitals included, for example, allegations that while in hospital a child had contracted TB, that another child had been strangled in its cot, that someone had been paralysed from a negligently administered injection and that another had died as a result of having been wrongly given two disinfectant tablets.

Aside from personal injury and medical negligence claims, Rose was instructed to draft claims in many other types of cases. Sale of goods cases provided an interesting mix and in her early days she acquired a particular expertise in food which was unfit for eating. Dead wasps in jam, flies in milk, insects in marmalade and cockroaches in bread were enough to put any plaintiff off his food and lose his appetite, as the pleadings alleged. There were also unruly horses sold instead of docile ones, deformed horses instead of fit ones, fur coats which had sleeves which were too short or fur capes which were not 'fashionable'. There were breaches of hire purchase agreements, wrongful dismissal cases, cases relating to purchases of business or shares, and false imprisonment allegations. There were claims for the return of furniture and personal effects and motor cars wrongly withheld, cases of trespass, claims for libel and slander and for breach of promise of marriage.

Then there were the cases where Rose acted for defendants and drafted defences. These provided a similar wide-ranging catalogue of cases, although relatively few personal injury cases. Barristers tended to become known as a plaintiff lawyer or a defendant lawyer, and Rose was principally the former. There were a handful of claims in which she alleged by way of defence that the claim was fraudulent, an allegation of fraud being something a barrister can make only if he or she has written instructions and credible evidence to support the allegation. In addition to Statements of Claim and Defences she would, where appropriate, draft additional pleadings such as Counterclaims and Defences to Counterclaims and Replies to Defences. Often Interrogatories would be drafted asking questions of the party in advance of the hearing or Requests for Further and Better Particulars of the pleading. Some pleadings would be accompanied by a note or Opinion, whereas others would be left with blanks for the solicitor to complete. While many of the pleadings were straightforward, others took time and all involved reading the instructions and considering the facts and relevant law. This work Rose did alongside her court work. Some of the work was devilled, ie drafted in the first instance by another more junior member of chambers. As Rose's work became more complex she would give lengthier Opinions citing detailed legal authority where appropriate.

Not all the instructions were well prepared. In 1949, for example, when in silk, she wrote a 12-page opinion on a partnership matter on which instructions she noted in pencil: 'This case is a complete muddle from start to finish'. In silk too her civil practice developed alongside her criminal practice, but once in silk she no longer drafted pleadings, as pleadings were always drafted by junior barristers, the burden of excessive paperwork being one of the main reasons a busy and successful junior applies for silk.

A substantial number of these cases would have come to trial and would have involved the same sort of detailed and lengthy preparation as for criminal cases, with opening and final speeches and cross-examination of both factual and expert witnesses. For example, Rose would regularly cross-examine doctors to establish the nature and extent of the injury involved and whether it was caused by the accident, as well as the recovery prospects for the injured plaintiff. It was often said that she acquired a particular expertise in medical matters as a result of being married to a doctor. It undoubtedly helped to be able to have one's own walking medical dictionary at home.

Rose also purchased a model skeleton and several medical dictionaries of her own to aid her knowledge and learning on the subject.

As an additional forensic aid Rose acquired some toy cars to assist in determining the cause of motor accidents. In her judicial years she would give them to small children to play with when they came to her room in adoption cases. The standard of proof in civil cases is proof on the balance of probabilities rather than the higher burden in criminal cases of proof beyond reasonable doubt. Sometimes the issues would involve liability and damages: on other occasions the issue was damages only. Damages would include compensation for injury and special damages, such as damage to property or loss of earnings.

Rose had acquired some very loyal clients in civil work. John A Behn, Twyford & Reece with her friend Betty Behn, and Silverman & Livermore, in particular the two eponymous partners, Sidney Silverman and Harry Livermore, provided the bulk of her plaintiff civil work in this period of her career, sending her a very large number of cases. Other firms also sent her civil work, but to a lesser degree—maybe because they had less of such work available—most notably Berkson & Berkson, the firm of Barney Berkson whom she had known since university days; Rayner & Wade, the firm of Stuart Rayner who unwittingly was to play a very significant part in her personal life; Ernest B Kendall & Rigby, the firm of Ernest Kendall who was her personal solicitor; Sidney W Price and others. There was the occasional brief from a London solicitor, for example WH Thompson, which firm in later years became a more regular client. In her defence work she was instructed by the Town Clerk of Liverpool as well as several other solicitors who did not usually do plaintiff work, not all from Liverpool.

BESSIE BRADDOCK MP

One of the libel actions in Rose's caseload came to court in June 1947, when Rose represented Bessie Braddock MP and three other Labour Councillors as plaintiffs. The case arose out of an election address given during local elections the previous year by Councillor Bevins, a Conservative. The address had subsequently been printed in a pamphlet entitled the 'Abercromby Labour Voice'. It was alleged that certain statements in the address were defamatory. In 1947 Communists were the new scourge of the Western world. It was the start of the Cold War. It was contrary to Labour policy to be a Communist. The gist of the libel alleged was that Councillor Bevins had imputed that the plaintiffs had an understanding with the Communists.

Unusually, the plaintiffs did not pursue a claim for damages, but sought to prove that the offending statements were untrue and defamatory. The case was heard before Mr Justice Stable and a jury. Rose appeared for the plaintiffs without a leader, but herself leading John Edward Jones, her former pupil, against Denis Gerrard KC (later a High Court Judge). The defence denied that the words were defamatory and raised the legal defences of fair comment and qualified privilege.

The case attracted considerable local publicity not least because of the involvement of Bessie Braddock who was the well-known local Labour MP for Liverpool Exchange, a position she held for 24 years. Bessie Braddock or 'battling Bessie', as she was sometimes described, was larger than life in every sense of the word: huge of girth and with an indomitable character. She was renowned also for being a great campaigner against poverty and injustice. Nor did she pull her punches, but said what she thought, as is evidenced by the following amusing exchange which allegedly took place between her and Winston Churchill in the House of Commons when the latter, somewhat intoxicated, stumbled into the former. An angry Bessie Braddock straightened her clothes and roared 'Winston, you are drunk, and what's more disgustingly drunk' to which he replied 'And might I say, Mrs Braddock, that you are ugly and what's more disgustingly ugly' and then added 'But tomorrow, I shall be sober and you shall still be ugly'.

Bessie Braddock gave evidence in her usual forthright manner. Although previously a member of the Communist Party, she described herself as a loyal member of the Labour Party. At times during her answers to questions in cross-examination she seems to have got a little carried away inviting on one occasion the riposte from counsel for the defendants that 'You are not going to take charge of this court or me'.

Rose ended her opening speech before the jury thus:

> We know that those taking part are not always meticulous in the use of their language, but there was a limit. That was not something done in the heat of the moment, but a deliberately written election address, and Mr Bevins, in this case, overstepped his limit. He has made a false assertion of fact, calculated to imperil their reputations ... Such behaviour is incompatible with membership of the Labour Party, and would be regarded as disloyalty to their colleagues and the electors of Liverpool ...

They want to make it clear to the electors that the passage in the pamphlet is a tissue of lies from beginning to end.

Such was the novelty of women at the Bar at this time that it drew the comment in one newspaper that it was a record for the longest speech by a woman barrister, as if it was a marathon race. At around this time too, Rose's first appearance against another woman barrister provided copy for the press on two occasions. The first occasion, as already mentioned, was as part of the first female duo in Manchester against her good friend Eileen MacDonald and the second, as part of the first women duo in Liverpool against Miss Monier Williams.

The Judge dismissed the action brought by the three Labour Councillors on legal grounds and concluded that the remarks concerning Bessie Braddock were published on a privileged occasion which restricted the grounds on which it could be libellous, but left certain issues for the jury to decide. Unfortunately they decided against Bessie Braddock. Whether or not it had anything to do with the fact that Bessie sat on the front row of the court apparently eating a punnet of strawberries is unknown!

Bessie Braddock, with Rose representing her and the other plaintiffs, appealed to the Court of Appeal. The appeal was heard in January 1948 before the Master of the Rolls, Lord Greene, and Lord Justices Asquith and Evershed. The appeal by the other plaintiffs was dismissed, but Bessie Braddock's appeal succeeded on the ground that the Judge had misdirected the jury. The Court of Appeal ordered a new trial and the case was subsequently settled. It became an important case on the circumstances when the defence of common interest qualified privilege exists in the context of elections and is reported in the law reports.[6]

Bessie Braddock and Rose became rather unlikely friends and when the family moved to their new home in the early 1960s, Bessie and her husband Jack (one time Leader of Liverpool City Council) came to visit and brought as a house-warming present a lovely magnolia tree, which is presumably still there and no doubt by now even larger than Bessie. Quite when and where the friendship began is not known.

However, it was two cases involving issues of law which reached the House of Lords that were of particular significance at this

---

[6] *Braddock and others v Bevins and another* [1948] 1 KB 580.

juncture of Rose's career: one was a civil case, the second a criminal case.

ADAMS v NAYLOR IN THE HOUSE OF LORDS

The first was the appeal to the House of Lords in *Adams v Naylor*, the case concerning the boys playing on the sand dunes, one being killed and the other injured by a mine. The appeal was heard in the spring of 1946.[7] Rose appeared on her own against the then Attorney General, Sir Hartley Shawcross. Not only was it the first time that a woman had appeared in a case on her own in the House of Lords, but she was appearing, still a junior barrister, against the senior law officer in the Government. The former posed practical problems as in those days there was no such thing as a ladies robing room. How it was resolved is not known, although in later years Rose used the peeresses' toilet.

The facts of this case have already been set out. As often happens, as cases ascend the court hierarchy, arguments are refined. In the House of Lords the issue ultimately revolved around whether the claim could be brought under the Personal Injuries (Emergency Provisions) Act 1939 which provided a statutory compensation scheme for 'war injuries'. If the statute applied then it barred a claim for common law damages which was the basis of the claim in the case. The House of Lords, despite what Viscount Simon described as Rose's 'excellent argument', said that the case fell within the statutory provisions as the mine was being used to combat the enemy.

The significance of the case, however, arises from the fact that a plaintiff could not in those days sue the Crown. To get round this, the practice was established of suing a servant of the Crown in tort in the hope or with the promise that, if the action succeeded, public funds would pay the damages and costs awarded against the defendant. The issue was thus whether or not that individual was personally liable which was often very difficult to prove. The procedure involved the Crown nominating an individual as defendant. The practice was criticised by the House of Lords. The bar on suing the Crown was a severe restriction on the ability to obtain compensation in many circumstances.

---

[7] *Adams v Naylor* [1946] AC 543.

Lord Simmonds stated:

[I]n such an action as this the defendant is merely 'nominal' and ... the real defendant before the Court is the Crown. No one who has experience of these matters will doubt that legislation on the subject of proceedings against the Crown and particularly in regard to tortious acts committed by its servants is long overdue.

Lord Uthwatt added 'and the increasing activities of the state in affairs which affect the ordinary man make the matter urgent'.

Apparently during the course of argument the Attorney General promised to bring in legislation, which in his capacity as a member of the Government he had authority to do, and the following year, 1947, the Crown Proceedings Act was passed enabling citizens to sue the Crown for the first time.

CHRISTIE v LEACHINSKY

Rose's most significant criminal case in legal terms during this period was *Christie v Leachinsky* in which she was led by Neville Laski KC, against Edward Hemmerde KC. Like Dunbell it was a false imprisonment case, but this time, instead of soapflakes, the goods in issue were remnants of cloth. Mr Leachinsky, a 'waste merchant', was arrested by two constables on a charge of unlawful possession of the cloth, a misdemeanour. He spent the night in a police cell and was then remanded in custody for a further week by the magistrates. This charge was withdrawn at a subsequent hearing, but Mr Leachinsky was immediately re-arrested on a charge of larceny, again without a warrant, requiring him to spend another night in the cells. The larceny charge was subsequently dismissed by the magistrates.

Mr Leachinsky brought an action for false imprisonment in respect of both periods of detention. One of the original defendants was Herbert (Bert) Richard Balmer, then a Detective Sergeant in the Liverpool constabulary, although he was later dismissed from the proceedings. Bert Balmer was to play a very significant role in many of Rose's cases, but in particular in a double murder case a few years later. The defence was that the arrest was made on the footing of a reasonable suspicion of a felony ie that Mr Leachinsky had stolen the goods, although the constables did not so inform Mr Leachinsky.

The case reached the House of Lords and established an important point of law which Viscount Simon, in the opening words of

his speech, described as an issue 'of great importance … for it concerns the liberty of the subject and the extent of the powers of the
police to arrest without warrant'. The case established that it is a
condition of a lawful arrest at common law that the party arrested
should know on what charge or on suspicion of what crime he is
arrested. Accordingly, a policeman so arresting someone without a
warrant must inform him, at the time of arrest, either of the charge
in respect of which he is being arrested or at least inform him of
the facts which are said to constitute a crime on his part, unless the
party is already acquainted with such information. On the facts of
the case Mr Leachinsky was entitled to damages for the first period
of detention, but only in relation to the night in the cells as the
remand in custody was by order of the court. Damages were left to
be assessed by a jury.[8] There is no record of a subsequent case and
it is likely that this aspect of the case then settled as the principle
had been established.

A PARTICULAR ADMIRER

Perhaps Rose's overall success in this period is summarised by
Lord Maenan, Presiding Judge of the Liverpool Court of Passage
from 1903 to 1948, the civil court where she had appeared many
times, when he replied to the letter she had written to him on his
retirement in July 1948 with these words: 'It was my privilege to
listen to the one superbly successful lady at the Bar of England.
I cannot forget her voice, so clear and musical, in which was
displayed her marked ability'.

[8] *Christie and anr v Leachinsky* [1947] AC 573.

6

Becoming a Mother and Taking Silk

THE BIRTH OF A DAUGHTER

1949 WAS ANOTHER momentous year in Rose's life, heralding immense changes both professionally and personally. In 1948, at the age of 33, after she and Nat had been trying for a family for some time, she became pregnant. Late parenthood was rare in the middle of the last century, particularly for a first child. Pregnancy did not, however, stop Rose working. It seems never even to have been an option she considered.

The only concession was that, alone among Liverpool barristers, she was given her own room in St George's Hall at the top of the main staircase where she could work during Liverpool Assizes and at other times, a room she kept until the end of her days in practice as a barrister. It was a cold and draughty, rather cavernous room, with a concrete floor and a very high ceiling. There were no side windows, the little natural light there was coming from some glass in the ceiling. In the absence of running water Rose made do with a large pitcher of cold water and a basin, although there was a toilet. The room was heated by a coal fire, but the toilet was freezing cold from the thick stone exterior walls of the building. The outside world was screened off with a panelled door with opaque glass panels. Rose created a one-way spy-hole by putting a small piece of sellotape on one of the opaque glass panels enabling her to see who it was who was about to knock on the door. It was hardly *House and Garden*.

Rose was lucky in that she did not suffer badly from morning sickness. She continued to work throughout her pregnancy, allegedly even taking papers wrapped up in customary legal pink ribbon into hospital with her when in labour so she could carry on working. She had had a relatively uneventful pregnancy, but her baby had other ideas! She was not in a hurry to enter this world. Whereas today the baby would have been induced, Rose had to wait for 10 months for her baby's appearance, which came via emergency caesarean section at the Liverpool Maternity Hospital in the early hours of 2 January 1949. By all accounts it was a worrying time and Rose nearly died in childbirth. The festivities of New Year had no doubt contributed to the crisis. Presumably, at least partly because of this, Rose and Nat never tried to have more children.

The baby weighed in at a hefty nine pounds with a shock of jet black hair. She was to be called Hilary, not after the legal term, but because it was the only name both parents liked. Hilary was given the middle name of Nora as it shared a Jewish derivation with Rose's late mother, Nellie. Rose apparently often called her baby her little 'Rosebud', a nick-name that she fortunately ceased to use as her baby grew older!

Nonetheless, the relief of a successful delivery and the joy of being a father for the first time at what was a late age of 43, left Nat drinking whisky and toasting crumpets with his good friend Bill Dove, also a doctor and one of his regular Thursday golfing partners. It was alleged that Bill Dove had first taken a peek at Hilary even before her father, as in those days, husbands, even if doctors, were not permitted to be present at the birth. The surgeon who had delivered Hilary joined them. The following morning, which was a Sunday, led to some poor patient of Nat's, who had the misfortune of being a florist, being woken up early to produce a bunch of flowers for him to take to his wife. According to Rose's records these comprised pink carnations, pink and white hyacinths and red tulips. Her cousin Dora's assistance was enlisted to produce new soft furnishings for the bedroom for the return home of mother and baby daughter. A large array of cuddly toys and baby clothes arrived from family and friends together with numerous bunches of flowers in a preponderance of pink, purple and mauve colours.

Although Hilary was delivered by caesarean—and in the days before epidurals, this was a major operation—Rose only took six weeks off before she was back in court. There was no maternity leave in those days or flexible working. More importantly, for her to have been away from work for a long time would have had a very deleterious effect on her practice. There never seems to have been any question of her taking it easy or stopping work for a few months. Attitudes to women were simply not forgiving. A maternity nurse was engaged to look after Hilary, followed by a nanny. On her daughter's birth Mary Ventris, a journalist on the *Liverpool Echo*, and friend of Rose's, wrote: 'The question now arises will the baby follow in her mother's footsteps and take up the law or in her father's and go in for medicine'. Eighteen years later she chose the former.

Apart from the personal joy of having a daughter, in the world at large Rose now became a role model and symbol of a working mother, something which was relatively unusual in those days, at least for a professional woman. Within a few weeks of Hilary's birth another event occurred in her professional career which would catapult Rose into a different stratosphere and accentuate the interest in her as a working mother.

TAKING SILK

In 1948 Rose had applied to become a King's Counsel, or to use the colloquialism, to take silk. A King's Counsel, or in these days, Queen's Counsel, is a senior barrister rather like a consultant in medicine. The appointment is made on application and only a small percentage of those applying, at least in 1949, obtained it, and not always on the first application. The decision was then that of the Lord Chancellor, after having consulted and taken soundings. Today there is a more transparent system with an independent body deciding the issue and making recommendations. On taking silk, a barrister obtains letters patent, is called to the inner bar of the court—ie sits on the front row in court—and does mainly larger and more important cases. In those days a silk always appeared with a junior barrister. Once in silk a barrister no longer has to draft written pleadings.

What prompted Rose to apply for silk at such a young age and when there had never been a woman silk before is not wholly clear, but Sir Hartley Shawcross, then Attorney General, had apparently encouraged her, as no doubt did others. It was clear, however, that she had a very successful practice of the type which, but for her age and her sex would have justified her taking silk in any event. Contemporaneous newspaper reports put her annual income at between £3,000 and £5,000 at this time, but this was probably a considerable exaggeration.

There still remained enormous prejudice against women at the Bar and it was far from certain that Rose, despite her qualifications for the position, would get silk at the first attempt. Rose's talents had secured the support not only of the two mandatory High Court Judge referees from whom she had sought references, but another High Court Judge, Mr Justice Cassels, volunteered an additional reference. The records of the Lord Chancellor's Office indicate that the matter went before the King on the recommendation of the Lord Chancellor, Lord Jowitt, and the King initialled the list of silks.

On 12 April 1949, Rose received a letter from John Hunt of the Lord Chancellor's Office which stated:

> I beg to inform you that, in pursuance of instructions received, a Royal Warrant directing Letters Patent to issue appointing you to be one of His Majesty's Counsel learned in the Law has been prepared, and I am directed by the Lord Chancellor to request that you will attend here on Tuesday the 26th April at 10am, for the purpose of making the usual Declaration before his Lordship ... The amount of Fees to be paid to the Exchequer in respect of the Letters Patent is £60....
>
> P.S. [In manuscript] Information regarding dress will follow tomorrow.

The following day Rose replied accepting the appointment. She was one of 19 new silks, of whom two were women. Rose was absolutely thrilled. She, along with Helena Normanton, who herself had had a distinguished career at the Bar, became the first two women silks ever made in England and Wales and thereby made legal history. Rose, being 34, beautiful, a wife and mother with a baby of three months old, caught the bulk of the public attention. Helena Normanton, aged 56, was nearing the end of her working life and retired a couple of years later, leaving Rose for several years the only female practising silk in the country. Rose was, and remains to this day, the third youngest silk ever made, and had only been in practice for 10 years, the minimum requirement for making such an application. It was exactly 30 years since the bar on women entering the professions had been removed by the Sex Disqualification (Removal) Act 1919.

After her appointment had been announced, Mr Justice Devlin (later Lord Devlin) congratulated Rose in open court at Liverpool Assizes saying:

> I cannot allow the court to start without some reference to the happy announcement in the Press this morning. The whole profession has watched with pleasure your brilliant career. They rejoice with you in the unique and well-merited achievement—double achievement—of taking silk at so early an age, and being one of the first women to be granted that honour. You have added yet another distinction to the proud record of the Liverpool Bar.

There were some further hurdles to overcome in the very masculine legal hierarchy to which she had just ascended. First, at the time it was traditional for practitioners on the Northern Circuit, once they took silk, not only to acquire chambers in London, a rule laid down by the Lord Chancellor, but also to move to London or at least 50 miles off the Circuit. The latter was a Circuit rule. This posed a problem for Rose, as Nat's medical practice was in Liverpool. A meeting of the 12 Northern Circuit male silks was called. Rose made representations explaining that to move would mean her separating from her husband. It was, as she often commented, both a worrying and humiliating experience for her. They relented, but only on condition that she kept her telephone number out of the telephone book. She thereafter continued to live in Liverpool with an ex-directory telephone number. Such rules no longer exist.

Rose still, however, had to seek chambers in London and give up her Liverpool chambers, as was then the practice on taking silk. She already had an association with chambers at 3 Pump Court in Inner Temple and so remained there where she was clerked by Charles Humphries who was blind. One of the young tenants in the chambers was Geoffrey Howe, later to be Chancellor of the Exchequer and Foreign Secretary in Margaret Thatcher's government, and to be instrumental in her ultimate downfall as Prime Minister. Some years later Rose moved to another chambers in Paper Buildings.

There also had to be an adjustment to the robes to be worn by a female silk, hitherto only worn by men. Rose received a letter from John Hunt of the Lord Chancellor's Office soon after her appointment. The letter stated:

> With the appointment of ladies to be King's Counsel, it has become necessary for provision to be made as to the style of dress to be worn by them, and I have been instructed by the Lord Chancellor for the information of the General Council of the Bar, to send you details of the style of dress that has been formally approved.

The letter then proceeded to set out the requirements for both 'full dress occasions' and 'less formal occasions'. The traditional formal or full dress robes required a barrister to wear a court coat, ruffles at the wrists and a lace frill round the neck, a silk gown with a pouch attached to the back into which money had historically been dropped by grateful clients, breeches, white gloves, tights and buckled patent shoes with a silver buckle and all topped with a full-bottomed white wig reaching over one's shoulders. For the less formal occasions, ie when in court, a wing collar and bands replaced the lace and frills and a short wig replaces the long wig.

Not usually known for its sartorial expertise, the Lord Chancellor's Department laid down in fine detail what was required. For example, the coat was to be 'made of black superfine cloth in the same style as a man's coat except that it should not be skirted but instead be short as in a lady's ordinary coat' and the skirt, which on formal occasions replaced the breeches worn by men, should be plain 'black superfine cloth', though for court wear it could also be in grey. The two-page letter also provided that 'those lady King's Counsel who attend Court functions should wear whatever dress is prescribed for ladies in general, and <u>not</u> the legal dress prescribed above [an old style velvet court dress]'.

The ceremony took place on 26 April 1949 in the House of Lords before the Lord Chancellor, which Rose, together with the other new silks, attended. The records of the Lord Chancellor's Office include the draft notes prepared for the Lord Chancellor's speech, not very politically correct by today's standards. The notes record the following:

> Nineteen persons made Silks by His Majesty on the Lord Chancellor's recommendation.
>
> A happy issue out of one of the Lord Chancellor's afflictions.
>
> Very special occasion—first English women K.C.s
>
> England not first to have them—Scotland, Canada, Ireland
>
> Two years ago there were women among the Clerks, now women among the K.C.s—you can never keep a good girl down ...
>
> You may like to mention Miss Heilbron's daughter, Hilary, who is about 3½ months according to the Evening Standard.

Rose's letters patent with the King's seal impressed upon it began:

> GEORGE THE SIXTH BY THE GRACE OF GOD OF GREAT BRITAIN IRELAND AND THE BRITISH DOMINIONS BEYOND THE SEAS DEFENDER OF THE FAITH To all to whom these presents shall come Greeting Know Ye that We of Our especial grace have constituted ordained and appointed Our trusty and well beloved ROSE HEILBRON one of Our Counsel learned in the law ...
>
> By The King Himself.

Rose also had to sign a declaration in far more flowery language than silks do today, reflecting the fact that she was a King's Counsel. It read:

> I, Rose Heilbron, do declare that well and truly I will serve the King as one of His Counsel learned in the Law and truly counsel the King in His matters, when I shall be called, and duly and truly minister the King's matters and sue the King's process after the course of the Law, and after my cunning. For any matter against the King where the King is party save in so far as I may be therein allowed or licensed I will take no wages

or fee of any man. I will duly in convenient time speed such matters as any person shall have to do in the Law against the King as I may lawfully do, without long delay, tracting or tarrying the Party of his lawful process in that that to me belongeth. I will be attendant to the King's matters when I be called thereto.

The publicity surrounding both her appointment and the ceremony later in the month was huge and gave her celebrity status. Her photograph appeared on the billboards in London Streets. Her photograph and appointment was in all the newspapers not just nationally, but as far and wide as Toronto, Johannesburg, Sydney, Bombay and British Guiana and in many other countries and places in the world. The headlines reflected the impact her appointment had at the time, including: 'Mother is KC at 34'; 'Well-earned Success'; 'Attractive and Clever'; 'Silks Without Breeches'; 'King's Portias' and 'Rose—KC'. She even appeared in *Illustrated London* with her photograph alongside the King, Princess Margaret, Rita Heyworth, Laurence Olivier, George Bernard Shaw and others as those who had 'made the 1949 headlines in romance, sport, world politics', although apart from journalistic licence it is hard to see under which of those headings she qualified.

Similar headlines greeted her attendance the following year at the opening of the Legal Year in Westminster Abbey. She was once again singled out for photography and news articles. She was photographed processing from the Abbey to the House of Lords for what is known as the Lord Chancellor's breakfast, namely wine and sandwiches, an event which had been re-introduced in 1949, following a gap of over a decade. As always the press reports were laudatory. For example, Norman Cook, a staff reporter at the *Daily Post*, wrote on her being appointed silk:

> Miss Heilbron's court technique has impressed me on scores of occasions. She has brought a refreshing sparkle into the most wearying of Assize civil actions. Her admirable air of confidence, her twinkling eyes, and—more often than not—the tilt of her wig with just that slight suggestion of rakishness, make her presentation of a case an affair of interest no matter how dull its content.

It is difficult, over 60 years after the event, to convey the impact in a male-dominated profession and a male-orientated world of a woman attaining silk. It was only four years after the end of the Second World War. There was still rationing, something brought home by the front page of the *Star* newspaper on 26 April 1949, the day Rose was sworn in as a KC. This had two equal-sized pictures: one of Prince Charles in the arms of his parents under the caption 'A New Picture for the Royal Family Album'; another of Rose under the Caption 'She Made History in a Wig', and the lead article began 'Fresh cream, ice cream made with real milk, and more chocolate should be freely available next year and there should be no real need for milk to go back on the ration'.

It was a time when women were only just beginning to climb the equality ladder. Rose's appointment to silk ranked alongside other notable female achievements in press articles. Several newspapers reported 'Thirteen "first footings" in 1949', additionally drawing attention to Professor Hilda Nora Lloyd, the first woman President of the Royal College of Obstetricians and Gynaecologists and Dame Debra Parker, the first female Minister of Health and Local Government and Cabinet Minister in the then Northern Ireland government and others. Another article entitled 'Suddenly they found the boss could be a woman—it's her century' addressed the issue of women attaining influential positions in business, academia and medicine, as well as the law.

Rose's photograph was frequently prominent and in the years to come she championed and supported many women's issues as her fame increased. There were many more firsts for her to achieve. In 1949, there were very few women barristers practising at the English Bar. Today, according to the latest published statistics for 2018, more than half the entrants to the Bar are women and just over a third of the independent practising Bar are women, including 275 female silks. It is a far cry from 70 years ago.

7

The Cameo Murder Trials

INTRODUCTION

ON SATURDAY EVENING 19 March 1949, the city of Liverpool witnessed one of the most notorious and shocking double murders in its history. The scene of the crime was the Cameo Cinema, three miles from the centre of the city, where that evening there was showing the film 'Bond Street'. It was a comedy-drama starring two relatively well-known actors of the time, Jean Kent and Roland Young. Part of the action included, coincidentally, a double murder. As in most fiction the crime was solved and the murderer caught and punished. But the real life drama that followed the end of the film that fateful Saturday night was of a very different order. It became one of Rose's most famous cases and launched her career in silk. It was also a fascinating and gripping story in itself. For all these reasons it justifies a longer exposition than her other cases.

THE MURDERS

As the final patron left the building following the last screening of the day, Leonard Thomas, aged 44, the manager of the Cameo Cinema, and John Bernard Catterall, aged 30, his assistant, were in the manager's office on the first floor of the building counting the confectionery takings. Shortly after 9.30 pm, the cashier came in with the ticket takings in a blue cloth bag. They amounted to £50.8s in cash, mostly in notes. She stayed about 3–4 minutes and left to go to the staff room. A few minutes later a masked man brandishing a gun burst into the room demanding the takings. Both men resisted and were shot at point blank range by the gunman, Mr Thomas receiving one bullet and Mr Catterall three. They both died from their gunshot wounds. The gunman escaped by blowing open the lock of the manager's office door, still brandishing his gun and telling everyone to 'stand back or I'll let you have it' and then running down the spiral staircase and into the side street. Two relatively young family men had lost their lives for the sake of just over £50 and in the end the gunman escaped without the money.

This brutal double murder executed in cold blood caught the public imagination and became headline news both locally and nationally. There was enormous pressure on the police to find the killer. The detective in charge of the case was Chief Detective Inspector Bert Balmer, later to be Deputy Chief Constable of Liverpool. It was not an easy case to solve. No witness was able to identify the gunman, as he was disguised, and in any event only fleeting glimpses of him running away were seen. Nor did anyone witness him entering the cinema. It was a case of building a case on circumstantial evidence, talking to informants, having some lucky breaks and finding a culprit. The investigation was a long drawn-out one with many thousands of people apparently interviewed and with many twists and turns before the alleged killer was eventually charged and tried. It was not until a half a century later that it became clear that the investigation had been deeply flawed.

JOHNSON

At the end of April 1949, Donald Thomas John Johnson, aged 22, a window cleaner and a Liverpool villain with a string of convictions for housebreaking and shopbreaking was charged, together with his brother, with robbing 30 shillings from a labourer on his way home. Apparently desperate to get bail he decided on a ploy. While awaiting trial on 2 and 6 May 1949 he made two unsigned statements to the police about the Cameo murders. These were to the effect that earlier in the week of the murders he had accompanied the gunman, whom he referred to by a false name, to reconnoitre a cinema for a robbery and had been shown the gun, an automatic pistol. The statements also explained that, as had been previously arranged, he met the gunman again near the cinema at 10.45 pm on the night of the murders and was given the gun to conceal.

Tantalisingly for the police, Johnson refused to disclose the gunman's name or where the gun was hidden or to sign the statements, contending that he had promised on the Holy Eucharist not to give the killer away. This was despite the fact that as inducements he was given bail on the robbery charge, with one of the police officers involved in the investigation standing surety for him in the sum of £20. Johnson's ploy back-fired and having given the police the run around by his refusal to give them this important information, he was charged on the basis of his unsigned statements of being an accessory after the fact to the Cameo murders.

Johnson was committed in custody to the next Liverpool Assizes. Rose was instructed to defend him. It was her first big case since taking silk the previous month. She was only 34 years of age with a young baby of five months. The case was heard on 14 June 1949 in St George's Hall at Liverpool Assizes before Mr Justice Lysnkey. It was also the first opportunity for any public airing of the events relating to the Cameo murders and aroused enormous public interest, with queues of several hundreds of spectators starting at 8 am trying to get into court.

After the charges were read out, Rose applied, in the absence of the jury, to have the indictment quashed on the ground that a man cannot be charged with being an accessory after the fact of murder before the murderer is charged, because if anyone was later charged with the murders he could either be acquitted or convicted only of manslaughter. She cited legal authorities in support of her submission, but the motion was rejected by the Judge.

The trial proceeded with Johnson pleading not guilty and Mr Dennis Gerrard KC for the prosecution opening the case. Rose then made a second application to exclude the admission of Johnson's unsigned statements as evidence on the grounds that they had been obtained by threats or inducements including the offer of bail and the provision of a surety. After hearing evidence from both prosecution witnesses and Johnson as to how the statements had been obtained, the Judge concluded that his second statement had been given as a result of the inducements and should not be admitted as evidence. This left the prosecution with insufficient evidence on which to convict Johnson and the Judge directed that the jury acquit him. It was Rose's first big success in silk and counsel apparently crowded round her to congratulate her. She had saved her client from 20 years in jail or a life of penal servitude.

Her success was widely reported in the newspapers: the *Daily Mail* headlines read 'Woman KC in 3-hour Duel with CID' and 'Miss Rose K.C. Wins her Case' and another 'Rose KC holds up the Assizes'. The novelty of a woman silk and the notoriety of the case led to reports of the case appearing in newspapers as far away as the *Egyptian Gazette* in Cairo, where the headline was 'Woman KC Wins her Case' and the *Montreal Star* in Canada which chose as its headline 'Woman KC Wins Acquittal in Sensational British Case'.

The Johnson case was not to be Rose's only association with the Cameo murders. The following year she was to tackle an even more difficult assignment. Nor was it the end of the involvement of Johnson with the Cameo murder investigation.

KELLY AND CONNOLLY

George Kelly was a 26-year-old small-time villain well known to the local police and with a criminal record. He and his brothers were part of a local gang. He mixed with those similarly inclined to crime, many of whom had been given amusing nick-names, such as Carpet Sam, so called because he kept nicking carpets, and flat-nosed Barney, a self-evident description. Kelly's mother ran a fruit stall on wasteland near Lime Street Railway Station in Liverpool and he used to help her with it. At the time of the murders Kelly lived with Doris O'Malley, a former prostitute, at a house in Wavertree, a few minutes' walk from the Cameo Cinema in Webster Street.

On 30 September 1949, over six months after the murders, and without any prior indication that he was a suspect apart from an initial call the day after the murder to check on his alibi, CI Balmer arrested Kelly for the murders alleging that he had actually fired the shots. On being charged Kelly said:

> I have never had a gun in my life. I don't know how to fire one: I have never handled one ... I don't know Charles Connolly: I have never seen him in my life. I have never seen the other people in my life [Jacqueline Dickson and James (Jimmy) Northam who had implicated him].

Earlier that day Charles Connolly, a former boxer and a married man with a small child, who as an adolescent had acquired a criminal record, but thereafter had gone straight, had also been arrested and charged with murder as being the lookout or 'douse'. He also protested his innocence from the outset and similarly maintained that he did not know Kelly.

THE COMMITTAL HEARINGS, THE EVIDENCE AND SUBSEQUENT APPLICATIONS

Kelly instructed Harry Livermore of Silverman & Livermore to represent him: Connolly instructed Mr Maxwell-Brown. Before the case could go to trial by jury the prosecution had to establish before magistrates that it had a prima facie case to answer. On 19 October 1949, a committal hearing in the case began before a magistrate and lasted four days. In those days the prosecution witnesses would all have had to give evidence, but the defence was not at that stage obliged to disclose its defence. Harry Livermore's request to hold the proceedings in camera to avoid prejudicing the trial was refused. Instead the case was very widely reported in the press and in considerable detail.

The Crown's case was based principally on the evidence of Jacqueline Dickson, a prostitute and her then pimp, James Northam, known as Stutty Northam, because of his stammer. Both had criminal records. Their testimony was that at about 7.30 pm on the night of the murders they had both gone to the Beehive Hotel, a public house in Lime Street, where they had met Connolly and later Kelly and another girl with dark hair. They alleged that they had discussed various robberies. They said that Kelly had asked Northam for a loan of his brown overcoat as it was cold, and Northam had handed it over. Connolly had then suggested a 'stick-up' at the Cameo Cinema whereupon Kelly allegedly produced a gun and bullets, six of which he proceeded to put in the magazine of the gun. When it had been suggested to him that someone might see him, Kelly is alleged to have said 'I don't care who sees me. I'm a Kelly'. Northam, professing not to like guns or the people who used them, alleged that he had refused to accompany Connolly and Kelly, as had Dickson. However they had allegedly arranged to meet the next day at the White Star pub in Brownlow Hill.

On Sunday 20 March, the day after the murders, Dickson and Northam alleged that they had all met up again at the White Star pub as previously arranged. They contended that Kelly had said: 'Balmer was up at my house this morning—if I'd still had the gun he would not have stood there so cocksure of himself'. Dickson and Northam also alleged that Kelly threatened them that if they did not keep their mouths shut they would be 'shut by him or his brothers'. Kelly was also alleged to have told Connolly to fix himself up with an alibi, to which Connolly had replied he would fix an alibi with his wife. The next day, Monday 21 March, it was alleged that when Kelly returned the brown overcoat to Northam, he had gone into some detail about the Saturday evening's events and had once more threatened Northam to keep quiet. Northam also said that his father had thereafter worn the coat which had been kept at his father's house, but the belt had been lost.

ROSE HEILBRON INSTRUCTED TO REPRESENT KELLY

On Saturday 22 October 1949, both men were committed to trial at Liverpool Assizes. The prosecution wanted the case to begin on 7 November. Rose, by then having been instructed by Harry Livermore to represent Kelly, requested more time in order to prepare the defence. She also applied to the court for the case to be transferred to Manchester because of the likelihood, following the widespread press coverage of the committal proceedings, of a prejudiced jury. Her application was supported by junior counsel representing Connolly, Gordon Clover. The Judge refused to transfer the case to Manchester, but adjourned the trial until January 1950 at Liverpool Assizes. With the benefit of hindsight had the trial taken place on 7 November, things might have turned out very differently, for a crucial piece of evidence did not become available until later in that month. But there are a lot of 'if onlys' in this extraordinary saga in which Rose played a significant part as Kelly's counsel.

Kelly had assumed, wrongly, that Rose's involvement with the application for the transfer of the trial was some sort of dock brief ie a barrister selected from those present in court to represent a defendant. According to George Skelly, the brother of Jimmy Skelly, Kelly's drinking companion, who had spoken to Connolly as part of his research for his book 'The Cameo Conspiracy', when told by Harry Livermore that she was a KC and was to defend him at his trial, Kelly was disappointed. The following conversation is alleged to have taken place between Kelly and Connolly, then both on remand together in the hospital wing of Walton prison: 'Hey Charlie, I'm not happy with this at all. Why couldn't I have a fella, like you've got? Whoever heard of a judy defending anyone?' to which Connolly replied: 'I don't know so much. I believe she's very good. She defended the Johnson fella didn't she? Got him off as well, so she can't be that bad'. However, when Kelly actually met her, his attitude apparently changed and he suddenly felt more hopeful than he had ever been since his arrest. As a result, his repertoire of songs, which he regularly sang each night and which reverberated around the hospital wing, was extended to include, in a voice imitating Al Jolson, the following: 'Rose you are my posy. You are my heart's bouquet. Come on out into the moonlight, there's something sweet love I wanna say'.

Rose was instructed under the Poor Person's Act and was paid only 15 guineas for the trial and its preparation. Her solicitors received their expenses and a fee of £2 per day paid for by the Crown. The cost of the prosecution, which was to run into several thousands of pounds, would be borne by the Crown. The preparation for the defence was extensive. Harry Livermore interviewed a large number of witnesses. Even Nat was brought into assisting and joined Rose and Harry Livermore for a view and a drink at the Beehive hotel. Nat also recalled being given the task of walking at a quick pace from the Cameo Cinema to the Leigh Arms, another public house, so that Harry Livermore and Rose could time how long it took.

One of the crucial decisions of any advocate is which witnesses to call at the trial. Many of Kelly's witnesses had criminal records which could affect their credibility if this came out. Sometimes a witness can be very helpful on one point yet damaging on another, so the lawyer has to decide whether or not to take the risk. These judgement calls are all part of the preparation of a court case. Similarly, the order in which witnesses are called is often crucial to winning or losing a case.

The public only sees the advocate in court, but hours and hours of work go into preparing for that performance. Rose had studied advocacy at length, reading many of the famous trials of the past to gain tips and techniques, as well as books on the subject, to improve on her own natural skills. Among her surviving papers on the Kelly case, for example, are manuscript notes entitled 'Notes on the Nature of Advocacy' in which she notes how one should approach different types of witness: the glib witness, the one whose credibility is in doubt, as well as many other tricks of the trade of an advocate. To an outside observer certain obvious questions may have been omitted, but there is usually a good reason for doing so, just as there may be for not pursuing a certain line of questions. Speaking to the Wallasey Soroptimist Club at the end of January 1950, shortly after the case had concluded, Rose also commented that the days of flamboyant advocacy in the style of Marshall Hall were over: 'It is no use trying to appeal to a jury's passions: the only way to succeed is to appeal to their reason' and that is, as the reader will see, what she tried to do for her client, George Kelly.

THE NEW EVIDENCE

The Crown had a fundamental problem in that both Dickson and Northam, on their own admission, were accomplices. Their evidence had therefore to be treated with extreme caution in the absence of any independent corroboration, a matter on which the Judge would be bound to direct the jury. They had turned King's evidence and so could not be charged in relation to the murders. At the time of the committal the only corroboration relating to the crime was the existence of the brown coat; the cinema witnesses said that the gunman wore a brown coat, some said with a belt: others without. The prosecution case was based exclusively on circumstantial evidence. No witness could identify the gunman who was disguised in a brown overcoat, a trilby hat with the brim turned down and a black mask and had dark eyes. No witness could identify the lookout. No gun was ever found. The trilby hat never featured in the evidence. No witness saw Kelly in a hat or coat that evening. No witness saw Connolly in the cinema. There was no forensic evidence of any blood stains on the accused or their clothing, nor was there any fingerprint evidence to associate them with the crime. DNA and CCTV evidence was not available in those days. One would have thought it was a thin case—and, so it was subsequently discovered, did the prosecution at the time, particularly before the evidence of one Robert Graham. However, it was an era when the police were rarely disbelieved and it was a brutal and callous murder for which the public wanted a culprit.

Towards the end of November 1949, the police had what, at the time, appeared to be a lucky break, although it was subsequently discovered not to be the product of luck, but of something far more sinister. On 21 November 1949, CI Balmer alleged that he had received a telephone call from the Preston police to tell him that a Robert Graham, then in Walton Prison, wanted to see him about the Cameo murders. At least three meetings allegedly took place altogether. The effect of Graham's evidence as set out in his consequent statement to CI Balmer, which does not appear ever to have been signed, was that he, Kelly and Connolly were in separate cells in the prison's hospital. Kelly and Connolly could not communicate with each other from their cells and were not allowed to exercise together. However, he, Graham, exercised with each of them on alternate days. They used him to pass messages to each other, and to find out what the other was going to do. He said that he had not known either of them before.

Graham stated that he had met Connolly before Kelly on 14 November 1949 and the next day he spoke to Kelly. His statement largely supported the prosecution's case and how Kelly came to be arrested and added some embellishments. In particular, according to Graham, Kelly told him that he had borrowed a coat from Northam, that he had shot the fellows, but that Connolly would not go in; then he had got rid of the hat and coat and 'was in my pub [ie the Leigh Arms] having a drink five minutes later. My life hangs on that five minutes'. This crucial piece of new evidence, which provided the corroboration which the police needed, was only formally tendered on the first day of the trial.

THE TRIAL OF KELLY AND CONNOLLY

On Thursday, 12 January 1950, Kelly was arraigned jointly with Connolly for the murder of Leonard Thomas at Liverpool Assizes at St George's Hall before Mr Justice Oliver and a jury of 10 men and two women. They both pleaded not guilty. The trial lasted for 13 days concluding on Saturday 28 January, the prosecution alone tendering nearly 50 witnesses. It was then the longest murder trial in British history. Basil Nield KC, MP for Chester and Recorder of Salford, represented Connolly leading Gordon Clover. William Gorman KC again led for the Crown. Rose led her former pupil-master, Dick Trotter, representing Kelly.

There was intense public interest in the case. There were lengthy reports each day in the newspapers setting out the evidence in great detail. Pictures of a young looking Rose in her full bottomed wig were daily splashed across the pages. Queues of several hundred formed early each morning trying to get into the public gallery, snaking back along St George's Hall. The police had to control the crowds when scuffles broke out as people tried to rush the doors. Members of the public fainted. On one occasion, when Nat was waiting to get into court, he heard someone he knew pretending to be a great friend of Rose's, which she was not, in an attempt to jump the queue and get a seat. In an age before television it was for many an intriguing, exciting and macabre piece of real-life drama with the possibility of the gallows looming at the end and in many ways, as is often the case, stranger than fiction.

The independent cinema witnesses put the time of the murder between 9.35pm and 9.40 pm. It was critical to the case for the Crown, on whom the burden of proof rested, to establish that Kelly had time after the shooting to dispose of his hat and coat, and presumably also the gun and mask, so that he was back at the Leigh Arms public house by the next sighting of him there by the prosecution witnesses at either 9.45 pm or 9.50 pm. To complicate matters, and the reliability of the witness evidence, the clock at the Leigh Arms was kept 10 minutes fast.

The prosecution witnesses gave evidence of the alleged movements of Kelly before and after the shootings and whether, when he was sighted, he was wearing a brown coat and a hat. All the witnesses were cross-examined by Rose who had some success in getting the witnesses to agree that Kelly was not wearing a coat when he was seen at the Leigh Arms; to accept that they were not sure about the time he arrived at the Leigh Arms; and to acknowledge that Kelly had said he had been on the bevvy, ie the booze, and did not look as if he had been having a fight.

CI Balmer gave evidence of certain 'verbals' allegedly made by Kelly, most of which were disputed. Importantly he gave evidence relating to an anonymous letter written in capital letters which had been received by the police on 4 April 1949, two weeks after the murders. The letter indicated that the writer knew about the planned robbery, though had refused to participate, but could identify the gunman and his accomplice. The writer alleged that he or she had a record and wanted to know whether, if he or she turned King's evidence he or she would not be prosecuted, and sought an assurance from the police by way of an advertisement in the Personal Column of the *Liverpool Echo*. The assurance was duly given, but, according to CI Balmer's evidence nothing further was heard from the writer until 29 September 1949, six months after the murders, when Northam and Dickson, who were at the time living together, ultimately admitted that they had written it jointly.

Northam and Dickson then gave evidence. They were cross-examined at length by Basil Nield KC for Connolly and Rose for Kelly to dent their credibility on a variety of issues in the case. During cross-examination Counsel elicited a number of inconsistencies between Northam and Dickson's story and the letter and drew attention to material omissions in the letter as well as to inconsistencies between the evidence of these two witnesses. Northam said he had written the letter and Dickson had helped him with the wording and the spelling. Dickson said they had both written it. Rose cross-examined Northam about the crucial brown coat, which was subsequently handed over to the police missing some buttons and a belt, as illustrated by the following exchange:

Was there any reason to bring it?
—Well no

Why did you bring it?
—I don't know. I thought it might have been cold in Liverpool.

And it might have been cold going back?
—Yes.

But you didn't take it back, you lent it?
—Yes ...

Did you not think it not a very wise thing to do to let your father wear this overcoat, knowing where it had been?
—I didn't think ...

You say Kelly suggested to you that you burn the overcoat?
—Yes.

And you said that you would have given it away but thought it might have been traced back to you?
—Yes.

Did it not occur to you that it might not have been very difficult for Kelly to have burned it?
—No

On the seventh day of the trial the prosecution called their star witness, Robert Graham. He admitted to having a string of convictions. He also admitted having been in a mental hospital the previous year for nine weeks. He, too, was cross-examined at length, but there was less material with which to shake his story.

On Thursday 19 January 1950, after the conclusion of the prosecution case, Basil Neild KC opened the case for his client, Connolly, who then gave evidence. Rose then opened the case for Kelly and he, too, gave evidence. Other witnesses were also called to support the respective alibis.

Kelly's and Connolly's account of their movements that night was very different. Kelly denied ever knowing either Dickson or Northam or Connolly, although Connolly said he knew Dickson by sight. Connolly's alibi was that he had been at a dance with his wife at the time of the shooting. Kelly said that in the afternoon and early evening he had been on a pub crawl with his friend Jimmy Skelly, but he denied ever going to the Beehive in Lime Street where the murders were allegedly planned. Shortly after 8.30 pm he left Skelly to make his way to the Leigh Arms where he had stayed until about 9.10 pm. He then left to go to the Spofforth, another public house, to look for Doris O'Malley, 'Dolly', the lady with whom he was then living, only to find that she was not there, so he had one drink and returned to his local, the Leigh Arms, at about 9.25 pm where he remained until closing which in those days was 10 pm, ie he was at the Leigh Arms at the time of the murders. The timings were not inconsistent with the evidence of Mr Ellis, the manager of the Spofforth, given earlier in the trial. Kelly also denied being at the White Star the following day. Kelly and Connolly both vehemently denied any alleged confession to Graham, explaining that they had no need to use him to pass messages between them, since they could communicate with each other from their respective cells without difficulty.

Who was the jury to believe? Did Kelly and Connolly know each other? Did either of them know Dickson or Northam? Were Dickson and Northam telling the truth about Kelly and Connolly to save their own necks or was the story a fabrication in whole or in part? Were Dickson and Northam actually participants in the crimes along with unidentified others but not with Kelly or Connolly? Were Kelly's or Connolly's alibis sound? Where did Kelly go after he left the Spofforth—directly to the Leigh Arms or indirectly via the Cameo Cinema? What impression did Kelly and Connolly, or for that matter the other witnesses, make in the witness box? How reliable was the alleged confession to Graham, a known convict with a history of mental problems? Would Kelly and Connolly, who vehemently denied their involvement in the murders, have suddenly after six weeks on remand unburdened themselves to a complete stranger, Graham? Was the existence of the brown coat and the confession sufficient independent corroboration to convict? Ultimately had the prosecution discharged its burden of proving beyond reasonable doubt that Kelly had shot and killed Leonard Thomas and that Connolly had participated in the joint venture?

Rose was acquiring a rapport with juries and the Kelly trial was no exception. Following the closing speech of Basil Nield KC on 25 January 1950 on behalf of Connolly, she rose to make her final speech on behalf of Kelly. After examining all the evidence at length, she concluded on the following morning:

> The police with all their resources, and after exhaustive enquiries, in my submission cannot produce, and they certainly have not produced, independent evidence ...

> There is no evidence of any gun having been sold to Kelly. There is no evidence from the Beehive of anyone who ever saw Kelly and Connolly together on March 19 ... There is no evidence that Northam and Dickson had been seen either with Connolly and Kelly alone or together, and there is no evidence whatsoever of any association at all. There is no evidence that Kelly left the Coach and Horses in time to go to the Beehive. There is no evidence other than Northam and Dickson that Kelly and Connolly were in the Star, either separately or together with Northam and Dickson on Sunday morning, March 20. There is no

independent evidence that anyone saw Kelly with a coat or hat on 19 March—indeed the only evidence is to the contrary ...

In my submission every part of the prosecution's case falls down under critical examination and analysis, and you may think in a matter so grave as this it would be unsafe to rely upon the evidence called before you to prove that George Kelly did this murder. Can you without misgiving accept the evidence of Graham? Is this the sort of evidence you can say without reasonable doubt is convincing? Are you satisfied beyond reasonable doubt that you know, in fact, who did this murder?

The murder was an appalling one, and I beg you let not your consideration be affected by prejudice or feelings of horror. If you are satisfied of the guilt of George Kelly you will not hesitate to say so, but if not, then your verdict must be one of 'not guilty'. In the perplexities, doubts and difficulties that pervade this case, can you, or any of you, with satisfying judgment, say that this man is guilty. You have a great, indeed, a tremendous responsibility, and everyone amongst you bears that responsibility fully.

I trust in your deliberations you will be guided by that consideration of justice of which we in this country are so very proud. After you have heard the final speech for the Crown and the summing up of his Lordship, I trust you will then clear my client from this dreadful charge and allow him to leave the court a free man.

The rest of that day and the next were taken up with the final speech for the Crown by William Gorman KC followed by the summing up of Mr Justice Oliver. The summing up took nearly six hours. At 11.08 am on Saturday morning, 28 January 1950, the thirteenth day of the trial, the jury retired to consider their verdicts. Queues had begun forming since 2 am to get into the public gallery and those lucky enough to be allocated seats remained in them while the jury was out, for fear of someone else taking their place. The local paper reported:

As the time of the jury's retirement lengthened a crowd steadily gathered outside St. George's Hall until by 12.45pm about a thousand people lined the pavement of William Brown Street ... All eyes were on the small black door at the end of St George's Hall. The sense of tension could be felt.

It had been the longest murder trial ever. After over four hours of deliberations the jury returned to ask the Judge, Mr Justice Oliver, for further information. When asked by the Judge whether he thought this would help, the foreman replied to the hushed court: 'I do not think that we will agree'. The Judge then said: 'If there is no chance of agreeing it would be useless to keep you here'. Majority verdicts were not then allowed. It was a sensational result. But it was also a pyrrhic victory, for both defendants were immediately ordered to be kept in custody and re-tried. Although unknown to the defence or prosecution at the time, the result might have been even more sensational if the Judge had allowed the jury a little more time, for it has subsequently been discovered from Home Office records that the jury were eleven-to-one in favour of an acquittal and only needed to swing one more juror round to the majority's way of thinking. This is yet another 'if only' in the story of Kelly, Connolly and the Cameo murders.

APPLICATIONS ON BEHALF OF KELLY

Any temporary euphoria was short lived. Rose was back in court the following Tuesday, 31 January 1950, this time to make two applications before Mr Justice Cassels. She first opposed the apparent decision to have split trials, which decision was stated to have been taken for the convenience of Connolly's counsel, Basil Nield KC. She had argued that such a decision was improper when the prosecution had alleged that this was a joint enterprise, where they had already been tried together, and where the evidence against one was substantially the same as the evidence against the other. She was told to re-make the application before the trial judge in the presence of the accused.

Secondly, Rose applied for the re-trial to be adjourned and for it to be transferred to another town on the ground of prejudice to her client. The trial had been re-fixed for the following day, leaving the defence no time to prepare the case. She argued that the line of cross-examination might be different, the whole burden of which would now be on her rather than shared with Connolly's counsel and that the preparation would have to meet the different circumstances. The prosecution objected on the ground that Dickson was very ill—she was allegedly suffering from tuberculosis—and was waiting to go into hospital. Rose was grudgingly given an extra day to prepare the case.

THE RE-TRIAL

On Thursday, 2 February 1950 George Kelly was for the second time put on trial for his life before judge and jury. The judge this

time was again Mr Justice Cassels. Rose, relying on legal authority, unsuccessfully renewed her objection to the split indictment
which was not supported by Connolly's counsel or the Crown.
The Judge made the decision in the exercise of his discretion.
The absence of Connolly made the case for Kelly more difficult,
not least because the evidence against Connolly was, if anything,
weaker than that against Kelly and hence Connolly's denials supported Kelly's story.

The second trial lasted six days. Most of the same witnesses were
called for the prosecution and defence. The prosecution called
42 witnesses. The evidence of Kelly and Connolly being seen
together was not wholly credible and the barman at the Beehive
said he had never seen them together. No one who knew them
well was called by the prosecution. The evidence of the two main
witnesses was even less convincing after they had been cross-
examined at length by Rose. The evidence of Graham was thus
once again crucial. Kelly explained that he had been foolish by telling everyone in the hospital wing about the evidence against him
given by others, but that he would not trust Graham as he had been
told he was mental. 'Well a mental man is not safe. You are liable
to tell him something and he is liable to say something else'. At
one point Kelly interrupted: 'Excuse me sir, Graham, McBride and
Johnson were in prison together, but nobody knows that, do they?'
When asked what was the relevance of his interjection, he said:
'because McBride was going to give evidence against Johnson and
now Graham has given evidence against me … well McBride was
willing to give evidence against an innocent man, because he was
acquitted'. Little did he know the whole truth, but he had correctly
sensed that something was not quite right.

The defence called six witnesses as to Kelly's whereabouts. The
last such witness was Mr Thomella, the licensee of the Leigh Arms
and a former police officer. He corroborated Kelly's evidence as to
the critical times he had been at the Leigh Arms and what Kelly
had said to him. There was then a bombshell, all the more unfortunate as it was the defence's last witness and being a former police
officer one who was likely to have been believed. He was shown by
Mr Gorman for the prosecution a statement he had made in which
he had said: 'I am quite definite that George Kelly was not in my
house at 9.30 pm on the night of the Cameo murder, but he was
in the buffet at ten to 10'. He denied that that was true and stated
that when CI Balmer asked him whether Kelly was in the house at
9.30 pm he said not to his knowledge, explaining that he signed his

statement subsequently without reading it in a motor car and did not notice the word 'definitely'. Was Thomella telling the truth?

At the conclusion of the witnesses' evidence Rose gave her final speech on behalf of Kelly lasting three hours in which she meticulously analysed and dissected the evidence against her client. She summed it up thus:

> Consider in retrospect the evidence of the prosecution. What do you think of Graham? Can you accept his evidence without some misgiving ... Do you believe Kelly, who never for one moment deflected from his denial of guilt, would unburden his soul to this perfect stranger in the detailed and circumstantial manner which Graham tells you he did? What of Dickson and Northam? ... This is a charge, members of the jury upon which evidence must be clear and unimpeachable. This charge must be supported by evidence upon which you can rely. Do you think the prosecution have called that evidence? They may have called sufficient evidence for you to say that there may be some truth somewhere. You may say: 'Northam and Dickson knew quite a lot', but you have seen Northam and Dickson in the box, you have heard their contradictions and read their lies.

Those of Rose's notes of her cross-examination and final speech that survive, some typed, others in her large handwriting, are witness to the detailed work that went into her preparation of the case. They demonstrate how she marshalled all the evidence on each individual point which enabled her to draw attention to the discrepancies and inadequacies in the evidence both for the purpose of her cross-examination and her final speech.

The final speech of Mr Gorman KC for the prosecution drew considerable attention to the absence of Doris O'Malley and Jimmy Skelly (who had been called for the defence at the earlier trial), whom he alleged would have been valuable witnesses. Mr Gorman then sought to paint a picture of Kelly as someone capable of the murders by reciting various threatening verbals alleged to have been made by Kelly, including statements made in the precincts of the court.

On 8 February Mr Justice Cassels began his summing up. He directed the jury that it would be dangerous to convict without corroboration and continued:

> Graham's evidence, if you accept it, may be corroboration, because you may think it strengthens the other evidence. That is a matter for you. Whatever description may be given to Graham—and you may think that he has laid himself open to many—but whatever description is given to that man, he cannot be described as an accomplice. A description of the

coat worn by the murderer that night may also be corroboration. That again is a matter for you.

He ended his summing up as follows:

'He fell to his knees'—according to Dr Grace the bullet that killed Catterall, the assistant manager, entered his back, struck his rib, went right down the body and went through the liver on the way down and was finally found on the inside of the thigh. Was Catterall shot while he was on his knees? Who knew that? Only one person. Has Graham imagined his evidence? If you have a reasonable doubt, you will find him not guilty. If, upon the evidence, you come to the conclusion that George Kelly is the man who, on that night of March 19th of last year, shot that cinema manager, Leonard Thomas, and thus brought his life of 44 years to an end, you will find him guilty. Will you now please consider your verdict.

The jury retired at 3.25 pm and precisely one hour later returned with their verdict. It was a verdict of guilty. The Judge, donning the black cap that it was customary to wear when sentencing someone to death, pronounced:

George Kelly, on that night of March 19th you committed a cruel and brutal murder of which the Jury have rightly found you guilty. A man who uses a gun to assist him in a robbery can expect no mercy. The sentence of the court upon you is that you be taken from this place to a lawful prison and thence to a place of execution and there suffer death by hanging and that your body be buried within the precincts of the prison in which you shall have been last confined before your execution, and may the Lord have mercy upon your soul.

AFTER THE VERDICT

Kelly immediately appealed. His amended grounds of appeal were that the Judge was wrong in refusing to grant more than one's day's adjournment for the re-trial and for ordering separate trials of Kelly and Connolly. The defence also relied upon 10 errors of misdirection in the Judge's summing up. On 15 February 1950, Kelly personally signed the notice of appeal. It has subsequently been discovered that in a letter dated 28 February 1950 from the Deputy Director of Public Prosecutions to the Under Secretary of State to the Home Office, the former wrote: 'I am of the opinion that but for the evidence that Graham gave before Mr Justice Cassels, Kelly would not have been convicted'.

The Appeal was heard in London on 6 March 1950 before Lord Goddard, the Lord Chief Justice, Mr Justices Humphries and Mr Justice Birkett. In addition to the pleaded grounds of appeal Rose raised a new argument as to whether or not one of the members of the jury, who ironically was a cinema manager, was disqualified as a matter of fact and law, which if correct, could have provided grounds for the court to rule the trial a nullity. Nonetheless, the court dismissed Kelly's appeal, delivering a reserved judgment on 15 March 1950.[1]

Kelly returned to Liverpool by train following the dismissal of his appeal. On the same train, though in a different compartment, was Rose. At some point during the journey the train guard came to Rose and asked if she would speak to Kelly as he was concerned about him, which she did. Kelly's parting remark to his young counsel was something Rose never forgot. As she was about to return to her compartment he said: 'Don't you worry about me luv, you just look after (take care of) yourself'. It was an extraordinary remark from a condemned man and it showed an altruistic side to Kelly that one might not have expected. But it also showed his appreciation for what Rose had done for him and the professional rapport that she had built up with him, as she did with so many of her clients, even though in this instance her efforts had proved unsuccessful. This was the last time that Rose saw Kelly.

Rose and her junior, Dick Trotter, immediately wrote to the then Attorney General, Sir Hartley Shawcross. They applied for his certificate for leave to appeal to the House of Lords on the ground that the juror disqualification issue involved a point of law of exceptional public importance and that such an appeal was desirable in the public interest. On 21 March 1950, the Attorney General refused his fiat for an appeal. Pleas were made on Kelly's behalf to the Home Secretary and even to the King, but to no avail. The Home Secretary, James Chuter Ede, said there were no grounds for clemency.

On 28 March 1950, Kelly was hanged at Walton Jail, protesting his innocence to his last breath. The night before his hanging, although he was already married, Kelly had become engaged to his sweetheart, Coleen Dutton, who had given evidence for him in his first trial. She had bought the ring.

---

[1]   *R v Kelly* [1950] 2 KB 164.

On 10 February 1950, two days after the verdict, Connolly was visited in Walton jail by his solicitor who introduced him to his new counsel Edmund Rowson KC. Mr Rowson told him that his previous counsel, Basil Nield KC, a Member of Parliament, had had to leave the case to fight the General Election. Connolly was advised that if he pleaded guilty to robbery the murder charge would be dropped and he would get 10 years in prison. It would save his life. He agreed. The Judge commended Northam and Dickson for their evidence rewarding each with £20 and said he would forward a recommendation regarding Graham. The Secretary of State at the Home Office subsequently recommended the remission of the remainder of Graham's sentence and his immediate release from custody.

Thus ended one of the most remarkable court cases in English legal history. It was not, however, the end of the story. As CI Balmer himself recalled in the *Liverpool Echo* upon his retirement in 1967: 'The Cameo murder had shocked the whole country, and certainly never before in the criminal annals of Liverpool, and for that matter the whole of Merseyside, had a case aroused such intense interest'. CI Balmer must have felt a degree of satisfaction at having been credited with resolving the Cameo murders. The convictions had the sobering effect of a significant reduction in armed robbery in the area for at least five years.

FURTHER DEVELOPMENTS

Those who believed in Kelly's and Connolly's innocence never gave up. Letters and articles were written alleging a miscarriage of justice, but to no avail. George Skelly, in his book entitled 'The Cameo Conspiracy' set out what he believed to be the 'real story of the cameo cinema murders'. Most of his findings have subsequently been substantiated.

Nor did Charles Connolly ever give up protesting his innocence. He was released from prison in about 1956 and died on 18 April 1997. Out of the blue, over 40 years later, on 26 October 1993, Charles Connolly wrote to Rose on seeing a recent photograph of her in the *Liverpool Echo*:

> Over the past 43 years the events of the CAMEO CINEMA murders have never left my mind and from time to time I have relived the proceedings as if it happened only yesterday. I remember very clearly the skill and sincerity in which you fought so vigorously to save George Kelly from

the gallows. But in the end it was not to be. My own view is that events overtook the reality.

I am now over 70 years of age and I have consoled myself over the years by the fact that, although I pleaded guilty to the Robbery and Conspiracy charges on the advice of my counsel Mr Rowson KC, I know in my heart and soul that I was absolutely innocent of any involvement whatsoever in the crime.

As for George Kelly I firmly believe he was also innocent of any involvement in the crime ... The truth of the matter is I did not know George Kelly or the witnesses NORTHAM and DICKSON. The first time I ever saw George Kelly was in the charge room on 30th September 1949 on the day we were both charged.

However, the question that has haunted me over the years is this: Having accepted the advice of my counsel Mr Rowson KC to plead guilty to the lesser charge of Robbery and Conspiracy, did I in any way jeopardise Kelly's chances of a successful appeal? ... To that end I have always thought that maybe Justice Goddard may have had at the back of his mind that Kelly's 'accomplice' Connolly had already pleaded guilty to his alleged part in the same crime so therefore Kelly must be guilty.

That thought has been, and still is, my dilemma ... I was released from prison in 1956 and had the good fortune to be able to pick up the pieces and raise a law abiding family of which I am very proud.

This concern was also expressed to others. In 1991 when working as a hotel doorman Connolly met Mr Luigi Santangeli, a businessman who was a guest of the hotel. As a result of what he was told, Mr Santangeli began to research the case. The firm of solicitors, E Rex Makin & Co was instructed and the matter was eventually referred to the Criminal Cases Review Commission, which in turn referred the matter to the Court of Appeal.

THE SECOND COURT OF APPEAL HEARING

The appeal was heard on 9 and 10 June 2003 before Lord Justice Rix, Mr Justice Douglas Brown and Mr Justice Davis. There were no queues outside the court and the reports in the newspapers were limited. The appeal was brought by Kelly's daughter, Kathleen Hughes, and Connolly's widow, Eileen Connolly. Mr Justice Douglas Brown, although considerably younger than Rose and a former member of the Northern Circuit, did remember the huge public interest in the case at the time. A reasoned judgment was given by the Court of Appeal on 28 October 2003.[2] Exactly 53 years and 5 months earlier Kelly had been hanged. It was the oldest criminal appeal ever to have been heard in the English courts.

The evidence which was put before the Court of Appeal included documents that had been discovered on police files, a statement from Mr Maxwell-Brown, Connolly's solicitor at the original trials, and recordings of interviews Connolly had made with journalists before his death. These were a revelation. There were three significant discoveries.

Graham's Earlier Statement

First, unknown to both defence and prosecution, on 15 September 1949, two weeks before Kelly and Connolly were even charged and three months after Johnson, whom Rose had also represented, had been acquitted of being an accessory after the fact to murder, Graham had made an additional unsigned statement to CI Balmer. In it, he stated that while he and Johnson had been in prison, Johnson had confessed to him that he, Johnson, had actually committed the murders and the robbery and had given him details of the events and that Johnson had made a similar confession to another prisoner, Bernard McBride. The police were also aware of McBride's detailed knowledge of the murder. Kelly had referred to McBride being in prison with Johnson and Graham when giving evidence at his second trial.

At the appeal the Crown, having carried out forensic investigations, accepted the authenticity of Graham's first statement. They also accepted that even under the more limited duties of disclosure on the prosecution which applied in 1949 it should have been disclosed to the defence and was not. In the course of his evidence at the joint trial, both CI Balmer and Graham had said that the first time they had met each other in connection with the case was two months later, namely on 19 November 1949.

The Court of Appeal concluded that:

> All that evidence was false and probably deliberately so. CI Balmer died on 3 May 1970, and thus no explanation from him regarding the non-disclosure of Graham's first statement or any other matter is available … and in the absence of any explanation for such testimony, the conclusion that such evidence amounted to deliberate concealment

[2] *George Kelly & Charles Connolly (both deceased) v R* [2002] EWCA Crim 2957.

becomes at least highly likely ... The importance of such non-disclosure is not in dispute, and that significance is enhanced if non-disclosure is viewed as concealment.

The mere fact that Graham allegedly received confessions of the murders from two different sources would of itself have cast doubt on the totality of his evidence. So would his inaccuracies or lies about his first meeting with CI Balmer, just as the latter's evidence would have been similarly undermined. Of particular importance, moreover, are the details of the shootings described in Graham's first statement.

From where did Graham get those details? It is not suggested that they were available in the press. They more or less accurately reflect Dr Grace's [the Home Office Pathologist] testimony. Graham could only have got them from Johnson or the police. Johnson could only have got them because he knew the gunman or was himself the gunman ...

If Graham's first statement had been disclosed, the judge could not have ended his summing-up in this way. The implicit reference to Kelly as the 'only one person' who could have known that Catterall was shot while he was on his knees could not have been made.

The Court of Appeal addressed the implications of this evidence on the evidence of Northam and noted that by the time of Graham's second statement he would have had an opportunity to read about the case in detail as the committal proceedings were widely reported. Moreover, at the appeal the Crown accepted that it was possible for Kelly and Connolly to speak to one another from their respective cells as Kelly and Connolly had said in evidence.

Northam's and Dickson's Evidence

Secondly, it was discovered that Northam and Dickson had made additional statements on 29 September 1949 and on 10 October 1949. In Northam's and Dickson's earlier statements of 29 September 1949 neither of them mentioned Northam lending the brown overcoat or the meeting on the day after the murders at the White Star. These were significant omissions which were subsequently rectified in later statements. The contents of these earlier statements were not known to the defence.

The Court of Appeal commented:

The significance is that a comparison of the earlier statements with the additional statements, and of the statements as a whole with evidence given at committal and at trial, may have affected those witnesses' credibility ... Balmer deliberately, as it would appear, obscured the point that not only had the evidence about the Sunday meeting at the White Star not emerged at the time of the first statements, but that those statements positively asserted that the witnesses had stayed at home in Birkenhead all day.

Mr Thomella's Evidence

Thirdly, a draft unsigned statement dated 4 October 1949 made by Mr Thomella, the licensee of the Leigh Arms and a former police officer, was discovered. Contrary to the statement signed in the motor car the unsigned statement recorded the following:

> Although I saw Kelly about 9.00 p.m. and again just before closing time, *I cannot say whether or not he was in the house between those times.* It would have been easy for him to leave between those times and I certainly did not serve him with any other drink. (emphasis added)

The Court of Appeal concluded:

> We are not sure whether Mr Thomella made two statements and stuck to his first rather than his second ... or whether Mr Thomella's remarks to the police were first drafted in one form and then drafted in another, in the form which he ultimately signed—in a motor-car. We would rather infer from the evidence which he gave at trial and the material we have seen (and we have not seen any signed statement) that the latter is what happened.

The Split Trials

Fourthly, the Crown conceded that no proper basis had existed for the trials of Kelly and Connolly being severed within five days of a jury failing to reach verdicts against either, where the essence of the case was that Kelly and Connolly were engaged on a common enterprise. Reference was made to the legal authority which Rose had relied on, but which the Judge had ignored. The Court of Appeal considered that Kelly had clearly been prejudiced in that the jury would have heard Connolly's evidence as well as Kelly's which would have added his contradictions to the evidence of Northam, Dickson and Graham. The court said that they found it disturbing and concluded that it was: 'a material and substantial ingredient in our overall conclusion that Kelly did not have a fair trial and that his conviction is unsafe'.

Connolly

Finally, the Court of Appeal concluded that Connolly was probably not consulted about the severance of his trial and that the advice that he was given to plead guilty to robbery and conspiracy 'must have amounted to enormous, indeed irresistible, pressure to take the course which would preserve life rather than gamble it ... and was left shortly before his retrial with a life and death decision whether to accept a deal, negotiated without his involvement, which involved pleading guilty to robbery'. His conviction was also found to be unsafe.

The Real Conspiracy

The Court of Appeal summarised what happened thus:

> As the Crown acknowledged the integrity of CI Balmer was of para-mount importance in the case. His evidence challenged Kelly's alibi at several points ... CI Balmer's evidence was in turn challenged in cross-examination by Miss Heilbron ...

> The non-disclosure of Graham's first statement, and to a lesser but cumulative extent the non-disclosure of Northam's and Dickson's statements, deprived Kelly and his lawyers of highly relevant material ... there is every sign that those non-disclosures, and particularly that of Graham's statement, were due to deliberate concealment. Indeed, the lies of Graham and CI Balmer in relation to when they first saw one another in relation to the Cameo murders are a strong indication of the need for concealment. The similar lies in relation to the time when the Sunday meeting at the White Star was first revealed to CI Balmer suggest the same conclusion in respect to the statements of Northam and Dickson. Disclosure of the statements would have enabled Miss Heilbron to go further than she was able in attacking the credibility of all three principal witnesses for the Crown.

Miscarriage of Justice

The Court of Appeal concluded:

> Did the non-disclosures make the conviction of Kelly unsafe? In our judgment, they did. The evidence against Kelly was ... far from overwhelming ... The essential corroboration presented to the jury was Graham's evidence ... On the prosecution's own case, Kelly's opportunity to commit the murders was very narrow ... The prosecution itself did not regard its case as strong.... A letter dated 14 October to the DPP from

the prosecuting solicitor says: 'You will probably agree that the evidence is not very strong' ... In all these circumstances we consider that Kelly did not have a fair trial, his conviction is unsafe and must be quashed ... there was in these cases a breakdown in the due administration of justice and a failure to ensure a fair trial, we consider that the consequence was a miscarriage of justice, which must be deeply regretted.

The verbals CI Balmer had falsely attributed to Kelly at an identification parade; 'If it's the last thing I do I'll get you for this Balmer' came back in death to haunt him as Balmer's reputation was shredded into tatters. There had been a tremendous miscarriage of justice and Kelly had been stitched up. It was not the first time such a thing had happened nor would it be it the last.

THE UNKNOWN QUESTION

So what did really happen? One strong theory espoused by George Skelly in his book is that the anonymous letter was written not by the dark-haired nameless girl who was alleged to be present at the Beehive nor by Northam or Dickson, but by someone called Norwegian Margie. According to the scene portrayed by George Skelly, it was at another public house, the Boundary, not the Beehive, as alleged by the prosecution, where the conspiracy was plotted and where Norwegian Margie saw two other men as well as Northam. One of these men she apparently alleged was called Johnny. She did not know the name of the other man who was wearing a brown belted coat and whom she saw slipping a gun into his pocket.[3] Norwegian Margie apparently committed suicide in mysterious circumstances on 11 November 1949, a week before Graham's second statement materialised and before Kelly's trial took place.

It is likely that both Northam and Dickson had some direct knowledge of the planned robbery and the consequent murders. To make up the story and stick to it through a committal hearing and two trials seems a little incredible, but to change the name of the pub and the names of the individuals involved and even play down their own involvement would have been much easier. They never knew Kelly or Connolly, but, according to George Skelly, Dickson had had an association with Kelly's brother Joey, who, unbeknown to George Kelly, had gone under the name George so that his wife did not find out about the liaison.

[3] Pages 98–104; 189–190 of "The Cameo Conspiracy".

What, if any, was Johnson's involvement? If Johnson made the statements to Graham, and for that matter to others, which Graham in turn relayed to CI Balmer on 15 September 1949, how did Johnson know of the details of the shootings? They had not been in the press and were, at the earliest, made public in the committal hearing in October and possibly not before the first trial in January when Dr Grace gave evidence? Was it from the Police or was it because he knew something of the murders? Was this the final irony—if Rose had not succeeded in getting Johnson acquitted of the charge of accessory to murder because of the police blunders in offering him inducements would Kelly have ever been charged and would Johnson have ultimately led the police to the killer?

AND THEREAFTER ...

Two years after the trial Dickson was sentenced at Manchester Assizes, in the company of her latest pimp, to two years' imprisonment for robbery with violence. She has not been heard of since. Northam married in 1951, changed his name, had a family and ran a successful motor business in another area of Merseyside. He died in 1989. Johnson completed his four years of corrective training and subsequently became a factory hand. He died in 1988, aged 61. Connolly's subsequent life has already been revealed. CI Balmer went on to become Assistant Chief Constable of Liverpool until his retirement in 1967 and died in 1970. Kelly's future was taken away from him.

Thus, despite two trials and two appeals, to this day the Cameo murders remain one of the great unsolved murder cases of the twentieth century. Rose played a significant forensic part in the legal outcome. Sadly, she never knew of the denouement for by the time of the second Court of Appeal hearing she was unwell. Had the real truth been known and the law fairly applied, Kelly's re-trial would not have been split and Kelly would probably have been acquitted. After all Rose had succeeded in getting the jury to disagree in the first trial. Her valiant efforts were made against a conspiracy of deliberate concealment and lies involving the police. Even with her undoubted skills as an advocate, in such circumstances the scope for success for her client in such a highly charged murder case was limited. Nonetheless the Cameo murder case sealed her already growing reputation as an advocate. She was still only 35, one of only two practising women KCs in the country, and had battled against the most senior of advocates and judges. It was a case she frequently mentioned throughout her life. A string of famous and fascinating cases followed.

8

Adjustment to Motherhood and in Demand as a Speaker

DOMESTICITY AND BEING A MUM

THERE WAS LITTLE respite for Rose after the Cameo case, which had taken a substantial part of her attention for many months, although she did many other cases as well during this period. Not only did she return to her varied practice of civil and criminal cases, but also her status as KC, together with her eloquent and 'powerful voice', made her in great demand as a speaker and guest at a variety of functions. She addressed legal organisations, women's organisations, Jewish Groups and others all around the country and, as her fame grew, the occasions became grander. Her portfolio of speaking engagements grew rapidly and the range of subjects she tackled was extensive: from women's issues to legal issues to a whole range of contemporaneous topics.

She also had a small baby. Rose's reaction to being a new mother was no different from any other new mother. Unfortunately she was unable to breastfeed her baby, much to her regret. The stylised professional photographs in an album of Hilary as small baby, the new found hobby of cinematography, the curl of Hilary's hair kept in a box, the thank-you cards produced on her birth and the love she showered on her were all testimony to a normal mother and baby relationship. On a letter to Nat from a trip abroad when Hilary was just two, she wrote the following PS: 'Tell Nannie I am delighted Hilary is taking to the pot'. She would often say that she was always brought down to earth when returning home to the perennial question 'Mummy—why?'

However, this naturally close relationship with her young baby was not necessarily the perception of others. She often recounted, with some wry amusement, the time when one of Nat's sisters visited from Dublin for the first time to see the baby, then about 11 months. She was taken to Hilary's cot in the nursery. Hilary apparently rose on her chubby little legs gurgling with delight at recognising her mother, to which her sister-in-law commented in surprise and amazement 'Gosh, she knows you!'. The idea that a baby and its working mother were somehow estranged was no doubt a fairly commonly held view in those days.

A working mother's needs were no different 60 years ago from today. Rose needed help both in her professional and in her private life. For many years she had had a housekeeper. After marriage and motherhood the domestic staff evolved into a nanny for Hilary, a cook and a cleaner, the permutations, job descriptions and those filling the posts changing from time to time.

After some initial bad luck with nannies, including one, with apparently impeccable timing, walking out while Rose was in the throes of some major case, 'Nanny' arrived to stay. Nanny lived in and had Sundays off. She sometimes accompanied the family on holiday. She stayed for seven years until her retirement when she went to live with her sister in the house they had built in North Wales which she aptly named 'Fingertips'. She died many years later in her eighties having moved back to Malta, the country of her birth.

As Rose had little time for cooking, something which in later years she enjoyed doing, she felt that she needed a cook. She was now married and she did not want Nat, who always loved his food, to be deprived of nice meals which, had she not been working, she would herself, as a wife, have been able to provide. She believed in 'husband care' as well as child care. There were no supermarkets as we know them today, but meat and groceries were ordered by telephone and delivered to the house, and Nat would buy the fruit and fish from stores owned by his patients as a result of which the quality was always excellent. The choice of food was, of course, much more restricted than it is today. There was no yoghurt or avocado, let alone mangoes or crème fraiche, though Nat would regularly go to the food department of Coopers in central Liverpool to buy smoked salmon and a few delicacies. Food shopping thus did not seem a chore, though quite regularly Rose and Hilary would go to the local shops at weekends for specific items.

Rose had to travel from time to time, mostly in England, either to the Court of Appeal, which was then exclusively in London, or to other Circuits in the country. It was still the age of the steam train and train journeys were much slower than they are today. A train journey to London in the 1950s was 4–5 hours, but on Sundays, which was when she frequently travelled, it could take a lot longer. Hilary would accompany her father on such Sundays to wave Rose goodbye at the station. As a small child, Hilary was frightened by the noise of the engines and would hide in the car while the engines gathered steam and the train edged its way south out of Lime Street Station.

Nat proudly recalled that he never let Rose return to Liverpool by train without meeting her at the station, whether it was from the midnight train from London or late at night at Exchange station when she was returning from Carlisle, a town in Cumbria and north of Lancashire. In later years Rose would more frequently drive to court rather than take the train, particularly if it was not too far away such as in Manchester. This tendency increased after she purchased her first Rover 2000 automatic, a car which she loved driving. Whenever she was away from home she would write almost daily letters to Hilary and Nat about what she was doing and how much she was looking forward to coming home, and they would write to her.

Although the family had live-in help until Hilary was much older, the fact that Nat's job kept him at home undoubtedly eased Rose's worries about leaving Hilary as a small child. General medical practice was very different from the medical trusts of the twenty-first century. Nat's practice at its peak had a patient list of 11,000 and there were three partners in the practice. He would be on call on a rota basis during the nights: there were no night duty schemes until the later years of his practice. He would have a surgery on Saturday mornings and one each morning and evening with one half day free: Thursdays, the afternoon he played golf. He would do many house calls before his surgeries each day and was telephoned each morning and afternoon with his itinerary by the lady employed by the surgery to act as a caretaker. However, there was a two to three hour break in the afternoon between surgeries when Nat would return home for lunch and a little afternoon nap. He could thus keep an eye on Hilary when she was tiny, or at home ill with the variety of the childhood ailments she seemed regularly to acquire, or in school holidays.

In the early years Nat would spoil Hilary, regularly bringing home little gifts from a shop run by one of his patients. The most memorable such toy was a ring with a rubber pouch which held water, which she could squeeze on some unsuspecting person who obediently bent down to admire this piece of red glass on her finger only to be rewarded by a shower of water! He was also there, if Rose was working at the weekends, as she often did, to entertain Hilary by taking her to feed the ducks or float her little boat on the lake at Sefton Park or on trips by ferry across the Mersey.

Although Rose worked long hours and travelled, the latter was usually only for short periods. She was able to carry out much of the preparation for her cases and her written work from home in the evenings and at weekends and this often coincided in later years with Hilary's homework. Rose also had long holidays when the courts were not sitting and so she would be at home for a large part of the school holidays. She was the one who took Hilary to the dentist, to buy her school uniform, pencil cases, crayons and geometry sets or lacrosse and hockey sticks needed for school. It was Rose who mostly took her to and from parties when she was small just like any other mother. She would have birthday parties for Hilary and when she was a young child, would have special birthday cakes made. She was there at mealtimes or to take Hilary to hospital when she had her tonsils out. In other words she always seemed to be there when Hilary needed her and, if not, Nat was there.

Any perception that Rose's work undermined her maternal role and love is unfounded. A story Rose told with pride was that on Hilary's first day at her first school, Beechenhurst, aged about four, she ran away after her and had to be taken back to school. Nat encouraged mother and daughter outings from an early age and in August 1958 Rose took a very excited little girl for her first visit to London where they saw the tourist sights. Hilary's own diary notes that they went on a 'desil' train, the steam trains gradually being phased out by this time. Hilary never really liked Beechenhurst, but settled well into her next school, Huyton College, where she remained for the rest of her school days. Sadly Huyton College no longer exists and the lovely buildings and grounds have been turned into a residential care home. Huyton College had the advantage of a school bus, which particularly when Hilary was a teenager, never being matitudinal by nature, she managed to miss each morning, necessitating Nat driving her the several miles to school before he started his visits, though it brought her home in the evenings. Taking Hilary by car to and from school was the one thing Rose's work prevented her from doing save on very rare occasions, but she always ensured that Hilary was met at the school bus until her late teens.

Rose, conscious of the importance of elocution lessons in her own life, engaged Miss Mulhearn to teach Hilary elocution each week and she took several elocution exams. Hilary remained as a child fascinated by Miss Mulhearn's different coloured inter-changeable spectacle frame lids, a rather pre-Gucci idea, and discussion of such life-enhancing matters always had to precede the rather more boring breathing exercises! As her own mother had given her, Rose wanted to give her daughter as broad an education as possible, from the ballet lessons she accompanied her to at the weekends when very small, to piano lessons, to sending her to ballroom dancing lessons, swimming lessons, arranging for Hebrew lessons, and, as Hilary got older, extra coaching for her exams. She left to Nat the more sporty side of life such as tennis lessons.

The legal vacations also provided the opportunity for Rose to catch up on all the things she had not had time to do when she was appearing in court, such as sorting and cleaning cupboards, attending to paperwork, clothes shopping, as well as spending more time with Nat and Hilary and having fun, such as visits to Chester Zoo when Hilary was a little girl. Family summer holidays were in the early years spent usually in England or in North Wales in places such as Llandudno, where Hilary would pester her parents to play the Nickelodeon on Llandudno pier, or in Devon where the family attempted a seaside holiday in very inclement weather. In the early 1950s the family took the car to France and Spain for a holiday with Nat's sister, Esta, and her husband Harry, also a doctor and Medical Officer of Health of Pretoria, who were over from South Africa. Buckets and spades in the rain eventually got Rose down and in later years, when Hilary was a teenager, the family would travel to France or Italy for the summer holidays most years.

People often ask—how did Rose manage with childcare? Other than the odd drama when someone gave in her notice, or was caught pilfering, it did not seem to be a big thing: just a bore and a necessary prerequisite to her working. If one employee left, the process of advertising in the local newspaper began, interviews were conducted, references taken up and a replacement was found in due course. It maybe that it was easier to find domestic staff 50 years ago. Domestically life at home seemed to move relatively smoothly. Rose kept her staff. They seemed to enjoy working for her and the people she employed were, for the most part, delightful. But such domestic comfort came at a price, literally. She would say that most of her earnings were spent on staff over the years. Having live-in staff is a constriction on one's lifestyle, but it is also a great benefit. She once remarked when she stopped needing permanent live-in help on how nice it was for the first time to be able to walk round the house naked if one wanted!

Being a wife and mother, running a home, having a full-time job and being in demand as a speaker left Rose little time for other hobbies. Nat was a very keen sportsman. When first married, however, she decided she would take up golf so as to be able to play with her husband, buying a set of golf clubs to show her seriousness. Nat, being an excellent all-round sportsman and with, at its peak, a handicap of five in golf, was no match for the divot-producing amateur with an advocate's ability to argue the toss. It was either a partnership in marriage or one in golf. The former took precedence and the temporary venture into sport stopped. In later life she would play a little tennis with Hilary on the tennis court she built in the family's future home, but apart from walking the dog, also later acquired, that was the sum total of her sporting and exercising activities.

ORGANISING HER PROFESSIONAL LIFE

On the professional side, although Rose had a clerk, Charles Humphries, in her London chambers, she engaged her own personal secretary who also acted as a junior clerk. She came to the house to help Rose deal with her increasing volume of correspondence, her filing and typing, the fixing of cases in court and organising consultations. Once in silk a client was supposed, rather oddly, to consult rather than confer and consultations replaced conferences. Rose had subscribed to the International Press-Cutting Bureau and additionally numerous press cuttings were filed regularly in large press cutting books, a progression on an earlier habit she had acquired at University of pasting important legal cases and information into a scrapbook. Over her lifetime this resulted in a collection of several thousand press cuttings featuring Rose both as a person and in relation to her cases.

As from October 1952 her part-time secretary was Mona Kelly. She worked in the small room at Rose's home which had become an office, Rose having requisitioned another of the bedrooms as her study. The two women would exchange tales of their young children, although Hilary never emulated the young Michael Kelly's desire for eating soap! Instead, perhaps in a foretaste of what was to come, she demanded her own brief, a piece of plain foolscap paper tied up in pink brief ribbon with which she would proudly play at being a make-believe barrister. In later years Hilary too was to qualify as barrister.

Rose was always very organised. For her increasing speech load she developed a colour-coded filing system, dividing copies of the speeches she had given into main groups with sub-topics, and each was placed in a separate file. Other files contained additional material again divided into topics, which she could use when appropriate. She always did considerable research for her speeches, although as she became more accomplished, she was able to adjust existing material and re-use it for another speech. The range of topics on which she spoke was extremely wide, as were the different audiences to whom she spoke. She spoke on medical issues, legal issues, the art of advocacy, legal reform, education, architecture and, of course, about women as well as other topics. Over the years she literally gave hundreds of speeches to magistrates, Jewish organisations and women's organisations, and spoke at many prestigious events.

Rose bought joke books which she would annotate according to topic such as education or legal. Over the years she accumulated a substantial number of jokes of the kind which could, in the 1950s, be given by a woman. It was quite unusual in those days for women to give speeches, let alone make toasts or give after-dinner speeches. Standard letters were drafted to respond to the different types of speaking requests and letters she received. She also received a large number of letters from members of the public, some from people with grievances who hoped she could solve their problems, others from people who were clearly unbalanced and others just genuinely nice letters from strangers and the occasional grateful client.

SPEAKING ENGAGEMENTS

The first couple of years after taking silk brought a number of speaking engagements, a pattern that was to continue throughout her working life. She developed themes which she could adjust to particular audiences and which she could expand in later years. In what she said, she was often way ahead of her time, particularly in her views on the role of women in society and on legal reform.

One common early theme was Law and the Individual. She would begin: 'Without justice or the rule of law there would be no liberties; without freedom of speech there would be no justice'. But other speeches suggested reforms. Opening a series of lectures organised by the Liverpool Co-Operative Society Limited, she suggested that there would be a distinct gain if a general study of the principles of law could be included in the last year or so of the general educational curriculum, for, as she said, law is the foundation of society. Many schools now teach law. She spoke at another function about the unequal punishments given for the same offence by judges in different localities, still something which occurs to a lesser extent today despite the introduction of sentencing guidelines. She was a guest speaker at the end of December 1949 at the annual Ladies' Day luncheon of the Liverpool Branch of the Institute of Export attracting the not so politically correct newspaper heading 'Justice and Nylons'. She raised with her audience the issue of the public's misunderstanding about whether a lawyer should defend a guilty man, explaining that he was innocent until proved guilty. She complained about the absence of training in cross-examination, leaving the barrister to learn at the expense of his or her clients, something rectified today with the introduction of compulsory advocacy training for young barristers.

The Jewish community was particularly proud of her achievements. In June 1949 the Council of the Jewish Chronicle held a reception at the Max Morris Hall, Liverpool in her honour. The following month the First Lodge of England of the B'nai B'rith gave a dinner in her honour in the Stern Hall, London. In her reply to the toast Rose returned to one of her women's themes. She criticised parents for thinking that it was better for a girl to be happily married than well-educated, because it disregarded the fact that a woman could be both, expressing her delight that many more women were now going into higher education. Sidney Silverman, the MP for the constituency of Nelson and Colne in Lancashire, and a founder of the campaign for the abolition of capital punishment, also spoke. He was the senior partner of Silverman & Livermore, the firm which instructed Rose in many of her famous cases including *Dunbell*, *Adams v Naylor* and the Cameo murder case. In his address, after acknowledging that women had a humanising and civilising influence, he incisively drew attention to the twin hurdles of prejudice that Rose had had to overcome, the latter usually remaining unspoken. He explained that Rose had had to prove not just that she was equal to the men, but also a little better than them, both because of her sex and also because she was Jewish.

In the autumn she delivered the Presidential address to the Birmingham Jewish and Literary and Arts Society on 'The Law and the Individual'. She spoke on the law of libel at the annual dinner of the Midlands area of the Trades Advisory Council in Birmingham. She was guest of honour at the inaugural function of the Parent-Teacher Association of the Liverpool Hebrew Schools; a guest at the Legal Group of the Friends of the Hebrew University; and a speaker at the Southport Jewish discussion group where she spoke about the dangers of delegated legislation and lack of access to the courts in a talk entitled 'Government Red Tape'.

The invitations were wide-ranging and her energy seemingly inexhaustible. In May 1950, she addressed the 129th annual meeting of the Gordon Smith Institute for Seamen in Liverpool Town Hall, where she spoke in favour of a motion to pledge all present to assist in furthering the welfare of the sailor by every possible means. Sir David Maxwell Fyfe, later Home Secretary in the post-war Churchill Conservative government and as Lord Kilmuir, Lord Chancellor in Anthony Eden's Government of 1954, and President of the Institute, also spoke. Rose was a principal guest at the University of Liverpool's annual dinner. In January 1950, she spoke at Liverpool Burns Club commenting amusingly on her reaction to the epithet 'lasses'. In April 1950, she presented the prizes at the Royal Southern Hospital Liverpool. On another occasion she joined Lord Derby in presenting the prizes at the Leggate debating society at Liverpool University. In July 1950, she was invited by the Lord Chancellor to meet the Delegates of the Third Conference of the International Bar Association in the Royal Gallery, Westminster. In November 1950, she proposed the toast at the Women's Chartered Accountants' Dining Society in London, and so the list continues.

WOMEN'S ISSUES

Her views about the prejudice suffered by working women and the need for change struck a chord with her female audiences. As a guest of honour at the Oxford University Law Society dinner in November 1949 addressing the topic 'Women in the Professions and Prejudice', she commented on the limited number of women in the professions, stating:

> There is still too much prejudice against women in the professions on the part of both men and women, but this conception denies the fundamental fact that skill has nothing to do with one's sex. However, there can be no doubt that these preconceived ideas will go and these old fashioned prejudices are going to die out.

Sir Raymond Evershed, the Master of the Rolls, was reported contemporaneously as repeating the age-old mantra about women barristers that: 'Their voices are not so good and they haven't yet overcome the prejudice against them'. Rose's retort to such assertions was always the same. She argued that women only needed more time at men's jobs and they would show them. She was, of course, right, but it has taken a long time and has not been completely achieved even today.

She also discussed more practical matters. When addressing the Bootle Townswomen's Guild she commented on the difficulties she had had as a woman when first joining the Bar knowing what to wear at the Police Courts where a barrister does not wear robes, explaining: 'I do think that if you feel that you are dressed for the part you have to play in life, then you can do it much more efficiently'. For work Rose always wore a smart black suit and, for many years, as was the custom, a hat. However, when she went out in the evenings she enjoyed dressing up, and became known for her elegant dress sense. She had a slim waist and clothes looked good on her.

Rose had, a few years earlier, become a member of the Liverpool Club of the Soroptimists. The Soroptimists are an internationally widespread women's movement which still exists today. Their current website describes them as 'a worldwide organisation for women in management and professions, working through service projects to advance human rights and the status of women'. The name derives from the Latin for sister 'soror, sorori, soro' and means sisterhood. In 1950 there were 190 clubs in the British Federation of Soroptimists with a membership in excess of 7,500.

A year or so earlier Rose had spoken at the Eleventh Annual Conference of the NW Divisional Unions of the Federation of Soroptimists of Great Britain and Ireland in Blackpool, giving an hour's talk on 'Women and the Law' and answering questions. At the beginning of February 1950, just after the conclusion of the re-trial in the Cameo case, Rose was again the guest speaker, this time at the fourth annual dinner of the Wallasey Soroptimist Club. She said there was a great deal of prejudice against women barristers, particularly in London. She also criticised the public and lengthy committal proceedings which existed in England comparing them with the Scottish system, no doubt prompted by the experience of the Cameo trials. The system has since changed and committal proceedings no longer involve the rehearsal of all the evidence.

Later in the month she was the guest speaker at the annual dinner for the Liverpool Soroptimist Club before catching the midnight train to London for a case. She encouraged women to vote in the general election and not to forget the pioneers and suffragettes of the past. She outlined the progress of women in the professions, business and politics, saying that there was still room for improvement and instancing the fact that if a married woman saved money from the housekeeping that money in law belonged to the husband.

This produced, to a roar of laughter, an interruption from a man in the audience who shouted 'hear, hear'. Her high profile meant that her speeches were often reported in the press, particularly where women's issues were concerned, adding to the public debate.

In November 1950, she attended two functions as guest speaker where she was able to propound some of her continuing themes about women's rights. She talked to the Manchester Rotary Club about the evolvement of the law in relation to women, pointing out that in the nineteenth century a man could restrain his wife from leaving him. Nonetheless, she noted that the perception of women as being infirm, weak and foolish, despite their advancement, still existed and gave as an example the fact that married women were grouped with lunatics, idiots and insane persons in the Income Tax Act of 1918.

She also addressed the Women's Group on Public Welfare in London. The title of her talk was: 'The Legal Position of Women, Yesterday and Today', and it received national press coverage. She tackled in particular two issues: the right of women to equal pay and the need in society for both working women and those who were homemakers. She acknowledged that: 'Prejudice against women is still rampant and I think it is up to us as women never to flag in our efforts to overcome the injustice and unreason of such an attitude' for, she continued, 'pressure of public opinion will eventually secure the adoption of equal pay for women'. She added: 'If women, however, are to be allowed to make their full contribution to national life, they must without doubt be placed not only legally, but economically, on an equal footing with men' emphasising that this would in due course be achieved by the pressure of public opinion. She also emphasised that women had the right to decide for themselves whether or not they worked outside the home and what work they did.

> The country needs both types of women. Not only has the woman at home a hard and difficult job to do, but we must not overlook the hard work and double hours of duty put in by the mother of a family who contributes to the family fund and the country's present needs by working outside the home in the factory or the office.

Her views on women's rights were ahead of their time. But perceptions die hard.

Her public profile also brought its lighter moments. One member of the public wrote wanting her to 'relieve my conscience' and apologise as, having read various reports, he had 'been given to forming a mental picture of you as being, quite frankly, "a crotchety sour old woman'". He then said he had seen a photograph of Rose and discovered that she was young and 'most attractive' and 'of a singular state'.

AN INTERNATIONAL COVENANT ON HUMAN RIGHTS

On Saturday 30 June 1950, Rose was to be the guest speaker at the Eighteenth Annual Conference of the Federation of Soroptimist Clubs of Great Britain, to be held at Southport. The International Soroptimist Federation had consultative status at UNESCO and had pledged to inform public opinion about the Covenant of Human Rights. The Universal Declaration of Human Rights had been adopted 18 months earlier on 10 December 1948 by the United Nations, but it had no legal force. The idea of a Covenant on Human Rights therefore came into being to produce a legally binding document, which in addition to setting out some of the rights in the Declaration, would also provide the means of enforcing or implementing such rights.

A Human Rights Commission was accordingly set up under the Chairmanship of Eleanor Roosevelt, the then widow of the former President of the United States and the US delegate to the UN General Assembly. She was a formidable lady. Its task was to consider and to formulate for the acceptance by Member States a draft Covenant embodying a number of the Articles of the Declaration. Thus Rose's address was entitled 'Measures of Implementation of an International Covenant on Human Rights'. She was to speak at the afternoon session. While her billing as guest speaker had been widely publicised and she was described as 'the chief attraction of the afternoon session', she had an unexpected surprise for her audience of an estimated 1,500 delegates.

The conference was opened in the morning by the President of the Federation, Miss D Warner FCIS JP, who read out a message from Eleanor Roosevelt. The message apologised for her inability to attend and stressed the importance of everyone knowing about the Implementation of the International Covenant on Human Rights.

The previous evening Rose had, coincidentally, been attending a dinner in London in honour of Eleanor Roosevelt. It was a very prestigious dinner. Other guests, all much older than Rose, included: Dame Edith Evans, the actress; Dame Myra Hess, the pianist; Professor Barbara Wooten (later Dame), the sociologist and criminologist; Florence Hancock (later Dame), the chief women's

Rose as a child with her mother

Rose aged 16

Rose age 17 as Petrucio in *The Taming of the Shrew*

Max and Nellie Heilbron - Rose's Parents

Rose in her 20s

Rose as a graduate of Liverpool
University

Rose as a young Barrister

Stylized photograph of Rose soon after her marriage, 1945

Rose processing from Westminster Abbey to Parliament following
service at beginning of Legal Year, October 1950

Rose with 7 month old baby daughter

Being a mum with a 2 year old

Family holiday in Llandudno

Rose on tour in Germany, January 1951

Rose and Nat at Regency Ball, October 1956

officer for the Transport and General Workers Union; and Lady Willingdon, the widow of the former Governor General of Canada and later Viceroy of India and a champion of human rights. They dined on crab salad, chicken, artichoke and strawberries and cream followed by coffee and cherry brandy.

Edith Evans was to become a close friend of Rose's, even offering Rose accommodation whenever she was in London (which she did not accept). In later years Rose introduced Hilary to Edith Evans at dinner at a restaurant called Luba. During dinner Edith Evans commented that 'the trouble with people today is that they never pronounce their consonants properly'. Such a comment conjured up her memorable and famous line as Lady Bracknell in Oscar Wilde's 'The Importance of Being Earnest', uttering surprise and shock when discovering that the baby had been found 'in a handbag', with its emphasis on consonants rather than vowels.

Rose spoke to Eleanor Roosevelt about her speech the next day and was given a message to send to the conference. Rose caught the midnight train back from London to be met by Nat, who took her home for a rest and a bath and then drove her to Southport in time to make her speech. As she rose to make her address, Rose was able to convey the personal message from Mrs Roosevelt which she had written down:

> Even if the Covenant does not go far enough, even if it does not cover all the rights you want, it is a step forward in translating human rights and freedom into law; therefore it is a big step forward and should receive the support of all women.

Rose began her speech, which lasted an hour and a half, with an explanation of the various organs of the United Nations and the background to and status of the Declaration of Human Rights and the Draft Covenant. Raising the question of what was the purpose and object of the Draft Covenant she answered:

> It is, is it not, to secure to all individuals in every corner of the globe, whether they reside in self-governing territories or in non-self-governing territories, whether they be white or whether they be coloured, whatever their language, their religion or their race, those inalienable rights which the enlightened conscience of mankind is beginning to realise belong to all humanity?

> To set forth the purpose, and it is a noble one, is easy: to achieve it is a vastly different proposition. When you consider that many of the nations

of the world are at present in a different stage of economic development, that there are many differing political climates, that no two legal systems are alike, that the legal consciousness of a people has been moulded over hundreds of years by many varying factors – tradition, habits of thinking, the wants and requirements of each particular country, prevalent moral and political theories, all of which have gone into the evolution of the Laws of that particular State – you will, I feel sure, realise the enormous complexities and difficulties attendant upon the proposed enforcement of the Draft Covenant.

She went on to highlight some examples of different legal require-ments in different nations and to explain some of the difficulties that the Commission were having in implementing the Draft Covenant. Her message was that means of execution and enforcement are of little use without sanctions, explaining that:

The protection of human rights is basic in the advance of civilization. The settlement of disputes judicially, the substitution of reason for force is also fundamental in the creation and maintenance of liberty and justice. I would go further and say that liberty and freedom for all will only be achieved when every nation voluntarily and freely offers to submit its problems and quarrels to an international judicial body, and what is even more important, to abide by the consequences of any decision it may make.

Once the International Court of Justice is by-passed, once the question of human rights becomes a political and not a juridical one, the Covenant may be in danger of becoming a dead letter. The fundamental freedoms have not yet been fully attained in any one country. How can we succeed in obtaining them for the whole world and still retain the independence of the Member States which was safeguarded by the United Nations Charter itself? Obviously general statements in the Covenant cannot in themselves alter municipal law. Domestic law cannot yet be written for a nation by the medium of an International Covenant. To what extent will adherence to the Covenant become a binding obligation and how is such an obligation to be enforced?

What about the treatment of racial groups, the existence of slave labour, the power of arrest, whose duty is it to decide? Surely these intricate problems will ultimately require the authoritative interpretation of a Court? The Court is ready, waiting and willing, and as the United Kingdom representative pointed out to the Commission, it is by no means overburdened with work. What better task could be offered to it?

The fact that the Commission on Human Rights has already achieved some measure of agreement is obviously an important contribution to the ultimate accomplishment of its aims.

She concluded:

> In the history of every nation has freedom ever been achieved without a long and arduous struggle? We in this country have not achieved freedom of speech or freedom of conscience or liberty without having fought long and bitter battles for them over the centuries ... Liberty does not happen overnight.

A copy of the address was sent to the Director of the Department of External Relations at UNESCO, to the Secretariat of the Commission on Human Rights and to the UK delegate on that Commission. A few months later Egon Schwelb, Assistant Director, Divisions of Human Rights, United Nations New York wrote to the Executive Officer of the Federation of Soroptimists:

> I have read Miss Heilbron's admirable statement with very great interest and I am drawing it to the attention of those of my colleagues whom it concerns, including the officials who pursuant to a resolution adopted by the Commission on Human Rights at its sixth session in March-May 1950, are compiling a bibliography on human rights.

It was to be almost 50 years before the Human Rights Act 1998 became law in England. The International Court of Justice at the Hague, established in June 1945 by the Charter of the United Nations, began work in 1946 and acts today as a world court. It has a dual jurisdiction: it decides, in accordance with international law, disputes of a legal nature that are submitted to it by states and it gives advisory opinions on legal questions at the request of the organs of the United Nations or specialised agencies authorised to make such a request.

Rose's tour de force was universally acclaimed and was widely reported in the newspapers. The Past President of the Federation of Soroptimists in her thank-you letter, wrote:

> You will let me say...that you won all our hearts, not only because of our admiration for the lucidity and clarity of your argument, not only for the arduous work which you gave in order that your contribution should be so outstanding, but for your wholly charming and compelling self.

A female journalist on the *Evening Express*, who had been present, wrote to Rose:

> May I say here, and very sincerely too, how splendid you were. The fact that you could keep more than a 1000 women as silent as the tomb for 1½ hours, was I think proof that your talk was masterly, your diction appreciated and that you yourself, by sheer personality captured your audience.

The *Liverpool Post* later said of her talk, with the typical qualification to her sex which was prevalent, that it 'is considered one of the most significant contributions to world thinking made by a woman'.

Although the address had a fundamental legal aspect, it was much more wide ranging in its overall content than a narrative of national legal issues. Rose had clearly spent an enormous amount of time researching her speech. The themes expounded illustrate Rose's wider appeal as a speaker and person than her role as a female lawyer, consistent with her multi-dimensional personality. For Rose was not just a barrister. She was a wife and mother, but was also well read and, even if she lacked the time to pursue other interests, was nonetheless well informed on a whole range of issues and never shy in expressing her views.

THE CASE OF ROSE YANTIN

This busy schedule of engagements did not mean any let-up in Rose's professional life. She continued with her increasing practice and a variety of cases such as defending a man on a manslaughter charge, defending a man of receiving stolen property, appearing for a six-year-old girl with a brain injury following being knocked down by a motor cycle and many more criminal and civil cases besides. Many of these were reported in the press and some in the law reports.

Apart from the Cameo murders, one other case in which Rose was involved attracted considerable press attention during 1950. Rose Yantin was a 23-year-old resident of the Darenth Park Mental Colony, where she had been residing since aged 15, although she had escaped many times. She had been sent there after absconding from a Jewish approved school where she had been for three years, because her parents said she was beyond their control. On 25 January 1950, she escaped and stole a coat and blouse worth £6.19s. The purpose of this escapade, she said, had been to draw attention to her plight and establish that she was in fact sane. She pleaded guilty before the Stipendiary Magistrate in London. With tears in her eyes, she told the court that she may have been out of control when younger, but was not mad:

> I don't see why I should go back. I'm just as capable of working as you are, Sir. There is nothing wrong with me. I have never had treatment since I have been in the place. My appeals and my mother's appeals have always been rejected. The next time I get a review is in 1952. Every time I run away I just get taken back without anything being said. I want my case

brought to light so that I can be given a fair chance. All I do all day long is work. Why should I work for a miserable 1s and 6d per week when I could have a place of my own and work and keep myself? I want to mix with sane people who are not imbeciles. My mother has offered to send an independent psychiatrist to Darenth Park but her letters and a solicitor's letters have been ignored. She has written to the King as well.

After hearing her, the Magistrate concluded that she appeared 'not only to be normal and to talk reasonably, but to talk sound sense too'. However, the prison doctor's report said she was certifiable as mentally defective and proposed that she should be remanded again so that she could be taken back for further treatment. Her case would not normally have come up for review at the mental colony until 1952. Her sentence was adjourned until 2 March 1950 because, Rose, who had been instructed on her behalf, was then appearing in the Cameo murder trial. She was sent home on bail of £10 into the care of her parents.

At the adjourned hearing the Magistrate indicated that he wanted to sentence her to one day's imprisonment, but her counsel pointed out that there was an order out for her return to the home. Rose suggested a way round was to put her on probation, as the Board of Control had agreed that they would not then exercise their power to bring her back. If she broke her probation she would go to prison for six months. She was put on probation for two years and went home to celebrate her 24th birthday. Friends had bought her new clothes and another friend had given her a job in a dress shop and it was stated that the family hoped to emigrate to Canada. This sad and poignant story was reported widely and led to headlines such as 'Rose Yantin wins freedom' and 'Rose got her wish for Happy Birthday'.

Rose had helped to secure her a future away from a mental institution, but there was to be an unexpected sequel, as in many of Rose's famous cases. The promised future of a normal life did not materialise. Eight years later in March 1958, having changed her name by deed poll to Rose Dugan, she was gaoled for three months for theft of a box of Camembert cheese and a comb worth 4s 6d and revealed nine previous minor convictions including two for shoplifting. Her defence was that her boyfriend was coming from Germany and he liked Camembert cheese, but she had no money to pay for it. She only disclosed who she was when she was sentenced. What her mental state was and what happened to her thereafter is not known.

If 1950 had proved a baptism of fire for the young female silk, the next few years were to produce some equally exciting and taxing challenges.

9

Getting into her Stride in Silk

ON 3 JANUARY 1951, after celebrating Hilary's second birthday the previous day, Rose left by train and boat for the Hook of Holland and then on to Hamburg in Germany. She had been invited by the Foreign Office to give a lecture tour in Germany. It was a tiring journey taking almost two days. On arriving early in the morning from the overnight boat she 'had breakfast with tinned milk as German milk not considered TT and cannot transport fresh milk there' and the train to Hamburg was 'full of troops', but the journey had views of snow-covered scenery. On arrival at Hamburg she was met by three officers and whisked to a reception at a grand venue. She was given a military permit and an identity card.

During her visit, she gave several lectures on a variety of legal issues taking questions afterwards, including the subjects of: 'The Law and Progress'; 'Women and the English Law'; English Law and Social Programmes' and 'English Law and the Individual', visiting four different locations: Hamburg, Neumunster, Kiel and Lübeck. In addition she was escorted to meet many dignitaries and working women. She visited the courts, attended various lunches and receptions, went to the opera and made a radio broadcast on the British Forces Network. The Inspector of Police also took her on a tour of the Reeperbahn or red light district of Hamburg, something she recounted in later years with great amusement.

Her contemporaneous and detailed manuscript daily notes of her visit bear witness not only to her full agenda, but also to what she saw and learnt about the difficulties of life in Germany and the international situation only seven years after the end of the Second World War. She also noted the differences she learned between the German and English legal systems, the former being inquisitorial with the judge asking questions, whereas the latter is adversarial with counsel doing the questioning. The following is an abbreviated extract from her notes:

> Spent morning of 5th sorting papers out and going round Die Brucke. Then in afternoon ... went to the office of the Commissioner and got Currency and Capitation Card and food coupons. Met one of the heads of Legal Dept; had tea at officers' club. Gave lecture at 6pm: large and appreciative audience and good questions. Reception at Public prosecutors. Very formal—a lot of clicking of heels. Welcome Herr General and gave ex tempore reply. Discussions about the differences between the two systems ... Mon: Writing this and feeling very very tried—didn't sleep well—too excited I suppose 'I must say this is rather like a royal tour' ... Tues. 9th ... Went to a Bavarian Bar ... in Bavaria no one under 40 could be a waitress ... Wed: Went to Naafi shop and asked for cigarettes but they are rationed ... got permission ... for 200 cigarettes which cost me £9. On way to Kiel ... Saw more courts; lunch. Taken on a navy launch up the Kiel Canal. Gave lecture at Scheslding.

Separately she noted amongst other things: 'bicycles on pavement; double and treble lorries; 1,500 Jews in Hamburg (all came since war ended); old judges not Nazis, but difficult to find enough'.

In one of her daily letters to Nat on 9 January 1951 she wrote:

> It's difficult to convey in writing what a terrific fuss they're making of my appearance here. I'm escorted everywhere, a car appears like magic and anything I suggest is done ... but very necessary really for my programme is so heavy and exhausting that I need comfort. There are so many receptions that I find myself changing 3 or 4 times a day so as to be correctly dressed.

She also learned about the German legal system and met some important and interesting people in the German legal world, as well as other working and professional women. She clearly found it all fascinating, if exhausting, but her daily letters to Nat and his to her show how much she also missed home and her family and he missed her. It was her first trip abroad alone since her marriage.

BACK TO WORK

On her return to England Rose was soon to be in the news again. In February 1951, she represented a Miss Florence Parry, a 61-year-old spinster formerly in charge of the St Helens Corporation Motor Taxation Department for 34 years. She was charged with fraud under the Falsification Act in relation to falsifying books and other documents relating to duty for road fund licences, such as substituting a different vehicle with a lower rating. She pleaded not guilty, contending that her actions were for an innocent purpose, namely to cover deficiencies in the books prior to audit which otherwise she personally would have had to make good. She argued that she did not act for gain and received no money herself. The trial took place at Liverpool Assizes before Mr Justice Ormerod. The jury found her guilty and she was sentenced to 12 months' imprisonment.

The following day Rose was back in court representing a seaman who had fallen from the mast of a ship. As a result of the accident, he was paralysed and suffered grave internal injuries. He was awarded £12,000 agreed damages, 'possibly the highest ever awarded in this court for his "terrible injuries"'. Her practice remained varied and included successfully representing a lady accused of cruelty to dogs; recovering damages for a young boy whose arm was injured when trapped under a bus; and representing one Norman Smith, before the Rhyl magistrates. He pleaded guilty to selling rock at Rhyl in breach of certain rationing orders and was fined.

Later in the year in 'a 165 minute Trial', the shortest trial in Manchester for many years, she unsuccessfully represented William Henry Nuttal on a charge of murdering the woman he was living with. In a fit of jealousy having found letters written by another man, he had picked up an axe and killed her. Rose had run the defence of provocation seeking a finding of manslaughter, but the jury thought otherwise, no doubt considering that the wielding of an axe might not have been as spontaneous as alleged. He was found guilty and sentenced to death. These examples of cases, chosen because they caught the public attention, give only a superficial idea of the size and variety of her practice at this time.

THE DOCKERS' CASE

The high points of Rose's professional career in 1951 were two other very famous cases. In the first she represented three Liverpool dockers whom it was alleged had gone on strike unlawfully. The case received widespread national publicity. Liverpool dockers were notorious for going on strike, as is epitomized by the joke told about them that when, one sunny spring morning, a mate of a Liverpool docker exclaimed 'I see the daffodils are out'. The docker responded 'does that mean we are out too?' The Dockers' Case, as it became known, was, however, much more serious.

Criminal proceedings had been brought against seven dockers who were charged upon indictment with three alternative counts, namely: conspiracy to incite dockworkers in contravention of the provisions of Order No 1305 (Count 1); conspiracy to induce dockworkers to commit a breach of contract (with their employers) (Count 2); and conspiracy to obstruct employers of dockworkers in the conduct of their business (Count 3). Counts 2 and 3 were late additions. The dockers pleaded not guilty to all counts. The prosecution had been authorised by Sir Hartley Shawcross, the Attorney General.

It was a case of high drama and national importance such that it warranted the trial being heard before the Lord Chief Justice, Lord Goddard, with a jury at the Old Bailey, London's famous central criminal court and the venue of many well-known trials over the years. The Crown was represented by Sir Hartley Shawcross, leading two junior barristers. Rose, leading David McNeil (later a High Court Judge) and David Turner-Samuels, represented the three Liverpool and Birkenhead dockers and Roy Wilson KC, with a similar team of barristers, represented the four London dockers. It was her first appearance at the Old Bailey as a silk. Rose was reported to have been paid 750 guineas on the brief with refreshers of 150 guineas a day, but one suspects that this is likely to have been wide of the mark and she earned much less, particularly as the fees which are known for work she did at the time are nothing like so high.

8,000 London dockers staged a spontaneous token one day strike on the first day of the trial, one of seven such strikes protesting against the Old Bailey trial. A large number of striking dockers formed a huge demonstration outside the court and officers with walkie-talkies stood at the entrance to the Old Bailey. There was a long queue of people trying to get a seat in the renowned No 1 court at the Old Bailey. A little background is now necessary to understand fully what happened next.

The Factual Background

Labour in the docks was organised into four different unions, the largest of which was the Transport and General Workers' Union (the TGWU) which had about 90,000 dockers as members. A dockworker's employment was covered by a statutory scheme which ensured a guaranteed week's employment at a guaranteed minimum wage.

Dockers were required to attend for work once a day at what were called 'stands' and then if ships were available, they were called off from those stands and asked to work on particular ships where they were employed by the ship-owners at higher rates of pay. If there were no ships available the dockers were able to go away, but had to return for a second call in the afternoon in case ships had become available in the meantime.

In 1947 at a biennial conference of the unions, the members had adopted the 'Dockers' Charter' as the official policy of the union. This provided for a wage of 25s a day, 2 weeks holiday with pay, a pension scheme for retired dock workers and one call per day instead of two, ie dockers had to turn up for work once a day instead of twice. By the summer of 1950 these demands had not been met. The prosecution alleged that from October 1950 until 14 January 1951, the Liverpool defendants concentrated on:

> fanning the discontent in the dock to a point at which the dockworkers of Merseyside would be in a mood to reject outright any terms that might be offered by the employers and agreed by the representatives of the union short of the full terms of the charter.

Unofficial bodies, called Port Workers' Committees were formed first of all in Birkenhead and then in London. Joseph Gerald Harrison was the chair of the Birkenhead committee. Two of the other defendants, Johnson and Crosbie, were members of the Liverpool committee and the remaining four defendants were members of the London committee.

In the meantime, on 22 January 1951, the workers' side of the National Joint Industrial Council, the recognised constitutional negotiating machinery between employers and employees for settling wage claims, decided to recommend to its men a 2s a day wage increase and a 7–10 per cent rise for piece work. On 1 February 1951, a docks delegate conference was held and representatives of the unions, by a majority, decided to accept the recommended proposal. A binding written agreement was then drawn up and signed.

The prosecution further alleged (although this was disputed) that on 2 February 1951, the day after the agreed settlement, as workers were arriving at the dock gates at Birkenhead, Harrison intercepted them by calling a meeting at the dock gates and asking the men to vote in favour of unofficial strike action, which they did. 1,732 dockers came out on strike and at its peak those on strike at Merseyside numbered 9,520, but for most of the time it was around 6,000. It was further alleged that the Liverpool docker defendants sought to persuade the London dockers to come out in sympathy and that similar activity was organised by the London docker defendants in relation to London dockers. However, the London dockers were not willing to strike.

As Sir Hartley Shawcross explained to the jury in opening the case:

> By that date, in spite of an agreed settlement of the dispute, there was, as a result of the concerted efforts of these defendants, a strike of considerable dimensions at Liverpool and at Birkenhead, but the defendants had so far failed in the efforts which they made to bring out the dock-workers of London in support of those who had been led to strike on Merseyside. Undeterred by that, unwilling to allow the strike to collapse, but apparently intent on renewing their efforts, although they knew, as one of their associates said, that a dock strike on a national scale would strangle the nation, they threatened to bring down from Liverpool and Birkenhead thousands of Merseyside dock-workers to march in procession, and, as they put it, to shame the London dockers into coming out on strike ... in the face of that threat ... the authorities could no longer hold their hand ... The complaint against ... [them] is that in order to promote what they thought, rightly or wrongly, was the interests of their fellow dock-workers, they were prepared to hold the nation to ransom and to defy the law of the land.

His opening speech led to headlines of extracts from the speech such as 'Dockers Aimed to Strangle Nation' (*The Star*); 'Dock Trial: 'Ransom Plot—Shawcross Talks of Blackmail'; (*The Evening Standard*); 'Dockers Tried to Strangle Us: Sir Hartley Accuses' (*The Daily Mail*). In the days before air freight and containers, sea transport was effectively the only means of importing and exporting goods and the loading and unloading of vessels was very labour intensive. A national dock strike could have been catastrophic for the nation.

The principal issue in the case was whether there was a breach of Order 1305, ie Count 1. Order 1305 provided that where there was a trade dispute between employers and workers, or between workers and workers, the employers could not take lockout action or the employees go on strike without first reporting the dispute to the Minister of Labour. The Minister of Labour was then given 21 days within which either to try to promote a settlement using whatever negotiating machinery was available or to refer the matter to arbitration by the National Arbitration Tribunal, an independent tribunal with representatives of employers and employees. Thus the key question was whether, as the prosecution alleged, there was a trade dispute, ie a dispute between dockworkers and the dockers' employers, or whether the dispute was between the dockers and their union and union representatives, who had agreed a deal with the employers, in which case there was no trade dispute and no breach of Order 1305.

The Trial at the Old Bailey

The trial began on Monday 9 April 1951, and lasted seven days. There was a considerable amount of evidence given. The prosecution called 26 witnesses. Representatives of the Ministry of Labour, the TGWU, the National Docks Labour Board, as well as many police officers who had been present at the various meetings, gave evidence of what was said. All these witnesses were cross-examined first by Rose, whose clients seem to have been more heavily involved than the London defendants, and then by Roy Wilson KC. The seven defendants each gave evidence and were also cross-examined. Most of the oral evidence went to the nature of the dispute, what the defendants had said in their speeches and whether or not the defendants were in dispute with their employers or merely in dispute with their trade union officials.

It was the defendants' case that the union officials, and in particular Arthur Deakin, the General Secretary of the TGWU, who were unelected representatives, were not doing their job properly in representing the interests of their members. The defendants were critical of the way the union officials were handling the negotiations on the Dockers' Charter. The defendants contended that the strike was the last resort having tried constitutional methods unsuccessfully, as they wanted to put pressure on the union officials to negotiate further with their employers.

By Monday, 16 April 1951, the sixth day of the trial, it was reported that almost 10,000 dockers had stopped work in protest. It was against this background that on the Monday morning, no doubt having worked all weekend, Rose gave her closing speech to the jury. She began:

> Now members of the jury, the Attorney General in his opening address to you ...—[at] the beginning of last week—told you that this was an ordinary criminal trial ... it is, of course, a criminal trial, but is this an ordinary trial? Are the offences with which these men are charged ordinary criminal offences? There is no charge here of violence, no charge of dishonesty, or seeking to make a profit out of another's loss; there is no

allegation suggested of personal gain. On the contrary, it was said that my clients, convinced, rightly or wrongly, of the justice of their claim, pursued the course of conduct with which they are charged without any hope of personal gain, but certainly seeking, and only seeking, an improvement in the conditions of their fellow men, without violence, but by means of the exercise of free speech, added to which, of course, as you have already heard from witnesses for the prosecution, that the men for whom I appear are men of the highest integrity—good, honest, decent working men.

She continued her powerful address, appealing to the jury about the basic freedoms of working men and women:

It may be on Counts 2 and 3 you are being asked to say that strikes are illegal. It is a strange commentary on the development of the law and the rules of law that you should be asked to say that now, in 1951. The right of workers to withhold their labour has been thought up to now to be one of the essential rights in this democratic country. No one says that strikes are pleasant, no one says that they can be conducted without hardship, not only to the workers involved, not only to their wives and families, but to a great many other people; no one would contend that a strike, be it important enough or sufficiently widespread, might not do great harm, but even during the war strikes were not made illegal. They were only made illegal if they offended against the Order ... If it is legal to have them, then it is legal to persuade, to organise, to encourage, or to lead. We have to go back a very long way ... before we find strikes made illegal, and any British jury will be very careful indeed, and very reluctant, before deciding that acts directed to exercise that right, the right to strike, are to be called criminal conspiracies ... No one is asking you to say whether you like or dislike unofficial strikes; that is utterly irrelevant to any issue you have to try. Voltaire once said: 'I detest what you say, but I defend to the death your right to say it'. Members of the Jury, you may also say: 'I detest what you did, but I defend to the death your right to do it so long as it is within the law'.

She then dealt with an exposition of the law and gave a detailed analysis of the facts by reference to the daily transcripts which had been provided to the jury, a facility which was rare in those days. She argued that on Count 1, which was the meat of the case, the prosecution had to prove three things: (1) An agreement to incite an unlawful strike; (2) that the strike which resulted from that agreement was illegal; and (3) that the intention of the accused was to bring that illegal strike about.

She examined such issues as who were the alleged employers and the lack of evidence on the point; she pointed to the failure to produce satisfactory evidence of the absence of notification of a trade dispute by the alleged employers which could have been given by employers had a trade dispute existed; she queried whether in law Counts 2 and 3 amounted to an offence, particularly when it was not known who the employers were; and argued that on the evidence it was clear that the strike action was started spontaneously by the Birkenhead men who were disgusted with the Union for not pressing forward to obtain the terms of the Dockers' Charter.

Her speech lasted three hours. It was also widely reported. Examples include: 'Woman KC Hits at Union Chiefs' (*The Star*) 'Woman KC Blames Dock Union Chiefs' (*Liverpool Echo*); 'Woman KC' Pleads 3 Hours' (*Daily Herald*). The next day Roy Wilson gave his closing address on behalf of the London dockers. Lord Goddard then gave his summing up. At the end he asked counsel whether there was anything that he had not raised with the jury or any particular matter which he had omitted on the facts which counsel wished him to stress which he had not. Rose's response was that 'I cannot say off hand: there are so many points in this case that one cannot pick them out'. Rose's contemporaneous manuscript notes indicate that Lord Goddard then turned to Hartley Shawcross and said very quietly: 'I don't blame her for not wanting to draft her notice of appeal now!'

Following the Judge's summing up, the jury retired. After seeking further directions as to the definition of a trade dispute, they returned with their verdict. They had been deliberating for about four hours. The jury indicated that they were unable to agree on Count 1 (Order 1305), but found the defendants guilty on Count 2 (conspiracy to induce a breach of contract). As the counts were alternative the jury was released from finding a verdict on Count 3. Rose immediately took the point as to the effect of the verdict as well as the risk of a re-trial on Count 1. The matter was left over for legal argument the next day. The verdict was immediately telephoned to the Prime Minister, Mr Attlee, who was in hospital and Mr Bevan, Minister of Labour. Rose, on the other hand was 2s 6d out of pocket. When the jury had retired Hartley Shawcross had made a bet with Rose that the jury would disagree on Count 1.

During the day, while awaiting the verdict, there had been scuffles with the police outside the Old Bailey when mounted police tried to move the crowd of about 1,000 striking dockers who had been singing such songs as 'Britons never, never will be slaves' and 'Keep right on till the end of the road'. When the verdict was announced the seven defendants were cheered and chaired in triumph from the Old Bailey to Holborn about half a mile away, temporarily disrupting the traffic. Bessie Braddock MP, not a light load, was also lifted off her feet and chaired with them to the strains of 'For she's a jolly good fellow'. She had been in court and had supported them.

The next day, the Attorney General announced as follows to a hushed court:

> My Lord, I have given a great deal of thought to the situation arising from the jury's failure to agree upon Count 1 of the indictment and their verdict upon Count 2. It seems to me that it is quite impossible to reconcile the jury's verdict on Count 2 with their disagreement under Count 1, and although I suppose this obviously was not the intention of the jury, I have come to the conclusion, subject to your Lordship's approval, that the illogical findings of the jury compel me, in fairness to the defendants, to discontinue the proceedings, and that, subject to your Lordship's better judgement, I propose to do so by not moving for judgment under Count 2 and by entering a nolle prosequi to the whole indictment.

> My Lord, important as this whole case is, it is even more important that the proceedings against these men should not in any way be unfair or oppressive ... it seems quite impossible for the jury logically to disagree upon the existence of a trade dispute under Count 1 and then to agree about it almost in the next breath in Count 2 ... I can only assume that some of the jury thought that these defendants ought to be convicted of something, and they were not quite sure what, and I do not think it possible to sustain the verdict in those circumstances.

The Lord Chief Justice entered an acquittal and discharged the seven defendants. There followed 'unprecedented scenes of rejoicing in London's dockland ... as jubilant dockers celebrated the release of their seven mates and what they believe is the end of Order 1305'. The Portworkers' Committee in Liverpool 'are preparing the greatest ever welcome for their leaders'. Expectations were high that Order 1305, introduced in the war to avert strikes, would be repealed, as indeed it was later that year. Even Rose was reported as smiling widely as she left the court. At the end of the case, one of her clients took her hand and said 'I can't kiss you Miss Heilbron—it would be bigamy'. Rose once again received fulsome praise for her efforts and ultimate success which was reported as adding 'lustre to her growing reputation as an advocate' and attracting headlines such as 'Rose KC Makes History Again'.

Fulsome Praise from All

Lord Goddard was regarded by many with fear, but he seemed to have had a soft spot for Rose and always treated her fairly, unlike some of his contemporaries. On the day the defendants were discharged, 18 April, he wrote to the 35 year old female silk thus:

Dear Miss Heilbron,

May I say a word of congratulation on the way you did the Dockers' case. In a case where it must have been very difficult to avoid going too far you made no mistake—in fact I thought your conduct of the case was in accordance with the best traditions of the Bar.

Yours sincerely,

Goddard.

Even during the trial Lord Goddard was flattering. When Rose asked a witness whether he could hear her voice as it had become hoarse while examining one of her clients who was deaf, Lord Goddard apparently turned to Hartley Shawcross and said very quietly 'and a very nice voice too!' The impression she made on Lord Goddard was lasting. Seven years later in 1958 in response to a letter from Rose on his retirement he wrote:

Your career has been one that has been of the greatest interest to watch and I have no doubt that you have many years of successful practice before you. I shall never forget the perfect manner in which you conducted the defence of the Dock strikers. It was indeed a lesson in advocacy.

On 2 May, Hartley Shawcross replied to a letter from Rose thanking her for her letter of congratulations on his recent appointment as President of the Board of Trade, in which he commented: 'I have been meaning to write and congratulate you on your great success at the Old Bailey—in the long run I think it was all for the best whichever way one looks at it'.

She received other compliments too. Frank Soskice, who was promoted from Solicitor General to Attorney General when Hartley Shawcross moved to the Board of Trade, wrote: 'Everybody tells me you did the dockers' case absolutely magnificently'. On 30 April, the Secretary, Chairman and another member of the Liverpool dockers' wives committee wrote: 'Although more than a week has passed since the trial of the seven dockers, we the undersigned on behalf of the Liverpool dockers' wives committee would like as women to express our thanks to you for the wonderful fight you put up for the Merseyside men'. Someone called 'Mersey Mike' even wrote a poem entitled 'The Epic of the Old Bailey', two verses of which proclaimed:

> Then a silver-voiced young woman, rose and faced the room
> And a ray of hope, as she spoke, swept aside the gloom
> She battled for our brothers as only women can
> With truth and facts and logic, she crushed the mighty man.
>
> And Shawcross looked astonished, then his head it bent low
> At last the Judge he turned and said 'I'll have to let them go'
> And right throughout the country as every docker knows
> When we get the Dockers' Charter
> We'll bless the lovely Rose.

But perhaps most memorable was the fact that as her train entered Lime Street Station in Liverpool on its return from London, Rose was met by a reception committee of a crowd of dockers waiting to cheer her along the platform. They were heady days.

THE BOOTLE BATH MURDER

The second high-profile case which Rose undertook in 1951 was much more distressing. Rose described the case to her junior as a harrowing one. For someone who was, by this time, pretty case-hardened and used to viewing upsetting images of dead people, this was clearly an unusual case.

100 Irlam Street in Bootle, Liverpool was the scene of the crime where there lived on the first floor Mrs Emma Grace and her children and, on the ground floor, Mrs Anna Neary, a 27-year-old French woman and her husband and three young children. They shared a front door. Late on Friday afternoon, 25 May 1951, Mrs Grace was found drowned in her bath with scratches on her face and blows to the neck, face and head. Anna Neary was charged with her murder. It was alleged that the two women had had a quarrel over money. She was defended by Rose under the Poor Persons Act. Rose earned 15 guineas leading Edward Youds. The case was heard at Manchester Assizes before Mr Justice Barry on 10 July 1951. An interpreter translated Mrs Neary's evidence. The case lasted four days and became known as the Bootle bath murder.

Mrs Neary, who was in tears during a large part of the trial, gave evidence, breaking down more than once when so doing. She was a rather pathetic figure. She responded to Rose's question whether she had killed Emma Grace: 'No, never, I never done it. Never'.

In her evidence she explained that earlier Mrs Grace had let a visitor into the house. Shortly afterwards she heard a large thud upstairs and went to see if Mrs Grace was alright, only to find her injured and bleeding leaning against the bath. She was then confronted by a man 'with big ugly hairy hands' who closed the door behind her, threatened her with a gun, lifted Mrs Grace into the bath and held her head under water until she drowned. When the man had gone she ran out of the house for help. Neighbours came to her aid and the police then arrived. It was alleged that money was the motive for the murder.

Rose's brief had contained the unusual comment: 'Counsel will no doubt paint a picture for the Jury of what normally happens when two women fight'. It is assumed that this was addressed to Rose's skills as an advocate! Under cross-examination the police surgeon accepted that the injuries to Mrs Grace were superficial and could not say how they were caused. In her final speech lasting three hours, Rose was able to point to the fact that Mrs Grace and her daughters had had a series of male visitors; to the absence of Mrs Neary's hair at the scene, which one would have expected if the two women had been fighting and pulling on each other's hair; to the absence of any signs of a fight upon Mrs Neary's hands, coupled with the fact that Mrs Neary bit her fingernails; and to the impossibility of Mrs Neary being able to lift Mrs Grace into the bath without showing signs of lifting her. Rose also drew attention to the fact that Mrs Neary was not short of money. She alleged that the police had arrested her client precipitously and had never properly investigated the likelihood that the murderer was a man. Rose summed the case up by saying that Mrs Neary was an innocent witness to the crime and that it was 'a tragic mistake'.

After deliberating for two hours, the jury returned a verdict of not guilty. Mrs Neary collapsed and lay weeping on the floor for several minutes after hearing the result and a doctor was called. Her husband also broke down in tears under the strain. Cheers, clapping and shouts of 'hurrah' were heard from the public gallery. In an interview after her acquittal for the *News of the World*, Mrs Neary explained that it had been difficult to make herself understood to the police through an interpreter, because she and the interpreter spoke different dialects. She spoke too of her fear that her children would have forgotten her—for had she been found guilty she would have hanged—and how she prayed night and day just to go back to her husband and children. The young children had been told their mother was in hospital. The family planned a new life away from Bootle.

Among the many press reports of the case, the *Daily Express* and even the *South China Morning Post* in Hong Kong announced 'Rose KC Wins her 'Harrowing Case'; the *Manchester News Chronicle* head-lined 'Woman Cleared of Bath Murder—Triumph for her Counsel— a Woman'; and the *News of the World* wrote: 'Brilliant Defence ... Another victory in a series of triumphant cases conducted by 36-year-old, petite, dark-haired Miss Heilbron ... Her brilliant defence culminated with a three-hour address to the jury at the end of which she smiled and asked them 'to rectify this tragic mistake'. The *News of the World* article juxtaposed two pictures of the two young mothers, Rose at her garden gate with the caption 'but out-side court she is just like any other housewife ... She is married to a doctor and has a two-year-old daughter' and a photograph of Mrs Neary with her three small children. Press interest in Rose was becoming intense and she was about to have to tackle some difficult issues on that front.

10

Welcome and Unwelcome Publicity and Another Famous Murder Trial

1952 STARTED UNEVENTFULLY. Rose returned to work after the Christmas vacation. She was beginning to do more work off Circuit as her reputation soared and demand for her services around the country grew. For instance on 3 January 1952 she successfully defended a former engineering company manager, Robert Morley, on an embezzlement charge at Quarter Sessions at Mold on the Chester and Wales Circuit. She led her good friend Emlyn Hooson (later Liberal MP and ennobled). Morley was alleged to have disposed of scrap metal, paint and other materials extraneous to the company's needs without crediting the company with the proceeds. His defence was that none of the money had gone into his own pocket, but instead he had used the money as petty cash to provide refreshments etc when workmen worked extra time at weekends. He was acquitted on the direction of the Chairman of the Bench. At the end of the month, briefed by WH Thompson, Rose represented the Fire Brigades Union before the City of London Coroner on behalf of the dependants of those killed in a fire at Broad Street.

LOUIS ARNOLD BLOOM

On 4 February 1952, Rose appeared at Durham Assizes in County Durham in a very high-profile case to defend 35-year-old Louis Arnold Bloom on a murder charge, instructed by a firm of solicitors from West Hartlepool and leading Norman Harper. She was the first woman barrister to appear at Durham Assizes. Bloom was a solicitor and son of the former Mayor of West Hartlepool, who had fallen in love with, and had been having an affair with, Patricia Hessler, aged 38, a former client. The relationship had been going on for some 16–17 months. Hessler had drink problems. She was an heiress, divorcee and femme fatale with a fairly chequered past—her previous lover's father had tried to end the affair and in the process shot his own son with a revolver.

Bloom had been trying to end the relationship, although apparently he still loved her. She had taunted him that he would never be rid of her. They spent the night of 14 November 1951 together in his office after having gone to the theatre. He had told her that he was moving to London and the relationship would end and that this was probably the last time they would see each other. Early the following morning, on his return from the newsagents, he found Hessler sitting in a chair the worse for drink and somewhat hysterical, screaming and shouting. She said 'I have meant trouble for every man I've come into contact with—nearly—trouble with a capital "T"'. There was no one else in the office at the time. He grabbed her throat to quieten her, pressing his thumbs into the front of her neck, as he had apparently done on previous occasions when she had become hysterical, but on this occasion, in the process, he throttled her to death. He then rang the police and admitted to the police that he 'did it'.

An admission, to put it at its lowest, of assaulting someone and inflicting the injuries which led to the death of that person was not the best way to begin a defence to a murder charge which, if proved, would lead to the defendant being hanged. His defence was that all he wanted to do was to silence Hessler, as the staff were about to arrive in the office, and that he had no intention of killing her. Rose had appeared in the magistrates' court at his committal for trial in December the previous year, but, despite cross-examining the Crown pathologist, had not succeeded in getting the charge of murder thrown out and the charge reduced to manslaughter. The national newspapers ran with the story at great length with long extracts from both the committal hearing and later the trial. Once again the headlines would frequently refer to 'Woman K.C.', emphasising the novelty of a female silk, for example, 'Woman K.C. Pleads: No Malice, so it Couldn't Be Murder' (*Daily Mirror*); 'Miss Rose Clashes with Doctor' (*Daily Express*); and 'Set Bloom Free—Woman Counsel' (*Daily Mail*) and, as usual, photographs of Rose would accompany the reporting.

The trial took place before Mr Justice Hallett. He gave Rose a hard time. Whether this was because he was not well disposed towards women barristers or because it was his normal judicial manner is not known. He was, however, an unpopular Judge and one of the very few High Court Judges who has been asked to resign by the Lord Chancellor, which he did in 1959. Crowds had queued outside the court for hours to get a seat and the police had to be called to control them. The issue revolved around the intention of Bloom—if he had been reckless as to the consequences of what he was doing or deliberately and maliciously throttled Hessler, then he would have been guilty of murder. The case was opened as a savage, brutal murder and the relationship as an illicit and sordid one. The nature of the injury and cause of death was highly relevant. It was alleged by the prosecution that she died from inhibition of the vagal nerve leading to a sudden stoppage of the heart and a stopping of breath which was different from strangulation or asphyxia.

Following the extensive publicity at the committal hearing Rose received unsolicited letters giving medical and other advice on the case. A two-foot-high red and yellow plastic model of a human neck was carried into court for the purpose of illustrating to the jury the forensic and medical evidence. Rose cross-examined the Crown pathologist at length about the cause of death and related issues. He accepted that there were no signs that death was due to asphyxia and that death from vagal inhibition could result without violence at all. The Judge constantly interrupted her cross-examination, but she stood her ground. As one journalist commented 'She showed sufficient knowledge of the human larynx to tackle a medical exam on the subject'.

Bloom gave evidence. To counter the allegation that he was trying to get rid of Hessler, the pair's love letters were read. He explained that he had put his hands around her neck with his thumbs to the front and had applied some pressure with his thumbs. Then he had taken his thumbs away and, as she was still making a noise, he had pressed again with his thumbs and when he removed them the second time there was no noise and her face looked lifeless. He said that he loved her to the end.

On 6 February 1952, when Bloom had finished giving his evidence the Judge announced that King George VI had died and adjourned the court for 10 minutes. Thereafter everyone wore court mourning—counsel swapping normal bands for white mourning bands. Overnight the King's Justices became the Queen's Justices and King's Counsel became Queen's Counsel.

The evidence in the case had concluded 10 minutes before the luncheon adjournment and Rose requested that she be able to begin her closing speech after lunch, but the Judge refused. Unlike the Dockers' case there were no daily transcripts. Rose therefore used the very full reporting of the testimony of the Crown pathologist in the local newspapers to dissect and annotate his evidence for the purpose of her final speech.

She suggested that Bloom was:

> a man who, all the times he was with this woman, was protective, kind, infatuated and foolish—but never cruel, and never wanting or ever thinking of doing her any injury, not even to want to hurt a hair of her head … You may have formed the view that this man cared a great deal about this woman. Far too much! … It was passion, infatuation, obsession; and you may think he never got it out of his system … If Bloom wanted to get rid of Mrs Hessler, can you think of a more ridiculous place to get rid of her than in his office? You may feel that a dead body in his office is even more dangerous to his practice than a live one … How truthful Bloom's story rings! There is a woman screaming. He had gone down on his knees to her to be quiet. What more natural thing than to press her on her neck and to tell her to be quiet … But if you make a mistake and press a little too hard, the damage is done. Bloom obviously pressed a little too hard. The whole thing happened like that. One, two three (Rose rapped on the bench three times) and she is dead.

Rose asked the jury to acquit her client on the basis of an accident, the alternative verdicts being manslaughter and murder.

The Judge summed up for a conviction for murder. As always the burden was on the prosecution to prove guilt beyond reasonable doubt. He explained to the jury that murder is not necessarily planned and is often committed on the spur of the moment. He further explained that to find Bloom guilty of murder, the jury had to be satisfied not only that, as an ordinary and reasonable man, he must have known that at least grievous bodily harm was likely to result from what he did to Hessler's neck, but also that what he did caused her death.

A reporter for the *Reynolds News* remarked on the Judge's sly reference to Rose's comely appearance in his summing up. The Judge commented on Rose's eloquence, but added, as she had noted he had done in another murder some eight years previously, 'Common sense should not be moved by oratory, however much you admire the oratory or orator'. The members of the jury were clearly moved. They came back with a verdict of manslaughter. Bloom was sentenced to three years' imprisonment. He had been saved from the gallows.

People crowded round Rose to congratulate her, but she said 'No fuss please' as she left the Court. *The News Chronicle* the next day ran a two-page spread entitled: 'Rose Heilbron Q.C. Ends Another Brilliant Case—Judge Talks of her "Eloquent Advocacy"'. Her junior, Norman Harper, wrote to congratulate her, indicating that he had heard that the sentence was lighter than another judge might have given Bloom 'so all the trials and tribulations re Hallett were worthwhile, after all'. He expressed his enjoyment at working with Rose and commented that: 'I continue to bask in the wonderful publicity you bring to your "so much older" juniors'. She also received a thank you letter from Bloom's mother not only conveying her and her husband's thanks, but also those of her son, Bloom, who could not write as he was only allowed to write one letter upon his reception in prison and he had written to his mother. Barristers rarely receive thank you letters from clients and when received they are greatly appreciated.

BAR COUNCIL PROFESSIONAL CONDUCT RULES

After the verdict Rose left to pack to return to Liverpool. She had been away from home for six days, including the previous weekend, preparing the case, meeting her client and representing him in court. She had worked into the early hours each morning in her hotel room, writing out everything in her large handwriting long before the days of computers and laptops. She was looking forward to returning to her family. However, her anticipated relaxation was disturbed by an incident which occurred concerning the press when she returned to her hotel to pack. It greatly upset her, as it had potentially serious professional implications.

Looking back over a half a century ago, the rules imposed by the Bar Council about what a barrister could and could not do in the 1950s and for some considerable time thereafter, look positively antediluvian. Barristers were not allowed to talk to the press or pose for photographs; they could not have visiting cards or advertise in any way; they could not visit solicitors' offices— the solicitor and client always had to attend upon counsel in his or her chambers. Breach of these rules was not some mere trifle, but a breach of professional conduct and, in a serious case, could lead to the barrister being disbarred. The rules have been gradually relaxed and today barristers operate in an environment which allows them to market themselves, give interviews to the press, visit solicitors' offices and have visiting cards, provided they act in a way which is not unprofessional and do not talk about their cases or disclose confidential information.

Rose had become good press copy. Not only was she involved in many fascinating cases whose facts in themselves caught the public interest, but her unique position of being young, female, attractive and a wife and mother, as well as her professional abilities, made her a role model. Added to this she regularly spoke on topics of the moment. From July 1951, when Helena Normanton KC retired from practice, she was the only female practising silk in the country and remained so for several years. Many reports of her cases headlined the unusual fact that she was a woman, as can be seen by some of the examples already given. As also can be seen the reporting was universally effusive and flattering.

The press coverage was wide ranging. There were the reports of her cases and of her role in them. There were articles about women's issues in which she featured, such as articles entitled 'A Woman Looks Around'; 'Career Women, the Law'. There were more general articles about successful or well-known people such as the *Picture Post* picking the 'New Elizabethans'. It included the names of eight famous people amongst whom were Earl Mountbatten, Rab Butler, the Chancellor of the Exchequer and Rose. Finally, there were articles exclusively about Rose or the speeches she had given. Her reputation was in the ascendancy. As the *Reynold's News* reporter wrote on 10 February 1952:

> So high is her reputation that I have noticed a strong note of mingled pride and satisfaction in the voices of solicitors who have told me 'I've managed to get Rose Heilbron for this case'. Their attitude suggests 'and who could ask for more?'.

But this consequent saturation press coverage brought with it some real problems.

At all times, however, Rose steadfastly kept to the professional rules. The press were persistent and, being unable to telephone her at home, because her telephone number was ex-directory, journalists often took to telephoning Nat at his surgery. When asked whether his wife was at home or when he would next see her, he would have to respond, tongue in cheek, that he did not know. If by any chance the press managed to telephone her at home and Rose answered, she would pretend to be her secretary and not admit that it was her. The whole family and employees were on alert and they were always very cautious when answering the telephone to a stranger.

It was thus with extreme concern that in August 1951 Rose read an article in the *Empire News* entitled 'Two Sisters, but they Live in Different Worlds'. Rose had the previous month been approached by a reporter from the *Empire News* when at Manchester, but had explained that she was unable to speak to the press. The article caused great consternation. It was the result of an interview with her sister without Rose's knowledge or consent. Her sister, although doubtless having been asked by Rose not to speak to the press, had clearly not fully appreciated the implications of what she had done. On reading the article today it seems relatively innocuous, but it was less what it said than the fact that it had been written as the result of an interview about Rose's childhood and lifestyle by a member of Rose's family that was the problem. Rose was not allowed to give interviews or authorise them and never gave one during her lifetime.

So concerned was Rose that she wrote to Mr Justice Devlin, who had offered her advice on previous occasions and also wrote to the Bar Council. Mr Justice Devlin responded that he could appreciate that she must be harassed 'by this sort of thing. But I think you are absolutely right to take it very seriously, as you are doing'. Rose hoped that this would be the end of the matter, but it was not to be.

At the end of the Bloom trial Rose was telephoned at her hotel by a *Daily Mirror* Reporter. She asked the hotel receptionist to say that she could not speak to him. Ten minutes later the telephone rang again and this time a photographer or journalist from the *Daily Mirror* had managed to get through. Rose explained to him that she would not see him. Ever persistent, a few weeks later on 14 March 1952, a journalist from the *Daily Mirror* called at her home address asking to see Rose. Although she was at home at the time she sent Mona Kelly, with whom she had been working, to speak to him. The journalist, Douglas Howell, asked to see Rose saying that he was anxious to obtain details concerning her and her private life such as her cooking and handed her a letter addressed to Rose. He asked Mona Kelly whether she knew if Rose contemplated taking any action against the *Empire News*, to which she replied that she didn't know anything about it having only recently commenced employment with Rose. The journalist then added that if he didn't get any corrected details, he could, of course, use the information which they then had. The letter explained that the *Daily Mirror* was 'anxious to fill gaps in the library about your career. I believe some cuttings are inaccurate'.

Concerned that the article in the *Empire News* would be reprinted or re-hashed, Rose contacted her London clerk, Charles Humphries, who in turn contacted the Bar Council and thereafter rang the *Daily Mirror* in vain to try to stop the article being printed. She then instructed London solicitors to advise her. They in turn sought a legal opinion from Sir Hartley Shawcross QC and Carl Aarvold as to whether the article was defamatory and as to what action, if any, Rose should take. Hartley Shawcross was then no longer in Government, the Conservatives having been returned to power in October 1951, and had returned to practice. She also wrote to Gray's Inn.

To those in the public eye today who are subjected to continual scrutiny of their private lives in the press, much of which is inaccurate or exaggerated, such a reaction must seem incredulous. But this was 1952 and things were very different. Added to which there were the concerns about possible allegations of unprofessional conduct. Her concern was less that the matters had been printed and the inaccuracies in them, but the implication that she might have directly or indirectly authorised the contents of the publication by giving an interview to the press and thereby been guilty of such unprofessional conduct.

Undeterred, on 27 March 1952, the *Daily Mirror* published the article by Douglas Howell entitled 'Rose' with a picture of her. It went into considerable detail about her private life, much of which was not entirely accurate. It purported to relate how she had met her husband, allegedly according to a member of the family, the kind of food she bought, the value of her house, her earnings and how she spent her spare time, the sort of clothes she liked according to an unnamed saleswoman, and gave details about her daughter and her parents and sister. Some of the material had come from the article in the *Empire News*, but some was additional. Thereafter these aspects of her private life were repeated in other articles.

Rose deeply resented what she felt was journalistic prying into her private life. She commented to her solicitor:

> The position at present is that I never open the door in case a press-man is outside. I am nervous of going to the shops in case what I buy is divulged to the public. My staff have always had strict instructions never to speak to the Press, not to answer any questions whatsoever, but apparently the Press are going round my friends, and the shopkeepers, and it is quite impossible to stop everybody from talking.

However, her colleagues at the Bar were very supportive and sympathised with her at having such articles written, even though it is inconceivable that there would not have been some envy at her huge press coverage, particularly as she was so much junior to many of her colleagues, some of whom, like Norman Harper in the Bloom case, were much older and had been at the Bar considerably longer than her.

The Under-Treasurer of Gray's Inn responded on 29 April 1952 in these terms:

> The attention of the Discipline Committee of this Inn has been called to two articles which recently appeared in the press: in the Daily Mirror of Thursday 27 March 1952 and the Picture Post of Saturday, 19th April [which stated 'Today Rose runs the home, shops, joins her husband at golf, studies at home and earns £5,000 a year']
>
> I am directed to ask you if you would care to supply the Committee with the following information:
>
> 1. Whether the statements as to your earnings at the Bar originated from you either directly or indirectly;
> 2. Whether the photographs in the two publications were in either case supplied by you or obtained with your knowledge or approval;
> 3. Whether any of the letter press was based on information supplied by you or to your knowledge by members of your family;
> 4. Whether you have taken any action to prevent a recurrence of publicity of this nature?

Following Rose's explanation, the Benchers of Gray's Inn decided to take no further action in the matter, but it must have been a worrying time for her nonetheless to have the issue raised before the disciplinary committee. Having taken legal advice Rose did not pursue defamation proceedings. Later that year she also received an enquiry from the Professional Conduct Committee of the Bar Council. This time the enquiry concerned a photograph of Rose, and she was asked whether it was a studio photograph, which was forbidden. She was able to refute the suggestion. Press intrusion and the risk of further issues about her directly or indirectly authorising articles became an occupational hazard and further incidents were to arise in the years to come.

MORE FAVOURABLE PUBLICITY

Alongside these troublesome articles were many more which did not cause her any problems, one of which in particular has more significance now than it did at the time. On 17 February

1952, Margaret Thatcher, later to be the first woman British Prime Minister, who was then studying for the Bar, wrote an article in the *Sunday Graphic* entitled 'Wake up Women' set in the context of the impending accession of Queen Elizabeth II. She said:

> I hope we shall see more and more women combining marriage AND a career. But the happy management of home and career can and IS being achieved ...

> But the name of Miss ROSE HEILBRON Q.C. whose moving advocacy in recent trials has been so widely praised, is known throughout the land.

> Unless Britain, in the new age to come, can produce more Rose Heilbrons—not only in the field of law, of course, we shall have betrayed the tremendous work of those who fought for equal rights against such misguided opposition.

> The term 'career woman' has unfortunately come to imply in many minds a 'hard' woman, devoid of all feminine characteristics.

> But Rose Heilbron and many more have shown only too well that capability and charm can go together.

But perhaps one of the most flattering reports of this time was an article about her in the *Liverpool Echo* in March 1952 headed 'The Law'. 'Liverpool is Particularly Proud of Miss Rose Heilbron Q.C.', the article began:

> She has gone from success to success ... Hard work plus talent had taken Miss Heilbron to the top of her profession ... She looks most elegant in court in a barrister's gown and wig, and has a charming dress sense for other occasions. She owns to being a keen feminist, but can also see the man's point of view ... Success has not spoiled Rose Heilbron Q.C. She is charming, unaffected, modest and likes nothing better in her spare time than doing her own shopping ... and taking her small daughter to buy the new clothes which little girls love and so quickly grow out of.

Such fulsome praise of a kind that is rarely seen in today's less deferential age continued in future years.

Rose had also acquired a sort of fan club. She received an offer of marriage from a man in West Africa and a request from a young gentleman of 19 for a photograph of her in a bathing suit. She had one particular anonymous fan, who referred to Rose as his 'Pin-Up', and wrote regularly. In one of his letters, following the Bloom case, he wrote that she should not go round persuading juries that men are entitled to strangle their lady friends!

11

A Series of High-Profile Cases

WHILE THE PROBLEMS with the press were being resolved, Rose continued with her practice. She barely had time to catch her breath on returning from Durham when, the following week, she appeared in another famous and notorious case, this time back home at Liverpool Assizes. The previous August, coincidentally on Rose's 37th birthday, Sunday 19 August 1951, a 52-year-old widow, Beatrice Alice Rimmer, had been left fatally injured in her home at 7 Cranborne Road, Liverpool where she lived alone. She had returned home from visiting her son and his family. She had probably just walked in the front door as she was still wearing her coat, and her keys and umbrella were found on or near her body. She had been subjected to numerous beatings, including 15 blows to the head from both a sharp and a blunt instrument and had been left to endure a slow and horrific death. There was a further coincidence. Cranbourne Road was the next road down from Webster Road, the scene of the Cameo murder two years earlier, the Cameo Cinema being about two minutes' walk from where Mrs Rimmer had lived. There were to be further coincidences of potentially much more significance.

Two Manchester lads, Edward Francis Devlin and Alfred Burns, both with previous convictions for larceny and similar offences and aged 22 and 21 respectively, were charged with her murder. It was accepted that either both were involved in the murder or neither of them was. They denied all knowledge of the murder, stating that they had been in Manchester on the night of the murder. At the time of the murder Devlin was actually on bail for an offence for which he was subsequently acquitted and so was on the run and Burns was a Borstal escapee. Rose, leading Jack Tarsh, appeared for Devlin. Sir Noel Goldie QC led Frank Nance for Burns. Basil Nield QC (later a High Court Judge) led A Baucher for the prosecution.

Rose's reputation had spread to the criminal fraternity. When arrested Burns wrote to a friend 'I expect we will be getting Rose Hildebrande [Rose Heilbron] defending one, or both, of us. She is an exceptional woman you know'. A little background to the murder is now needed.

The Prosecution Case

The prosecution story, in summary, starts on 27 July 1951 at Bill's café in Liverpool. There Devlin was alleged to have met a stranger, one, George McCloughlin, who told Devlin that he was going to 'screw', ie break and enter, his aunt's house at Cranbourne Road, to which Devlin is alleged to have responded that he had a 'job', ie a criminal breaking and entering there too. Later that day they allegedly went to 'case' No 7 Cranbourne Road, Devlin's 'job'. The plan, according to the prosecution, was to carry out the 'job' at a weekend, but not until after 17 August.

A few days later, on 2 August, according to the prosecution case, Devlin and June Bury, a girl with whom he had been associating, went to another public house, the Dive, where they met Burns. They then began a trawl of the local hostelries which lasted all night, at the second of which they once again met McCloughlin. In the presence of Bury the three men are alleged to have discussed the 'job'. Devlin was keen on her keeping 'nix', ie acting as lookout. There were alleged to have been subsequent meetings between Devlin, Bury and Burns and another girl of 17 called Marie Milne, where the crime was planned, including discussions as to which of the girls should act as lookout.

During August the two men went to stay in Manchester only returning to Liverpool for one day on 8 August. The key issue was whether they returned to Liverpool after 8 August as they had allegedly said to the two girls they would. From the moment they were arrested, Devlin and Burns vehemently and independently denied being in Liverpool in the 10 days after 8–9 August. Two witnesses gave evidence of sightings of the men in Liverpool a few days before the murder.

The evidence of 17-year-old Milne was crucial. According to her version of events, she had met Devlin and Burns in Liverpool on Friday 17 August as allegedly had been previously planned. They had discussed the job including details of the house, Devlin and Burns explaining to her that she had to keep the old lady talking at the front door while they got in through the back. Devlin is also alleged to have threatened her with a knife. She said she had also seen them the following day.

On 19 August, the day of the job arrived, so the story continues, Devlin and Burns picked Milne up at a pre-arranged place and time and took her to the house for a second reconnoitering of the place. A taxi driver, who knew Milne, said he had driven her and two strangers at this time to Smithdown Road Hospital. It was alleged that she had met the two men again later when it was dark and that the three of them had set off together for Cranbourne Road. Milne alleged she had been asked to wait at the corner of the road and then go and talk to the lady, but had not done so. Instead she alleged that she had taken the tram back to town where she had once again met up with the two men and they had discussed the 'job' which they told her they had done.

The Trial

The case started before Mr Justice Finnemore and an all-male jury on Tuesday, 12 February 1952, having been adjourned one day because the judge had been indisposed. It must have been a welcome breathing space for Rose having had only a few days since the Bloom trial to make her final preparations for the case, although she may well have had the papers for some time. The case lasted 10 days. Twenty prosecution witnesses were called and 21 defence witnesses including Devlin and Burns. There were large queues of people trying to get in to hear the case, allegedly even longer than for the Cameo trial.

Rose had, as usual, prepared copious cross-examination notes for each witness, some of which had been typed and some of which were in manuscript in her large distinctive handwriting. The documentation she was provided with was heavily underlined in important places and various coloured inks used to highlight different parts and annotate others. The cross-examination involved a careful analysis of the evidence given by the witnesses at the committal proceedings, so as to be able to point to any discrepancies with the witnesses' evidence given at trial, as well as questions relating to the improbabilities in their respective stories and the inconsistencies between the evidence of each of the witnesses. She was provided with copies of the committal evidence and some grisly photographs of the deceased and her home. In addition she had to study the proofs of evidence of the two defendants and the defence witnesses, and additional evidence which would not necessarily have been evidence at the trial.

It is the duty of counsel to put to the prosecution witnesses the defence's case in so far as it affects each witness. Preparation of a detailed and effective cross-examination is a time-consuming process. However well prepared counsel is, only a detailed knowledge of the case and a recollection of what other witnesses say in evidence enables a good cross-examiner to adjust the questions to the answers previously given and to make the best points. The questioning thus has to be adjusted as the trial progresses and daily and lengthy work outside court hours is essential. As with all cases, a shorthand note was taken by a court reporter and a transcript available, but, unlike in the Dockers' case, it would not have been available during the trial. Both counsel and the judge would therefore have had to rely on their own respective manuscript notes of the evidence. In addition Rose had to prepare an opening speech and a final speech, analysing in great detail the conflicting evidence on every point—and in this case it was a huge task. Rose was acting on legal aid and was paid 15 guineas for the 10 day case to cover her court appearances and all the preparation before and during the trial. Her counterpart for the prosecution would have been paid a much larger fee, one of the advantages of acting for the prosecution.

The main players relied upon by the prosecution were largely discredited under cross-examination by Rose for Devlin and Sir Noel Goldie QC for Burns. McCloughlin, the first main witness, a Liverpool man, whom Devlin and Burns denied knowing, had a long history of larceny and housebreaking and admitted to 40 previous offences and 'leading a persistent life of crime'. He was arrested on 17 August, conveniently enabling him to say in his statement, given to the police when in custody, that the robbery was to take place the weekend after 17 August. His evidence was not only inherently inconsistent, but also inconsistent with his earlier evidence at the committal proceedings. For example, he was reduced to admitting that when he had suggested to Devlin that he was going to burgle his aunt's house, what he meant was that he was going to iron his uniform, the real burglary having taken place before he met Devlin. He was forced to admit that he had a poor memory, something which should have been apparent from his evidence.

The testimony of Bury and Milne was equally discredited and inconsistencies between their evidence shown. The two witnesses to the sightings of Burns and Devlin were also unimpressive witnesses, both failing to pick out one of the men at identity parades. The taxi driver gave evidence, as did the arresting officers who testified as to what was said by the accused, which was challenged. There was also forensic evidence as to the blood group of blood stains found on a fawn gabardine suit said to belong to Devlin and a brown coat belonging to Burns, but under cross-examination the forensic scientist accepted that these stains did not match the blood found at the scene of the crime.

There were many similarities to the Cameo murder. The case was based on circumstantial evidence; there were no witnesses to the crime; no fingerprints were found at the scene of the crime; and no direct evidence was given as to whether the murder had been carried out by one person alone or two acting in concert. There was a confession from a prisoner, McCloughlin, whom the defendants denied knowing. The three main prosecution witnesses who either overheard plans for the 'job' or, in the case of Milne, agreed to participate in it, were probably or actually accomplices whose evidence needed to be corroborated by independent evidence. The accused denied that they were anywhere near the scene of the crime and produced alibi evidence. Chief Superintendant Bert Balmer, whom the Court of Appeal severely criticised in the 2003 Cameo murder appeal, but who was at the time a highly respected police officer in the public's eyes, was in charge of the investigation and participated in the taking of some of the statements.

The Defence Case

After four days of prosecution evidence, Rose then opened the case for her client, Devlin. She pointed to the many inconsistencies and improbabilities in the prosecution evidence and outlined the evidence for the defence, emphasising that although her client had a criminal record 'because a man is a thief does not mean to say that he is a murderer'. It is a principle of legal practice that if in pursuance of one's client's defence, counsel attacks a prosecution witness's bad character by reference in particular to his or her criminal past, as was the case here, then the criminal record of the defendant is also open to scrutiny in evidence. As most witnesses in the trial had a criminal record of some sort, this was fairly inevitable. Her client, Devlin was then called.

Devlin's story was rather different. While he admitted knowing Burns and Milne, the dates, venues and discussions during their meetings were largely at odds with the prosecution case. In particular he denied their allegations about the alleged planning or commission of the job or their evidence as to what happened after 8–9 August. He admitted stealing a bale of linen in Manchester earlier in the month with Burns where Bury was the look-out. He stated that the last time he had seen Bury was in Manchester on 11 August and explained the reference to putting the date as 17 August in his statement thus:

> Actually, I could not remember the exact date when I made the statement and Mr Balmer, who asked me questions when arrested, *suggested that date to me* ... but since I have been able to think back and I know it was 11th when I last saw her. (emphasis added)

He gave a detailed account of his movements and explained that on Sunday evening 19 August he and Burns together with another man, Alan Campbell, were in fact breaking into a warehouse, Sun Blinds, in Manchester and so could not have committed the murder. He gave an explanation as to the blood stains on his suit. He denied knowing McCloughlin and could not explain why McCloughlin, a stranger, had known he had been in prison. He denied ever using the phrase 'keep douse' and had other words for look-out. A string of witnesses were called to corroborate different parts of the defence evidence, some more satisfactory than others. Many had criminal records although usually for only one offence.

One of the most critical issues was the defendants' alibi for the time of the murder on 19 August. The director of Sun Blinds testified that the burglary had taken place between 12.30 pm on Saturday, 18 August, and 7.30 am on Monday morning, 20 August, when the warehouse was re-opened after the weekend. When the original charge had been put to Campbell it was alleged that the break-in had occurred between 18–20 August. Campbell pleaded guilty to the charge. It was his first offence. However, the indictment for the breaking and entering charge changed the dates, limiting the offence to 18 August and so removed the defendants' alibi for 19 August. The date of the indictment is not known, but the court case was after the arrest of Burns and Devlin for the murder. Campbell's evidence was that he could not remember the date, but he confirmed that it was a Sunday night in August (19 August was a Sunday) and had signed a statement to that effect when initially arrested for the warehouse break-in. He explained that when he had pleaded guilty he did not realise what day of the week it was. His evidence was that the police tried to help him with the date. Despite an application by Rose, the Judge refused the defence permission to see the original statement made by Campbell to the police about the date of the warehouse theft. There was no evidence before the court that the warehouse was broken into on the Saturday.

Rose's final speech went through the evidence in great detail. She said that McCloughlin was a liar. She queried why the men would want do a job out of the blue in Liverpool which 'by a strange coincidence, happens to be the same road as that of the house in which McCloughlin's aunt lives'. She drew attention to the fact that they were doing a large warehouse in Manchester where the rewards were substantial and would not have needed the money. She questioned whether Devlin's police statement was made without prompting by the police as some of what appeared to be answers did not flow from the obvious follow-on questions. The questions had been put by Chief Superintendent Balmer, who has since been severely criticised in the Cameo murder case for concealing evidence.

There is a tradition that if the defence does not call any witnesses, his counsel has the last word. In this case, Rose called all the witnesses on behalf of her client, Devlin. Sir Noel Goldie only called his client. This meant that her final speech was first. Basil Nield QC then gave his closing speech for the prosecution which was followed by Sir Noel Goldie's closing speech. One suspects that there were some tactics involved and that as the two were accused of a joint enterprise, there were certain advantages in one defending counsel having the last word before the jury and some agreement was probably reached between the two legal teams.

The Verdict

On the tenth day of the trial, the Judge concluded his summing up and the jury retired. Their deliberations were swift. After only 75 minutes the jury returned with guilty verdicts. Both men, though stunned, made short statements from the dock. Both said they had told the truth, but Burns added:

> As far as the evidence is concerned I think it has been quite a fair trial, but as far as the Judge is concerned, I think he gave a very prejudiced view of the case. I cannot understand how they managed to bring in a verdict of guilty considering the evidence.

After such a long trial the short period of deliberation undertaken by the jury tends to indicate that the all-male jury must have formed a clear view of the evidence and formed impressions of the defendants and other witnesses. The Judge sentenced them to death.

It was reported that as he passed sentence his voice sank to a whisper and his head was cupped in his hands.

After the Verdict

In early March 1952, both men lodged an appeal and their execution was temporarily stayed. The grounds of appeal pointed to errors in the summing up. At the appeal on 31 March 1952, before the Lord Chief Justice, Lord Goddard, Rose made an application to adduce new evidence from a 15-year-old girl relating to a statement allegedly made by June Bury that the murderer had been someone else. The statement had come to light a few days previously. The Court of Criminal Appeal refused to admit the evidence, though it indicated the new evidence might be a matter for the Home Secretary, and dismissed the appeal.

Rose immediately saw the then Attorney General, Sir Lionel Heald, who referred the matter to the Home Secretary, Sir David Maxwell Fyfe, who the following day, ordered an inquiry into the statement, only the second time that such an inquiry into new evidence had ever been held. The execution of the two men was further postponed. Denis Gerrard QC (later a High Court Judge) was appointed to chair the Inquiry. The Inquiry began on 4 April 1952 and was held in private, but counsel and solicitors were present. Counsel were able to make suggestions as to lines of questioning, but Denis Gerrard QC asked all the questions of the witnesses. The key witnesses were given immunity from prosecution in relation to their evidence and their evidence was not given under oath. The terms of reference were as follows:

> to inquire into (a) the statement made on 27th March 1952, by Elizabeth Rooke to the effect that June Bury had told her and other persons that the prisoners, Edward Francis Devlin and Alfred Burns, had not committed the murder of Beatrice Alice Rimmer and that it had in fact been committed by another unnamed person who is alleged to be the father of June Bury's child and of another child she is expecting, and (b) the confession made, but subsequently recanted, by Joseph Ernest Howarth, to the effect that he had committed the murder of Beatrice Alice Rimmer; to consider any further relevant information laid before him which may have come to light since the conviction of the prisoners at the Liverpool Assizes on 27th February 1952; and to report whether, in his opinion, the result of his investigation of these matters affords any reasonable grounds for thinking that there has been or may have been any miscarriage of justice.

Following a thorough review of all the new evidence from 11 witnesses, much of which was discredited, but some of which was favourable to the accused and other parts of which were unfavourable, Denis Gerrard reported to the Home Secretary on 21 April 1952. His report was then presented to Parliament and was published as a Command Paper the following day. Rose's copy was sent by the Home Office by the 2.30pm train from Euston Station, London and collected at Lime Street Station, Liverpool at 6.43pm. Denis Gerrard had concluded that there had been no miscarriage of justice. 'Devlin and Burns: Death' was the succinct headline in the *Liverpool Echo* that evening. Rose had been in court all day on another matter, but had been telephoned the result of the inquiry. The men were due to be hanged in 48 hours. 'Woman Q.C. in Race to Save Two' read the headline in the *Daily Express*. The Home Secretary had indicated that any new request for a reprieve had to be received by 9am the following morning and the lawyers worked until late drafting the request in order to catch the midnight train to London. There were no faxes or emails in those days. It was to be of no avail. Devlin and Burns were hanged on 25 April 1952.

Both Devlin and Burns wrote letters from prison to family and friends protesting their innocence. Burns also had a rather morbid sense of humour. In a letter to a friend he wrote:

> Ted [Devlin] wanted to know what I thought he would do when this is over with. I said you'll be hanging around as usual. It's pretty cold round here and I told him it was simply topping weather. He doesn't like my sense of humour.

After the inquiry had ended Devlin again wrote to his friend maintaining that he had been framed. 'It makes one wonder how many innocent men have gone to the gallows in this present-day England of ours'.

The case of Devlin and Burns has always been regarded as one of a miscarriage of justice and there remain many unanswered questions. It still holds a fascination and two books have very recently been written about the case.[1] Is it likely that Bury and Milne, as was probably the case of Dickson and Northam in the Cameo trial, were embellishing the facts and transferring their knowledge of the crime to the wrong men? To what extent were the witnesses who

---

[1] M O'Connell, *Where Lies the Truth?* (Country Books, 2012); G Skelly, *Murderers or Martyrs* (Waterside Press, forthcoming).

testified against them involved in the murder or seeking to frame Devlin and Burns? Why would Devlin and Burns suddenly do a job in Liverpool when their patch was Manchester? What was the explanation for the police confining Campbell's indictment to the Saturday rather than leaving the time between the Saturday and Monday morning?

Bert Balmer, in an article in the *Liverpool Echo* dated 5 December 1967 on his retirement, wrote that McCloughlin had put the original plot for the murder not at 27 July, but 'eight or nine days before the murder' possibly at a time when both Devlin and Burns said they were in Manchester? How did McCloughlin know about the crime? He gave his statement from prison which conveniently scheduled the murder for two weeks in advance and for the two days after he was arrested. He clearly had some inside knowledge, as he referred to aspects of the deceased's house about which he would otherwise not have known and he identified the defendants in an identity parade. Where did he get that information from? Was he telling the truth or did Rose alight upon another theory in her final speech when she alleged that there had been prompting by the police? We may never know.

There was to be one positive outcome to the case. It started a debate in the House of Lords as to whether the Court of Criminal Appeal should be entitled to receive new evidence rather than the cumbersome procedure of an inquiry. Lord Goddard criticised as 'an extremely dangerous proceeding' the need for witnesses at such inquiries as the Devlin and Burns inquiry to be given immunity from prosecution. He urged that powers be given to the Court of Criminal Appeal to order a new trial and received support from both sides of the House. The law was reformed to allow new trials in such circumstances by the Criminal Appeal Act 1964 as amended by the Criminal Justice Act 1988.

THE FAMOUS PROFESSOR

The Burns and Devlin trial was not, of course, Rose's only case in the spring of 1952, nor did it halt her travelling to other Circuits. On 6 March 1952, she appeared for the first time in Birmingham, at Birmingham Quarter Sessions before the Recorder and a jury, defending Professor Lancelot Thomas Hogben, who was at the time Professor of Medical Statistics at Birmingham University and a famous mathematician, biologist and authority on human genetics.

He was charged with driving his car when under the influence of drink following a collision. The circumstances of the accident were straightforward: his car had been stationary at a junction, but instead of going forwards when free to cross, he went in reverse and his car hit another stationary car about four yards behind him.

Professor Hogben was a brilliant academic and during his career held various professorial chairs. He was a prolific writer on a variety of subjects and the author of *Mathematics for the Million* (a best seller) and *Science for the Citizen*. The police are used to all sorts of strange requests, but Professor Hogben's must have been one of the most bizarre. When at the police station he asked for a piece of paper to set out an algebraic problem. Not perhaps the normal reaction to finding oneself charged with an offence, but Professor Hogben explained that this was a well-known habit of his to indulge in some intellectual work to keep his mind active when in a difficult situation. As for the algebra—he was apparently developing 'an original line of thought' on the abstruse 'Chi-square test', a formula for proving the truth of presumed premises. Recital of this research alone might have raised eyebrows as to his sobriety at the local police station. The hieroglyphics, incomprehensible to most people, were produced as an exhibit in court.

The issue was whether he was actually drunk or merely appeared to be drunk as his peculiar mannerisms, untidiness and general demeanour were those of a man influenced by drink. This case was, of course, before the introduction of the breathalyser in England. Thus, the question of whether or not someone was under the influence of drink while driving was a factual issue to be determined on the evidence and not merely a question of whether or not someone had in excess of a certain amount of alcohol in his or her blood. The prosecution called evidence as to his demeanour at the time of the accident, including testimony from the police surgeon, whom Rose cross-examined.

Professor Hogben seems to have had a catalogue of woes. He explained to the court that his car's hand gear mechanism had an irritating habit of going into reverse rather than second gear; that he had thyroid trouble on the day of the accident which affected his speech; that he had something wrong with his feet which necessitated wearing specially made shoes which made normal walking difficult on slippery surfaces; and that he had had several teeth extracted a fortnight before the accident and had had dentures fitted which made his speech indistinct, commenting 'I wasn't used to my new crockery'.

His colleague, Professor Philip Cyril Cloake, Professor of Neurology at Birmingham University, gave evidence on his behalf and said: 'When I first heard of this case I at once offered to help Professor Hogben, for there is no other man I know more likely to be mistaken for a drunken man when he is quite sober'. Even the Recorder, Paul Sandlands QC, was driven to ask him whether he had been drinking before he gave evidence because of the manner of his giving evidence.

The Recorder directed the jury to bring in a verdict of not guilty. Today he might not have been so lucky given the strict limits on the consumption of alcohol when driving, peculiar mannerisms or not. He had apparently drunk two and a half double whiskies 'slowly'! He clearly appreciated what Rose had done for him, as after his acquittal he wrote her a beautiful letter of thanks.

A MIXED DIET OF CASES

The cases which hit the headlines, which tended often to be the murder trials because of the looming gallows, continued to represent only a small part of Rose's practice at this time. She was doing a wide range of work, most of which went unnoticed in the press, while other cases were reported briefly. Her practice now took her more regularly around the country and to London.

March, for example, saw Rose in the Court of Appeal in London, but this time in a divorce case where she appeared for a husband against whom his wife had alleged cruelty as a ground for divorce and he had cross-petitioned on the same grounds. The original judge had concluded it was 'six of one and half a dozen of the other'. The Court of Appeal dismissed the appeal and the pair were left to live in tempestuous disharmony.

On 4 April, Rose successfully represented an architect, Sidney Morris, on various false pretences charges relating to frauds against the War Damage Commission arising out of certificates which overcharged for building works.

A few days later she represented Mrs Rachel Skuse at Liverpool Assizes, also charged with obtaining money by false pretences, though not successfully. This time the charge related to something more luxurious, namely a 'new look' Persian lamb fur coat with leather pockets. She was alleged to have received a cheque for £700 from her insurance company following a burglary at her flat. The issue was whether or not the fur coat, which represented the bulk of the insurance payout, had been stolen at the time of the burglary. Unfortunately for Mrs Skuse a fur coat was later redeemed from the pawnbrokers by her husband. She claimed this coat was her 'shopping' coat, but the jury did not accept her tale. She was found guilty and that night took an overdose and collapsed before sentencing, but survived. There was an unusual postscript. After the verdict a worried prosecution witness sent a note to the judge saying that he had been worrying about a matter he did not disclose. He was re-called and stated that he had not checked for himself whether the pockets were leather!

Also in April, at Manchester Assizes, leading her good friend, Eileen MacDonald, Rose represented Alfred Williams, a bus driver originally charged with manslaughter, but whose charge was later reduced to death by dangerous driving. The charge arose out of a cross-roads collision between the bus and a van. It had been a horrific accident in which five children waiting at a school bus stop had been 'mown down' and killed. Although Williams was on the major road, it was alleged that he had ignored the crossroads warning sign. However, the jury obviously accepted that the van had shot out of the minor road hitting the bus violently and wrenching the steering wheel out of Williams' hand causing the bus to mount the pavement. Following his acquittal the bus driver declared that he wanted to go back to being a bus driver.

On 19 May, Rose was at the Assize Court at Ruthin defending Harry Huxley, charged with the murder of Mrs Ada Royce, with whom he was alleged to have had an adulterous relationship during a period when her marriage had been unhappy. Edmund Davies QC (later Lord Edmund Davies) prosecuted. Huxley had killed her with a shot gun, possibly because she had lost interest in him and then turned the gun on himself, but the shot hit the metal buckle on his braces saving him. He seemed to think the youngest child was his and had written to his mother asking her to look after the child. His defence was that he had only tried to frighten Ada Royce and did not know that the gun was defective. Rose in her final speech dramatically held the gun and said to the jury: 'Witnesses can imagine, but this gun cannot lie ... A shake of the gun sets it off. What a gun! The trigger need not be pressed to set it off. What a defect in a weapon!'

The jury were sufficiently concerned to ask the Judge whether it was murder if a gun was cocked and loaded and placed against the woman's body without the trigger being pulled and were directed accordingly in the law. Huxley was found guilty and sentenced to death, but the jury made a recommendation for mercy. A subsequent application against conviction, made by Rose on his behalf to the Court of Criminal Appeal, failed. He was executed on 8 July 1952.

On 13 June, she defended a Dr Mansour at Liverpool Assizes. Dick Trotter, Rose's erstwhile pupil-master, prosecuted. Dr Mansour had been charged alongside a chemist, Eric Wild, on a Bill of Indictment of conspiracy to defraud the Ministry of Health between certain dates by means of false prescriptions, and of 11 offences of causing the Ministry to deliver cheques for a total of £1,876.4s. The Bill of Indictment was an unusual legal procedure and brought about because the magistrates had found no case to answer. The National Health Service had been introduced only four years earlier. Dr Mansour's defence was that he wrote out prescriptions so that he could have available stock at his surgery. He argued that this was justified on the grounds that all patients on his list were entitled to free medical service even if the prescription was procured for the wrong patient, explaining that he never procured the prescriptions for himself. Many appreciative patients were called in support. Rose contended on his behalf that he may have been guilty of a breach of the regulations, but not of fraud, saying in her final speech: 'This doctor was trying to be a doctor and not merely a clerk handing out prescriptions'. He and the chemist were both acquitted.

Some of Rose's civil work also caught attention. In May she appeared, leading Eileen McDonald, before the Court of Appeal in a case reported in the Law Reports, for a deckhand who claimed negligence against his employers. His leg had had to be amputated when caught in a rope, but the appeal failed and the court held it was an accident.[2] Although Rose normally acted for plaintiffs, this was not always the case. In June, for example, she acted for the Liverpool Corporation defending a claim made by a cabinet maker, Samuel Taylor, who, as a result of a tram overturning, injured his right arm and fingers preventing him working as a cabinet maker. He was awarded £4,000.

At the end of July Rose appeared in London before Lord Goddard representing a 17-year-old girl, Georgina Hobbs, who had wanted to be a nurse. She had sued her employers for damages following a serious accident when she had bent down to pick up envelopes in a factory and her hair had been caught in an unguarded machine. They had admitted negligence and the issue was one of the amount

---

[2] *Martin v Manchester Ship Canal Company* [1952] 1 Lloyds Rep 539.

of damages. The young girl had suffered dreadful injuries, had endured nine operations and had to wear a wig. Lord Goddard commented that the photograph showing the change in the girl's appearance gave one a shock. He awarded her £7,000 for the disfigurement.

Later in the year Rose appeared for a young mother, Ann Hickey, burned by a hot water bottle at Walton Hospital, half an hour after her baby was born. There were many more such cases of claims for damages for injuries sustained at work or on the roads. Health and Safety regulations were much less sophisticated in those days.

Abortion has always been a controversial subject. In 1967 it was legalised in England within certain parameters, but this was not the case in the 1950s. On 20 November 1952 Rose, leading Christmas Humphreys (senior prosecuting counsel for the Crown), defended Dr William Arthur Chanmungan Nason. He was charged with using instruments to procure an abortion. The case took place at the Old Bailey before the Recorder of London, Sir Gerald Dobson. In a lighter moment the defendant explained that he had changed his name to Nason from Chanmungan because people had mispronounced his name as 'chewing gum'. His defence was that he only treated women in a routine way for the consequences of their own personal interferences with themselves when otherwise they might have died from sepsis. He was found guilty and was sentenced to three years' imprisonment.

Rose had also started doing some more work for the prosecution and, for instance in February 1952 she prosecuted a young mother charged with murdering her 11-month-old child. It was alleged that she had wanted to get rid of the evidence of her adulterous relationship with another man before her husband came out of prison.

The above cases are only a snapshot of life at the Bar for Rose at this time. All these cases required detailed preparation, often travel and nights away from home and working long hours into the night and at weekends. As previously explained, while much preparation can be done in advance of the trial, there nonetheless remains considerable work during the trial. The court hours, usually 10.30am to 4.15pm with an hour for lunch are the culmination of this preparation and in terms of time may represent only a small part of the work for a case. Cross-examination has to be honed each night to take account of developments in the case and the final speech, particularly to a jury, has to be given without any break in the proceedings, yet it needs to distil all the evidence in a persuasive way for one's client. There is often no option but to work until

3 or 4 in the morning and Rose would sustain herself with coffee and soup.

By now Rose had joined two women's clubs where she stayed when in London and where the charges were more modest than hotels. She either stayed at the Forum Club at 42 Belgrave Square, with a membership in excess of 1,000 and whose President was Princess Marie Louise, grand-daughter of Queen Victoria, or at the Cowdray Club at 20 Cavendish Square. Rose was made a Vice-President of the Cowdray Club along with Valerie Hobson, the actress, and Dame Ninette de Valois, founder of the Royal Ballet and others. These women's clubs had some idiosyncrasies in terms of guests and rules. One frequent titled guest at the Forum Club would arrive carrying her stuffed dog under her arm. The doors would close early—as befitted ladies—and although husbands were allowed—at least at the Forum—it was the not the most comfortable of experiences. Neither club exists today.

THE CASE OF MARY STANDISH

Two cases before the year was out need special mention. On 5 November Mrs Mary Standish was arraigned before Mr Justice Oliver and a jury, charged with murdering her husband with a knife. She was 35 years old. She was defended by Rose. Once again queues formed outside St George's Hall. She lived in a one bedroom flat with her husband, the 17-year-old daughter of her first marriage who was pregnant (her first husband had died naturally) and a child of three from her second marriage. She explained that she had had a row with her second husband, who had been drinking and had earlier in the evening hit her. He had also attempted to hit her elder daughter and she had picked up a bread knife to frighten him. He had then rushed for her, there was a struggle and the knife had penetrated his heart. There had been a previous row with the elder daughter, when she had been punched in the face by the husband when trying to separate the husband and her mother.

In her final speech Rose said that it had been proved that Mrs Standish was very fond of her husband, yet she was the woman charged with his murder. She continued:

> Apart from raising the knife there is no evidence of using it ... Mrs Standish was not frightened for herself. She could take a blow on the chin—and she did—but she was not going to let him attack her daughter, a young girl five months pregnant. She did what anyone would

do in defence of her daughter. She turned a foot or two away, snatched up a knife—it might have been anything—and used it in a way that a teacher uses a ruler, to admonish.

The jury only deliberated for 17 minutes. She was acquitted of murder and manslaughter. She wrote to Rose to thank her 'with all my heart for what you have done for me as I know only you could have done for me, although I know myself I hadn't harmed my husband'.

She subsequently told a reporter from the *Sunday Express* that Rose

> wasn't at all what I expected, a stern poker-faced sort of woman. When I first saw Miss Heilbron I whispered to the policeman 'That's not her is it?'. She was so friendly and quiet, the kind of woman whom when she asks you a difficult question you don't think twice about giving an honest answer to ... And I'll never forget it—she remembered to smile at me across the court. I don't expect to meet anyone like her again.

MURDER IN A MANSION

The second case related to an incident in high society, at Knowsley Hall, the home of Lord and Lady Derby. Lady Derby had been watching television after dinner in the smoke room when she was attacked and wounded in the neck by Harold Winstanley, a 19-year-old trainee footman in her employ who had run amok with a gun. She was lucky to escape with her life, because immediately thereafter he murdered her butler, Walter Stallard, and under-butler, Douglas Stuart. He also shot Lady Derby's valet in the hand. 'Everyone in the country was shocked beyond words at the tragic death of two such fine men and the fearful experience of Lady Derby on the night of October 9th' said Rose to the jury.

Rose's engagement to represent Winstanley once again brought a flurry of publicity highlighting the fact that a woman QC was defending him. 'Portia Q.C. is to Defend Harold Winstanley' (*The Star*); 'Woman Q.C. for Footman' (*Evening Chronicle*); 'Woman QC will Defend Footman' (*Daily Mail*); 'Woman Q.C. for Defence' (*The Daily Telegraph*) and many more. The epithet 'woman' reflected the fact that she was unique at the time and no doubt this intrigued people.

The case, described as the 'Murder in a Mansion' was heard at Manchester Assizes. Rose was instructed by E Rex Makin. The only issue was as to Winstanley's mental condition. Lady Derby gave evidence as to the incident. The defence called Dr Francis Herbert Brisby, senior medical officer at Walton Gaol, as its only witness to testify as to the defendant's state of mind. Winstanley's mother had been sent to a mental institution and he had been brought up in an orphanage. Rose explained to the jury: 'This normally pleasant young man had become a man with staring eyes [after the shooting]. He had become completely changed. The manner of the shooting indicates that this man went berserk with the gun'. The jury found him guilty of the murder of Stallard, but insane. He was sent to Broadmoor. The other murder was left on the books. Lord Derby ordered that the doors of the smoke room where Lady Derby was injured be locked indefinitely.

Some weeks later Rose and Nat were attending a function in Liverpool in the presence of the Duchess of Gloucester. Rose was chatting to Lord Sefton, who had clearly temporarily forgotten the incident that Lady Derby had recently endured and apparently said to Lady Derby that if one was ever had up for murder Rose was the woman to get to defend you. Lady Derby just smiled.

But for having been instructed in this case Rose would probably have defended 16-year-old Christopher Craig in the famous Craig and Bentley case at the Old Bailey according to several contemporaneous newspaper reports. She was not briefed in the end partly because the trial clashed with her defence of Harold Winstanley. The two were alleged to have murdered a policeman during a bungled break-in. Bentley, who had learning difficulties, was 19. He was alleged by police witnesses to have shouted 'let him have it, Chris'. Both were found guilty and Bentley was hanged. Craig who fired the shot was too young to be hanged and served 10 years in prison. It became a cause célèbre and Bentley's conviction was quashed 45 years later in 1998. But even without appearing in this case, 1952 had been a very significant year professionally for Rose.

12

Rose Cements Her Reputation

PREJUDICE AND THE WORKING WOMAN

'OUR ROSIE', AS she endearingly became known on the Northern Circuit and in Liverpool, or plain 'Rose', as she was known elsewhere by the criminal fraternity at the one extreme to her personal friends at the other, was certainly acquiring a phenomenal reputation. Were it not in black and white, it would not seem believable. By this stage in her career the press coverage was quite extraordinary. The year started well with the *Liverpool Post* exclaiming 'Miss Heilbron, it is being said, is well on her way to establishing for herself a place in legal history as the female Marshall Hall'. However, this laudatory exposure belied the prejudice that still existed at the Bar for women, even for Rose, as became evident in the disparity between her public profile and the restrictions on her progress up the professional ladder.

The coronation of a female monarch, Elizabeth II, on 2 June 1953 led the interest in women in the nation. 'Career Girls Storm the Man's World—Women from Victoria to Elizabeth' proclaimed the *Illustrated News* in January 1953, showing a picture of Rose. The House of Lords considered a Bill to make women life peers. Rose was one of 10 candidates named by the *New Chronicle* asking 'Can you think of a better "top ten"?'

Over the next couple of years Rose became increasingly involved with the Soroptimists. In February 1953, for instance, she responded to Sir David Maxwell Fyfe, the Home Secretary, at the annual banquet at the Adelphi of the Soroptimists Club in Liverpool. In the spring of that year she gave an hour-long conference address at the eleventh annual conference of the North West Divisional Unions of the Federation of Soroptimists Clubs of Great Britain on 'Women and the Law':

> You could have heard a pin drop, so engrossed were the ladies in her every word, spoken so clearly and so cleverly. Her talk was followed by a discussion, and many intricate questions were put to her. She answered

them all...What a charming woman Miss Heilbron is, and well-tailored too! She was wearing a small black felt boater hat graced with a quill and a red rose. A rich silver fox fur cape was worn over a thin black coat, which topped a grey and black pin-head suiting. Elegantly cut, it favoured the double-breasted highwayman's fastening and had large military pockets.

On 29 April 1954, Rose was elected at their annual meeting as the new President of the Liverpool Club of the Soroptimists, then the largest Soroptimist Club in the world. She had been a member since 1946. 'Success has not spoiled Miss Rose Heilbron and it is perhaps her charm, modesty and genuine friendliness which has endeared her to the heart of her club members' wrote Dorothy Rimmer in the *Liverpool Evening Express*. There was discussion of a plan for an old people's home and Rose urged an early start on the scheme. Rose embarked on her role with her usual dedication and enthusiasm attending regular meetings and functions. At one of the weekly luncheons she asked members to stand up and state their classification, describing herself as a bit of a lawyer.

At times Rose would hold committee meetings at her home. On one such occasion when Hilary was about five Rose watched aghast as Hilary interrupted the proceedings without warning, going over to the radiogram and to Rose's horror, in front of her guests, she put her finger along one of the grills, stuck her finger in the air and proclaimed 'filthy'. To Rose, who was very house-proud, this must have been an acute embarrassment. Whether there was dust on the grill or whether, as a naughty youngster, Hilary was simply copying what she had seen her mother do when checking on the thoroughness of the dusting cannot be recalled!

Rose once commented on the 'yards and yards' of hands she had shaken as President and the types of grips. She added, tongue in cheek, that when she had time she might write a book on handshakes—the hard hand, the soft hand, the brave and frightened hands and the shy person and the chatty one—not leaving out the most amusing—when she had to receive her husband, Nat.

Simultaneously Rose continued to speak to other audiences on women's issues, pressing home her various themes and ideas for reform. The financial dependence of women was one such theme and in 1954 she tackled it from two angles. On Saturday January 1954, she addressed the annual conference of the Standing Conferences of the Women's Organisations and Women's Group on Public Welfare in London. Her female audience was naturally receptive to her criticism of the fact that a married woman still laboured under difficulties which did not attach to the single woman, with savings from her housekeeping belonging to the husband and yet having no claim on his earnings.

In October she was much braver. She addressed an all-male audience at the Liverpool luncheon club on the subject of 'Women'. 'The Woman Who Dared', 'Portia Among the Panthers' proclaimed the *Liverpool Evening Express*. She complained that women should know what their husbands earn, commenting that there was still prejudice: a mental attitude, 'an invisible hindrance of archaic prejudice' and urged that a law should be passed entitling a woman to a fair share of her husband's income. She added:

> I should be the last to decry that a woman's place is in the home. My place is very often in the home. Because I happen to be a lawyer does not mean that I can neglect my place in the home. Some women would not go out to work for all the money in the world. And it is often an endurance test for women to do two jobs.

Other pet subjects surfaced too. In a speech in February she is reported as reiterating her view that clothes are important 'particularly to women who have to wear a sort of uniform for their job'. She endeared herself to those women who stayed at home to look after their children by often saying that 'nevertheless, I am a home-lover and the last to ... attempt to diminish the importance of the work a woman does who stays at home to look after her husband and family'.

But Rose's own success highlighted the difficulties for other women at the Bar, encapsulated in this press comment: 'Barrier at the Bar: Miss Heilbron's star, though glittering, remains a lonely feminine light in the legal firmament'. As the *London Evening News* reported in July 1954 there were more women entering for Bar examinations than ever before, a trend which had been most noticeable over the previous five or six years. The article also noted that, senior male colleagues considered that there could not have been more than half a dozen among hundreds of women barristers who earned enough through briefs to pay the rent of their chambers, despite 35 years since the Sex Disqualification (Removal) Act 1919. The early years remained particularly difficult for women, having to overcome not only the prejudice of solicitors, but also clients who were reluctant to brief women.

Even fellow women could be condescending about the chances for a woman barrister. One female journalist wrote in the *Birmingham Post*:

> [I]t is true that many of the qualifications essential to success at the Bar are not always those found in a woman. A barrister must, for instance,

have stamina, must be able to concentrate intensely over short periods, must not be put off easily and must be prepared, if necessary, to be ruthless and perhaps even a little cruel.

While not all of these traits are necessary to be a successful barrister, there is no doubt that Rose had both stamina and determination and, as her family learnt, an ability to shut out the rest of the world when concentrating.

A RAFT OF SPEAKING ENGAGEMENTS

Rose also continued with a number of speaking engagements around the country on a variety of other subjects. She was in constant demand as a speaker and had to limit the engagements she undertook. So numerous were the requests that she had a variety of standard letters which she used to reply to invitations when refusing requests to speak, suitably amended depending on the nature of the engagement and source of invitation. This scheme was later developed into 24 different pro forma letters ranging from qualified refusals of invitations, second request invitations, and acceptance of invitations to requests for autographs, requests for interviews, and many others. She was also beginning to receive many more letters from members of the public. Some had genuine grievances and asked for her advice and help not realising that they could not go straight to a barrister, but had to instruct a solicitor first. Others were from cranks or the mentally unstable. The latter were not answered. Carbon copies typed by Rose's personal secretary of the time were kept of all letters sent, as were the letters themselves. Most Saturday mornings were devoted to sorting out this personal correspondence with Rose's secretary.

In February 1953, Rose addressed the dinner of the combined Legal, Medical and Accounting Committees of the JPA (Joint Palestine Appeal). In the autumn of 1953, she spoke at the 39th festival dinner of the Solicitors' Managing Clerks' Association at the Connaught Rooms in London or as one newspaper described the event 'A Glamorous QC Goes to a Party'. Managing Clerks, a species of litigators which no longer exists, were very much the backbone of solicitors firms. They were not qualified solicitors, but did have lesser qualifications. Rose also appeared on a brains trust at the Crane Theatre Liverpool in aid of the Lord Mayor of Liverpool's War Fund alongside Professor Sir Henry Cohen (later Lord Cohen of Birkenhead) and others. Sir Stafford Cripps, Minister of Aircraft Production, was guest of honour. In July 1954, she attended a birthday dinner in honour of Princess Marie Louise. In April 1954, she spoke on child welfare to the Liverpool Child Welfare Association. In September 1954, she was the principal guest in Glasgow launching a scheme to raise £20,000 for a Glasgow tuberculosis clinic in Israel. She was one of the guest speakers at the 1919 Club dinner, where she responded alongside other speakers including the Right Hon Sir Alfred Denning (later Lord Denning and the famous Master of the Rolls) to the toast 'Bench and Bar'.

An engagement in November 1953 illustrates the sometimes frenetic pace of her life. She addressed the Annual Dinner of the Leeds University Union Law Society where she urged the need for student barristers to have a school of practical advocacy. This was another of her forward-looking themes, something which only recently has come to pass a half century later with the introduction of extensive advocacy training for young barristers run by the Inns of Court. She had been at Manchester Assizes all day and had to leave immediately after her speech to catch the train to Birmingham to appear in court the next day. Her talk was clearly appreciated. In the rather deferential language of the times the *Yorkshire Post* described her as: 'A speaker who combines charm and elegance with intelligence'.

QUEEN ELIZABETH II

The coronation of the young Queen Elizabeth II in June 1953 engendered a mood of national celebration after the austere war years and continued rationing. Rose and Nat were invited to the first Royal Garden Party on 16 July 1953, given by the new Queen at Buckingham Palace. The invitation brought great excitement. Rose and Nat posed in the garden of their home for a preview photograph, Rose in a new sage green printed silk suit and matching hat and Nat in morning coat. They travelled to London for the occasion in July, the first of many such garden parties they were to attend over the years. However, an event the following year involving the new Queen was to prove even more exciting.

On 21 October 1954, Rose, in her capacity as President of the Liverpool Soroptimists, accompanied by Nat, was invited to a reception at the Liverpool Town Hall where the Queen and Duke of Edinburgh were to be present as part of their first royal tour of Lancashire. Rose was not one of the dignitaries chosen to be presented to the Monarch. Rose wore a turquoise blue suit with matching hat. The story can best be told in Rose's own words:

> Curiously enough I was exceptionally nervous and excited going though I knew we were to be amongst 400 guests.
>
> At the Town Hall the guests were divided into two rooms. The MPs, Councillors and official guests were in the Ballroom where the Queen, the Duke of Edinburgh, the Mayoral Party and the Judges (Sellars and Lloyd Pearce JJ) had tea.
>
> We were in the Dining Room chatting with Maud, Andrew Semple [the Medical Officer of Health of Liverpool] and Henry [Lord Cohen]. It was most enjoyable.
>
> About 4.45pm the Queen and the Duke entered the Room and we all curtsied. She passed out of sight and we all got ready to go.
>
> Suddenly Brizel, the Lord Mayor's Secretary followed by Alker [the Town Clerk], came rushing in calling 'Miss Heilbron'. I was stunned. Alker said 'Come quickly, the Queen wants to meet you'. My knees felt weak, and handing my programme to a lady near the door I was ushered into another room. The Queen and the Duke were standing with the Lord Mayor on one side and the Judges on the other.
>
> Either Alker or Alderman Griffin introduced me—I'm not sure—and I shook hands and remembered to curtsey to both.

Following a conversation with the Queen and Duke of Edinburgh the note continues:

> I curtsied (very badly) and returned to the Dining Room, where there was great excitement and many congratulations at having been singled out and honoured. That night many people phoned and I felt and still feel two days later a tremendous thrill. The Lady Mayoress was kind enough to phone to tell me what happened.

This was the first time that Rose had been presented to the Queen, although she was to meet her again several times in future years. The event also hit the local newspapers: 'The Queen Asked to Meet Her' ran the headline in the *Liverpool Evening Express*.

THE CAUSE OF ROSE'S SUCCESS

At the other end of the spectrum her fame had reached the Old Bailey where the previous year a defendant, when asked to choose any barrister in court for what was known as a dock brief (for which the barrister was paid £2.3s.6d), announced 'I'll have Miss Rose Heilbron'. Alas for him she was not in court.

Why had Rose caught the public attention from everyone from the Queen at one extreme down to a defendant at the Old Bailey at the other? She was, after all, on one view, not doing a particularly glamorous job, often defending rogues and alleged murderers or trying to eke out some damages for a badly injured client or arguing some abstruse point of law in the higher courts. She was a woman and women were just beginning to emerge from the chrysalis of being second-class citizens on the path to equality. She was young and attractive and glamorous, but that alone would only have given her ephemeral fame. The enduring public obsession with her was grounded in the fact that she excelled at what she did.

In the spring of 1953 Drusilla Beyfus of the *Sunday Express* sought to examine her success from the perspective of contemporaries' impressions of her both as a woman and as an advocate. She wrote:

> The town [Liverpool] wears Rosie like a medal. She will always be bright and new and young to the ordinary people there. 'I wouldn't miss a word of Rosie', they say. The local people will tell you about the day the late Recorder got up in court and put all the men out of sorts by saying to Miss Heilbron: 'I am delighted to see you here; I do hope you will come again'... or the way she looks in evening dress. 'Rosie was the first woman in the town I saw wearing a black ballet length frock,' a woman friend told me... I listened to the fellow silk: 'She got her chance during the war—but her distinction is that she kept the lead when the first-class men came back. Rose has a sense of form in court. She's no mumbler and she puts over a case with lucidity, persuasion and perfect courtesy. But she's a pugilist at heart; you can't knock Rosie off her feet with an unexpected thrust of thought' ...Another stroke on the canvas came from a top solicitor. 'She's good, she knows her stuff and she's a woman... In court she gives you the feeling that she stays awake at night over a client. She defends a person more than a set of facts. I think it shows that she is a woman—and it helps her.

It certainly helped on occasions to have a woman's intuition as was recognised by some of her clients. One client, presumably in a divorce case, assured her 'I would like you to appear for my case. You understand women—you will be able to cross-examine my wife'.

A LITTLE BIT OF GAMBLING

Meanwhile, her catalogue of cases continued to include many fascinating as well as sad stories. Since 1933,[1] the right of a plaintiff to a jury trial for personal injury actions had been at the discretion

---

[1] Administration of Justice (Miscellaneous Provisions) Act 1933.

of the judge. In practice the discretion was infrequently exercised. In 1966 the Court of Appeal ultimately laid down guidelines for the exercise of such discretion where damages are claimed, indicating that the judge should not order trial by jury in such personal injury cases save in exceptional cases.[2] In 1981 jury trial in civil actions was abolished save for a limited number of categories such as libel, malicious prosecution and false imprisonment.[3]

One such instance of a civil jury trial was the case of a four-year-old girl, Marjorie Slater, who had been crippled as a result of losing a foot infected with gangrene when, as a baby, she had been admitted to hospital suffering from gastro enteritis. It was alleged that the hospital had been negligent in their care of her, causing the foot literally to drop off. Rose was instructed to represent the child on legal aid, one of the early cases using the recently introduced legal aid scheme for civil cases. The case lasted eight days with six doctors and specialists giving evidence and attracted considerable nationwide publicity. Unfortunately, Rose did not prevail and the jury, after only one hour of deliberations, rejected the claim. Nonetheless, she made a hit with the little girl who, according to her mother, was always asking about the nice lady who gave her the toys, and impressed the girl's mother who wrote to thank Rose for 'the magnificent way in which she fought the case against all the odds'.

Other personal injury cases over the next couple of years were less newsworthy and not substantially different from those she had been doing as a junior, save that the injuries were more serious. Some involved issues of liability: others were contentious as to damages only. They ranged from a serious head injury for a young pedestrian knocked down by a motor cycle to a lady who was para-lysed when a 35-foot chimney had fallen on her. Two cases involv-ing injuries loading cargo on ships went to the Court of Appeal and were reported in the Law Reports.[4]

However, Rose was also getting a name in a wider range of heavy civil work other than purely personal injury cases. Two such examples were a case relating to the dissolution of a book-making partnership and the application for a licence for a theatre for the public to use a balcony during performances. She also appeared before Lord Goddard and Mr Justice Cassels and Mr Justice Slade,

---

[2] *Ward v James* [1966] 1 QB 273.
[3] Section 69 of the Supreme Court Act.
[4] *Sims v Thos & Jas Harrison Ltd* [1954] 1 Lloyd's Rep 354 and *Marcroft v Scruttons Ltd* [1954] 1 Lloyd's Rep 395.

for Daniel Brandon seeking to quash a decision of the Liverpool Dock Labour Board by the old writ of certiorari. The Board had removed his name from the register of registered dockworkers and the application was to have it restored. She did not succeed.

Rose also had a double foray into the world of household gambling. Henry Burton QC was a very successful silk on the Northern Circuit. In October 1952, he was tragically killed in a train collision at Harrow in foggy conditions whilst travelling from London to Manchester. He had been instructed to represent one Arthur Madden de Haut-Ville Bell, a retired wing commander and aero engineer, who had sued Cecil Moores, the Managing Director of Liverpool Football Pools, and Liverpool Football Pools Ltd over an allegedly lost 'treble chance' winning coupon which Littlewoods denied ever having received. Rose was instructed to take over the case, which had had to be adjourned to June 1954 because of the death of Henry Burton.

The issue was whether the coupon, together with a postal order for 3s 6d, had been received by a porter at Littlewoods and stolen by the porter. Littlewoods relied on its rules and as the coupon could not be traced, refused to pay out the winnings of £57,000, a substantial sum of money. Rose called Owens, the former porter, who went back on his story when giving evidence in the witness box and denied stealing the coupon. Rose therefore applied to treat him as a hostile witness so that she could cross-examine him. Owens said that he had been offered £200 by the investigators to sign a false statement. It was not to be Arthur Madden de Haut-Ville Bell's lucky day. The judge, Mr Justice Pearson, found that he had not proved his case. The press, as ever, found this a compelling and newsworthy case.

Rose's next involvement in the world of pools, this time racing rather than football, proved equally unsuccessful. A few days later Rose appeared for Cyril Carter in a libel action against the Empire Pools, Blackpool and Leonard Edwards, a director of the company. This time the action was before a judge, Mr Justice Barry and a jury. Cyril Carter was the sole survivor of a destroyer which had sunk during the war. Churchill had asked him to give an account of the action for his memoirs. He had forecast the results of five races on the 'Teasy Five' correctly, but Empire Pools did not pay up. Instead it accused him of filling in his coupon after the races were over despite the postmark of 1.30pm before the race in issue started.

The alleged libel was contained in a letter from Empire Pools to Carter's MP which stated that the entries were made after the result was known and put in an envelope which had already been postmarked, the implication being that he was a criminal. The issue arose out of when it was known that one of the winning horses would ride and whether or not the statement was given on an occasion of qualified privilege. The defendants did not seek to justify the statement as being true.

In opening the case, Rose said that her client:

> Mr Carter having come through the war with the scars of battle ... a hero to his family, his friends and to his country ... had been falsely castigated as a low mean crook and he sought such damages as would indicate to the world at large that even in these materialistic days 'he who steals my purse steels trash, but he who filches my good name leaves me poor indeed'.

Empire Pools was represented by Colin Duncan. The Judge ruled that the letter was privileged and withdrew the case from the jury. Afterwards a juryman ran across the court and shook Carter by the hand and said 'Hard luck, old chap'.

Professionally Rose had had to learn about gaming in this case in the same way as she had to learn about other matters relevant to her cases. On a personal level she seems to have been a bit naive about gambling—at least according to a tale Nat would relate. Rose and Nat rarely went to the races. However, on one occasion they went to watch the Chester Cup. Nat had made a sizeable bet on a horse which won at 4:1. Rose's reaction, far from being pleased, was to castigate Nat—no doubt in a teasing way—for not putting more money on the horse!

A FEW MORE MURDERS

Although Rose undertook a variety of criminal cases in this period, it was once again the more salacious murder and abortion cases which received the widest publicity. Not all Rose's cases were susceptible to her eloquent and persuasive advocacy. On 8 April 1953, she defended 20-year-old John Lawrence Todd accused of murdering 82-year-old Hugh George Walker at his 'Old Curiosity Shop'. It had been a brutal murder, the deceased receiving 32 blows to the head. Todd was unemployed, but apparently liked tinkering with clocks and watches and admitted visiting the old man. Despite the severity of the injuries and the bloody mess left all around, his defence was that the old man had 'tripped' over an axe and had had a nose bleed.

Although there were no fingerprints or blood matches, it did not help Todd's case that he admitted making a false statement to the police. Mr Justice Cassels told the jury that 'Miss Heilbron has conducted this case with her usual ability on behalf of the defence'. Todd was found guilty and sentenced to death. His appeal to the Court of Criminal Appeal was subsequently dismissed, as was the last-ditch request to the Home Secretary to appoint a panel of medical experts to examine Todd's mental condition. He was hanged on 19 May 1953 at Walton Prison.

In another murder trial three months later Rose was more successful. At Manchester Assizes, instructed by a Salford solicitor, she defended John Waddington charged with murdering a 25-year-old former Accrington and Stockport footballer, William Robinson, who had been associating with Waddington's wife in Salford. Waddington's marriage had been unhappy and he and his wife had separated during which time his wife became pregnant by another man. However Waddington had pretended that the child was his, looking after the boy as his son and acknowledging him as such.

Unfortunately the marriage broke down again and they separated once more, but Waddington wanted his wife back. Something appeared to snap when he saw Robinson with his wife one evening. He went home for his revolver acquired during the Normandy invasion, when he had served as a chief petty officer in the Royal Navy. He wanted to frighten his wife into returning to him. A struggle ensued between the two men in the street, maybe because Robinson was trying to protect his lover. Waddington did not recollect shooting his rival. He thought he had shot his wife. Unknown to him she was pregnant and she lost her baby as a result of the incident.

His wife's father gave evidence which was clearly pivotal in that he was strongly critical of his daughter's behaviour. In her final speech Rose said 'You have heard from the lips of Mrs Waddington's own father words no daughter would ever want her father to say about her. He obviously thought her conduct was deplorable'. The case indicated a not untypical form of domestic disharmony that led to tragedies of this sort. Waddington was saved from the gallows and found not guilty of murder, but guilty of manslaughter and given five years' imprisonment by Mr Justice Lynskey.

Aside from these two murder trials, Rose defended at the Old Bailey Edward Harrington Sanders, accused of shooting a detective with intent to murder him and with another conspiracy to rob. She appeared at Manchester Assizes pleading for leniency for a 47-year-old former nurse, Marion Vallance, who pleaded guilty to using an instrument to procure the miscarriage of a 17-year-old girl and of supplying a poisonous substance, ergot, knowing that it was to be used to procure a miscarriage. She had apparently performed six previous operations for friends. She received £15 from the American GI who had made the girl pregnant. Mr Justice Donovan imposed a £20 fine or six months' imprisonment in default. Rose also prosecuted Margaret Elizabeth Gorman, a pathetic figure of poor intellect, who pleaded guilty to a charge of infanticide at Liverpool Assizes. She had asphyxiated her baby with a button. Mr Justice Oliver bound her over on condition she remained in the convent where she was then residing. Rose also travelled to Leicester to represent Joseph Mahon who had allegedly pickpocketed three men at Padby races.

As the above selection of the many cases she undertook in this period indicates, 1953 and 1954 saw Rose consolidating her silk's practice. She was developing further her own method of working. She continued to write everything out in longhand, including relevant extracts from the legal authorities, as there were no photocopiers. When she could, she had her notes for speeches or cross-examination typed. Often she had her speeches typed in capitals in short paragraphs dotted across the foolscap pages and sometimes the paragraphs were typed alternatively in red and black.

What is noticeable from her contemporaneous papers and a consideration of her court advocacy is the consistent thoroughness of her preparation and the time it must have taken her. In many of her cases, as well as studying the factual evidence of the witnesses, the maps, the plans, the photographs and similar evidence, Rose would often have to analyse and understand difficult technical expert evidence so that she could cross-examine the relevant expert witness. This might be a doctor in a medical or personal injury case or even a murder, for example, as to the cause of death in the Bloom trial, or it could be a forensic witness in a criminal case or an expert in a particular industry where an accident had occurred. In her civil practice she also had to learn about various industries from loading ships to machinery in factories and even gaming. In addition she had to research the relevant law.

While she would receive assistance from her juniors in her cases, the ultimate responsibility for the presentation of any case in court remained with Rose. Many of these cases were on legal aid and poorly paid. But as she often remarked, her work was also her hobby. Rose continued to work evenings and often at weekends in legal term time, sending Nat to play golf or to take Hilary out. These were not years of particularly famous cases, but ones which nonetheless caught public attention. More spectacular cases were to follow in the next few years. However, her public profile continued in the ascendancy.

ILLUSTRATIONS OF THE PRESS' COVERAGE OF ROSE

The Star, April 1949

Housewife Who is Britain's Portia

(Sunday Tribune Special Correspondent)

LONDON, Saturday.

SHE is 39, happily married to a doctor and the mother of a girl aged seven. Seeing her shopping in her home town, Liverpool, you would note her as a rather handsome, pleasant, quietly-dressed house wife, with a faint trace of the Merseyside in her accent; just like thousands of other well-to-do Liverpool housewives, in fact.

Durban Sunday Tribune, SA, June 1955

WOMEN SHOULD KNOW WHAT HUSBANDS EARN

Rose Heilbron tells an audience of men

Manchester News Chronicle, 1954

THESE WASTED WOMEN

By Rose Heilbron

MISS ROSE HEILBRON, Q.C., wife of a surgeon and mother of a 3½-year-old girl, took up another "brief" last night—on behalf of professional women who, having married and had children, want to resume their careers.

News Chronicle, 1952

'EQUAL PAY SOON' SAYS WOMAN K.C.

PRESSURE of public opinion will eventually secure the adoption of equal pay for women, declared Miss Rose Heilbron, one of England's two women K.C.'s today, when she addressed the Women's Group on Public Welfare in London.

Birmingham Evening Despatch, 1950

WHAT WOMEN ARE TALKING ABOUT
Brilliant woman K.C. in murder trial

IN the corridors of the Law Courts several years ago a well-known K.C. pointed out a slim, dark-haired girl and said to a colleague: "You'll be hearing a good deal about that girl—watch her."

The K.C.'s prophecy has been well justified. The girl was Miss Rose Heilbron.

Yorkshire Evening News, Leeds, 1950

The Liverpool Echo, February 1950

Counsel Opens Defence In Cameo Murder Trial -

Miss Heilbron's Reference To "Incredible Story"

The defence of George Kelly, aged 27, labourer, of 39d Trowbridge Street, off Copperas Hill, Liverpool, who is accused of the murder of Leonard Thomas, manager of the Cameo Cinema, Wavertree, on March 19, last year, was opened at Liverpool Assizes to-day, before Mr. Justice Cassels, by Miss Rose Heilbron, K.C.

Rose, K.C., holds up the Assizes

JURY ARE SENT HOME

MISS ROSE HEILBRON, who two months ago became one of Britain's three women K.C.s, twice held up a trial at Liverpool Assizes yesterday.

The second time, argument between her and Mr. Justice Lynskey lasted so long that the jurors were sent home for the night.

In her first big case since she was appointed K.C., Miss Heilbron was defending Donald Thomas John Johnson, aged 22, accused of harbouring the man who murdered cinema manager Leonard Thomas at Liverpool on March 19.

Rose Heilbron, K.C.

DAILY EXPRESS THURSDAY FEBRUARY 7 1952

LET THIS INFATUATED MAN GO FREE
Miss Rose pleads

Judge starts summing up in Bloom tria.

Express Staff Reporter : Durham, Wednesday

MISS ROSE HEILBRON, Q.C., told the jury of five women and seven men at Durham Assizes today that Louis Arnold Bloom, 35-year-old solicitor and son of a former mayor of West Hartlepool, never thought of injuring a hair of Mrs Patricia Mary Hessler's head.

She said: "Perhaps one should not use the word love in connection with this case. It was infatuation.

Daily Express, February 1953

Woman KC Blames Dock Union Chiefs
9,880 Out As Trial Nears End

Liverpool Echo, April 1951

Curlers prove Vicki innocent
JURY TOLD

IT'S just one of those things with women. They won't be seen with their hair in curlers— not if they can help it.

A woman, Miss Rose Heilbron, Q C, reminded an Old Bailey jury of this foible of her sex yesterday.

It shows, she said, that Mrs. Violet Clark is innocent of murder.

WOULD SHE?

For 35-year-old Mrs. Clark (known as Vicki Wright) put her hair in curlers on the night the houseboat Windmill caught fire at Benfleet Creek, Essex.

Would she have done this if she planned to start the fire? Miss Heilbron asked.

Would any woman be prepared to face firemen, neighbours and police with her hair up if she could avoid it?

The prosecution says Mrs. Clark did start the fire, killing her two-year-old twins, Colin and Reginald, who were burned to death.

ROSE HEILBRON, Q C
She was eloquent

Daily Herald, 1956

RECORDER ROSE WINS AGAIN

Reese is led away by U.S. military police after the verdict.

GI cleared of murder

Daily Mail, November 1956

ROSE HEILBRON
MADE HISTORY
BY BECOMING
A JUDGE...

Is she our cleverest woman?

ROSE
HEILBRON,
Q C.

Manchester Evening
Chronicle, 1957

Rose, Q.C., is to defend Mrs. Wright

By VICTOR SIMS

MISS ROSE HEILBRON, Q.C., is expected to defend Mrs. Violet Lavinia Clark, 35—known as Mrs. Vicky Wright—mother of the two-year-old twins who died in a houseboat blaze.

Sunday Pictorial, London, 1956

Woman cleared of bath-murder

Triumph
for her
counsel
—a woman

Manchester News Chronicle, 1951

'THAT GIRL ROSIE

...the greatest lawyer in the world'

It's no hold barred when Rose QC pleads
BUT AT HOME SHE'S JUST THE DOCTOR'S WIFE

South China Sunday Post, Hong Kong, October 1955

Reynolds News, September 1955

DAILY MAIL; SATURDAY, SEPTEMBER 24; 1955

Miss Rose, QC, triumphs

TRIBUTE AFTER OLD BAILEY VERDICT

By Daily Mail Reporter

MISS ROSE HEILBRON—brilliant 39-year-old Queen's Counsel, surgeon's wife, and devoted mother—had a crowded day yesterday fulfilling all three rôles.

At the Old Bailey, in London, she had added to her long list of legal victories when Jack "Spot" Comer, whom she defended, was acquitted in the Soho stabbing case.

Then—with moments to spare—she doffed wig and gown to rush home to Childwall, Liverpool, to join husband Dr. Nathaniel Burstein and their seven-year-old daughter.

She was home for a well-earned restful week-end—before Mrs. Burstein must become Miss Heilbron again. The attractive daughter of a Liverpool hotel proprietor showed no signs of strain after the arguing at the Old Bailey the fine legal points of a case which has made news for weeks.

Mrs. Comer insists: "We go straight home to the family."

JACK SPOT BOWS THANKS TO JURY

Daily Mail, September 1955

Rose, QC, does it again

A 39-YEAR-OLD doctor's wife from Liverpool brought off another victory yesterday. As Jack Comer walked out of the Old Bailey a free man, he said:

Daily Herald, September1955

ROSE HEILBRON, Q.C., ENDS ANOTHER BRILLIANT CASE

Judge talks of her "Eloquent advocacy"

NEWS CHRONICLE REPORTER

MISS ROSE HEILBRON, 5ft. 2in. tall, at 37 the country's youngest woman Q.C., ended another successful case yesterday at Durham Assizes. Her client, Louis Arnold Bloom, was cleared of a charge of murder and found guilty of manslaughter.

News Chronicle, 1952

WOMAN Q.C. GETS RESPITE FOR MEN IN DEATH CELL

Johannesburg Sunday Times, 1952

THE AMAZING CAREER OF ROSE HEILBRON

Times of Ceylon, 1967

4th 'SAVE' FROM THE GALLOWS

Daily News Correspondent

LONDON, Wednesday.
MISS ROSE HEILBRON, Q.C., has for the fourth time in her career at the Bar saved a man from the gallows by her brilliant advocacy.

The man freed from the death cell, 29-year-old Manchester dealer Dennis Patrick Murtagh, walked out from the Law Courts and the shadow of death yesterday into the bright sunshine of the Strand and into his mother's arms.

Five judges in the Court of Criminal Appeal had quashed the sentence of death passed on him. He had been convicted on a charge of murdering William Joseph Jackson, a stock car racing driver, by running him down with a car.

When Murtagh's appeal had succeeded two wardens from Pentonville Prison handed him a railway ticket and brought him down from the court to the side entrance. Then, as Murtagh stopped to shield his eyes from the sun, they gave him a friendly shove. On the pavement his 64-year-old mother, a tiny, stooped figure in a worn-out coat, ran forward crying: 'Dennis, it's me, your mother.'

WAS CONFIDENT

Murtagh, who spent nine weeks in the condemned cell, said: "I was confident that my appeal would not fail." He added that the only thing he had to look forward to when he was in the cell were the half-hour visits of his mother "who never for a moment doubted my innocence."

Mrs. Murtagh's first words, on hearing that her son was once more a free man were: "Thanks be to God and His Holy Mother."

Freed with Murtagh was 24-year-old Kenneth George Kennedy, who was a passenger in the car when Jackson was killed and who had been sentenced to seven years' imprisonment for man-

Daily News, May 25, 1955

Miss Rose Heilbron Q.C. Is Britain's Portia

Christchurch Press, New Zealand, January 1962

CAREER WOMAN

The DOUBLE life of ROSIE OF THE OLD BAILEY

A DOCTOR'S WIFE

Sydney Sun, 1955

13

A Series of 'Triumphs'—On the Brink of Legal History Once More

THE PROSPECT OF A JUDICIAL APPOINTMENT

IN JUNE 1955, the *Manchester Evening News* wrote: 'A woman as a judge? Could it be ...? Will Rose Heilbron one day become Britain's first woman judge? Many in the legal profession believe she may, for this latest triumph is only one of a long series of successes'.

By this time Rose had been in silk for six years and, had she been a man, would undoubtedly already have been appointed a Recorder of Quarter Sessions. A Recorder is a part-time judge. Originally the office of Recorder was created by the Mayor and Aldermen of a borough to 'record' or keep in mind the proceedings of their court, as well as the customs of the city. The term evolved to refer to the principal legal officer of a city or borough, having a separate court of Quarter Sessions of which the Recorder is sole judge of the court.

When appointed a Queen's Counsel a barrister became eligible for such a position and would be assigned to a particular city's Quarter Sessions. Quarter Sessions sat, as the name suggests, at least four times a year, once each legal term: Michaelmas, Hilary, Easter and Trinity. Recorders hear cases of a certain seriousness sitting with a jury and also take appeals from magistrates. They exist to this day, although they are no longer assigned to particular Quarter Sessions and the procedure for appointment is very different. There had never been a female Recorder in England, but Rose had to wait a little longer before she took on such a judicial role. As Rose herself often said: 'Just let women have a bit more time at all the men's jobs. Then they'll show them'. She had to be patient throughout her career. Meanwhile, there was no shortage of famous cases and 'triumphs'.

MURDER BY MOTOR CAR

The first famous triumph of 1955, and the one referred to in the article above from the *Manchester Evening News*, involved Rose's defence of one Dennis Murtagh. Dennis Murtagh was aged 29, and had a string of convictions for larceny and similar offences. He was charged, together with his younger brother Derek and a friend, Kenneth Kennedy, with the murder of a friend of his, William Jackson, a stock car racing driver, on the night of 20–21 November 1954. The murder weapon was stated to be a Ford Zephyr motor car owned and driven by Dennis Murtagh, which he allegedly deliberately drove onto the pavement where the deceased had been standing and rammed him against the wall of a house near his home causing his death. The case provoked considerable interest because of the novelty of a car being relied upon as a murder weapon.

The alleged murder followed two previous incidents that evening when the three accused had repeatedly driven down the road where the deceased lived following a fight earlier in the evening in a public house. On the first occasion the deceased's wife had allegedly thrown a brick at Dennis Murtagh's car, smashing a window. On the second occasion, the deceased himself had hurled an iron coal grid at the car breaking the windscreen of the car. Dennis Murtagh had reported both incidents to the police and the police were on their way to the scene at the time of the alleged murder.

The trial was held at Manchester Assizes in March 1955 before Mr Justice Glyn-Jones. The issue for the jury revolved around the third occasion the three accused had driven past the deceased's house. The question was whether the accused had intended to murder the deceased, as the prosecution contended, or whether, as the defence argued, the driver, Dennis Murtagh, had accidentally lost control of the car, which had swerved and mounted the pavement, as he ducked to avoid an iron coal grid which the deceased had picked up apparently to throw at the car for a second time. Despite less than convincing evidence, the jury found Rose's client, Dennis Murtagh, guilty of murder and he was sentenced to death. His brother was found not guilty and Kennedy was found guilty of manslaughter.

An appeal was immediately lodged by the two convicted men. The main ground of Dennis Murtagh's appeal being that the Judge had misdirected the jury on the issue of burden of proof. The hearing took place in May 1955, but the three-man Court of Criminal Appeal disagreed and for the first time in legal history a second appeal was heard, this time before a five-man court. 'A Hush fell in the courtroom ... Rose Heilbron had begun her fight to save a man from hanging' proclaimed the *Weekly News*.

Rose explained:

> In this case the dividing line between murder and accident is so thin, so narrow, and so close that it was exceptionally important for the judge to put accurately, clearly and in full, the direction as to burden of proof ... This is a somewhat unusual case for it is not often that a motor-car is alleged to have been used as a lethal weapon in a case of murder.

She added in her reply:

> It has always been the pride of these Courts that a man was presumed to be innocent before he was proved guilty, and the right of an accused coming before an English jury was that the case should be proved beyond reasonable doubt. Unless the jury were told that, they could not possibly know what standard of proof was required.

The appeal was allowed and Murtagh was immediately freed after spending nine weeks in Stangeways prison as a condemned man with only his mouth organ for company. Outside the court the crowd held up the traffic. People were shouting for Murtagh's counsel to appear and receive their congratulations and chanting: 'We want Rose ... where is our Rose?' But disliking the limelight, she had slipped away to catch her train back to Liverpool.

'Man from Condemned Cell is Set Free' and similar banner headlines appeared in many national and local newspapers with personal stories of the weeping mothers at their reunions with their sons, Murtagh and Kennedy (who was also freed). It was a sensational legal victory at the time attracting headlines for Rose both nationally and internationally such as: 'Miss Heilbron Does it Again' (*The Daily Mail*); 'Fourth Save from the Gallows' (*The Daily News*); 'Rose QC Does it Again' (*The Daily Herald*); 'Woman QC Thwarted Hangman' (The *Sydney Sun*, Australia); 'Housewife Who is Britain's Portia' (*Sunday Tribune*, Durban, South Arica), and foreign language headlines in newspapers from Buenos Aires to Rome.

JACK SPOT

Her second, even more sensational case of the year, concerned Jack Comer, otherwise known as Jack Spot from a childhood nickname 'Spotty'. Jack Spot was a notorious and famous gangster in the 1940s and early 1950s. He became the self-confessed leader of the criminal underworld in London or 'King of Soho', the base from which he operated. Born into humble and impoverished beginnings in a Jewish ghetto in East London, his progressive and ruthless criminality led in his heyday to a superficially opulent lifestyle and a reign of terror as he suppressed opposing gangs to gain supremacy.

He ran his operation like a business empire, living on the profits of protection rackets and other forms of organised crime. This extended to racing and other types of gambling, the running of bars and clubs, together with robberies and other criminal activities, all serviced by numerous other gang criminals with a variety of criminal specialities. Jack Spot prided himself on meticulous planning of his crimes and ensured that he himself avoided direct involvement in them. His stock in trade was the razor and cutting or 'chivving' his target as the means by which he instilled terror into those who got in his way, but table legs filled with lead and fists were additional forms of ammunition. A special recipe of his followers was to create mayhem by throwing a sackful of razor-filled spuds or potatoes. These were not men one would invite round for tea with an elderly maiden aunt!

By the early 1950s new rivals began to emerge and in particular one, Billy Hill, and later the Kray twins. Jack Spot's Godfather-like position was beginning to be threatened. In September 1955 Spot was involved in a fight in Soho with one Albert Dimes, also known as Italian Albert, one of Billy Hill's henchmen. Spot alleged that Dimes had issued a warning to him to keep away from the racecourses. Spot at the time had a monopoly of certain betting pitches at racecourses. Knives were used and both men were seriously injured. They were both charged jointly with several offences relating to the incident including unlawfully fighting and making an affray.

Rose was instructed by a London firm of solicitors, Peters and Peters, to represent Jack Comer at the Old Bailey at his trial in September 1955. Her junior was Sebag Shaw (later a Court of Appeal Judge), and the Judge was Mr Justice Glyn-Jones. Her brief fee was 100 guineas. Once again the mere act of her being instructed to defend Jack Spot provoked considerable press interest. The issue was who had started the fight and who had the knife and used it first, or whether one or both of them was acting in self-defence.

After two days, at the conclusion of the prosecution case, the Judge, following legal argument, ruled that Dimes and Comer should be tried separately on a charge of wounding with intent to cause grievous bodily harm. Comer was also charged with being in possession of a knife. The Judge also ordered the jury to acquit

on the affray charge and withdrew from the jury the charge against
Dimes of unlawfully possessing a knife.

Two days later Jack Comer's trial began in the famous No 1 Court
at the Old Bailey. This time he was tried alone before the Recorder
of London, Sir Gerald Dobson, and a different jury. After the prosecution evidence, Comer was called to give evidence in his own
defence. He said that it was an unprovoked attack on him by Dimes
and that he never managed to retrieve the knife from Dimes. Trying
to explain the injuries received by Dimes to exculpate himself he
responded to a question from the Recorder, rather incredibly, that
Dimes had caused his own injuries. Comer called another witness,
who had a criminal record, Christopher Glinski, who said that
Dimes drew the knife first.

A key and surprise witness was the Reverend Basil Claude
Hudson Andrews who had approached Comer's solicitor late in the
day offering to give evidence. As a man of the cloth and an independent witness with no apparent gangland connections, his evidence
would carry great weight. Rose's instructions gave no clue as to how
his evidence came about. All she was told apart from the contents
of his proof of evidence was that:

> [He] is 88 years of age and his memory does not appear to be too good, in
> addition to which he is slightly deaf. If, however, the witness can be kept
> to the point and not allowed to ramble into his life history, his evidence
> should be of great assistance to the Defendant Comer.

Little did the legal team know of the 'real' Reverend Andrews or
how he came to approach Comer's solicitor. This deception was to
be revealed much later.

In her impassioned closing address Rose referred to the 'Alice
in Wonderland' aspect of the case in which Spot was accused
of wounding the very man who had inflicted extremely serious
knife injuries on him. She also drew attention to the unexplained
appearance in some bushes nearby of a knife some 16 days after
the incident which had not been proved to be the knife in question and which could not have been put there by Comer as he was
hospitalised.

After retiring for only 65 minutes, the jury returned a verdict of
not guilty. On hearing the verdict Comer danced in the dock and
clasped his hands above his head like a victorious boxer. 'God be
praised. Justice has been done!' he shouted until the Judge told
him to behave himself. Whether the jury took the view that Dimes
and Comer deserved each other, or whether they were swayed by

the evidence of the Reverend Andrews or whether they felt that the prosecution evidence was, as Rose contended, unreliable and confused, is not known.

On the steps of the old Bailey, Comer paid tribute to Rose: 'Don't write about me, write your story about Rose, greatest lawyer in history'. Apparently Comer had a picture of Rose framed which he kept on his mantelpiece and he together with some of his gangland friends described her as his 'pin-up girl'. 'Rose QC is the Toast of Soho' exclaimed the *Sunday Pictorial*. It had not always been so. Comer had initially been very doubtful about hiring Rose as his counsel, exclaiming: 'A woman defend me—you're crazy', but his solicitor persuaded him to engage her.

Despite such praise and her outward professional calm, the trial with its gangland involvement had clearly not been a particularly pleasant experience for Rose. She noted how on the Sunday evening before the trial she had gone 'in trepidation' with her solicitor and junior to view the scene of the fight in Soho where she saw 'swarthy, tough unpleasant characters'. Later she went for another view with police protection and recorded that prosecution witnesses had asked her to buy fruit. She described how outside the Old Bailey during the trial a sinister Italian deliberately crossed her path and almost bumped into her and how when she went to speak to Comer's wife, who had two bodyguards, they had to move away from four of the opposition gang. She also referred to the 'battery of press photographers' taking photographs of her on the first day of the trial as she entered the Old Bailey. Rose would clearly have been glad to get the train home to Liverpool after the trial was over.

Such was Comer's notoriety at the time, that his acquittal received huge national press coverage. But the case had an unexpected twist. The verdict had been a surprise and it was followed by the prosecution withdrawing the charge against Dimes. Thus two notorious gangsters, who had undoubtedly been in a fight and who had each received extensive knife wounds, had got away scot free. The police and the press started digging. Concerns were raised as to jury and witness tampering. The Home Secretary ordered a full report on the Dimes/Comer affair and the Attorney General was kept informed. The possibility of a public inquiry was raised.

The national newspapers started a campaign with front page banner headlines concerning 'The Amazing Battle that Never Was' (*The Daily Sketch*). Witnesses started to come out of the woodwork and the bumbling old clergyman, the Reverend Andrews, was metaphorically speaking defrocked as the 'Knocking Parson' who had a string of unpaid gambling debts. A week to the day after the verdict, Reverend Andrews finally confessed that he had never seen the Soho fight and that he had been paid £25 to give perjured evidence. Having been acquitted, Comer could not be charged with the same offence again. However his wife and friends, Moisha Bluebell (Morris Goldstein), Sonny the Yank (Bernard Schack) and 'Tall' Pat MacDonagh were all charged with conspiracy to pervert the cause of justice and all were convicted. The three men received custodial sentences and Mrs Comer a fine.

The following year two 'associates' of Billy Hill, then self-styled king of the underworld, namely Robert 'Bobby' Warren and Francis 'Mad Frankie' Fraser were found guilty of beating up Jack Spot in an outburst of gang warfare between the racecourse gangs. They were identified by Comer's wife. They were each sentenced to seven years' imprisonment. Jack Spot eventually lost his gangland supremacy. His wife and two daughters emigrated to America and he died alone, aged 84, in a nursing home.

THE HOUSEBOAT TWINS MURDER

The following year, 1956, saw Rose appear in two further sensational murder trials. The first, the 'houseboat twins' murder trial, as it was known, concerned the alleged murder of twin boys aged two years, by their mother in a houseboat fire on the night of 16–17 May 1955 at Benfleet Creek, Canvey Island. The horror of a mother allegedly deliberately setting fire to her home and leaving her babies to die provoked widespread national interest. Violet Lavinia Clark aged 35, known also as Vicki Wright, was accused with Mrs Grace Richardson, 47, of murdering Mrs Clark's twin sons. Rose represented Violet Clark. Her trial began on 29 October 1956 and people queued from early in the morning to get into the packed No 1 Court at the Old Bailey where the case was tried before Mr Justice Hilberry and a jury.

Mrs Clark had lived for some time on a houseboat called the 'Buchra' with her late second husband, Mr Wright, but when he died in mid-April 1956 she went, taking the twins with her, to sleep with her then friends, the Richardsons, on a neighbouring boat, the 'Windmill', while she redecorated the Buchra. Both houseboats were part of a colony of rather squalid houseboats at Benfleet Creek. The Buchra had caught fire two days before the Windmill.

The father of the twins was a third man, Stephen Taylor, and Mrs Clark admitted to having several men friends. The one who was key to the trial was a Bill Smith whom the prosecution alleged she had been having an affair with for many years, although she denied this. She was not liked, probably because of her penchant for associating with married men, and was called a prostitute.

The prosecution alleged that the motive for the murder was clear from a conversation which had taken place between Mrs Clark and Mrs Richardson, in the presence of Mrs Richardson's daughter. This conversation allegedly revealed that Bill Smith, who was a married man, was going to take her to Australia, but would not take the twins as well. As a result, it was further alleged that, possibly emboldened by an earlier fire on the Buchra in respect of which by implication it was contended she had also been involved, Mrs Clark had suggested burning the Windmill. It was never established how the Windmill caught fire, but it went up in flames suddenly with several people, including the twins, on board. It was also alleged that Mrs Clark knocked one of the twins out of the arms of Mrs Richardson and into the flames. The main prosecution witnesses were Mrs Richardson's son and daughter and one or two other houseboat dwellers and they were cross-examined at length by Rose.

Vicki Wright's version of events was very different. She denied ever saying she wanted to go to Australia or having any involvement in starting the fire. She claimed that she thought others had taken the twins off the boat and tried in vain to get back to them when she realised they had not been rescued, but was restrained by the police. There were some awkward pieces of evidence to overcome: Mr Smith did have a son and daughter-in-law living in Australia and had been to Australia to visit them. It was alleged that Vicki Clark had applied for a passport to go to Australia without mentioning the twins and a letter was produced written in intimate terms from Mrs Clark to Bill Smith when he was in Australia, which was put in evidence.

Rose, in her final speech dealt deftly with the issue of Vicki's various lovers. She told the jury:

> She is an immoral woman, but immorality is not a crime and, if it was, she is not being charged with it ... Is it likely that a woman is going to paint and renovate a houseboat only to burn it? ... She knew someone had written what are commonly called poison letters [admittedly written to the police and Bill Smith's wife by her co-accused Mrs Richardson]. There was great hatred of Mrs Clark along the creek—she was hated with a malevolence and spite that is hard to believe until you see those anonymous letters ... There was a good deal of reason for Vicki Clark thinking that one or other of people who hated her had set fire to the boat ... There is no evidence that Mrs Clark made any preparations whatever for setting fire to the Windmill that night.

Then came the feminine angle:

> There she was going to be in her pyjamas with her hair in curlers. Would she have gone to bed in curlers and then face firemen, police etc if she planned to set fire to the boat?

She ended her final speech with an impassioned plea using hand gestures as appropriate:

> If ever a woman went into the dock up to her neck in prejudice and bias, and covered by malice and hatred, that woman was Vicki Clark. It is for you to clear away these tissues of lies and malice that have surrounded her. I ask you to say that the prosecution evidence is neither credible nor convincing—that it is unsafe and dangerous. I do NOT ask you to decide this case on pity or passion, but on logic and reason. I say there can only be one verdict in the name of justice. That verdict is one of not guilty.

After a hearing lasting two weeks, Vicki Clark was acquitted of murder and saved from the hangman, but found guilty of manslaughter for the criminal neglect in the duty to her children and was sentenced to three years in prison. Bill Smith was outside the courtroom at the end of the hearing, but declined to comment. Mrs Richardson had previously been found not guilty of murder and discharged on the direction of the Judge. The case still has a lingering fascination and has given rise to a blog on the internet.

A VARIED PRACTICE

On 26 November 1956, a day of great significance in the professional life of Rose for reasons which will be revealed in the following chapters, she attended the assizes at Stafford to defend GI Freeman Reese, alleged to have murdered Police Constable Brindley James Booth at Burton 10 years previously. His skull had been fractured by a blunt instrument, probably a jemmy. Reese and another man had earlier in the evening of the murder stolen a safe from a cinema, but finding it too heavy to carry had borrowed a pushchair, when they were spotted and chased by the deceased policeman. Reese's defence was that it was his accomplice who had hit the policeman, who was at the time suffering from hardening of the arteries. No weapon was ever found and the evidence was entirely circumstantial.

He was acquitted—the fifth man Rose had saved from the gallows, exclaimed the press—but his freedom was short lived as immediately he went out into the street, the US military police snapped handcuffs on him and drove him away to face a charge of deserting the US army in 1944. He was court martialled and on 7 January 1957 he was sentenced to 20 years' hard labour for desertion.

While the above cases attracted enormous publicity, Rose's criminal and civil practice in 1955 and 1956 continued to flourish generally. Some cases were reported in the press. In her criminal practice she continued to represent murderers, robbers, women charged with infanticide, thieves, shoplifters, rapists, those charged with other forms of sexual offences, dangerous drivers and clients charged with a gamut of other criminal offences. Sometimes she was successful: on other occasions she was not. Among them was 'Champagne Charlie', described subsequently as the prince of confidence tricksters. Then there was Michael Woodfall, who had mental health problems. In May 1956 she unsuccessfully sought on appeal to reduce his sentence for theft of a valuable diamond clip from a London jeweller. She represented a young American airman, Norman Dean Griffith, accused of attacking a hotel chambermaid. As Rose exclaimed to the jury:

> It is an accusation easily made, but difficult to refute. It is difficult for a man in a vulnerable position, alone with a chambermaid in his room, to deal with such an accusation ... Women often make false accusations against a man, either for an ulterior purpose or from selfish reasons.

The jury clearly took this on board and acquitted him of rape and on the direction of the Judge found him not guilty of the other charge and he was discharged.

In July 1955, she appeared at Warwick Assizes defending two Indians, Brij Bhusan and Makhan Singh, both labourers who gave their evidence through interpreters. They had been charged with murder. It was alleged that on 5 March 1955, during a street fight in Coventry between three or four Indians, they had stabbed a man through the heart. Prosecution counsel, Richard Elwes QC, began his final speech thus:

> Members of the Jury, I preface the few observations I am now to offer to you with my tribute of respect and admiration to my learned friend for her conduct of the defence. You will wish me to pay tribute because it is not only the prisoners who profit by it, you profit by it as well. There is a deep satisfaction to everybody who has the serious responsibility, which each of us has in our different ways, of dealing with a crime of this gravity. There is a deep satisfaction from the knowledge that here, in a foreign country, and in a foreign tongue, men accused as these men are should be able to call upon the great talent of my learned friend for their defence.

He then presumably proceeded to put the boot in for they were both found guilty and sentenced to death.

Rose's civil practice also continued to prosper, acting for negligent doctors and injured plaintiffs from all walks of life. Several cases went to the Court of Appeal and were reported in the Law Reports. One related to the extent of the statutory duty owed to an injured seaman under the Shipbuilding Regulations 1931.[1] Another concerned the ambit of the disclosure of documents by the British Transport Commission relating to similar accidents following injury to Rose's client, Andrew Edmiston, when he fell from one of their engines and injured himself.[2] A third reported case at first instance concerned issues of master and servant and the system of working.[3]

These high-profile successes produced even more flattering publicity around the globe for Rose, but such incessant press coverage also continued to bring its problems.

[1] *Bryers v Canadian Pacific Steamships, Limited* [1957] 1 QB 134.
[2] *Edmiston v British Transport Commission CA* [1956] 1 QB 191.
[3] *Spring v JJ Mack & Sons Ltd* [1956] 2 Lloyd's Rep 558.

14

An Unwitting Public Persona

THE PUBLIC FASCINATION WITH A WORKING
WIFE AND MOTHER

THE PUBLIC FASCINATION with Rose's dual role as professional lawyer, on the one hand, and wife and mother, on the other, continued both nationally and internationally. 'Wife, Mother and Advocate: Britain's Portia Succeeds As all Three' proclaimed the *Rhodesia Herald* in September 1955. 'It's no holds barred when Rose QC pleads, but at home she's just the doctor's wife' echoed the *South China Sunday Post* in a long article. 'The Double Life of Rosie of the Old Bailey' was a full page spread in the *Sydney Sun*, Australia, in the following month. An extract conjures up the contemporaneous reaction:

> Every Queen's Counsel in Britain has a healthy respect for the woman known to them as 'Rosie'. But to the ordinary man she is more than that. To them she is a second Portia, who might well have stepped out of the pages of Shakespeare's Merchant of Venice. For she is, above all things, a woman in legal disguise ... She is one of those women who have learned the secret of how to be a complete career woman and yet stay happily married. Judges recognise that there is no other woman of her stature at the Bar ... She enjoys a good clean fight, does not wince at the sound of bad language, has not grown conceited with success, and fights to the last ditch ... her magical appeal to the British public goes on. For whenever she appears in a great criminal trial, they will flock into court to listen to their Portia.

Similar articles and full-page spreads appeared in the national press attracting various epithets, including 'one of the fabulous women of today' and 'the first lady of the law'.

In the mass circulation paper called *Tit-Bits*, Joanne Heal, one of the best known names in musical theatre, wrote of meeting Rose:

> At this gathering I met one of the women I most admire in the country, Rose Heilbron QC. The surprise was to find her attractive and smart in such a 'wifely' way. Very much there with her doctor husband and not

the other way about, and for all her fame and brain anxious to talk not of famous legal struggles, but of the thrill of owning a new dish-washing machine.

Such a conversation would undoubtedly have taken place, for Rose was an avid gadget collector, a trait she passed on to her daughter, and every new gadget around, provided it was affordable, would be purchased well ahead of it becoming the norm. Whether it was the first dishwasher on the market, rather primitive by today's standards, involving turning a knob for every rinse and lifting out the racks of dishes from the top, or the latest spit (which Rose and Hilary spent hours trying to work to stop the chicken flopping until they discovered that it needed a prong at either end!) or the infra-red grill proudly brought back from London, all were bought on the pretext that they were labour saving, but probably also because Rose loved playing with such 'toys'. When Hilary was staying in Brussels to improve her French in her teens she apparently wrote telling Rose about a new gadget she had seen. Rose replied 'I'd be delighted to have <u>any</u> gadgets you can find (By the way there is a "d" in "gadgets")'. Some of these gadgets turned out to be less labour saving than others. On one occasion when Hilary was a teenager she had a girlfriend to supper. Rose proudly showed off her new coffee maker and the facility for getting rid of the coffee grains by simply lifting out the paper container straight into the bin. Unfortunately, as she lifted the pedal of the rubbish bin, she missed and coffee grains went all over the floor to much amusement!

THE INCESSANT PRESS COVERAGE

The press coverage of Rose was incessant. Journalists vied with each other to portray her in laudatory terms and tried to analyse the secret of her success. Her qualities were variously described as a clear brain, immense industry, a very thorough knowledge of her craft, a logical approach, incisively worded questions without intimidation, a flair for the job, being a fighter, a confident air without being aggressive or dominating, and what a colleague described as her astonishing capacity for 'mental athletics', developing her tactics as the case moved forward. '[U]nder this cloak of passive, apparent calm, there is a rapier' (*Evening Chronicle*). Journalists and colleagues pointed to her clear and musical voice and absence of theatrics. She herself would say that charm never appeals to a jury: the only way to succeed is to appeal to their sense of justice and this is what she strived to do. A more unlikely explanation was one given by the *Weekly News:* 'Rose Heilbron's large solitaire diamond [engagement] ring is the court's barometer. When it flashes in the light as she eloquently pleads, the case for the defence is going well'.

Her publicity also had a lighter side. She was chosen in October 1955 by members of the public as one of 500 best-dressed women in the country, and one of the seven best-dressed people in Liverpool. This article in turn prompted an unsolicited letter from Z Kopelovitch Ltd of 92 Berwick Street:

> We note with interest that the 'Daily Express' named you as one of the 500 best dressed women in the United Kingdom ... We are writing to you because we would add to our congratulations by helping you to keep your pre-eminent position in the world of fashion. You have not acquired your present reputation without being aware of the value of lace as an integral part of your wardrobe. We are specialists in lace, and we have in stock some of the world's loveliest laces ... May we ask that on your next visit to London, you may honour us with a visit.

It is unlikely that she did!

Rose also began to feature in cartoons. A *Smile* cartoon showed a constable about to arrest a man committing a violent assault on another man. The caption attributed to a passer-by, read: 'Why worry, officer?—they'll only engage Rose Heilbron for the defence'. Another cartoon in the *Liverpool Echo*, following a publicised theft at St George's Hall in Liverpool in which Rose and other barristers had lost their wigs and gowns, showed a man without trousers with a caption balloon over a policeman's helmet saying 'Probably the same bloke as stole Rose Heilbron's wig'.

Such was her fame and selling power by this time, that she started to receive the first of many inquiries to write her life-story, from famous publishers, potential authors and literary agents alike which requests continued until her retirement. Her stock response was that, as a practising member of the Bar, she was not permitted to write an autobiography nor permit publication about her life or work by anyone else, as this would amount to self-advertisement and would be prohibited by the Bar Council. Her first recorded such response ends with the comment that 'one day I expect I shall retire, and when that time comes I might well wish to tell my story'. Unfortunately she never did.

CONCERNS ABOUT SELF-ADVERTISEMENT

The rigid attitude of the profession towards any self-advertisement in those days continued to bring unwelcome problems for Rose. On 25 September 1955, there began a series in the Sunday newspaper, the *Reynolds News,* by Harry Loftus entitled 'That Girl Rosie—the Story of the Greatest Lawyer in the World, First Lady of the Law', which proceeded to examine her cases and repeat personal details about her. It was an extremely flattering series. Rose was concerned because it repeated some of the material which had caused her problems in the past and gave the impression that she had consented to the article, which was forbidden. She immediately contacted the Bar Council. The matter came to the attention of the Attorney General as leader of the Bar. On 17 October the Attorney General, Sir Reginald Manningham-Buller, wrote to Rose: 'I sympathise with you very much indeed and will certainly do what I can to make it clear that you are in no way responsible for all this publicity. I am glad you brought the matter to my attention'.

She also received the following response from Mr William Boulton, Secretary of Bar Council from 1950–74:

> Your representations to the Attorney General concerning the current series of articles in Reynolds Weekly have been duly reported to and considered by the appropriate committee of the Council.
>
> I have in consequence been asked to invite you to request that the whole matter be made the subject of enquiry by the Professional Conduct Committee. In the event of your following this suggestion the Committee would invite you to attend a special meeting. It would then be the task of the Committee first to satisfy itself that you are in no way responsible directly or indirectly for the publication of the articles or the material contained therein, and secondly to make recommendations as to any action which could be taken by the Council and which might be of assistance to you in the present circumstances.

The meeting duly took place and according to Neville Laski QC (then Recorder of Burnley) Rose 'charmed all'. Nonetheless, it must have been quite worrying at the time. However, that was not the end of such issues. The following year a similar problem arose in relation to articles appearing in a South African newspaper, called *Outspan* (home of oranges), which had been drawn to Rose's attention by Nat's sister who lived there and which gave the impression, wrongly, that she had given her consent to the articles. Once again she was compelled to write to the Bar Council who advised her to take the matter up personally with the newspaper, which she did through her personal solicitors, Ernest B Kendall & Rigby. She also again sought advice from Hartley Shawcross who advised an apology be published. This was achieved and the South African publisher paid all her legal costs.

RADIO AND TELEVISION

Rose was also being asked to appear on radio and television, the latter still in its infancy. The line between self-advertising and other programmes was a thin one. The Bar Council did give her permission to appear on 'Question Time', but it is unlikely that she in fact did so. However, as it amounted to what might be deemed personal advertising, Rose had to decline an invitation to appear on a television programme called 'At Home' which televised the homes of famous personalities and had previously broadcast programmes from the homes of the Duke of Norfolk; Lady Isobel Barnett, a well-known television personality; Field Marshall Lord Montgomery; and Mrs Pandit, the High Commissioner for India. She also declined an invitation to appear on a programme called 'Personal Call' which again involved an interview at the personality's home. Other participants on the programme included Graham Sutherland, the famous artist; Hermione Gingold, an actress; and Sir Alan Herbert, a well-known author. Rose was also asked to appear on a popular programme of the time called 'Brains' Trust', but it is not believed that she did so.

Apart from requests for personal appearances, Rose's success inspired a popular television programme. Ernest Dudley was a well-known playwright, author and writer for television and radio. His most popular TV series was called 'Judge for Yourself'. It was one of the earliest viewer-participation shows, in which after a half-hour 'trial', viewers were invited by Dudley to send in their verdicts, 'Guilty' or 'Not guilty'. His catch-phrase, spoken to camera at the end, was always 'Remember—you are the judge'. In 1955 he introduced for the first time a woman Queen's Counsel to his series. The actress who played the part, Hannah Watt, as part of her preparation for the role, went to the old Bailey to listen to Rose in the Jack Spot case.

The following year the film star, Anna Neagle (later Dame) was to play a female QC in the film to be released in 1958 'The Man Who Wouldn't Talk'. Spotted by a *News of the World* journalist soaking in the atmosphere of the Old Bailey, she declared that she was longing to meet Rose and that a friend was trying to arrange such a meeting.

'Judge for Yourself' was not the only television programme modelled on Rose's career. Several years later, in September 1969 Margaret Lockwood, a well-known British actress, stage and film star, starred in 'Justice is a Woman', a courtroom drama produced by Peter Willes for Yorkshire TV. She played Julia Stanford, a woman barrister. This inspired Yorkshire Television to create a new fictional series starting in 1971 called 'Justice' which ran for three series. Margaret Lockwood played Harriet Peterson, a female barrister from the Northern Circuit who aspired to becoming a Queen's Counsel and in the last series did so. It was always assumed that the character was based on Rose, Margaret Lockwood sharing Rose's dark hair and good looks. The indirect attribution seems to have been the inclusion of the part for a scatter-brained secretary called Rosie.

But perhaps Rose's most famous television 'moment' was a reference to her in 1957 by the late and great comedian, Tony Hancock, in his highly successful show 'Hancock's Half Hour'. The scene in the sketch called 'The Lawyer' was a discussion between Tony Hancock, playing a barrister, and his Head of Chambers. The latter was complaining about Hancock's dreadful performance in his recent criminal trials including the occasion when he went to court 'drunk and spent the entire afternoon trying to sit on Rose Heilbron's knee!'

REQUESTS FOR PHOTOGRAPHS

There were the first of many requests for photographs from the serious to the frivolous. They ranged from requests for photographs of Rose in a bathing suit, to a photograph to go in the magazine *Girl*, to a photographic portraiture as a mother and daughter 'conversation piece' by Madame Yevonde, a well-known and respected portrait photographer of the time, to retain as a stock photograph for the *Illustrated Press*. The 'Tail-Wagger Magazine' even asked for a photograph of her and her favourite pet—'a budgerigar would do'—the letter said! However, when *Men Only* wrote to her, they refrained from asking for a photograph and confined their request to an interview! It was nonetheless declined. While Rose was widely photographed in her court dress, such as each year at the opening of the legal year in October or in a business suit and hat when entering or leaving court, save for the occasional photograph at a function, photographs of her in the public domain in 'home guise' were non-existent. This was what the press were after—a new angle, but this was what was forbidden under the Bar's professional rules. Thus all requests for photographs were politely refused by typed letter which Rose would have dictated to her secretary or written out first in longhand.

There is, however, no shortage of photographs of Rose, for over the years the family acquired a large collection, many taken by Hilary, but these were not for publication. Rose's own hobby, developing around this time, when Hilary was small, was not still photography on which she relied on others, but cine photography and some 70,000 ft of 16mm cine film was shot by Rose during her lifetime with cameras of increasing sophistication leaving a lovely memory of family life. Although the family would watch these films when Hilary was a child, some of the later ones were not even opened after their return from processing until Hilary had them all reduced to DVD after Rose had passed away. Nonetheless it was in time for Nat to see some of them before he died which he enjoyed, commenting when he saw Hilary running around the garden aged two, that he did not realise that she was 'such a lively little thing'.

OTHER ACTIVITIES

Rose remained in demand as a speaker and was invited to many glittering functions, both locally and nationally. She opened garden parties. She spoke at University functions, to Rotary Clubs, groups of women, a variety of charitable events and many others. She returned to her themes on women and to the prejudice they suffered in the law, such as where a woman is injured in a car driven by her husband she could not sue him for damages. She spoke commemorating the centenary of the birth of Margaret Ashton, an English suffragist and first woman City Councillor for Manchester. She addressed the difficulties facing women combining a profession and a family and recognised the need for reform long before the days of maternity leave and re-training programmes:

> Of course that isn't to say that a woman cannot combine the running of a home and the care of a family with a professional career. But in certain circumstances she may require extra help at home, but this can be provided for out of the extra income which her work brings into the family fund. These handicaps sometimes face the professional woman and one is left with the position that it is wasteful not only to the woman

herself, but also to the community, that a woman, who takes the time and trouble, and whose family incur the expense of having her fully trained and qualified for the professions ... should probably on marriage and certainly on the advent of a family, have to relinquish her outside occupation.

For it is difficult, and in some cases impossible, for a woman to continue a career in such cases. Little attention however has as yet been paid to the fact that when her children grow up they release for the community a skilled and trained woman, who after a busy life tending her home and children and still in her prime, will probably find that she is unable for many reasons to take up the threads of her original career.

If, for instance, at the Bar a woman were to leave that profession and then say in 10 years to come back, she would find it difficult, if not impossible, to gain another foot-hold. That must nearly always be the position in those occupations where a person builds up a personal practice. It may not be the same in occupations where she can join with a group of other members already established ...

For a woman who returns to professional life after an interval provided she has kept in touch with the recent trends and developments in her own sphere of work, can bring to bear a maturity of judgement and an experience of life which must be invaluable. This problem of the woman returning after an interval can and should be tackled. It will become of added importance with the increase of trained women.

The following year she was invited to undertake a paid lecture tour of the United States by the 'Manager of the World's Most Celebrated Lecturers' on whose books were also Randolph Churchill and Alistair Cooke. Again she had to decline.

Together with Nat she attended several Jewish functions including, in May 1956, the Tercentenary Council's banquet at the Guildhall to commemorate the 300th anniversary of the resettlement of the Jews in the British Isles in the presence of HRH the Duke of Edinburgh; the then Prime Minister, Sir Anthony Eden; and the Chief Rabbi, Israel Brodie.

Rose went to the Regency Ball in October 1956 where she was presented to the Duchess of Gloucester with whom she had a long chat. In November 1956 she attended a masque and revel, 'The Prince of Purpoole III', at Gray's Inn which had originally been performed in Gray's Inn in 1594. The Treasurer of Gray's Inn at the time was Sir Leonard Stone. It was his flat in Gray's Inn many years later where Rose and Nat were to spend the last chapter of their lives. She attended a dinner at the Forum Club in Belgravia in the presence of Princess Marie Louise, then President of the Forum Club, one of two women's clubs where Rose stayed when in London.

Rose had been invited, along with other famous women of the time, to the very first Women of the Year Luncheon held on 29 September 1955. It was the brainchild of the Marchioness of Lothian in aid of the Greater London Fund for the Blind. But the novelty of the first year's invitation was eclipsed the second year, 1956, by the 'Sabrina' factor. Sabrina, born Norma Sykes, was an internationally famous star of the time with a voluptuous hourglass figure who moved from being a 'dumb blonde', whose ample bosom became the butt of many jokes, to acting and appearing in shows. Rose was originally billed to speak alongside Sabrina and Rose's friend, Dame Edith Evans. In the end neither Rose nor Sabrina spoke, the former, according to the *Evening Express*, because professional etiquette debarred a member of the legal profession from figuring in a programme which included a 'spotlight personality like Sabrina'.

AND ...

Despite all the fame, the lingering question remained—would Rose become the first female judge in England? In September 1955, an article appeared in *The Daily Telegraph* under the heading 'The Woman Who Might Be A Judge', commenting:

> It is said that Rose Heilbron might in due course be Britain's first woman judge ... Rose Heilbron would have been distinctive in any age—in this she is a phenomenon ... Many adjectives have been applied to judges ... but if Rose Heilbron is made a judge it will be the first time that 'charming' will be appropriate.

The catalyst was an occasion in September 1956 when Neville Laski QC, previously Recorder of Burnley, was appointed Recorder of the newly opened Liverpool Crown Court at St George's Hall, described as the first Old Bailey of the North. There was thus a vacancy for a new Recorder. Rose had recently made an application to be a Recorder, but as Hartley Shawcross said in his letter to Rose in September 1956:

> I will certainly do what I can to support your application. I have no doubt that the difficulty lies only in the question of your sex and I am not sure whether the present Lord Chancellor [the Conservative Lord Kilmuir] will feel able to depart from precedent in this regard, although someone someday will have to make the departure.

Although over 35 years had passed since the bar to women entering the professions had been removed by statute, in 1956 there were still only 64 practising women barristers including Rose, the sole female QC, representing only 3.2 per cent of the independent Bar. Would Rose, despite these discouraging statistics and the negative attitude towards women in the profession referred to by Hartley Shawcross, himself a loyal supporter of Rose throughout her career, break another barrier and become the first female judge? It was far from certain.

15

First Woman Recorder and a Trip to Benin

ROSE MADE RECORDER OF BURNLEY

ON MONDAY 26 November 1956 it was announced that Rose was to become Recorder of Burnley and England's first woman senior judge. It was an historical moment in the 800-year history of the English judiciary.

The same day the then Lord Chief Justice, Lord Goddard, wrote to Rose:

Dear Miss Heilbron,

I am not sure that I agree with ... the 'Miss', for the tradition of the Bench and Bar is that the former address the latter without prefix! But this will not make me hesitate in sending you warm congratulations on establishing a precedent—and our law depends on precedents. And I am sure the administration of the law in Burnley is in safe hands ... On the Bench we address each other as 'Brother' and I believe the construction of the Interpretation Act would be that Brother includes Sister. But some day I think it may have to be decided if it is 'my Brother ... or my Sister'. Not I fear in my time for I am very old and retire soon, very soon I suppose make way for another, but I keep in my memory a defence at the Old Bailey against an Attorney General, in which with every temptation to introduce politics not a foot was put wrong [the Dockers' case].

If an old man's good wishes are of any value you have them.

Goddard.

Rose treasured this letter from the Lord Chief Justice of England, as she did his earlier letter to her following the Dockers' case, and she framed them and had them on view.

What followed her appointment as the first female senior judge in England can only be described as an avalanche of publicity nationally and internationally. Rose had broken through another barrier for women and there were more such achievements to come. Being the first woman to break through the barriers in a male-dominated profession steeped in traditional attitudes, as Rose was so often to do in her career, was a remarkable achievement at the time. She repeatedly made legal history. She led where others followed.

Although, in 1945 Sybil Campbell had become the first female stipendiary magistrate at Tower Bridge Magistrates Court, a full time appointment as a professional judge, a position she retained until 1961, Rose's appointment was hailed as being the first female judge. This was no doubt because the magistracy is different from the rest of the judiciary and regulated by its own legislation. Magistrates deal with smaller cases, have more restricted powers of punishment and neither lay nor stipendiary magistrates wear court robes or judicial wigs. It was this last reason which no doubt was what caught the public attention when they saw Rose in her wig.

Her success also heralded a new dawn for women generally. 'After Recorders Let us have Women Brokers' exclaimed the *Daily Express* 'Another Male Bastion Falls'. The Editorial in the *Evening News* on 28 November, under the heading 'Madam Recorder', stated:

> The elevation of a distinguished QC to the Bench is naturally a matter of private congratulations among his friends and perhaps some discreet commemorative celebration in the Hall of his Inn; but it is not often the occasion of widespread popular comment. The appointment of a new Recorder of Burnley is, however, in a different category. For the new judge … is Miss Rose Heilbron QC, the first woman to achieve this particular eminence. When the necessary decision has been made as to how she should be addressed … it should be possible to ponder the wider implications of this interesting appointment.

> It is interesting not only in respect of Miss Heilbron's very remarkable qualities of character and achievement but because it is something large sections of the public in this generation have come to take for granted. Miss Heilbron is the first but there are bound to be others. The tradition of the great profession to which Miss Heilbron belongs have not been shattered, but on the contrary strengthened, by women's entry into it. They have, as outstanding individuals, made their mark.

> It is so too in many other fields of public life and service which they have entered: the outstanding individual has triumphed and earned, as of right and not on sufferance, high position, reputation and respect.

> Examples are not difficult to cite … For women like these their careers are part of that fuller life which the long struggle for 'emancipation' won for all women. Because we take it for granted nowadays we should never forget how it was achieved.

Cartoonists had a field day:

> A female judge is shown in a full bottomed wig leaning over from the bench exclaiming: 'I washed it this morning and I can't do a thing with it!' (*News Chronicle*).

> Two judges are standing in judicial robes talking to each other holding up a paper which reads: 'Miss Rose Heilbron QC Madam, M'lady, Your Worship'.

> The question of how she was to be addressed was a hot topic of debate at the time and led to a caption based on Shakespeare: 'Personally—Rose by any other name is just as sweet'. (*Liverpool Evening Express*).

> A defendant is pictured preening himself and combing his hair outside court when the policeman says 'Relax, Romeo. It's not M'Lady, it's M'Lud'. (*Evening News*)

> Two old lags are shown looking at a bill-board which read 'Miss Heilbron: will she be addressed as madam, m'lady or your ladyship?' The caption proclaimed: 'I called her "Ducks" and copped three more months for contempt'. (*Daily Express*)

> An old lag holding a bunch of flowers is depicted being held by a police-man in an arm grip as he walks along the street. 'Yes Miss Heilbron is judging your case' answers the policeman ... why?'

Congratulations came from far and wide. Literally hundreds of telegrams and letters were sent from family, friends, some of whom she had not seen for many years, colleagues, members of the Jewish community, various women's and other associations and admirers, both those she knew and complete strangers. Some letters were simply addressed to Rose Heilbron, London, England, but they reached her. Many commented that the next step would be the High Court Bench. At the time of the announcement Rose was representing GI Freeman Reese at Staffordshire Assizes and away from home. 'We are very proud of you and send our congratulations and love. Daddy and Hilary' was the telegram sent by Nat to his wife. Someone wrote her a poem. The *Women's Sunday Mirror* sent her two dozen red roses.

Lady Sefton wrote on behalf of herself and Lord Sefton: 'Everyone I've talked to in Liverpool is very proud of you and pleased about it'. Her cousin wrote: 'Congratulations on becoming Recorder—you are the talk of London'. A Martin Rosenhead wrote:

> A very junior student at Gray's Inn writes to you to add his name to the myriad of acquaintances who must have flooded your home with congratulatory messages. I hope that you will accept my warm

congratulations among the rest. I know in my bones that when I am become old ... and wise, the flock of grandchildren at my knee will revere me for one thing—that in my youth I served tea and sandwiches to Rose Heilbron in my parents' lounge. And I shall pat them upon the head, and know they were right!

The National President of the National Federation of Business and Professional Women's Clubs of Great Britain and Northern Ireland, Mrs Margaret Thompson wrote:

> Not only is your appointment as the first woman Recorder a milestone on the long road for women towards full citizenship and equal status, but your own success and integrity as a barrister and QC have done even more to dissipate prejudice against women in public life, and to reassure the doubters who thought that women were unfitted for a legal career.

Mr Justice (Jimmy) Cassels wrote, as 'an old friend', giving her two pages of detailed and useful advice on how to deal with cases as a judge.

Rose's good friend Lord Donovan said:

> Yours is a unique achievement and I congratulate you upon it. I congratulate Burnley even more ... If ever I am there again I shall stop and make enquiries: for brains <u>and</u> beauty upon the Bench is also unique and too good a thing to miss ... My love to you, Terence.

But perhaps the most poignant comment was from her old friend and fellow barrister, Eileen MacDonald, who said: 'And in the midst of all the honour and glory, one of the most endearing qualities to me is your modesty. How you manage to retain it, is to me a source of never failing wonder'. Yet the comment rang true. Rose remained always very modest about her achievements.

On 4 December 1956, Rose made her first visit to Burnley to attend the Burnley Law Debating Society's Annual Dinner where she responded to the toasts and announced that it had been decided that she would be addressed as Madam Recorder. She wore for the occasion a long, low-cut sage green dress adorned with diamante and looked very glamorous, prompting the *Manchester News Chronicle* to write:

> It was left to Miss Heilbron too, to provide an object lesson to any woman who has ever been tempted to confuse feminine with feminist. She managed to give the law due dignity without losing one iota of feminity ... She contrives to be beautiful and brilliant—and intelligent enough not to use her intelligence as a battering ram.

This was an accurate summary, for Rose was a great supporter of women in every way: yet she was never what one would call a strident feminist. She believed that women's time would come. She recognised that women would have to wait longer than men at times in order to succeed. She believed in the work ethos and the fact that women by their own ability would in due course succeed. Yet she also acknowledged the importance of homemakers. These were the days before sex equality laws, maternity leave, quotas and targets. Women just got on with the job.

Burnley is a Lancashire market town, about an hour and a half's drive from Liverpool. It dates back to Anglo-Saxon times when a settlement was established on the banks of the River Brun in the area around where St Peter's Parish Church is now located. It was from the Brun that Burnley got its name, derived from Brun Lea, 'the field near the Brun'. The industrial revolution of the nineteenth century saw its population rapidly increase as people moved into the area for the jobs in the mills, coal mines and foundries. By the late nineteenth century Burnley was producing more cotton cloth per year than any other town in the world and making more looms than any other place in the country. By the time Rose became its Recorder the cotton industry had long since ceased to be a dominant force, but it remained a thriving town with, at the time, a very successful football team. It boasts Towneley Hall, a historic house dating back to mediaeval times, but now an art gallery and museum, whose magnificent banqueting hall is where King James I knighted a loin of beef 'Sir Loin', nowadays a familiar cut of beef. Over the years Rose and Nat developed many friendships with the people in Burnley.

1956 ended on a high note for Rose. *The Daily Mirror* nominated her its 'Woman of the Year' and many other newspapers included her in their lists of women of the year alongside other prominent names, including one list where she shared a stage with among others, Grace Kelly, Marilyn Monroe and Margot Fonteyn. William Hickey of the *Daily Express* wrote that she should be made a Dame in the New Year Honours List. Her fan mail continued and on 23 December she received her second anonymous letter in turquoise ink addressed to 'My pin-up'.

Because sitting as a part-time judge had to be fitted around her practice, Rose would usually go to Burnley during legal vacations. As Quarter Sessions tended to coincide with school holidays, in later years Hilary would sometimes accompany her mother, sitting discreetly in the well of the court. Hilary would watch mesmerised as each case was called and the evidence given. She would then listen to her mother sum up the case and await the verdict of the jury. On one occasion she had to duck as the defendant threw the Bible at the person administering the oath and Rose sent him down to the cells 'to cool off'. On another occasion Hilary was given a tour of the police offices and had her fingerprints taken, a memento retained— happily unused!—to this day. These visits to Burnley were one of the factors which sparked Hilary's own interest in the profession of the law, although she eventually took up practice in a different area of the law.

THE OATHS OF OFFICE

On Sunday 6 January 1957, Rose and Nat travelled up to Burnley and stayed at the Thorn Hotel. The Mayor had invited Hilary, but having only turned eight the week before, Rose considered that she was too young. The following morning Rose was picked up by car at 9.55am. She wore for the occasion a mushroom coat with a fur collar and a brown and white hat. She was met in a private room in the Court House at 10.10am by the lady Mayor and Clerk of the Peace. In civic constitutional order, the Recorder came second after the Mayor. She then met the magistrates and said a few words to them. At 10.30am, wearing full ceremonial robes, including her full-bottomed wig, and accompanied by the Mayor, she processed to a packed court, people having queued to get in. Many of her friends from the Northern Circuit were there including Eileen MacDonald. Sitting with her on the Bench that morning were the Mayor, other dignitaries and Nat. She read and signed the Oath of Allegiance and Judicial Oath and made the Declarations required by statute.

The Mayor then gave an address of welcome to the new Recorder on behalf of the Town Council and the Citizens of Burnley. This was followed by addresses given by Mr C E Goolden on behalf of the Bar, Mr Slater on behalf of the Burnley District Incorporated Law Society and finally, Mr Thornley, the Clerk of the Peace, on his own behalf and on behalf of the Officials. The new Recorder replied, her speech having been written out in longhand:

> I am greatly indebted to her Worship the Mayor for her gracious and charming words of welcome. I am most grateful for all your very kind and generous tributes. Conscious as I am of the great responsibility which devolves upon me, aware of the high traditions of the office of

Recorder, it is gratifying for me to know that I will continue to have in my work, that cooperation which traditionally exists between Bench and Bar and which in large measure is responsible for the maintenance of those high standards of justice for which this Court has always been known.

I am particularly pleased that the happy and agreeable relationship that has always existed not only between the solicitors' branch of the profession and the court, but also between the Town Officials, the Court Officials and the Bench shall continue, for they are an important factor in the maintenance of the best traditions of Law and Order.

I am not unmindful of the departure from precedent in appointing me your Recorder and for this reason particularly I am more than happy to be assured in such warm terms of your continued loyalty and support.

It is especially agreeable to me that I should have been accorded this Honour in the County of my birth, to which as you may imagine I am deeply attached.

Following as I do a distinguished line of predecessors, the two most recent of whom Sir Noel Goldie and Mr Neville Laski, it is my privilege to know, I shall do my utmost to maintain the high standards they have set.

Burnley is a fine and ancient borough. It has a long and proud history and its citizens have wide and varied interests. I am glad to be a part of your Town, and I shall always endeavour to take an interest in all its activities. I am proud to be associated with Burnley and honoured to be your Recorder.

At the conclusion of the ceremony the court adjourned for five minutes before the formal business of the court began and Rose changed back into her short wig. Rose's first case as a judge concerned Granville Briggs who pleaded guilty to unlawfully wounding his wife, but the couple had since reunited. Giving him an absolute discharge she told him: 'You are being treated leniently. Don't abuse it'. There were 12 cases in her list altogether, of which 11 were guilty pleas. They were dealt with as follows: Two were sent to jail, one for 18 months for breaking, entering and stealing, one for nine months for housebreaking and larceny; one was sent to Borstal for larceny, five were given conditional discharges and two put on probation. Her next Quarter Sessions was in early April.

It was a very special day for all concerned. As the *Daily Herald* reporter explained in its article 'Gentle Justice—That's the Heilbron Way':

It was the most exciting quarter sessions Burnley has known: Because the Recorder was a pretty woman; because barristers stumbled over the new address; because all Burnley turned up to see what was going on. A pushing curious crowd strained to find seats in the crowded courtroom: in the public gallery were women shoppers who had brought out their best hats for the occasion; in the Press seats were 16 men on a bench made for six.

Policemen guarding the doors told the Press that there was no room left; told the jurors to push their way through. They even told one of the prisoners to go away, but he obligingly persisted in establishing his identity and they let him through. The prisoners, indeed, were nearly overlooked. They were the men with the walking-on parts in a cast that had bigger stars.

Worldwide publicity followed. Articles appeared for instance in the *New York Times* 'Woman is Chief Judge of Textile town'; the *Adelaide Advertising*, South Australia; the *Christchurch Star Sun*, New Zealand; the *Otago Daily Times*, New Zealand; the *Malay Mail*, Kuala Lumpur; the *Buenos Aires Herald*, Argentina; the *South China Daily Post*, Hong Kong; the *Ceylon Daily News*, Colombo; the *Times of Ceylon*, Colombo; the *Nagpur Times*, Central India; the *Iraq Times*, Bagdad; the *Indian Express*, Madras; the *Mombasa Times*, Kenya which exclaimed 'Mother Makes Legal History'; and the *Dublin Evening News*, as well as in many national and local newspapers in Britain.

Yet, as usual, Rose remained humbled by it all and at lunch with the Mayor said that 'there is a novelty in my position which causes undue interest and excitement. I hope it will die down soon'. She had her practice to run and there were domestic issues to attend to alongside her professional job—the dual role so often referred to. Her energy seems remarkable, for she was no dilettante and everything she did was thoroughly considered and researched, whether it was a professional matter or otherwise.

THE CELEBRATIONS CONTINUE

The fallout from Rose's judicial promotion continued through 1957. In March of that year 25 women MPs of all parties held a dinner in her honour at the House of Commons to mark her appointment as the first woman Recorder, presided over by Dame Florence Horsborough. In the same month, the Forum Club also gave a dinner in her honour. In her speech Rose said:

> The distinction of my appointment is merely its novelty, but the achievement of which I am most proud is the demonstration that women can, given equal opportunities, compete on equal terms with men in the professions as well as other types of work.

The following month the Jewish Representative Council of Liverpool also held a reception in her honour to mark her appointment as Recorder. In her speech she said:

> Discrimination against women is still marked. If my appointment has done just a little towards easing the path of those who now and in the future—who feel they would like to order their own existence and fulfil their own destinies, then I am content ... the Bar is indeed a hard task-master. One requires patience, physical stamina, hard-work, confidence and above all a deep and abiding regard for the law.

At the end of May Rose was invited to speak at the jubilee celebrations of the British Federation of University Women, whose patron was Nancy Astor, who had been the first woman Member of Parliament, in the presence of the Queen Mother and Princess Royal. It was held at the Senate House of the University of London. Rose was presented for the first time to both the Queen Mother and the Princess Royal. This was followed by an evening reception. She wrote out in longhand the detailed instructions she had been given as to what to do in the presence of royalty including: 'Don't cross legs' and 'dark suit or dress and white gloves ... White tie for evening'.

In her speech Rose surveyed a momentous 50 years, in which she traced the influence of women in the changed structure of the Social Welfare State as not the least of feminine contributions to history. Men, she suggested, take more interest in and have more knowledge of the running of a home than they did. She added:

> Never in World History had there been such a half century of change, through the pattern of which can nevertheless be clearly discerned the steady advancement of women from partial subjugation to almost total equality; from a position in which they had recently emerged from being virtually their husbands' chattels, in which they were acquiring advanced education, with difficulty prevented from entering the occupation of their choice, lacking the franchise, from all of this, to almost complete emancipation.

A month later she attended another function in the presence of the Queen Mother when she was invited to a luncheon given by the Lord and Lady Mayoress at Liverpool Town Hall in honour of the visit of the Queen Mother to mark the 750th anniversary of the granting of King John's Charter to Liverpool in 1207. There were many other invitations too.

Some invitations Rose was forced to decline because of reasons of professional etiquette. In February she received a telegram from

Christina Foyle inviting her to be the guest of honour and propose the toast of Monsieur Christian Dior at a luncheon in his honour at the Dorchester hotel to mark the publication of his autobiography. Other guests included the French Ambassador and distinguished women from many different walks of life. Rose must have been rather disappointed not to have been able to attend as she always loved glamorous gowns and fashion.

Throughout her life Rose always had a dressmaker of varying skills. In the early 1950s, a Miss Brennan in Dublin, a couture-standard dressmaker, introduced by Nat's sister, Stella, made her some fabulous beaded long evening gowns and cocktail dresses. Miss Brennan used materials purchased from Europe at a time when, so soon after the War, the selection of dress material in England was limited. Rose would have fittings for clothes when she went to Dublin on family visits to stay with Stella and her family, and the finished garments were then posted to her home in Liverpool. The surviving dresses have now acquired the soubriquet 'vintage'. Having clothes made had several advantages: it saved Rose time, it meant that she could have something distinctive which would not be worn by anyone else, it was cheaper and it enabled her to get exactly what she wanted, particularly in later years when the range of dress fabric on offer increased.

Rose also had a milliner in Chester. She was a friend and from time to time Rose and Hilary would make a trip to Chester on a Saturday to purchase a new creation while Nat was playing golf. This did not stop Rose shopping elsewhere and other outfits were purchased in Liverpool, Southport and, in later years, in London. She wore clothes well, accentuated by her narrow waist and beautiful face. Had she been able to afford it a Christian Dior outfit would have looked wonderful on her.

In July 1957 the American Bar Association organised its first convention in London with 2,000 American lawyers, including a large number of women lawyers. On 22 July Rose attended a dinner at the House of Commons for the American Association of Women lawyers who were attending the ABA conference and whose retiring president, Mrs Neva Talley, lived in Little Rock, Arkansas. Rose, together with five other eminent women, were given the keys to Little Rock and a parchment stating they 'shall hold a place of high esteem in the minds and hearts of the people'.

While Little Rock is nowadays more readily associated with President and Hillary Clinton, the former coincidentally sharing a birthday with Rose, some two months after this event, in September 1957, it acquired a much more infamous reputation. Three years earlier the historic decision of the Supreme Court of the United States in 1954 of *Brown v Board of Education* had declared all laws establishing segregated schools unconstitutional. However, the Governor of Arkansas sent in armed troops to bar nine students from attending white schools in Little Rock causing widespread protests and condemnation worldwide. This left the recipients of the freedom of the town, including Rose, in a rather embarrassing position, but there was little they could do. The tiny key, made of silver and inscribed on blue enamel, exists to this day.

On Wednesday 24 July, Rose chaired a luncheon at the Lancaster Room in the Savoy Hotel given by the American Adjustment Board (an organisation to help forward the economic and political status of women) to honour the American women lawyers visiting for the ABA Convention. She proposed the toast of the Queen and that of the guests was proposed by The Right Hon Sir Norman Birkett. An address was also given by Lady Colville DCVO, DBE, JP, President of the American Adjustment Board and Woman of the Bedchamber to the Queen Mother.

A CASE IN BENIN, NIGERIA

It was a rushed day. Rose had to catch the afternoon BOAC flight to Lagos, Nigeria. She was to represent James Moru Egbuson, a senior police superintendent, at the Benin High Court at Benin Assizes in the city of Benin in what is today southern Nigeria (previously the Kingdom of Benin). He had been charged with corruption. The prosecution case was that any constable who wanted to be posted to the Urban Motor Traffic Unit had to pay monies, ie bribes, to James Egbuson and the only way a constable could fund such bribes was to find fault with motorists and in turn get money from them. The defence was that the charges were concocted.

Rose was instructed by a London firm of solicitors, John Morris, Wilkes & Co. Her team included five juniors from the Nigerian Bar. Mr NG Hay QC, the Attorney General of Western Nigeria, prosecuted. Rose's brief fee was 800 guineas which in those days was a huge fee. The judge was Mr Justice WAH Druffus. There was no jury and the court sat from 9 am to 5 pm each day.

The story of that day and what followed can now be taken up in Rose's own words. The following day, which happened to be Nat's 52nd birthday, she wrote the first of her daily letters home:

Yesterday, [Wednesday] was simply hectic ... I had my fitting and the uniform is lovely [see below] ... Then I rushed back to the hotel and completed my packing ... Then with Lady Colville I received nearly 300 guests including two Ambassadors ... I was given a lovely horseshoe with roses which I have kept. Then there was the luncheon ... There I sat in the Chair between the Indian Ambassador and the Nepalese Ambassador with many titled and distinguished guests and I had to run the show! ... My speech ... was ... short but I think suitable and Sir Norman [Birkett] went out of his way to congratulate me. Then he spoke for so long that I was getting the gitters. I was due to leave the Savoy at 2.30pm.

She did catch her flight and appeared to enjoy her first long-haul plane journey. It was by Stratocruiser. She travelled first class and commented on the excellent food and the cocktail bar downstairs. The plane touched down at Rome and Kano to re-fuel. She was met at Lagos by a crowd of press and the Chief of the West African Airways.

Her accommodation both in Lagos and Benin was a matter of chance. A week or so before Rose's trip, she and Nat had been invited by their old friends, Vernon and Peggy Sangster of Vernons Pools, to their son's, the late Robert Sangster's, 21st birthday party. Robert Sangster was later to become a famous racehorse owner and breeder. At the party, Nobby Roberts, an orthopaedic surgeon who was a friend, noticed the plaster on Rose's arm which she explained was from a vaccination she had had in preparation for her trip to Nigeria. This led to him introducing her to the chairman of a shipping line, a Mr Gates. Mr Gates then arranged for Rose to stay with the Holts in Lagos where she had the luxury of air conditioning and eight servants and then in Benin with the local bank manager and his wife, the Meadows, who also looked after her marvellously. Her solicitor, John Morris, was not so lucky and he rang Rose from his hotel in Benin, the Catering Rest Centre, to see if she could help as he had terrible accommodation and he was then put up with someone else from the Bank.

The next day she was sworn in at the High Court in Lagos, the ceremony taking about an hour. Afterwards her hosts drove her around Lagos, which she found very primitive. She then flew to Benin, the oldest city in Nigeria and the home of the famous Benin bronzes. She was the first white barrister ever to have set foot in Benin. On the Sunday morning she began working on the case with her juniors and in the afternoon was given a tour of the city. She noted the dreadful conditions in which people lived, the open sewers and the dirt everywhere with children wearing no clothes, and commented on the tremendous poverty.

In her letter of Monday 29 July, Rose writing to Nat from her bed lying under a mosquito net and with a fan whirling in the ceiling, recorded:

> This morning the case started. We pushed ourselves through crowds ... all staring into the court house. It is a nice building (different from most here which are mud shacks with straw roofs) with glass in the windows. The Court room is very large but it gets hot as the sun rises, though it is amazing how you get used to it.

She remarked that she was now armed with a flit gun and as the days passed she became more proficient at 'flitting' the mosquitoes.

The case took longer than expected and the following week Rose was clearly getting homesick. She wrote that she was fed up 'with flitting mosquitoes and insects' and anxious to get home and, although the Meadows' house was very comfortable, it was clear that the novelty had worn off. She remarked that all the water had to be boiled and filtered and there was no fresh milk and the precautions were 'a blessed nuisance'. As for the case, she commented that all the men had four wives and about 20 children, probably a slight exaggeration, although her own client had two wives and a girl-friend and nine children. She noted that the witnesses against her client were dreadful liars. She added: 'I am having to talk "Pidgin" English to the witnesses', which must have been a bit of a strain.

Despite her despondency at having to stay longer than antici-pated in Benin, the case was going well. She began her final address to the judge thus:

> I shall address your Lordship at some length, but in the course of prepar-ing my address it occurred to me that the witnesses for the prosecution were so completely discredited that it is really with the greatest respect and with the utmost sincerity that it is inconceivable that anyone, let alone a man with Mr Egbuson's record and position, could be convicted. I have found it impossible, as no doubt your lordship has, in reconciling the witnesses' accounts or to see what the prosecution's case is.

The case had lasted eight days and the defendant was acquitted on all charges.

Home life was never far from Rose's thoughts and she sent details of how to pickle brisket for salt beef, a Jewish family recipe, so that the cook could prepare it in her absence. She also asked Nat to arrange for her post to be sent to her solicitor's wife who was meeting them at the airport so she could read her mail on the train home to Liverpool. There were no e-mails or even faxes in those days.

She made an impression in Nigeria, for not only was she to return the following year for a case in Lagos, but some years later on 21 November 1962 a Nigerian law student studying at Holborn College of Law and a member of Middle Temple and also an MP in Western Nigeria wrote to her saying that:

> I got my inspiration to study law since I watched you defend Mr Egbuson, a police officer, in Benin City in Nigeria years ago. Since then, you have been a legal hero I have worshipped and I have since then on that account decided to study law some day.

He said he wanted to find out when she was appearing so he could come and listen to her.

As for James Egbuson, he continued to send Rose Christmas cards for several years. He left the Police Force a few years later following his failure to be promoted. He hoped to get a job in New State which was to be split from Yoruba West to augment his meagre pension.

HONORARY COLONEL OF THE WRAC

The uniform for which Rose had a fitting en route to Nigeria was following her appointment as the first Honorary Colonel of the 320 Battalion (East Lancs) of the Women's Royal Army Corps (WRAC) (Territorial Army). It comprised a splendid bottle green jacket and skirt, approximately 14 inches off the ground to comply with Army regulations, all lined in red with brass buttons and a matching gold braided cap. The unit had been formed in 1947 as a General Duty Battalion. The Unit Headquarters was located in Salford with Company Headquarters at Salford, Eccles & Blackburn. The unit covered a wide area in East Lancashire and Platoons were situated in Drill Halls in most East Lancashire towns. Trades and employments of those in the Territorial Army or TA were varied and women were trained as drivers, cooks, clerks, orderlies, storewomen and pay clerks.

Rose took the salute at her first parade at Wellington Barracks, Bury on Saturday, September 1957. 'Colonel Rose on Parade' was one of the headlines (*Northern Daily Telegraph*). So excellent was her salute after one brief lesson that an experienced drill sergeant remarked: 'I wish my recruits picked up drill as quickly as that'.

Her notes on the plan given to her for her first parade state, some-what obviously: 'Whenever saluted—return it' and 'probably very little time between two salutes'. She was also provided with detailed instructions of what was going to happen. She had wanted to take Hilary along. Unfortunately she had flu, but accompanied her mother the next time she took the salute.

MEDICAL EXPERTISE

Although now both a part-time judge and an Honorary Colonel, Rose still had a practice to maintain and while the murder and criminal trials caught the limelight, Rose increasingly preferred the civil side of her practice and the legal issues that it threw up. She was in court almost every day during Liverpool Assizes and trav-elled round the country to other Assizes paying the fee required to appear on another Circuit. She appeared once more in the House of Lords in the case of *Bryers* which she had won in the Court of Appeal the previous year, and succeeded in having the appeal dismissed.[1] She travelled regularly to London for trials, appeals, and functions enduring a train journey of at least four and a half hours each way, but always with the pleasure of having Nat waiting at Lime Street station to meet her.

She was also establishing some expertise in the medical negligence and medical disciplinary arena and was often instructed by Peter Baylis of Hempsons, the solicitors to the Medical Defence Union. Today such general practices are rare and medical negligence has become a legal speciality in itself, but in Rose's day, barristers took what came their way. Moreover, Medical Defence Union work was paid, whereas legal aid provided only a very modest income.

In March she represented Dr Katharina Dalton in a disciplinary appeal hearing before the General Medical Council (GMC) on charges of oversubscribing expensive hormone drugs for the treat-ment of patients with pre-menstrual syndrome. Dr Dalton was one of the authors of what the board described as the first important paper on the subject in England. The Middlesex Local Medical Committee had found the case not proved, but the Minister of Health appealed.

---

[1] *Canadian Pacific Steamships Ltd v Bryers* [1958] AC 485.

The issue seems to have been whether she should have prescribed less expensive drugs. Having examined her method of prescribing, including a trial with less expensive drugs, the members of the GMC acknowledged that since medicinal art is largely experimental, the efficacy of a remedy had some bearing on the reasonableness of its cost. Nonetheless they were satisfied that the cost incurred in this case was reasonably necessary for the treatment of the patients. They recognised that women would tend to gravitate to Dr Dalton because of her expertise.

In the last week of October Rose represented a surgeon, Mr Segar, one of the defendants accused of negligence arising about of a misdiagnosis of cancer, when in fact the patient did not have cancer. The hearing was in London before Mr Justice Hilberry and lasted a week. Mr Segar was discharged. The Judge commented that a difference in diagnosis did not necessarily involve negligence.

The following week at the Old Bailey she defended Dr Joseph Adewunmi Ademiluyi, a General Medical Practitioner in north London, on a charge of using an instrument upon a female student with intent to procure her miscarriage for which he had been paid £50. His defence was that he had performed the operation because his patient was suffering from acute melancholia and that her mental state justified it and she paid him nothing. He was found guilty and given four years' imprisonment.

In between these two cases on Saturday 2 November, Rose attended at the Grosvenor Rooms, Grand Hotel, Birmingham, where she gave the BMA lecture 'Doctors and the Law'. Continuing this medical association, in December she delivered the annual BMA lecture to the St Pancras Division entitled: 'The Legal Responsibilities of Doctors'.

'Rose QC Seeks Drug Guard'—was the headline. She argued that three factors contributed to an increase in cases against doctors, namely: the National Health Service introduced in 1949, the changes in the law about liability of hospitals for the negligence of their staff, and legal aid. Before 1946 hospitals were voluntary, but the changes had brought about a change of attitude from the public. She continued:

> With anaesthetics, if adverse symptoms were due solely to the personal idiosyncrasy of the patient, the doctor was not liable, of course. But if the wrong drug were administered, then there was likely to be a finding of negligence against the hospital, the doctor or the nurse, or against all three. 'Is it not possible to invent some infallible system of labelling or handling over such drugs—a system which could overcome the fallibility of human nature?

MORE PROBLEMS WITH THE MEDIA

The perennial shadow of the Bar Council's Code of Conduct was constantly present, for almost everything Rose did in public appeared in the press. Following a weekly serialisation in the *Picture Post* of Rose's cases and achievements, the Bar Council received a complaint. The Secretary of the Bar Council, Mr Boulton, accordingly wrote to Rose in April saying: 'I would be glad to know whether these Articles have been or are to be published with your knowledge and approval'. The following day Rose sent a letter to the Editor of *Picture Post* explaining that she had been approached by the Treasurer of Gray's Inn and that she might have to answer to her Inn of Court about the Articles. She requested either that the newspaper stopped publishing or make it abundantly clear that she was in no way concerned with these articles or had supplied any material. The *Picture Post* apologised and opted for the latter alternative, issuing a disclaimer. The matter went before the Professional Conduct Committee of the Bar which unanimously accepted Rose's explanation.

There were two further exchanges with the Bar Council at around this time, when Rose sought permission to make broadcasts. The first concerned a request to participate in an interview for NBC to be broadcast only in the United States for which she was granted permission provided it was confined to general questions about the legal profession and that nothing in the interview should bear on her life practice or earnings at the Bar. Rose in the end decided on balance that it was better not to do it.

The second related to a broadcast on a non-legal subject which she was informed therefore did not require any consent of the Bar Council. The letter from Mr Boulton highlighted the tight restrictions that applied:

> The relevant paragraph of the Council's rulings on advertising provides that a barrister who broadcasts on a non-legal subject may do so under his own name but may not disclose his qualification as a barrister, or cause or allow it to be disclosed. I would also draw your attention to an earlier paragraph of these rulings which provides that there is no objection in general to a Silk describing himself or permitting himself to be described as a Queen's Counsel or Q.C. in conjunction with his name, but he should refrain from so doing in all cases in which the spirit of the rulings relating to advertising would otherwise be infringed. Although I think it is a matter of taste you may consequently wish to consider whether to ask for the letters 'Q.C.' to be omitted when you are introduced.

Such restrictions on advertising which Rose encountered are light years away from the position today. Barristers are now generally free to advertise, subject to not disclosing confidential client information and not acting with impropriety or otherwise acting contrary to the Bar's Code of Conduct. Most barristers' chambers have dedicated marketing personnel. Exchanging visiting cards, visits to solicitors' offices, giving interviews to the Press, participating in conferences, and posing for photographs for web-pages or brochures, are all commonplace today, but would have led to disbarment in Rose's time.

THE PROGRESS OF WOMEN

As Rose had said when addressing the British Federation of University Women and as many journalists continually wrote, women had come a long way by the end of 1957. The Lords Reform Bill in 1957 leading to the Life Peerages Act 1958 gave women the right to become peeresses. There was much talk as to who would be the first female member of the House of Lords. Rose's name would crop up regularly in various articles as a possible nominee alongside a range of other famous women of the day, from Lady Astor to Vivien Leigh to Edith Summerskill, the last of whom was in fact made a peeress in 1961. However, Rose's ambition was one day to become a High Court Judge rather than a peeress and the two were incompatible. Meanwhile, aged 43, she continued in her busy practice and remained very much in the public eye.

ROSE Q.C.—FIRST WOMAN JUDGE

Daily Mirror Reporter

MISS Rose Heilbron, Q.C., who won fame as leading counsel for the defence in murder trials, yesterday became Britain's first woman Recorder.

Daily Mirror, November 1956

Official—CALL ME MADAM

News Chronicle, 1956

Wives Queue To See Miss Heilbron Installed

A CROWD of housewives and schoolgirls waited almost two hours today to see Miss Rose Heilbron, QC, Britain's first woman Recorder, installed with traditional ceremony at the opening of Burnley Quarter Sessions, the first since her appointment in November.

Evening Telegraph, January 1957

The WOMAN who last night made legal history

THE ASTONISHING RISE OF ROSE HEILBRON

Daily Mail, 1956

MADAM RECORDER'S FIRST HISTORIC DAY

She wore a full-bottomed wig, pale make-up and a dark lip-stick

Manchester News Chronicle, 1957

'Madam Recorder' Makes History In Britain

Otago Daily Times, New Zealand, January 1957

The first woman judge

Manchester Daily Herald, 1956

"Yes, Miss Heilbron's judging your case...why?"

"I washed it this morning and I can't do a thing with it."

"Relax, Romeo. It's not M'Lady, its M'Lud!"

Billboard reads: 'Miss Heilbron: Will she be addressed as Madam, M'Lady or your Ladyship?' Caption reads: "I called her Ducks and copped three more months for contempt."

A WOMAN AT THE TOP OF A MAN'S WORLD

How Britain's first-ever woman 'judge' spent the first hours of her new life

Daily Express, 1957

Today the Mirror chooses...

THE WOMAN OF THE YEAR

Daily Mirror, 1956

Gentle justice–that's the Heilbron way

HERALD REPORTER

Daily Herald, 1957

The New York Times

TUESDAY, JANUARY 8 1957.

The Malay Mail, Wednesday, January 9, 1957.

Judge Rose is a happy wife and mother too

The Malay Mail, 1957

WOMAN JUDGE PIN-UP GIRL OF BRITISH COURTS

LONDON (A.P).—Petite and good looking, the judge came into the musty English court room like a breath of fresh air.

Morning Bulletin, Rockhampton, Australia

Woman Is Chief Judge Of British Textile Town

Associated Press, 1919
Miss Rose Heilbron

January 1957

A HUSH FELL
the COURTROOM...

FABULOUS WOMEN OF TODAY

Rose Heilbron had begun her fight to save a man from hanging

The Weekly News, September 1955

DAILY SKETCH Friday, July 3 1964

ROSE HEILBRON, QC, AND JUDGE CLASH

SUMMING-UP IS QUITE RIDICULOUS, SHE SAYS

By JAMES NICHOLSON

MISS ROSE HEILBRON, QC, was in an astonishing clash with the Isle of Man casino trial judge yesterday.

Daily Sketch, July 1964

ONE WORD
and
Rose, QC, saves killer

By Daily Mail Reporter

A MISTAKE of just one word in a law textbook—and an error in a judge's note — saved hammer-killer Joseph McCrorey from the hangman's noose.

Scottish Daily Mail, Edinburgh, July 1962

Free, he steps from the dock to embrace his mother

BOY CLEARED OF MURDERING AUNT
No thug, says Miss Heilbron

BY A "DAILY POST" REPORTER

Eighteen-year-old Daniel James John Browne stepped from the dock at Liverpool Crown Court last night and into the arms of his mother — cleared by a jury of murdering his fifty-year-old aunt.

Browne's aunt, Miss Mary Josephine Aberdeen, a nurse at Rainhow Hospital, was found murdered at Browne's home, Rossmini Road, Aberdeen, on December 31 last year.

Liverpool Daily Post, February 1965

JUDGE BARS
NO-BABY OP

Miss Justice Heilbron...who overruled a specialist

September 1975

'To reproduce is the basic human right of every woman'

By LESLIE TOULSON

A WOMAN judge yesterday barred doctors from sterilising an 11-year-old mentally handicapped girl.

Drugs Act threatens morally innocent, says QC

HEADMASTERS, hoteliers, university hostel wardens, housing managers — and even prison governors — risk prosecution for drug offences about which they know nothing, a woman QC suggested to five Law Lords yesterday.

Miss Rose Heilbron claimed in a test case that this was the effect of a High Court decision dismissing a schoolteacher's appeal against her conviction of an offence under the 1965 Dangerous Drugs Act.

The teacher was found guilty of "being concerned in the management of premises used for cannabis smoking" although the prosecution accepted that she knew nothing about it.

Miss Heilbron recalled that 24-year-old Miss Stephanie Sweet let an Oxfordshire farmhouse to students who, without her knowledge, smoked drugs there. She was convicted by the magistrates at Woodstock, Oxfordshire, in September, 1966, and fined £25.

Miss Rose Heilbron

A Queen's Bench Divisional Court held that the 1965 Act created an "absolute offence," the state of mind of the accused person being irrelevant.

Nottingham Guardian Journal 1968

July 1980

EVENING NEWS and STAR

Tuesday, July 15, 1980.   Price 10p

Upon my oath!
M'lud is a lady

Evening News, 1975

'Save rape victims from name ordeal'

VICTIMS of rape should remain anonymous, says a report out today.

A woman's sex life is her own affair says judge Rose

MRS. JUSTICE HEILBRON
Headed inquiry group

WEDNESDAY FEBRUARY 25 1987

One of the quickest legal actions in British judicial history

Lords reject father's appeal over abortion

The Times, February 1987

16

Premieres, Parades, Parklands and Practice

SOME INTERESTING INVITATIONS

1958 BEGAN MORE quietly for Rose than the previous year when she had been sworn in as Recorder of Burnley, but the last two years of the decade nonetheless brought their fair share of excitement in all areas of her life.

In 1959 Rose, a doyenne of defending murderers, was asked to consider murder from a wholly different angle. She was invited by the Chairman of Columbia Pictures Corporation Ltd to the film premiere of 'Anatomy of a Murder' held on 1 October 1959 at the Columbia Theatre, Shaftesbury Avenue and afterwards to a party at Claridge's in honour of Otto Preminger, the producer-director of the film. The film starred Lee Remmick and George C Scott with music by Duke Ellington. Rose wore one of Miss Brennan's creations, a three-quarter-length royal blue flowered dress which she had nicknamed her 'underwater dress', because the colours resembled the colours of the barrier reef. The party was attended by a glittering array of famous people including: Sir Mortimer Wheeler, Earl and Countess of Harewood, George Sanders, Otto Preminger, Mr and Mrs Lewin (Editor of the *Daily Express*), Sir Bernard and Lady Docker, and several judges.

She also met Ed Murrow. He has more recently returned to our screens, played by David Strathairn, in George Clooney's acclaimed film 'Good Night and Good Luck'. In 1959 Ed Murrow was at the height of his fame. He was America's foremost exponent of the television interview, interviewing all the leading world figures of the time and was the anchor of such programmes as 'Person to Person', 'Small World' and 'See it Now'. A chain smoker, he died in 1965. Rose described Ed Murrow as one of the most mesmerising and attractive men she had ever met. He asked Rose if she would appear on 'Small World'. Her contemporaneous note records her reply as saying it would be wonderful, but that she was too nervous. He also autographed the Claridge's menu 'To Nat Burstein a "small but pleasant world" Ed Murrow'.

The letter of invitation to the premiere had referred to the fact that the distinguished American Republican attorney, Joseph Welch—who defended the Army against McCarthy and who appears in the film as the judge—was paying his first visit to London for the purpose of the premiere. Rose was asked if she could meet him when he was in London, which she did. A few weeks after the premiere on 11 November she received a cable from him which said:

> Understand you have some misgivings about doing a television program as discussed with Ed Murrow in London last month period just wanted personally to assure you that the idea of a transatlantic conversation with Rose Heilbron and the eminent Justice William Douglas of our Supreme Court and Justice John D Voelker of our Michigan Supreme Court and myself is one that I view with great enthusiasm stop I can assure you that it will be done modestly and with a sense of dignity that you would approve of and I urge you to accept stop I would even go so far as to predict it will be so painless that you will hardly know you were on television stop Please cable me collect Warmest regards

So different were the Bar's professional rules 50 years ago that this exciting prospect was immediately threatened by the ever-present concern about the Bar Council professional conduct rules. The rules applied despite the fact that this was intended to be a serious legal programme relating to Anglo-American issues and featured a Supreme Court Justice. Rose, although she wanted to do the programme, was compelled to respond that she was unable to accept the invitation without the approval of the Bar Council and Benchers of Gray's Inn, but that if she received permission she would accept.

Meanwhile she received an encouraging letter from Joseph Welch assuring her that she 'have no anxiety about it, since you will be protected by Mr Friendly [played by George Clooney in the recent film] in Mr Murrow's office as he edits it, as well as [it being edited] by me when we tape it'.

Rose contacted Mr Boulton, Secretary of the Bar Council, and had discussions by telephone with Ed Murrow. Various conditions were laid down by the Bar Council including that there be no preliminary announcement about her; no discussion of any personal subjects, and that it would be advisable that the Bar Council view the programme prior to broadcasting, which conditions were agreed to by the programme makers.

On 10 December 1958, the Professional Conduct Committee of the Bar and the Lord Chancellor gave approval for Rose to appear on the programme, but laid down further conditions. She could not be introduced as a QC, but as 'Miss Rose Heilbron, Recorder of Burnley'; no one should refer to her in eulogistic terms relating to her work such as saying that she was a famous woman lawyer; and there should be no reference to her career at the Bar. Such petty rules seem very strange today, but even at the time Rose was clearly frustrated. She noted on a piece of paper that two months earlier Gerald Gardiner QC (later Lord Chancellor) 'took a big part in a television debate on capital punishment and was listed as Gerald Gardiner QC ... If I ever go on television there appears to be now no reason why I should not also use QC'. Unfortunately by the time Rose received approval, the programme had run into timing difficulties and she had been replaced by Lord Birkett. Rose was naturally very disappointed.

There were other glamorous invitations and speaking engagements around this time, but there were also the more mundane. She was particularly assiduous in attending local events and in supporting the local Jewish community, although she was not particularly religious. In the middle of November 1958 she was presented to the Duchess of Gloucester at the Liverpool Town Hall. In December 1958 she was present at a reception when Harold McMillan, the Prime Minister, opened the rebuilt Holker Library at Gray's Inn, destroyed in the Second World War. Lord Justice Holker, later Lord Bowen, had been a Lord Justice of Appeal from 1882–93 and, although promoted to the House of Lords, never sat because of ill health. He apparently had a ready wit. For example, when it was suggested on the occasion of an address to Queen Victoria, to be presented by her judges, that a passage in it, 'conscious as we are of our shortcomings', suggested too great humility, he proposed the emendation 'conscious as we are of one another's shortcomings'! Rose had of course been a Lord Justice Holker scholar many years previously, which funding had set her on her career path.

The following Christmas Rose spoke at the Eleventh Annual 'Ambulances for Israel' Dinner at the Dorchester hotel in London, sporting a new hairstyle which she dubbed the 'chrysanthemum', because it was shaped like the petals of a flower. In May 1958, she attended a dinner held by the Compound Animal Feeding Stuffs Manufacturers' National Association in Liverpool where Lord Cohen of Birkenhead spoke and she replied for the guests—one assumes she was not chosen for her expertise in the products sold by the Association! There were other social engagements, both local and national.

On 3 December 1959 Rose proposed the toast in the presence of Lord Kilmuir, the Lord Chancellor, of 'The Printed Word' at the Seventy-second Annual Festival dinner of the Lloyd Memorial (Caxton) Seaside Home at the Connaught Rooms, attended by 400 guests. The home had 150 beds for the convalescent members of the printing and allied trades. Rose said that the invention of printing was undoubtedly one of the greatest blessings conferred on mankind. It was difficult and impossible to imagine a world bereft of books. She talked of the days before press freedom, commenting:

> The value of the printed word is beyond price whether contained in books or magazines or the Press. What a nation of newspaper readers we are! Now we have a Press which is free to publish, to criticise, to condemn, to praise, to disclose, to display and what charms are often displayed. The newspapers inform and entertain us every morning, every night and all day Sunday.

Rose took her position as Honorary Colonel seriously and regularly attended parades and on one occasion attended with Lord Derby in the pouring rain. In early March 1958, Rose took Hilary, aged nine, for the first time to Blackpool to watch her take the salute, she having been prevented from doing so the previous year because of the flu. Hilary was alleged to have said to a journalist that 'Mummy looked very smart'. Her photograph, dressed in her school uniform of navy blue coat and beret, appeared in the newspaper for the first time under the heading 'Such a Big Day in a Little Girl's Life'. Likewise the papers were full of Rose taking the salute with headlines such as 'What, No Wig!'

There were also regimental dinners to attend. Nat recalled the amusing incident how, when leaving late and rather the worse for wear after one such dinner, he picked up the last coat in the cloakroom and discovered, when he put it on, that it was very short in the arms—Nat was over six feet tall. Realising that his own coat had been taken by someone else, he delved into the pockets only to discover mothballs and that the owner was a Colonel Snodgrass. His charitable verdict was that the Colonel must have been even more drunk than he had been, as Nat's coat would have drowned the obviously much shorter Colonel with sleeves hanging down over the Colonel's hands. The coats were exchanged the next day.

PARKLANDS

For several years Rose had wanted to move house. She had lived at 22 Menlove Gardens North since her own childhood and wanted a home which she could put her own mark on. Many weekends were spent driving round Liverpool looking for a larger property, but nothing quite fitted the bill. However, in 1956, Rose began negotiations to purchase an acre of land in Allerton Road, close to Calderstones Park, from Sir Alan Tod, a wealthy ship-owner. He lived at Maryton Grange and owned the neighbouring land. He also gave her an option personal to her for a further acre if he ever sold his estate. The land had not been on the market, but Rose knew Sir Alan, who had lived there since 1920. Her desire to build a single house was consistent with his own wish 'to try and preserve the area where I live in quietness and privacy'. Completion took place on 2 November 1956, only three weeks before her appointment as Recorder was announced. It was quite a month.

Thus began the long road to the culmination of what became Rose's dream house. But first the land, which was a complete wilderness, had to be cleared of weeds and detritus, all done by hand with a variety of labourers and the odd intervention by family; a very long wall needed to be built to delineate the boundary of the property; planning permission needed to be obtained; an architect had to be found and the project started.

The house project also became a way of increasing Hilary's pocket money. On one occasion her father had promised her a penny for pulling up a certain number of weeds, thinking that she would help pull out the large polygonum weeds which had overgrown the land and that the enterprise would be modest. Spotting an opportunity, and maybe the budding lawyer in her realising that no particular type of weed had been specified, Hilary instead plucked out the little chickweed and similar small weeds achieving a remarkably large haul for which her surprised father rather grudgingly paid up. The request was not repeated!

For the next few years, Rose spent every spare minute on the house-building project. Converting an acre of barren land covered with weeds into a five-bedroomed house with a beautiful landscaped garden and tennis court required vision, energy and determination, but somehow, with Nat's help, she managed to achieve her dream house and yet simultaneously pursue her career and enjoy family life.

Rose and Nat were not rich. Both had started life with nothing. As Rose often said, a large part of her income went on paying for staff: in the early days a nanny or mother's help, a cleaner, a cook, a secretary and clerk. Thus to keep the cost of building the house within budget she decided to sub-contract directly with the various workmen and effectively project-manage the house, rather than employ a builder. This imposed a huge extra workload on her, even though Nat assisted. Regular trips to what became known as 'the Land' therefore became the norm, as the family watched the weeds gradually disappear and the house rise from its foundations.

The house project became a family hobby, most weekends being spent visiting the Land. Nat's patients were brought in to ply their various trades, trips were made to brick foundries, or to gardens in Hoylake to see the work of a landscape gardener, and Hilary practised her gymnastics by climbing in and out of the wooden structured frames. It was a slow process, but it was also fun. As with everything associated with building works, no less 50 years ago than today, nothing was straightforward. Rose was a perfectionist. Lists were made, articles and pictures torn from journals, advice sought from friends, comparative quotations sought and plans reviewed, traits which she passed on to her daughter.

As Rose was project managing the building and directly employing sub-contractors to save money, rather than using a builder, Rose and Nat had to choose everything and organise the supply themselves. This extended from the bricks to the type of pointing, the roof tiles, the floor, the types of windows and plaster, the fireplaces, to the more decorative aspects of the house. Rose wanted the best quality she could afford and paid great attention to detail. The architect chosen devised a rather unusual and controversial 'butterfly' roof. He was not a very practical architect. The butterfly roof may have looked attractive, but it produced enormous headaches when it came to finding windows and curtains to fit the design. The kitchen layout included a step in the middle of the floor placed conveniently so, without too much difficulty, one could trip whilst holding a pan of boiling water or oil. Rose's keen eye, however, spotted the defect and the plans were adjusted. Cost was an important consideration and the size of the rooms had to be reduced from the original plans to accommodate Rose and Nat's budget. Like everyone else they had to borrow money for the project, which they subsequently paid off.

Rose was lucky, however, to have access to good tradesmen through Nat's patients and through friends. She had help from at least one landscape gardener who drew plans of the proposed garden and listed numerous unusual plants for consideration. She had also been introduced to Dennis Lennon, a famous contemporary architect and interior designer, whose commissions had included the Royal Opera House and the liner, the Queen Elizabeth II. He produced colour schemes for the main rooms in the house which she largely adhered to, though there was far less choice of fabrics and furniture available then, than there is today.

Progress was inevitably slow, despite, by the end, daily visits to chivvy the workmen. Eventually, fed up with the continual delays, Rose and Nat decided that the only way to finish the works was to move in, albeit that the house was far from complete. Accordingly, on Friday 22 May 1959, the family moved into their new house. A name had to be found. As it was less than five minutes' walk from Calderstones Park, this proximity combined with the family description of the property as the 'Land' led to 'Parklands'. The house had no carpets, the garden remained without plants or even grass, the walls were not decorated, there were no tiles in the bathrooms, there were few cupboards, but within a few months everything started to take shape and by the end of 1959 it was beginning to look like a home, though still not finished. In August 1959 Rose took Hilary to London to purchase some items of furniture and fabrics for the house, as the selection in Liverpool was very limited and they made a bit of a holiday of it, going to some shows in the evening. As ever, the latest gadgets were purchased including an infra-red grill which Rose had discovered was the means of cooking the delicious steaks she and Hilary had eaten most nights at a steakhouse.

That Christmas Hilary presented her parents with a little book she had typed called 'Grand Removal and Settling In'. It provides an interesting contemporaneous insight through the eyes of a 10-year-old of the whole process. 'We have been greatly inconvenienced for the last year, but now we have moved we are getting straighter' she wrote. She also wrote of the actual removal:

> We had a very exciting week-end but it was hard work for Mummy ... Mummy has been very busy since the removal arranging things. We will be uncomfortable until we are really settled. I am sure we will remember the removal, especially the concentration and headaches.

The year after moving Rose began to concentrate more on the garden. First, however, the garden, once cleared of weeds, had to be dug over back and front, the foundations of two cottages removed from the large front garden and the soil made ready for sowing the grass. The garden also had to be levelled, which involved dispersing hundreds of wheelbarrows of soil from the back garden to the front. Special grass seed was ordered. Literally hundreds of unusual plants were purchased from Hilliers, the famous nursery, and other nurseries. Weekend trips would be made to various nurseries in Cheshire. Rose was no dilettante: she studied the plants, learning their names and attributes, choosing rare and unusual plants to provide year-round cover and colour, selecting many rare evergreens and taking account of whether the plants would be shade-loving or like sun. She also selected many established plants to give some maturity to the garden. Her enthusiasm instilled in Hilary her own love of gardening. Then, however, aged 11, she decided she wanted her own garden and her indulgent mother allocated to her a small plot in the vegetable garden which she planted and looked after until she eventually got bored with the idea and grew out of it.

Ultimately the garden comprised a large rockery area, a herbaceous border, a rose garden, a fully equipped tennis court, a large vegetable garden and orchard where everything from asparagus to potatoes to raspberries were grown and two greenhouses. While Nat entered into the spirit of the garden and was to be seen occasionally digging and weeding, and transporting rocks for the rock garden in the boot of his car, it was really Rose's baby, Nat preferring his golf. This was clearly Hilary's contemporaneous perception as is exemplified by an entry in her own diary shortly after the family had moved which states: 'Daddy is digging the garden—it is a miracle'. The garden remained an on-going hobby and soon Mr Belcher, who had an encyclopaedic and professorial knowledge of plants, joined as a full-time gardener and really transformed the garden with Rose's help into something quite magnificent.

It was a huge accomplishment to have turned a brown-field site into a wonderful house and an acre of garden given everything else Rose was doing. It undoubtedly brought the family enormous pleasure living in such lovely surroundings. Over the years Rose and Nat collected antiques, pictures, porcelain and various other items from antique shops around the country to complement the modern décor. It became Rose's dream house and it was a terrible wrench for her when in later life she had to leave it and move to London.

CONTINUING MATERNAL GUIDANCE

The upheaval of moving did not affect other aspects of Rose's life. By now Hilary was no longer a little girl, but still needed a close maternal eye kept on her. Rose ensured that she played with friends and did her homework and that there was always someone there to look after her. Whenever she was away she would write Hilary loving letters often with good maternal advice, such as when she told her to practise her spelling for her 11-plus examination. The summer after the move, Hilary took ill and the doctor visited. The family was lucky that as a result of Nat being a doctor himself the doctor would always visit rather than having to attend a surgery. Rose was advised to take Hilary away for a holiday and they spent a week in La Baulle in the Loire, France. It was the first time that Hilary had been on an aeroplane. Unfortunately, soon after arrival, Hilary promptly took ill again. This resulted in Rose sitting by Hilary's bedside in a small bedroom reading Nancy Mitford's *Love in a Cold Climate* and laughing her infectious laugh out loud, instead of enjoying the sunshine.

PROFESSIONAL STAFF

Since taking silk, Rose had always had a personal clerk on Circuit, although professional rules demanded that she was also a member of a set of London Chambers, which was initially 3 Pump Court, where Charles Humphries was the clerk. This was an unusual set up, precipitated by the fact that she lived on Circuit rather than in London. In 1958 her then clerk, Rosetta Andrews, left and was replaced by Kay McCall, a widow, who stayed with Rose for many years and only left because she was getting remarried. Rose had a contract of employment drawn up including a confidentiality clause. Kay McCall's role was a mixed one of a traditional clerk fixing cases in the list, sometimes accompanying Rose to cities away from Liverpool, answering calls from solicitors, being Rose's personal assistant and doing her typing. She would come to the house on Saturday mornings when Rose would attend to correspondence, filing and other matters which she had been unable to do during the week.

In 1964 Rose employed an additional personal secretary, a Mrs Sheppard, to whom she would dictate her opinions and speeches, whether for juries or audiences. On occasions, they would both sit up until the early hours of the morning drinking coffee or soup as Rose prepared her final speech and Mrs Sheppard typed it. She became a friend as well as an employee. Mrs Sheppard had a car and on rare occasions she was known to pick Hilary up from school after exams and even walk the dog.

A YEAR FOR WOMEN

1958 was a year which resonated with women: 14 July 1958 was
the centenary of the birth of Emmeline Pankhurst, the famous suffragette, and the year that the Life Peerages Act was passed entitling
women to become peeresses for the first time.

In October 1958, along with Helen Pathick-Lawrence, Nancy Astor,
Thelma Cazalet-Keir, (Dame) Vera Laughton Mathews (Director of
the Woman's Royal Navy Service during the war and Life President
of the Association of Wrens), A Louise McIlroy, Mary Stocks and
Sybil Thorndyke, the actress, Rose wrote a letter to *The Times* about
building a memorial to Christabel Pankhurst who had recently
died. In 1904 Christabel Pankhurst had been refused permission to
become a barrister. They wrote:

> This month will be remembered in our constitutional history as the one
> in which women first sat in the House of Lords. This event calls to mind
> the advance that women have made in status in recent times ...We recog-
> nize the debt we owe to the pioneers who pressed women's enfranchise-
> ment on reluctant Governments. Notable among them was Christabel
> Pankhurst, who, as a young law student, struck a new note of defiance by
> adopting what later became known as militant tactics and thereby made
> 'Votes for Women' front page news. During the nine years in which the
> conflict raged she displayed courage, political insight, and leadership
> to a high degree and devoted the whole of her youth to obtaining the
> enfranchisement of her sex. Dame Christabel died a few months ago and
> many people feel that a national monument should be erected to her.

The ladies formed a committee to raise funds and a proposal to
add a low wall to Mrs Pankhurst's (her mother's) statue in Victoria
Tower Garden, adjacent to the House of Lords was approved by the
Ministry of Works.

Although 1958 was an historic year for women, four being
appointed peeresses, there were still many barriers to be broken.
In the law, out of 1,600 practising barristers, only 70 were women.
There was still no female High Court Judge, although Rose was
tipped in various newspapers to take that honour. As an article
entitled 'Handicap in Court' in the *Evening Standard* written in
September 1958 recalled:

> A woman barrister advertising today for 'suitable employment' com-
> plains that her stumbling block in making a success at the Bar is her sex.
> Is there a prejudice against women as barristers? I discussed this today
> with law experts. They say women have one natural handicap in court:
> having less voice power they often have difficulty in making their cases

heard. Clients, briefing through solicitors, tend to choose experienced male barristers rather than women. An exception is in the criminal courts. Prisoners granted State legal aid often ask for a young girl barrister, believing she will receive greater sympathy from the court. But poor prisoners' defence briefs are notoriously low-paid, and barristers cannot earn a livelihood by these alone. A few women barristers achieve great success, notably Miss Rose Heilbron QC. But there are about 70 women practising at the Bar. The names of only a handful are known outside legal circles.

In another article in the *Liverpool Echo* describing the problems facing women at the Bar, Rose was described as 'a swallow without a summer'. The old excuse about women's voices was still trundled out. Despite her success, Rose was not immune to the prejudicial customs of the time, as will be revealed.

Her fame continued to attract its lighter moments. She was one of several people nominated by the public as Woman of the Year; a reader disagreed with the Professional Photographers Society's choice of Joan Collins as 'the most beautiful girl in the world' and suggested Rose, ex-Queen Soraya and Claire Bloom as more beautiful. As an avid watcher of 'Dynasty' in later years, Rose would have been quite tickled by this article had she remembered it.

In October 1958 in an article entitled 'Can't Husbands be Honest?' in *The Star*, Ann Ford, a friend of Rose's and Fashion Director of the Bear Brand Stocking Company, wrote:

> I admire two women particularly. They are Rose Heilbron, Recorder of Burnley and Marlene Dietrich. Rose Heilbron I admire because she somehow manages to be a sweet simple housewife in her home and a brilliant powerful lawyer in her work. A difficult combination of jobs which she does to perfection. Marlene Dietrich I admire because she had kept beauty captive through the years.

THE SMITHFIELD FIRE INQUEST

Among the many cases Rose undertook in this period, three stand out. The first was the resumed inquest on 28 February 1958 into the fire at the famous Smithfield meat market in London in which two firemen had been killed. They had died from asphyxia due to fire fumes when working in the unventilated maze of underground chambers in the basement of the building. Issues arose as to whether they had had proper supervision. Their oxygen cylinders were found to be empty. Rose, representing one of the deceased firemen, posed detailed technical questions to the well-known pathologist Dr Keith Simpson. Recording verdicts of misadventure, the coroner recommended the adoption of an automatic warning device designed to be fitted to a fireman's breathing apparatus which would sound when the oxygen was running low. The coroner was informed these would be fitted within the following 2–3 weeks. The cause of the fire was never ascertained. The General Secretary of the Fire Brigades Union wrote to Rose thanking her, saying 'how impressed I am, once more, at what a splendid job you did on our behalf—in very difficult circumstances'.

THE WIDOW OF WINDY NOOK

The second case was more sensational. It became a cause célèbre and was widely reported in the press. The 'wicked woman' of 'Windy Nook', Mary Elizabeth Wilson, was charged with two murders. Not content with allegedly poisoning her second husband, Oliver James Leonard, she was further accused of poisoning her third husband, George Lawrence Wilson, whom she married a year later. Each marriage had barely lasted a fortnight. Mrs Wilson was clearly not someone who procrastinated. Neither the victims nor the murderess were in the first flush of youth. Both deceased were in their mid-seventies and the accused was 66.

Rose was instructed to defend her. Mary Wilson pleaded not guilty. The trial opened at Leeds Assizes on 24 March 1958 before Mr Justice Hinchcliffe and a jury. Rose sought to have the two murder charges dealt with at separate trials, but the judge rejected the application on the basis that the evidence in one charge was admissible in the other. That really sounded the death knell for her defence.

The evidence was that Mary Wilson had inveigled both husbands into marrying her with the intention of terminating their lives for the 'paltry' financial benefits she would receive on their deaths. There was considerable evidence to this effect including her asking the first deceased for money. Leonard had left her about £45–75, but her attempts to insure his life had failed. She added to this with the inheritance from Wilson which also included payment from an insurance policy on his life. Both bodies had been exhumed and phosphorous present in rat poison had been found in them.

The defence principally revolved around questioning the doctors about the reliability of their respective death certificates. Rose also carried out a detailed probing of the forensic evidence as to the existence of phosphorous in the bodies and its effect and the likelihood as to its being the cause of death on the facts of the case. The defence called Dr Francis Camps, the well-known Home Office pathologist, whose evidence was that the cause of death in each case was unascertainable, the findings being contradictory pathologically such that he could not exclude natural causes. Rose did not call her client to the witness box. A further less technical line of defence was that pills containing phosphorous could be purchased over the counter and were used as an aphrodisiac.

On the fifth day of the trial Rose began her final speech. It lasted three hours during which she dissected the factual and scientific evidence. She also ran what might these days be called the 'Viagra' defence. 'What was more natural', she asked 'than that these men, 76 years of age, both finding a wife in the evening of life ... should have purchased those pills for the purpose for which they are apparently known?' The jury were having none of the 'Love Pills' defence and after a deliberation lasting only 85 minutes found Mary Wilson guilty on both charges. They no doubt had in mind the truism in the well-known quotation of Oscar Wilde: for one husband to die after only a fortnight of marriage may be regarded as a misfortune; for two to do so looks like carelessness—or in this case murder.

Mary Wilson was sentenced to death, the first woman to be sentenced to death since the Homicide Act of 1957. Her subsequent appeal against conviction failed and the Attorney General refused to grant a certificate entitling her to appeal to the House of Lords. However, on 31 May 1958 the Home Secretary, Rab Butler, recommended a reprieve and thus the last woman to be hanged in England still remains Ruth Ellis in 1955.

HARRISON GIBSON, THE FURNITURE STORE

The third case which attracted particular public attention concerned the late night opening of a well-known furniture store of the time, Harrison Gibson, with branches all over the country. It was charged under the Shops Act for permitting late night opening on Tuesday evenings at its Ilford store. It closed at 5.30pm as usual and then re-opened for late night viewing between 7pm–9.30pm, although nothing could be purchased or ordered at that time. Apparently 1,500 people visited the store every Tuesday evening. It was a test case. Rose was instructed to defend the store at the magistrates in November 1959. The issue was whether serving a customer within the meaning of the Shops Act 1950 was confined to selling. The store was convicted and fined £6. It appealed by way of case stated, but the appeal was not successful. Late night opening had to wait many years before it became legal.

ANOTHER TRIP TO NIGERIA

Rose's Nigerian practice also seems to have been flourishing. In late September 1958 she returned to Lagos for an appeal court hearing confined to points of law. Mandilas & Karaberis Ltd, a very substantial company, and Leslie Fitton, their one-time area manager and later director, were both charged with larceny relating to two lorries. The case only took two hours and Rose succeeded in getting both convictions quashed. She was immediately offered another case, but it never materialised, probably because the client would not pay her fee. She seemed to have enjoyed her trip, staying with Mr and Mrs Howard of John Holt & Co in considerable comfort. She had been introduced by Mr Gates, who had helped her find accommodation on her previous trip to Benin. She was entertained at Government House and managed to do some sightseeing, noting in her letters home that she had seen houses with butterfly roofs. The new house was clearly on her mind because in a letter to Hilary, which shows her attention to detail, she told her to 'ask Daddy to tell Mr Little to carlite the sides of both chimney breasts in the living room and the lounge'. Carlite was then a new form of quick-drying plaster which did not crack so easily.

SADNESS BACK HOME

Two days after Rose's return from Lagos her father passed away. He was in his mid-seventies, but had spent the last few years of his life in a nursing home near the family home disabled, deaf and blind, having contracted diabetes some years earlier. His main pleasure, apart from family visits, had been his pipe. He had been a widower for over 20 years. He had lived long enough to see his younger daughter achieve great fame and become the first woman Queen's Counsel and Recorder.

A SPLASH OF COLOUR

Rose continued to have cases reported in the Law Reports such as a case concerning a system of working relating to injuries suffered by a dockworker.[1] Another reported case concerned an application by the Attorney General on behalf of the Lord Mayor, Aldermen and Citizens of the City of Manchester, for an injunction restraining flower sellers from operating outside the Manchester Southern Cemetery, contrary to the Manchester Corporations Acts. These statutes, among other things, prohibited the sale of flowers on the footpath. Rose appeared for the flower sellers, Mr and Mrs Harris, leading Ivor Taylor. The Harrises had form. Between them they had over the years been convicted 237 times, usually being fined, for using their stall or obstructing the footway. The matter was eventually referred to the Attorney General.

Mr Justice Salmon, in a reserved judgment, refused the application for an injunction, stating they were not committing a nuisance.[2] 'They were providing a splash of colour in a somewhat otherwise dismal landscape' said the Judge. The decision was later successfully appealed, but that was for another year.

---

[1] *Lawler v AE Smith Coggins Ltd* [1958] 1 Lloyd's Rep 1 (CA).
[2] *A/G v Harris* [1960] 1 QB 31.

17

A Flourishing Practice and a Royal Invitation to Lunch

A VARIED PRACTICE

B Y THE END of the decade, Rose, aged 45, had been in silk for over 10 years and had established a wide and varied practice as well as a substantial professional and public reputation. Hilary was growing up and the family were settling in to their new home. Rose's energy undiminished and her love of her job, of family and life undimmed, she was ready for the challenges of the years ahead.

1960 was rare in Rose's career at the Bar for the absence of any high-profile or sensational case, unless of course, one can so categorise 'the case of the "X" bosoms', which caused a little local interest. Rose appeared before the local licensing committee representing the Scala Cinema in Lime Street, Liverpool, which was seeking a renewal of its licence. Objections were made to full colour posters of naked and near-naked women on the walls of the cinema, which were alleged to corrupt young children's minds. A string of objectors including housewives, teachers and clergymen, gave evidence. Rose lost the case and the cinema's licence was not renewed on the ground that proof that posters are objectionable is that people object to them. It was held that provided that the objectors were reasonably representative of the general body of citizens, the authorities had little option in the matter.

It may come as no surprise to learn that evidence was given that when the posters were pulled down for two weeks the audience dropped from 20,000 to 2,000. Rose, presumably a little tongue in cheek, argued that: 'Everyone is used to seeing pictures of women with blown-up bosoms. In the past few years they seem to have become the fashion'.

The absence of a headline hitting case did not mean that Rose was not busy nor that the year was uneventful. On the contrary, she continued with her varied practice and had two Court of Appeal cases reported in the Law Reports because of their importance. The first concerned the construction of statutory provisions relating to deductions from a loss of earnings claim made by an injured machinist.[1] The second was the appeal to the Court of Appeal in the case of Harris, the flower sellers, referred to previously, where the appeal succeeded and an injunction was granted. The Court of Appeal granted leave to appeal to the House of Lords, but it does not however seem to have been pursued, Mr Harris moving his stall into the roadway.[2]

By the early 1960s Rose had been put on the Attorney General's list which meant that she was chosen to prosecute murders and other serious crimes from time to time. She was not part of the 'establishment' and so obtaining prosecution work took time and being female no doubt was an additional impediment. She was also building up her practice in medical negligence cases. In addition, the following selection of the sorts of cases she was doing at the time illustrates that her practice was not short of variety, for the age of specialism had not yet come about. Nor was her practice confined to Liverpool and Manchester. She would often appear in several different cases or even different courts in one week, many involving travelling some distance either by train or car each day and some even requiring her to stay away from home. Some of her work was privately paid: some was funded by legal aid.

In 1961 Rose defended a woman charged with murdering her 20-month-old son. She had strangled him with a scarf because he had been screaming. She was found guilty of manslaughter on the ground of diminished responsibility and was put on probation. Rose represented a young boy of 16 who had lost three fingers in a bacon-slicing machine and was awarded £2,294 by way of damages. She appeared in the High Court in London for a former shipwright, William Cuddily, who was injured when he fell 27 feet to the bottom of one of the holds on a ship at Tilbury Docks and recovered damages of £5,325 against ship-owners for his injuries. The case was reported in the Law Reports.

Rose also represented Harold Dorfman, the managing director of a bank, the General Issue and Investment Co Ltd, at Marlborough Magistrates' Court in London, who was charged with conspiring with

---

[1] *Hultquist v Universal Pattern and Precision Engineering Co Ltd* [1960] 2 QB 467.
[2] *Attorney General v Harris* [1961] 1 QB 74 (CA).

a commission agent and others, to cheat and defraud Henry Smith, a chinchilla farmer, of his money. It was a complex case involving exchange control issues. As part of her research she read up about chinchilla farming and learnt useful pieces of information including the fact that 'A fourteen stone man can be pulled around with a single pellet!' Back home at Liverpool Crown Court she represented two men who pleaded guilty to conspiracy for using pocket radios to enable them to place bets after the result of the race was known and thereby defraud bookmakers. They were fined £800. Rose represented Freda Squires at Lancaster Assizes. She had stabbed her cruel husband after a 20-year marriage and was charged with murder. Rose commented to the jury that: 'After being beaten, punched and wounded, suffering the humiliation of not one mistress but several, she was a tormented soul and her mind just snapped'. The jury found her guilty of manslaughter on the ground of diminished responsibility and she received three years' imprisonment.

1962 brought a similar spectrum of cases of which the following are examples. In early January at Blackpool Quarter Sessions Rose successfully defended a director of a transport firm charged with stealing. He had sold tyres from 10 tipper trucks he was buying on hire-purchase, replacing them with cheaper ones, allegedly because they were blowing out, but without telling the finance company.

The following month she appeared at Liverpool Assizes for a motor cyclist, Richard Joseph Osborne, who had suffered brain damage and had become a permanent invalid following a collision with an ambulance. He was awarded damages of £9,725. On 2 March she appeared for a plaintiff who had received serious leg and brain injuries in a car accident. Later that month she defended Selvin Leslie Bernard who pleaded guilty to manslaughter at Manchester Crown Court. He had been attacked with a broken bottle earlier in the day by the deceased. This had prompted him to go home and get a rock from the garden which he threw at the victim. He was given three years' imprisonment. She defended Edwin Musgrove charged together with a Mrs McCusker, whose lodger he was, with murdering Mrs McCusker's husband with an axe, then a non-capital murder, but the outcome is not known. They were two of life's unfortunates: she was an orphan who had spent 16 years in a mental home and had been a prostitute; Rose's client was a man with a criminal record and a history of suicide attempts.

In April, she appeared in the Divisional Court in London representing William John Jones, a hospital porter, who had been inoculated against polio three times as a condition of his employment which led to an acute onset of rheumatoid arthritis. He claimed incapacity benefit on the ground that he had suffered an industrial accident which was ultimately refused by the deputy Industrial Injuries Commissioner. After the oral hearing the Commissioner had obtained advice on the case from a specialist in rheumatology without informing the parties or giving them an opportunity to comment. Rose moved for an order for Certiorari to quash the decision as that of a quasi-judicial tribunal on the grounds of a breach of natural justice and the relevant statutory and regulatory provisions. An order for Certiorari was granted.[3]

In October, Rose appeared at Birmingham Assizes for former company director, George Sharp aged 60, who admitted offences against young children and was given 10 years' imprisonment. Also in October, this time at Lancaster Assizes, she defended John McCormack accused of attempting to murder his wife. He had been deeply in love with her, but when she refused a reconciliation following a separation he dragged her into his car and stabbed her. He was cleared of attempted murder, but found guilty of wounding with intent to cause grievous bodily harm and jailed for 12 months.

Slightly out of the ordinary was her appearance at Bow Street Magistrates' Court in London representing five men from the committee of 100, a committee which included Bertrand Russell, the well-known philosopher and pacifist, among its membership. This committee organised the anti-nuclear war campaign. The five individuals were charged under the Public Order Act 1936 and accused of inciting demonstrators to charge the police cordons present at demonstrations in Trafalgar Square on 17 September 1961. Earlier there had also been a sit-down at the American Embassy. They pleaded not guilty, but guilty to disregarding the directions of the Police Commissioner. At the hearing on 30 October two were found not guilty and the other three were fined £30 and ordered to pay £20 costs. The successful outcome resulted in considerable publicity, but one article in the *Socialist Leader* is noteworthy for its praise of the way Rose conducted the case, describing her cross-examination as 'brilliant'; and her final plea as 'a masterpiece of lucid exposition'.

PUBLIC FASCINATION DIMMING

Whereas 10 years earlier murder cases had received saturation press coverage, it is noticeable that by the early 1960s this was becom-

---

[3] *R v Industrial Injuries Commission, ex parte Jones* [1962] 2 QB 677.

ing the exception rather than the rule. They were still reported, but less extensively. This was probably as a result of the Homicide Act 1957 which restricted capital punishment in murder cases to five types of murder: murder in the course or furtherance of theft; murder by shooting or causing an explosion; murder while resisting arrest or during an escape; murder of a police officer or prison officer; and two or more murders committed on different occasions. These restrictions produced some anomalies: why should someone who strangles a person not be eligible for hanging, whilst someone who shoots someone could be executed? Why should murder in the course of theft be punishable by death, while murder in the course of rape was not? This fuelled further public disquiet against the death penalty and capital murder convictions became less common.

Capital punishment was finally abolished in 1965 by the Murder (Abolition of Death Penalty) Act, introduced by way of a private member's bill by Sidney Silverman MP who had long campaigned for its abolition. The last men to hang in England were Peter Anthony Allen, aged 21, who was hanged in Walton gaol, Liverpool and Gwynne Owen Evans, aged 24, who was hanged in Strangeways, Manchester. They were both convicted of the murder of John Alan West while robbing him in his house on 7 April 1964. They were hanged on 13 August 1964.

The removal of the shadow of the gallows in turn removed the grim spectre that had undoubtedly led to the intense public interest in murder trials in the 1940s and 1950s. In addition television had arrived and people could watch detective stories and murder trials on a daily basis on their televisions instead of queuing for a seat in the public gallery of a court, albeit that they were works of fiction. Some murder cases still caught the public imagination, particularly those which remained a capital offence, but by the 1960s there was an undoubted shift in public fascination with them. Nonetheless there remained cases which attracted huge public interest.

One such category of cases was that concerning sterilisation and abortion. Such cases are always controversial and require sensitive handling, for people have deeply held and differing views on the subject. In her career as a barrister and, later as a judge, Rose had to deal with both. Over the years Rose had represented doctors and others who had unlawfully attempted to abort babies and were criminally charged. Even as late as 1962 at Manchester Assizes she defended Dr John Maurice O'Grady on a manslaughter charge following an attempted abortion. His defence was that the victim was more likely to have died from a reaction to penicillin to which she was sensitive, but he was found guilty and received five years' imprisonment. Abortion was not legalised in England until the Abortion Act of 1967.

In June 1961, she represented a Mrs Waters, a mother of six who sued a surgeon for negligence and breach of contract for a failed sterilisation operation which had been performed because she had a weak heart. The operation was unsuccessful and she became pregnant again giving birth to a stillborn child. She later underwent a successful sterilisation operation. The issue revolved around whether the surgeon should have told her of the risk of a further pregnancy. The Judge found for the surgeon concluding that there were mixed medical views as to whether it was good practice to tell a patient of the risks.

Rose still appeared in capital murders, though inevitably they were much less frequent. In July 1962, for instance, at Manchester Assizes she defended Bernard Joseph McCrorey for the capital murder of the wife of the licensee of Kendal Castle Hotel in Preston. The defence was diminished responsibility, but the jury found him guilty of capital murder and Mr Justice Lyell sentenced him to death. Rose appealed on behalf of her client to the Court of Criminal Appeal where she succeeded in having the conviction quashed on the basis that the Judge had misdirected the jury on the impact on premeditation of the defendant's impairment. 'One Word and Rose QC Saves Killer' was the headline.

HENDERSONS' FIRE

Civil cases did not normally create as much interest as criminal ones. An exception was a fire in the afternoon of 22 June 1960 at Hendersons department store in Church Street, Liverpool, in which three men and eight women lost their lives. The store, which was in the process of renovation, was completely burnt down. Hendersons was then part of the Harrods Group. It was a regular haunt of Rose and Hilary on their Saturday shopping trips and its dramatic destruction with tragic consequences had a particular resonance— they could so easily have been there themselves.

Rose represented two widows, Mrs Mary Murphy and Mrs Margaret McBride, who had lost their husbands in the fire. The trial began on 22 October 1962 at Liverpool Assizes before Mr Justice Stable. The two men who died had been employed in the on-going construction work. McBride was a labourer and Murphy was a sheet-metal worker. McBride was asphyxiated and Murphy was killed when, heroically rescuing two women, he fell from a ledge. The Fire Service had arrived within two minutes and found the ground floor full of smoke, but customers and staff were still behaving as if nothing had happened.

The claim was for damages for negligence against Hendersons and based on a failure to take precautions both before and at the time of the fire. There were three main issues: the adequacy of the escape routes; whether a state of urgency was created sufficiently quickly; and whether the organisation for dealing with that state of urgency after it had arisen, was up to standard. The more detailed allegations included the failure to obtain approval from Liverpool Corporation over a period of six years as to the fire precautions, including the means of escape and the adequacy of the design of the timber staircase, which was not consistent with fire prevention.

As to this last ground, Rose commented to the Judge:

> It is a sad commentary and a reflection on the concern by Henderson's for the safety of the public that this elementary fire precaution which had been the subject of conditions by the Corporation since 1954 had not been started in 1960 at a time when the documents will show the work of reconstruction was to all intents and purposes completed. It is an interesting speculation—and may be a live issue in this case—as to whether the staircase (concrete) was to be put in.

The case lasted over two weeks. The claim was successful. Mrs Murphy was awarded damages of £5,500 and Mrs McBride £2,452. The Judge concluded that in his judgement:

> [T]he defendants had no right under the Corporation by-laws to throw that floor open to the public unless and until the plans which they themselves had sent to the Corporation and which the Corporation had approved had been carried out.

An appeal by the defendants to the Court of Appeal failed.

A FAMILY VISIT TO THE UNITED STATES

The early 1960s were not exclusively taken up with work. In August 1960, after some dithering because of the cost involved and preparation needed, the family went for the first time to America to attend the American Bar Association Conference in New York and Washington. They had been planning it for several months with 'exhausting shopping expeditions Saturday after Saturday'. Rose had several dresses made by a local dressmaker. It was touch and go whether the family would be able to travel, as Nat, with impeccable timing, had injured both his knees; one was in plaster and he was hospitalised. However on 19 August, Rose's birthday, the family all managed to scramble aboard the Cunard Liner the MV *Britannic* at Prince's landing stage in Liverpool, for the voyage to New York, not helped by an unofficial strike of seamen.

The voyage was, as was intended, a relaxing holiday which was enjoyed by all and included the sighting of whales and dolphins in the Atlantic. On arrival the family travelled by coach to Washington to stay with Chuck and Alice Vetter who had kindly agreed to put them up and who remained life-long friends. The round of parties at the conference included a reception at the White House given by President and Mrs Eisenhower which Rose and Nat attended.

Hilary, having managed to catch the flu on arrival in the States, was nonetheless fit enough to attend a reception at the British Embassy. On a balmy summer evening in the gardens of the Embassy, much against her better judgement, Rose was persuaded by either the then Attorney General, Sir Reginald Manningham-Buller or Lord Kilmuir, the Lord Chancellor, to let Hilary try her first glass of champagne. It is a tale Hilary has retold with some amusement on more recent visits to the British Embassy in Washington, though the effect of champagne on an 11 year old has obscured such nice-ties as to certainty as to which of the two gentlemen of high office it was! This judicial tradition was taken one step further a couple of years later when Mr Justice Stable introduced Hilary on a visit to Liverpool Judicial Lodgings to her first champagne cocktail! But such impish behaviour was not the ultimate reason why Hilary herself decided to enter the profession! While in Washington, the family was also taken one evening for dinner at the Watergate Inn, at that time unaware of the significance the building would have in later years under the Presidency of Richard Nixon.

A week in Washington was followed by a week in New York and the round of sightseeing from Times Square to the Empire State Building. The family stayed with the Rileys and spent a couple of days at their lovely country home. Rose attended a tour of the United Nations along with other women barristers. She also purchased towels for the new house as the selection was much better than in England at that time. The trip home was on the RMS *Parthia*. Rose and Nat saw little of their daughter as she spent most of the time preparing a headdress 'Lady Luck' which won her a set of cocktail glasses which she still has.

FOOTBALL

The other notable event that year was Burnley becoming Football First Division League Champions for 1959–60. On 18 October 1960, Rose, as Recorder of Burnley, accompanied by Nat, attended a celebration at the invitation of the Burnley Football and Athletic Co Ltd at the Imperial Hotel in Blackpool. The evening comprised an eight-course split dinner followed by dancing which went on until the early hours. Unlike Nat, a keen sportsman, Rose was no cognoscenti of football. The nearest she got to being involved in a game was, according to Nat, a lifelong supporter of Liverpool Football Club, when she was taken to watch Everton play—and lose—at home in Liverpool. The sports editor of the *Liverpool Echo* apparently wrote an article about the match in which he asked if Rose could defend the team for losing!

LUNCH WITH HM THE QUEEN AND HRH THE DUKE OF EDINBURGH

If 1960 was the year of distant travel and football success, the highlight for Rose in 1961 was undoubtedly an invitation to a private luncheon with the Queen and the Duke of Edinburgh on 8 November. This was one of the first such lunches the Queen had held. Rose wore a dark sapphire blue dress with a black design and matching hat. Other attendees included: Lord Luke, Chairman of the National Playing Fields Association and a member of the International Olympics Committee; George Woodcock, General Secretary of the TUC; Sir Stanley Rous, Honorary Secretary of the Football Association; and Sir Aubrey Burke, Chairman and Managing Director of de Haviland aircraft.

As she tended to do on momentous occasions in her life, Rose wrote and retained a contemporaneous note of the day's events in her distinctive large handwriting. She had travelled to London the day before and stayed at the Carlton Tower Hotel. In the evening she met a solicitor about a forthcoming murder trial at the Old Bailey. The following morning Rose went to her London hairdresser who styled it specially to wear under a hat. She was dressed and waiting three quarters of an hour early for the car she had ordered to take her to Buckingham Palace. To her astonishment she found herself at the top of the guest list and the only woman guest.

In advance of being received by the Queen and Duke of Edinburgh, Rose was greeted by two lively five-month-old corgi puppies and one 12-year-old corgi bitch. Rose noted that the Queen wore the most enormous diamond brooch and commented on how attractive she was. She sat next to the Duke of Edinburgh at lunch and had coffee with the Queen. A combination of etiquette 50 years ago and Rose's own approach to matters which she regarded as private, meant that she would not discuss what was said during the conversations she had with the Queen or the Duke of Edinburgh. Reading the notes of these conversations, they appear very innocuous by today's standards a half a century later, but in deference to her desire to keep them private they shall remain so. She did however comment to herself: 'It was unbelievable. If only Nat and Hilary could see me they'd have been very proud of their "old Mum"'. A loftier comment came from the *Christchurch Press* in New Zealand, which in an article entitled 'Miss Rose Heilbron QC is Britain's Portia', referred to her attending a luncheon given by the Queen and commented 'It was a small item, but a significant one—a pointer to the growing stature of "Rose QC"'.

TANDY

Whatever the pressures of work, domestic issues could not be avoided and staff would leave or, on rare occasions, have to be sacked, their departure usually timed to occur at the most inconvenient moment. Some were excellent: one according to Hilary's diary when she was aged 14, was a bit 'nye eve'! By this time Rose had quite a large staff: a Mother's help, one, and later two, part-time cleaners, a full-time gardener, a clerk in Liverpool, Kay McCall, as well as her London based clerk and by 1964 also a part-time private secretary. Expensive though employing such a large number of staff was, she could not have coped without domestic and other employed help. Moreover, income tax was around this time very high and the top rate ultimately reached 83 per cent on earned income.

In 1961, Gladys, the mother's help, who had been with the family for several years, retired. This had two consequences. First, it led to the employment of Mrs Simms as cook/housekeeper. Hilary was now getting older and no longer needed to be looked after in the same way. Mrs Simms stayed with the family for some 12 years, with breaks in between, and worked part time into her eighties until Rose and Nat moved to London permanently in the early 1970s. She was a lovely lady and became part of the family and is remembered with much affection. Her wise sayings are likewise remembered to this day, such as her admonishment of Rose when she refrained from using the good crockery: 'What is good enough for your visitors is good enough for yourselves'. Mrs Simms was a wonderful cook and taught Rose and Hilary many culinary skills.

During the family trip to America in 1960, Hilary had fallen in love with the Vetter's Dalmatian dog 'Sultana' and thereafter, like most children of that age, had consistently badgered her parents for a dog of her own. Rose having previously had a dog was willing, but Nat was less keen. However Gladys disliked dogs and the dog was deferred, Hilary having to make do with two goldfish called 'Whipper' and 'Kipper' instead. However, with the retirement of Gladys, the possibility of a dog re-emerged.

One July afternoon in 1961, at the beginning of the school holidays, a very excited 12-year-old and her mother arrived at the car park of Bear Brands, the well-known stocking manufacturing company. There in a small cage sitting in the back of a Rolls Royce was this tiny bundle of white fluff with a blue moustache from the medicine he had been given following an upset stomach on the journey up from London. The puppy, a white miniature poodle, was a present from Ann Ford, a colourful personality, who with her husband owned Bear Brands, the stocking manufacturers. They were friends of Rose and Nat. The bundle of white fluff became known as Tandy.

Although four legs would normally disqualify him from a place in a biography, Tandy was so much part of the family and wheedled his way into everyone's heart that he deserves more than just a mention. Moreover, when found on one occasion sitting opposite Mrs Simms at the kitchen table apparently having dinner à deux with his paws on the table, Rose naturally chastised Mrs Simms. Never one to miss the unanswerable riposte Mrs Simms replied: 'But he is only human!'

This 'human' dog was exceptionally intelligent. He had been taught to act as ball boy for Hilary when she practised her serve on the tennis court, ultimately realising that if he did not return the ball and drop it at her feet he would not have another throw; he was able, like a seal, to bounce a plastic beach ball, obtained free with a breakfast cereal, up and down on his nose without it touching the ground; he could close a door on demand by pushing it hard while standing on his two hind legs; and he had learned the topography of the house so could fetch objects—which he could differentiate—from a particular room. He even had a special bark for milk which sounded phonetically very like the word, which he would utter as he sat in front of the fridge, but that was the limit of his vocabulary. He was, however, a very fussy, ie spoilt, eater. He would not eat tinned dog food: only fresh meat or tinned chicken bought by Rose for him at Woolworths; home-made sweet biscuits—never pre-packed; and he had a penchant for gorgonzola cheese!

Like many dogs he reserved a particular hatred for the postman. The *British Medical Journal*, which was delivered weekly and came wrapped in a roll in brown paper somewhat resembling a bone, attracted an energetic thrashing until the wrapping was removed and it merely resembled a magazine at which point he lost interest and this chewed-up journal was then ready for Nat to read. He was, however, a useless guard dog and on the one occasion the family suffered an attempted burglary he slept right through it, although the ladder had been placed directly in front of the window by his basket.

Tandy had originally been Hilary's dog, but as with any other teenager, the initial enthusiasm for the less fun aspects of having a dog descended on Rose. Tandy adored Rose and would guard over her lying on her bed when she was not well, particularly when she was suffering from one of the migraines she regularly endured: the days of Tandy not being allowed past the utility room having long gone. Just as a doctor, he instinctively knew when she was ill and no one could get near her. More regularly he would wait with his nose up against the landing window at the same time each evening for Rose's car when she came home from work and when he heard the car would go berserk with excitement.

Rose spoilt him too, buying him a little blue coat with a black fake fur collar on one of her trips to London and making sure that Hilary in her enthusiasm did not overtire him and looked after him properly, especially when he was a puppy. In one letter she wrote:

> I do hope you are being a good girl and not forgetting to feed and exercise 'our' little fella. Tell him Grandma sends lots of love—I wonder if he'll recognise me when I return … Look after yourself & Daddy. With all my very dearest and deepest love, affectionately, Mum".

He was a 'modern' dog and did not mind his mistress working or her daughter going to school. Provided Rose was dressed in a black suit and Hilary was wearing her school uniform he was resigned to staying at home. But at weekends, when dressed in mufti, any attempt to leave the house without him caused misery and dejection. On many occasions he came along. On one Saturday when Rose and Hilary went shopping in Southport, they stopped en route at Blundellsands where Tandy was let out for a run—and run he did, for he had never come across sand before and he ran and ran such that his return to the car looked problematical. On another occasion, one springtime, when Nat was playing golf, Rose and Hilary went on one of their drives to the countryside in North Wales and stopped somewhere in the Snowdonian hills among the lambs and sheep. Tandy could not believe his eyes and barked incessantly—all those white poodles like him!

He brought the family much fun and laughter, but aged nine developed a heart condition. He was taken to see a veterinary specialist who was a Professor at Liverpool University. In a rather manly, but booming voice, and finding a fellow professional in Rose she declared 'What a working woman needs is a wife'. She unfortunately was not able to cure Tandy, but her pearls of wisdom have been repeated many times thereafter. Tandy died while Hilary was at University and was never replaced—life had moved on and having another dog was not practical. He is still remembered and missed.

A BUSY LIFE

Rose had other distractions from practice and sitting as Recorder apart from domestic and 'doggy' issues. She had been asked to sit for a bronze bust in her full-bottomed wig by a sculptor, Hilda Littler, whom she knew. The end product, of huge weight, sat in the dining room at Parklands for many years. Hilary has since given it to Gray's Inn where it is now displayed. There were events to be attended such as the opening of the Manchester Law Courts in the presence of the Queen in May 1961; the premiere of 'A Taste of Honey' with Rita Tushingham in September 1961; a Gala Performance at the Liverpool Playhouse, the local repertory theatre, of 'The School for Scandal' by Richard Brinsley Sheridan in the presence of Princess Marina in November 1961; a dinner at the Law Society in London in the presence of Queen Elizabeth, the Queen Mother; prize-giving at the local hospital; speeches to be made; and official dinners at Burnley in her role as Recorder, including a banquet at the Cafe Royal in London in May 1962 when Burnley reached the football Cup Final against Tottenham Hotspur, but unfortunately lost 3:1.

One activity did, however, come to an end at this time. In 1962 she was informed that following the reorganisation of the WRAC (TA) and the consequent disbandment of 320 (East Lancashire) Battalion WRAC (TA), her tenure of appointment was to terminate on 30 April 1962, but she was to retain the title of Honorary Colonel.

PREJUDICE AT THE BAR

Although by now the initial novelty of Rose's position was beginning to wear off and other women were reaching the higher echelons of their respective professions and business paths, the position of career women remained the subject of much debate. Regular articles under a kaleidoscope of different women-related topics continued to appear on the subject in which Rose was featured, often accompanied by a photograph of her, such as: 'Would You Look Good in a Wig', an article about the difficulties facing women barristers (*North Western Evening Mail*, 24 September 1960); 'Should the Lady be a Lawyer' discussing the dress code for women barristers (*The Mirror*, 22 September 1960); 'Woman's Place is Not Only in the Home', describing Rose as 'a famous and brilliant woman' (*Liverpool Daily Post*, 7 December 1960); 'Should Girls Play Second Fiddle' (Teenage Topics in the *Jewish Chronicle*, April 1961); and 'A Woman's Best Age' an article by Barbara Cartland in *Woman & Beauty* in 1962.

Women may have been 'on the march' as was said in one article, but there was still a long way to go. Women barristers remained ostracised in relation to social events on Circuit. It was not until November 1961 that women barristers on the Northern Circuit, including Rose, were for the first time invited to a social occasion with their male colleagues at the Bar, when a cocktail party was held to celebrate the opening of the new Law Courts in Manchester. It was still some years before they were allowed to attend Bar Mess.

Bar Mess are the twice weekly dinners held during Assizes. It is an opportunity to get to know one's fellow Circuiteers and for young members of the Bar to learn from their elders in convivial— and no doubt at times not very sober—circumstances. Tales of the happenings at Bar Mess are legion, but it also has a more useful function in that if anyone behaves badly in court it is soon known. The Junior of the Circuit, an elected young barrister, has the role of determining when people should sit down and, in the days when smoking in public was allowed, when permission should be given to smoke and, rather like dining in the Inns of Court in London, it is similarly ritualistic.

Women barristers were, however, barred from such events on the pretext that rude stories were told. Rose was also barred from attending judges' dinners and would have to write to the judges apologising for her absence. It was something which rankled with

Rose. When her colleagues would be dining together at Bar Mess and she was away from home—she would have to eat alone save on one occasion in 1960 when Rose was in Lancaster doing a case at the Assizes. She was sitting alone in the dining room of her hotel with a novel when Alex Karmel QC invited her to join the Mess for dinner. 'But I've just finished my dinner' she exclaimed. 'Never mind' said Alex, 'come and have another'—and she did. It certainly rattled cages for there was no knowing where it might end—women might even attend Grand Court! This is the Northern Circuit's big night where no ordinary guest is allowed and 'the most eminent members of the Circuit are gleefully deflated in carefully written speeches of studied insult and outrage'.

Presumably some of the comic questions, turns of phrase and repartees of Sir Noel Goldie, Recorder of Burnley in 1929 and of Manchester in 1935, were repeated, for he attended until his eighties. He was a much-loved character on the Northern Circuit such that a book of his 'sayings' entitled 'Goldiana' was compiled. It was said of him that he won more cases before juries, and then lost them in the Court of Appeal, than any other advocate. In that court he was once asked, 'Mr Goldie, have you considered the case of *Smith v Jones*?' 'If your Lordship pleases', said Goldie, 'with the greatest possible respect, the case, if I may say so, can be easily distinguished from the present'. 'That's a pity Mr Goldie', said the Lord Justice of Appeal, 'because I thought it was in your favour!' On another occasion during a trial he asked a little girl whether she attended St Luke's school to which she replied in the affirmative. He then asked 'And St Luke's has a boy's department and a girl's department?' 'Yes' she replied. 'And which department were you in, Marjorie?' asked Goldie without pausing for breath. Perhaps the most memorable of his sayings was when in his final speech he commented 'Members of the jury, so disfigured has my client's jaw become that never again will he be able to bite his bottom with his top teeth'.

Rose had to wait for 30 years of practice on the Northern Circuit before she and other women were allowed to attend Bar Mess at the end of the decade and enjoy the camaraderie and fun of such evenings. Apparently there was a postal vote—presumably of the male members of the Northern Circuit—to determine whether women should be admitted to Bar Mess. Even then a compromise was originally proposed and the Northern Circuit introduced a Ladies Night. Rose considered this a ridiculous idea and the lady members of the Northern Circuit, in solidarity with her, refused to contemplate the idea. The male members also determined that if women were admitted there should never be a woman leader of the Circuit. Astonishingly it was not until 1973, when Rose defied that rule and became the Leader of the Northern Circuit, that women were allowed to attend Grand Court.

Progress for women in the law had not moved forward greatly since Rose had been made a Recorder in 1956, although another female silk had been appointed when Dorothy Knight Dix was made a Queen's Counsel in 1957. It would still be a few years before the next rung on the judicial ladder was taken by a female.

18

Some New Experiences

THE MURDER OF A ROCK 'N' ROLL SINGER

A CAPITAL MURDER committed on the Glasgow to London express train leading to the death of a rock 'n' roll singer was a heady mix. Add to that Rose appearing for the defence and the papers had a field day. Thus began Rose's year in 1963.

David McKay, aged 28, and an engineer, was accused of shooting Thomas McBain, 'Big' Tommy McBain, a 14 stone, 20-year-old Glasgow rock 'n' roll singer and a Glasgow teenage idol, on the evening of 29 September 1962 as the train left Glasgow station. He was tried at Carlisle Assizes in January 1963 before Mr Justice Cantley and a jury. The story is best described in an extract from Rose's final speech:

> Very much the worse for drink, McBain eventually disturbed the peace of a compartment containing five sleepy men and women. There, McBain for the first time in their joint lives, met the accused, and McKay for the first time clapped eyes on McBain. Out of that meeting arose this tragedy. McBain lost his life and McKay sits here charged with capital murder ... McBain was boorish, unpleasant and disgustingly drunk. McKay was forebearing. Everyone was heartily sick of the whole incident, heavy with fatigue and longing for sleep. McKay pulled out the gun, which tragically he had with him, and showed it to McBain, hoping it would scare him. That did not happen and McKay pressed the trigger accidentally—negligently if you like—but with no intention of doing so. Do you really think he deliberately aimed to kill that man in a crowded railway compartment, with no possibility of escape from the moving train? Words fail me in trying to describe the gross stupidity in carrying that gun, but negligence is not murder. Some people have fishing for a hobby, some have golf. This man has guns. It was a ghastly coincidence that these two men should meet—one belligerent, needing to be quietened, and the other with a gun. Wasn't it cruel fate that put McKay, not an aggressive man, in that compartment?

He was acquitted of murder and found guilty of manslaughter. Saved from the gallows, he was sentenced to four years' imprisonment.

A week later the ballistics expert called for the defence sent Rose a very flattering letter as to her conduct of the case enclosing as a gift a print of the spent cartridge used in the murder—blown up 100 times—as a perhaps somewhat unusual and rather gruesome memento.

The local Glasgow evening paper recorded in an article entitled 'Star in a Wig and Gown':

> [I]t is not just in the world of entertainment that fans have their 'idols' ... Every day [in the Carlisle murder trial], more than 50 women packed the public benches to hear Miss Heilbron ... it was standing room only, with a handful of men sprinkled among the fur hats ... and the women listened intensely to every word spoken by this small woman who wore a smartly tailored black suit beneath her gown ... The women also gathered in the street outside to look as she left the court-room at the end of the day ... They were more like some hypnotised fans of a teenage "rockstar" than ordinary housewives. In Scotland we have two QCs but if, as seems likely, more are appointed, will they ever command the same following as Rose?

A WIDE-RANGING AND BUSY PRACTICE

The following month saw two defendants charged with murder successfully represented by Rose resulting in the verdicts being commuted to manslaughter. The first involved the horrific murder of a 12-year-old girl, Leslie Hobbs, by a 15-year-old boy who had a psychiatric disorder and whose plea of diminished responsibility was accepted by the jury at Liverpool Assizes. He was sentenced to be detained for life. Given the young age of the deceased and the accused, the case attracted much publicity. The second concerned a 32-year-old woman accused of murdering her husband who had been violent to her and had terrified her. But she was far from the Merry Widow of Franz Lehar's operetta. As she left the court she said that it was wonderful to be free, but that she was so very sorry to have lost the man she loved.

Then in April there was Rose's client, 'Uncle Eddie', vice-captain of his public house's darts team, whose wife went down to the cells to persuade him to plead guilty to murdering a 12-year-old girl, who was the daughter of his best friend. The next month at Lancaster Assizes there was the trial of Adrian Ayres accused of brutally killing 'Blackpool Albert', Albert Porter, his widowed father-in-law, in his bed with an axe or a chopper. He was acquitted following a submission by Rose on the ground that someone else had previously been tried and acquitted of the charge and the jury were being asked to say which of two men was the murderer. The murder trials kept on coming in all shapes and sizes: many, but not all, were domestic murders: a husband accused of murdering his wife (reduced to manslaughter); a man accused of murdering his eight-year-old step-sister (he got life imprisonment); murder of an invalid wife with barbiturates; a 16-year old boy shooting his father in self-defence; a mother who killed her 16-year-old daughter with an axe and was sent to the mental institution, Broadmoor. Rose did not win them all, but no more of her clients were hanged. Of course, defending alleged murderers was not the only form of criminal defence Rose undertook.

The flow of personal injury cases kept coming too, Rose trying to achieve as high an award of damages as she could for the unfortunate victims who had suffered so much as a result of their accidents. She was now only instructed in cases where the injuries were serious. A difficult judgement area was always whether to accept a sum paid into court, because if the judge awarded a lower sum, the plaintiff would not recover all of his or her costs. Rose still mostly acted for plaintiffs, but occasionally she did do defence work. Damages awards Rose achieved for her clients during this period included: £16,163 for a dock labourer who was paralysed from the waist down and condemned to a wheelchair for the rest of his life after falling down a ship's hold; £3,009 for a deaf and dumb boy of 12 who suffered very serious leg injuries after being knocked down by a van; £7,500 against the Motor Insurance Bureau for a 64-year-old lady who had been crippled and likewise condemned to a wheelchair when knocked down as a pedestrian by a 20-year-old uninsured driver; damages for a young boy who had severely injured himself by drinking cleaning fluid used by his mother to clean her public house; and £1,250 for a female passenger who sustained a serious head injury when the vehicle she was travelling in mounted the pavement and hit a lamp-post. These are only a random selection, but they exposed Rose to the hardships people had to endure as a result of such unfortunate accidents. It was no wonder that she always admonished Hilary to 'watch the traffic'.

These were the cases which made the newspapers, but, as throughout her career, there were a vast number and range of other cases which attracted little public interest, yet were naturally immensely important to the client for whom Rose acted. Rose's notes and at times some of the papers once the case had been completed, were neatly filed away by her then clerk under specific categories so they could be retrieved in the future for comparative purposes when preparing similar cases. Some of these cases reached trial; other civil cases Rose merely advised on and were settled before trial. Some of the personal injury cases concerned issues of liability and damages: others damages only. Civil cases were not confined to personal or medical injury cases and some involved interesting points of law, which Rose really enjoyed tackling.

In both her criminal and civil work Rose continued to appear at all the Assize towns of the Northern Circuit, namely: Liverpool, Manchester, Preston, Carlisle and Lancaster. She would commute whenever she could either by car or train, but Carlisle involved staying away from home. The larger Assizes would last for about three weeks during each of the four legal terms, depending on the list. Her professional client base remained large and solicitors instructed her from all over the country, though some of her instructing solicitors were particularly loyal and regular clients: Silverman & Livermore, Berkson & Co and in later years E Rex Makin & Co, WH Thompson and Hempsons to name just a few. As her practice was in criminal and common law she was not instructed by the large London City firms. Commercial work was not then, in practical terms, open to women at the Bar: that was not to occur for another decade.

SITTING AS RECORDER

As Recorder of Burnley, Rose heard appeals from magistrates. In August 1963 she heard a resumed planning appeal concerning Burnley Corporation's plans to create a new town centre. The appeal was brought by tenants and shopkeepers and businesses affected. Silks represented the parties and the case lasted six days. She reserved her decision until 22 November when she rejected Burnley's plans in part. Burnley also gave her the opportunity to be generous with other people's money! She gave £1 each to three boys who turned detectives when they heard two burglars plotting to break into a house as a 'Practical demonstration of the court's approval', commenting that this would be better appreciated by the boys than mere words. They had kept watch and had thrown a ball over the wall so that they had a reason to go and see what the thieves were up to.

Burnley sessions also had its lighter moments, or so it is said, though the story may be apocryphal. On one occasion prosecuting counsel was reading out a police record of antecedents of a defendant whom Rose was about to sentence. It said: 'The Defendant resides at 1 Duke Terrace with his common law wife, Mrs Ada Smith. He also cohabits with a Miss Johnson. His cohabitee lives at 43 York Street. His home conditions are good'. To which Rose allegedly retorted 'I'll say they are'.

THE ISLE OF MAN CASINO CASE

Perhaps the most interesting and unusual of Rose's cases of this period of her career was a case in the Isle of Man in June 1964. The Isle of Man is a self-governing Crown Dependency. The head of state is Queen Elizabeth II, who holds the title of Lord of Mann. The Crown is represented by a Lieutenant Governor. The island is not part of the United Kingdom, but foreign relations, defence, and ultimate governance of the Isle of Man are the responsibility of the government of the United Kingdom. It is a small island measuring only 52 kilometres long and 22 kilometres wide at its widest point. Its current population is approximately 84,000, a quarter of its population living in the capital, Douglas.

Its legal system is different from that in England and Wales. Lawyers in the Isle of Man are known as advocates, combining the roles of English solicitors and barristers, and are organised into partnerships. Although English law does not extend to the Isle of Man, the Manx legal system is based on the principles of English common law, like the legal systems of most Commonwealth countries. Manx criminal law was codified in the nineteenth century and is closely based on English law. The Island's High Court judges are the two Deemsters (a term dating from Viking times), who have jurisdiction over all the criminal and civil matters that in England would fall under the High Court, County Court and Crown Court. The Manx Appeal Court consists of the Deemsters and the Judge of Appeal, a part-time position filled by an English QC. The final appeal, one that is rarely pursued, is to the Judicial Committee of the Privy Council in London.

Rose was instructed by her old university friend, Barney Berkson, to appear on behalf of four former casino employees, all American: William Paris, aged 39, of Las Vegas; Frank O'Neill, aged 49; Raymond Gavlin, aged 45; and Arthur Anderson, aged 23. None of the four men had any previous convictions. They were charged with conspiring to steal money from the Isle of Man or Manx Casino between 1 May and 18 December 1963 and receiving stolen money. Anderson was also charged with stealing £18 from the Casino company.

The Manx Casino was the first and, at the time, only public casino in Britain. It had been set up following the coming into force of the Gaming, Betting and Lotteries (Casino) Act 1962. A Mrs Saul had put up most of the capital for the casino, but was a sleeping partner and not a director. The Casino was run by a William Arthur

Albury Junior and a Mr Hickey who were directors of the company and who, along with Mrs Saul, had been granted the Manx Casino concession.

Rose had to obtain a licence from the Manx Law Society at a cost of £50 and be admitted to appear as an advocate for the particular case, such an appearance being a rare occurrence for an English barrister. She also had to learn all about gaming and the various types of games such as blackjack, her previous knowledge being limited to a very basic game of family roulette, the family having somehow acquired in the distant past a roulette wheel. Her juniors were Jack Corrin and Martin Moore, both from the Isle of Man. Rose was paid 3,000 guineas for the case. The case involved a huge amount of work and trips to the Isle of Man to meet her clients and visit the casino.

The Trial before the Deemster

The trial began on Monday, 22 June 1964 before Deemster G E Moore. It was held in the Tynwald Court Chamber. The Attorney General of the Isle of Man, Mr David Lay, prosecuted. It was to be a case of dramatic twists and turns. It attracted extensive daily front page press coverage in the Isle of Man, was reported widely in the English newspapers and was even mentioned on television.

Day 1 started with Rose challenging 27 jurors before the seven-man jury was selected. The prosecution case was that there had been various fiddles at the casino including inflating the record of winnings made to winning punters, which meant that half the defendants' pay was made up from what were termed 'cuts from the top'. The defence claimed that it was their legitimate wage paid by arrangement with Hickey and Albury, their bosses, on whose instructions the fiddle had been carried out: there was thus no question of the monies being stolen without the company's knowledge.

The first and main prosecution witness was James Gilson aged 21, a cashier at the Casino. He had originally been charged, along with the other four defendants, and had similarly been represented by Rose and Barney Berkson to whom he had made a statement. He later turned Queen's evidence and appeared for the prosecution, Rose and Barney Berkson ceased to act for him and the charges were dropped against him. Unbeknown to Rose and her instructing solicitor at the time, he had in fact given the police the tip-off for the original raid the previous December.

Gilson was cross-examined by Rose for over a day. He was forced to accept that Hickey and Albury knew what was going on and were evidently receiving sums of money. He admitted that the statement he had made to Barney Berkson, at a time when he had already become a police informer, had been false. He supposed, that as he had by then become a police informant, he must have told the police that he was making a false statement to his solicitor. He was then questioned about his original statement to the police at the time of the raid the previous December, which he said had been written out in longhand, allegedly done at the home of a detective sergeant in the case. Rose asked for production of the original statement. The Attorney General said his instructions were that they were only notes and had been destroyed. At this Rose retorted:

> It is nothing short of scandalous that this document should not be available. It is a very important document that this man dictated and it should be here. A policeman's notebook and notes are not just destroyed. Any note made at the time must be kept by a police officer.

Other witnesses were called to support the prosecution case, including Luigi del Blanco, a Casino director, and were cross-examined by Rose. The last prosecution witness was Albury, 'a most material witness', but despite the IOM Police and the CID contacting the FBI, he failed to appear. At the end of six days the prosecution closed its case. Rose made a submission in the absence of the jury that there was no case to answer on the evidence adduced by the prosecution, the onus of proof of course being on the prosecution, but the Deemster rejected it.

The following day Rose said that she intended to stand by her submission and would not call any of the defendants. Instead she addressed the jury for three hours. Rose argued that the prosecution case had crumbled and collapsed. She questioned why the four defendants had to suffer the agony of being incarcerated in the Isle of Man for six months and have their passports and work permits taken from them. She described Albury and Hickey as 'these two despicable creatures' who fled the island, who not only allowed the scheme to continue for their own mercenary ends, but involved their employees in it too. It was a scheme she said 'to produce a rich harvest' of untaxed wealth for Albury and Hickey.

She stressed that the hand that should have arrested Albury, ie the police, was stayed and instead he was handed back his passport and waved off at the airport, leaving with 'indecent haste'. She pointed to Albury's opulent lifestyle and commented rhetorically that someone along the line did not want Albury prosecuted. She was particularly scathing about the police planting an informer in a conference between the four accused and their legal advisers when preparing their defence, describing it as an abuse of privilege.

Her criticism did not end at the prosecution's evidence. As the newspaper headlines put it 'Woman QC Raps Judge' 'Rose QC Attacks Judge In Casino Case'. 'Rose Heilbron QC and Judge Clash'. During the Deemster's summing up to the jury, seeing Rose shaking her head, he asked her if there was anything wrong and if she wanted to address him. She replied: 'I was rather astonished about a remark you made. I thought the jury was going to decide this case. When your Honour tells the jury what Your Honour has decided I am just lost for words'. To which he retorted: 'If you don't like it you have a remedy in another place'.

The jury found all four men guilty of conspiracy to steal. Instead of the usual plea of mitigation, Rose courageously told the Judge: 'My clients are so shocked at the summing-up they have instructed me not to ask for mercy. All they wanted was justice. I am instructed to give immediate notice of appeal'.

The run in with the Judge did not end there; the four having been found guilty on one charge, the judge said that he would next deal with the other charges against them to which Rose commented: 'That makes the whole summing-up bad in my opinion. Obviously Your Honour cannot sum up on half the indictment. It is quite ridiculous'. The jury was then directed to find the men not guilty on the other charges. The four men were sentenced to six months' imprisonment and fined and told they would be recommended for deportation. One of the defendants, Frank O'Neill, jumped up and declared: 'I speak for all of the defendants and we all feel this is a tremendous travesty of justice'.

The Four Accused Appeal

An appeal was lodged the same day setting out seven grounds of appeal and alleging that the summing up was heavily biased and unfair and contrary to every principle of natural justice. An application was made to the senior Deemster, S J Kneale, who granted them bail pending appeal. The appeal was heard on 30 September 1964 before the Manx Court of Criminal Appeal comprising Joe Cantley QC (later an English High Court Judge) and Senior Deemster

S J Kneale. Rose and Jack Corrin did the appeal pro bono, ie without a fee, as the four men were destitute.

The Attorney General conceded that the judge had never explained the legal definition of larceny, ie theft. This was crucial because during the trial the defence had submitted that a second weekly wage packet for each man was paid with the full knowledge of the casino company, namely Hickery and Albury, whereas the prosecution had alleged it was paid with money stolen from the company.

The Appeal Judge said that the judge had directed the jury impeccably on the charge of conspiracy, but not on the charge of stealing, nor had he put all the relevant facts to the jury. He analysed the evidence and concluded that there were three alternative explanations for the defendants' actions, namely: first, that they had in fact conspired to steal the money; secondly that they were attempting to defraud the Manx government (a 15 per cent tax being levied on all gaming), but they were not charged with that; and thirdly, that the company by its agents, Albury and Hickey, had agreed to pay the amount as a salary to the defendants.

He concluded that the jury must have been misled by the Judge's summing-up and that the judge had not put the issue of conspiracy to defraud the defendants' employers fully to the jury, adding that such a fundamental omission was fatal to the resulting verdict. 'For those reasons I am of the opinion that the convictions cannot be sustained and that the appeal ought to be allowed and the appellants discharged'. The Senior Deemster concurred telling the defendants: 'If there had been other charges you would have been in a very grave position. You have nothing to congratulate yourselves on'.

The four accused were inordinately grateful to Rose. The *Daily Express* accordingly, with a little embellishment, headlined an article on 2 October 1964 'Casino Men Kiss Their QC'. But this was 1964, not the twenty-first century, and it led the next day to the following apology:

> In our report it was stated that after the case these four men kissed Miss Heilbron. We are asked to point out that although the men expressed their thanks to her, at no stage did they kiss her. We apologise to Miss Heilbron for any embarrassment caused.

Rose was in turn very grateful to her junior whom she rewarded with a red bag used for carrying court robes, a tradition of the English Bar which occurs when a junior is in his or her first major case and provides his or her leader with particular assistance.

The four men, having spent all their savings to clear their name, were penniless and, with the help of the American Consul in Liverpool, immediately made their way back to the United States. It is believed that Paris subsequently returned to England to open a club in Nottingham. The following March an inquiry was held into matters relating to the Casino by a tribunal of three, chaired by Sir Benjamin Ormerod. Its terms of reference concerned the granting of and the operation of the concession and the delay in instituting judicial proceedings leading to the above trial. One of the issues was why Albury had not been charged, but it was said that there was insufficient evidence to charge him at the time and this was largely accepted by the Tribunal.

HOME LIFE AND A TEENAGE DAUGHTER

Rose tried to have a balanced life, though when she was very busy she could not always achieve it. She was happy just being at home with her family, watching not very highbrow television, pottering around the house, talking to the gardener about the garden, doing household chores, taking Tandy for a walk, shopping, having her hair done and enjoying her lovely home. Despite her fame, at home, apart from having domestic help to assist her, she was just a normal housewife and mother doing the things wives and mothers do. Rose and Nat both had strong personalities and the house was always fully of lively discussion and lots of laughter. Nat was a fund of jokes and Rose was susceptible to uncontrollable fits of the giggles.

As with many families, and before YouTube, videos and multiple televisions, there was occasional family discord as to which television programme to watch. Nat usually knew when he was beat and gave in to the demands of the distaff side of the family wanting to watch the latest thriller or TV drama. However, Match of the Day on Saturday evenings was sacrosanct and Rose and Hilary would escape once the theme music started.

Somehow Rose also found time to entertain a large circle of friends and family at Parklands and to join Nat in a busy social life in Liverpool. Rose was always very vivacious in the company of her friends and colleagues, though remained inherently diffident on more formal occasions, which over the years she learnt to overcome. Nat was likewise very popular. According to a story told by Nat, which has probably been embellished over the years, Rose had been less worldly when they first met. He recalled giving her

her first gin and tonic which she apparently gulped down as if lemonade, with the inevitable consequences.

In vacations friends or Nat's relatives would come to stay. Every three years his sister Esta and her husband, Harry Nelson, who lived in South Africa, would visit their wider family in England, Scotland and Ireland, usually spending three weeks with Rose and Nat either in Liverpool or on holiday. As Rose became more senior she would also regularly entertain the High Court Judges to dinner when they were on Assizes in Liverpool, often doing some of the cooking herself in conjunction with Mrs Simms. Chicken Kiev, then a new and fashionable dish, was a particular favourite. Rose produced lists of menus reflecting her habit of list-making as an aide-memoire. This habit extended to both professional and non-professional matters and encompassed lists for such things as packing and cleaning.

Other forms of entertainment included visits to the cinema and the theatre and to the local Liverpool show. Visits were made to see relatives in Liverpool, Glasgow, London and Dublin. On Jewish holidays the family went to synagogue, though Rose became much less religious as she grew older. There were also long holidays when the Assizes did not sit: three weeks at Christmas, 10 days at both Easter and Whitsun and the whole of August and September and these provided a much needed respite for Rose to catch up. It was during these breaks that Rose would usually go to Burnley to sit as Recorder. Rose tended to drive more once she had bought her first automatic car, a Rover 2000, not only to courts, but also enjoying a drive into the countryside with Hilary, though she did tend to drive fast, much to Nat's disapproval.

Once ensconced in Parklands, holidays continued to provide the time for cleaning, tidying and reorganising cupboards, polishing the copper pans (a regular chore which the staff failed to do!), picking apples from the orchard in the garden and storing them in trays in the store cupboard, filing her press cuttings assisted by Hilary, catching up on non-court work such as opinions, as well as seeing the friends and relatives whom she had little time to see during legal terms. Rose also began to develop an interest in cooking, inspired by Mrs Simms, and acquired a seemingly endless selection of cookery books and recipes. Sunday evenings, Mrs Simms' day off, would be the day to experiment and she would try out new recipes for dinner while Nat went to the golf club. Infuriatingly, he would often arrive home late, such that the precise timing of the relevant dish sometimes went awry.

As Hilary became a teenager, the child care and other domestic needs changed. Rose's career obviously impacted at a practical level in that arrangements still had to be made for looking after Hilary and for providing meals for Nat and Hilary when she was not around. A teenage daughter still required some supervision. There was the perennial juggling of staff to make sure there was always someone to meet her at the bus stop and be there when she got home from school or in the school holidays, particularly after Gladys, the home help, left and Rose relied more on part-time help. There was Tandy to be walked every day and taken on Saturdays to be clipped and washed, though it was Hilary's duty to bath him in the interim, an experience which he did not like. There were tennis games to arrange on the tennis court. Rose played occasionally, but Nat was the better player.

Rose had to learn, like other mothers, to adapt in other ways too to living with a teenager, as Hilary's own life at the time grew increasingly absorbed with exams and boys. Parties were no longer afternoon affairs, but Saturday evenings and with mixed company, where the latest hits from the many Liverpool groups which were around at the time including the Beatles and Gerry and the Pacemakers, were usually aired. But Rose always entered into the spirit of things. On one occasion Hilary was invited to a fancy dress party and decided she wanted to go as Goldfinger. Rose engaged her then dressmaker to make her an outfit in gold material and bought her some gold nail-polish to finish off the ensemble. Rose also gave parties for Hilary and her teenage friends with the strict instructions that her guests could not wear stilettos as these would dent the lovely wooden parquet floors. Christmas and birthday presents produced such things as a sewing machine and a record player. Peer pressure led to requests for more sophisticated clothing from the 'sloppy joes', the large sweaters that were fashionable at the time, to the heels on shoes that Hilary asked for—and, of course, got. Hilary's friends would come to stay and she would stay with them. Rose tried—and succeeded—in keeping family life as normal as possible.

Rose, as did Nat, undoubtedly spoilt their daughter. Such over-indulgence was no doubt partly because Hilary was an only child, but partly, one suspects, because of a misplaced guilt felt by Rose about not always being around. However, she was also a disciplinarian from the time when Rose told her daughter as a small child that there was no such word as 'no' in the English language when asked to do something, to chastisement for other aspects of her misbehaviour as she grew older.

Rose's chatty, loving and daily letters from London and elsewhere about what she had been doing and her longing to be back home with her family give some flavour not only of her maternal role, but also of her warmth. They would regularly contain exhortations such as 'do not go to bed too late'; 'No I won't take your gramophone away <u>this</u> time, but please darling for your own sake don't let it happen again—you know how tired you get and how difficult it is to get up in the morning'; 'do be careful sweetie of the traffic and if you walk alone along Allerton Road, don't talk to strangers'; 'wrap yourself up well and wear your boots if it is still cold, but see they are clean. Comb your hair and don't rush'; and 'Do as much work as possible while I am away and then we can have lots of time together'. As parents Rose and Nat were however probably a little over-protective, but one can understand why. Other letters promised treats: 'I saw our friend too and he has given me quite the loveliest of colours for your carpet—in fact I think he's much more interested in your room than any other'; 'I am looking forward to the hols ... and to our first shopping expedition—was it for a sewing machine ...? I'll soon be home and ... we're going to have a whale of a time. Get the list ready for your birthday and start thinking of games'.

Absorption in the casino case did not let Rose off nagging from Hilary. 1964 was when the Beatles were at the height of their fame. They had recently captured the United States and had many hits at the top of both the UK and US hit parades. They were sons of Liverpool and the talk of Hilary's teenage peers. Rose and Nat's friendship with Harry and Queenie Epstein, parents of the Beatles manager, Brian Epstein, led to Hilary getting tickets to concerts and various memorabilia. On Friday 10 July, Liverpool held a civic reception in their honour. Rose had access to an invitation via the Lord Mayor of Liverpool. Hilary's contemporaneous diary entries indicate that Hilary had pressed her Mother during her time in the Isle of Man, as only teenagers can, to get her tickets so that she and a friend could attend the reception, which ultimately she did and Hilary 'stood very near them'. The lyrics of the Beatles single 'A Hard Day's Night', released at this time, could not have more aptly described Rose's sojourn in the Isle of Man: 'It's been a hard day's night, I have been working like a dog'.

Inevitably, as Hilary grew older, her own horizons widened and she began to absorb more of what her mother was doing when she was working. Rose would talk about her cases and her work in lay terms to Nat and Hilary, as well as about the various personalities she came across in her work and in the other activities she undertook. Although Hilary accompanied her mother on visits to Burnley in school holidays to see her sitting as a judge, she did not listen to her as an advocate in court until she was about 17 and then it was only occasionally. Somehow tagging a young daughter along to watch her mother in action did not seem to arise. However, Rose's enthusiasm for her career must have rubbed off onto Hilary for once she addressed herself to the issue when she was about 15, it was always a career as a barrister which beckoned, though at that stage she had not envisioned the area of law that she eventually entered. There was no pressure from her parents as to which career to follow. In Hilary's gap year, before going to Oxford University, Rose arranged for her to spend some time in a solicitors' office in Liverpool to make sure that she had chosen the branch of the law which she liked best.

How Rose packed so much into her life seems remarkable, but she always had unstinting support from Nat. She undoubtedly got tired and at times fed up with all she had to do. Nat would write to her when she was away, encouraging her to relax or have a rest. On one occasion for example she wrote from her chambers in London: 'I am a little bit overwhelmed with work at the moment, but I expect I'll cope'.

VARIOUS FORMS OF ENTERTAINMENT

The previous year Rose had had her own first foray into the entertainment world, when in December 1963 she was invited to become one of the board of governors of London Independent Television Producers Ltd. This was the company formed by a group of 125 writers, producers, directors and show business personalities who had applied to the Independent Television Authority for one of the principal network company licences which lasted for three years. Other governors included many famous names from the word of theatre and the arts such as: Dame Peggy Ashcroft; Anthony Asquith; John Betjeman; Rose's good friend, Dame Edith Evans; Ivan Foxwell; Christopher Fry; Jack Hawkes, Bernard Miles; John Mills; Mrs JB Priestly (Jaquetta Hawkes); Sir Michael Redgrave; Dame Flora Robson, Sir John Rothenstein and Peter Ustinov. Chairman of the board of directors was Sidney Box, the film producer and director of Tyne Tees Television. They had already secured studio space at Shepperton Studios and acquired over £3 million working capital. Despite the impressive list of governors, the endeavour does not appear to have been successful.

Earlier in the year Rose appeared on British television for the first time. 'Panorama', a weekly news programme, dedicated a whole episode to Liverpool in April 1964. The late and much admired commentator, Richard Dimbleby, anchored the programme which was filmed at the Adelphi Hotel. Many local dignitaries attended the occasion. Richard Dimbleby introduced the programme thus:

> We have come to Liverpool because it is bursting out all over ... I think the reasons for Liverpool's pre-eminence spring from a number of factors, but one of the main reasons must be because it is such a cosmopolitan city. Because of your tremendous and terrific cross-section of personalities and people—I think you have the reason why Liverpool is such a great and famous city today. The Beatles aren't the be-all and end-all of Liverpool. You have two famous soccer sides [Liverpool and Everton], two wonderful cathedrals and some magnificent public buildings, besides a city rich in cultural heritage. It's a great city in its own right.

Richard Dimbleby spoke to Rose and in response to a question, Rose replied: 'I think it is a wonderful thing to be a native of Liverpool. I am very proud of being a Liverpudlian'. That was the end of her television career—she never appeared on television again—not for want of asking.

SOME IMPORTANT SPEECHES

Rose did, however, continue with her speaking roles and attendance at other formal events. She proposed the toast of the Magistrates' Association at the annual dinner of the Merseyside Branch in January 1963; she attended a conference organised by the Federation Internationale des Femmes des Carrieres Juridiques at the House of Commons where the reply was given by Maître Marlise Ernst-Henrion, Presidente de la Federation. The following year Rose arranged for Hilary to stay with the Henrions and their sons and daughter in Brussels to improve her French. Madame Henrion's husband was a well-known banker and later became Minister of Finance in the Belgian Government. While there, as usual, Hilary received motherly advice in her daily letters, as the following extract from a letter she wrote illustrates:

> My darling,
>
> Just received your <u>most</u> welcome letter. We are absolutely delighted you are having such a 'fab' time, and we are not a bit disappointed you are

not missing us. I gather Francois' friends are very nice, but don't neglect him for his friends. Remember you are <u>his</u> guest. I hope you are helping Madame Henrion ... I managed to get your lipstick ... Everything is much the same here—I took Tandy to the Park this morning and then to Allerton Road to get your lipstick. That cost me £5 because I saw all sorts of things I needed in Tesco, Reeces, Boots etc. I am writing this in Mrs S's room and Tandy is looking at me out of the corner of his eye ...

All my very dearest love ... xx Mum xx

In July 1963, Rose spoke at the annual dinner of the British Federation of University Women: 'This is still a man's world although men in this country are dependent on 8 million women who work'. Her theme was that she thought women could do more to help themselves. 'If we were to analyse our own feelings, I think we would realise that many women are suspicious of working women. They are surprised when women can give a practical demonstration that home and work can be combined'.

She urged that the power for good and peace which the women of this country possessed must be realised, commenting:

> But we do not speak where the voices count. How many important women can you think of in the international scene? How many women speak for us on the national scene or even locally? I think it is very important that in the next years women harness that power. They have to do good and to do something to check this sense of futility in what is becoming an insane world.

In July, Rose attended the Society of Labour Lawyers Annual Dinner at Waldorf. The guest speakers were: Harold Wilson MP, who was made Prime Minister the following year and Anthony Wedgewood Benn, who became a Cabinet Minister in the Labour Government of 1964. Dingle Foot QC MP, later Solicitor General, was Chairman. Those present also included two future Lord Chancellors: Gerald Gardiner QC and Elwyn Jones QC. Rose was never an active politician. In her university days had stood as the Conservative candidate in a mock election. She changed allegiance as she grew older, and no doubt influenced by the poverty Nat saw in his practice and the deprivation she saw among some of her own clients, she became a member of the Society of Labour Lawyers for a time.

On 22 October of the following year, she gave the key address to 500 magistrates at the opening of the Magistrates' Association Annual General Meeting in the New Hall, Lincoln's Inn. It was a wide-ranging speech with themes which still resonate today and had considerable press coverage.

First, she attacked a 'noticeable and steady decline' in British morals:

> What was once wrong, fraudulent or dishonest is now euphemistically called a fiddle. There is the commercial exploitation of sex. There is an excessive and unhealthy interest in violent crime both real and imaginary. This inevitably produces a society in which delinquent attitudes thrive and grow. It seems that whatever we try to do to or with offenders there is still an upsurge of crime.

Secondly, she directed her thoughts to young people, whom she commented seemed little interested in living: only in having. Thirdly, she advocated hostels to rehabilitate 'inadequate' criminals in a sheltered atmosphere. In prison, she said, the petty offender was often 'infected' by the vicious professional criminal. She then referred to a television play in which the opening scene was one in which a girl was stabbed in the back with a dagger:

> It was horrifying. I'm glad my teenage daughter wasn't there to see it. I don't think television would make a criminal out of a normal level-headed person, but I do think things like this could be toned down a bit.

Next, she also reiterated her suggestion that regional courts of appeal should be set up within the existing framework of Circuits and Assizes in a few different centres up and down the country to hear appeals from a particular area. She argued that there should be, from time to time, itinerant judges of appeal and that this would benefit the rest of the country greatly and save time and expense, as well as enhance the status of the regional centres of appeal. This issue, nearly 50 years on, remains the subject of much debate, although there are now some appeal hearings on Circuit.

Finally, she returned to another old theme of hers: a restriction on lengthy public committal proceedings. This was eventually introduced into law many years later. She contrasted once again the position in Scotland. She explained that she was a defender of the rights of the press, but that in such cases publicity was not avoided, merely delayed.

> Why should a man be virtually tried twice in the full glare of publicity? How can a jury, especially in sensational trials, be expected to approach the matter with an open mind after reading all the details of a preliminary hearing?

As is apparent, Rose's reforming ideas were regularly ahead of her time.

BLOOD BROTHERS

Her views on publicised committal proceedings were brought into sharp focus again shortly after this speech in a case in which she herself was later to be instructed on behalf of the accused. At about 10pm on 20 October 1965 Mary Josephine (Maureen) Adamson of 3, Rosedale Road, Allerton, a 50 year old single lady and nurse at the Rathbone hospital, was strangled and raped by someone who was lying in wait for her as she returned from work. The culprit seized her before she barely crossed the threshold of her front door. There were no signs of forcible entry and the electricity had been switched off. The attacker had escaped by the back door. Her nephew, Daniel James John Browne, aged 17, rang for an ambulance from a public call box saying he had found the body of his aunt. Browne was subsequently charged with his aunt's murder.

At the committal hearing in December held before the stipendiary magistrate, the accused's solicitor asked for the press to be excluded from the committal proceedings because of the wide publicity and potential prejudicial effect on future jurors. The response from the Stipendiary Magistrate was clear: 'This is a most unusual form of application. You are asking me to exclude the press from reporting committal proceedings. I have never heard of such an application being granted'.

The trial took place at Liverpool Crown Court in early January 1965. Rose represented the defendant. Browne's family had been preparing to emigrate to Australia at the end of October and had moved out of their house, Miss Adamson taking over the tenancy. On the night before the murder Browne's mother stayed in the house with her sister, the deceased, but Browne went temporarily to stay with his friend Jones and his family. Browne retained a key to the house.

Browne maintained that he had been cycling around Sefton Park and had been to the house earlier in the evening about 7.30pm on October 20, the night of murder. He said he had asked Lyn, the younger brother of his friend Haydn Jones, to accompany him to the house and when he opened the front door there was something obstructing the front door. The attacker had left by the back door.

The defence revolved principally around two issues: timing and the forensic evidence. Browne said that he had returned to his lodgings at about 6.45pm and had then gone to see a neighbour of his aunt's in Rosedale Road at about 7.45/50pm. He had next visited his aunt's house, which had previously been his home, to nose around for about 15–20 minutes before meeting up with his landlady's son, Haydn Jones, with whom he remained all night. The neighbour's evidence, based on what he was then watching on television, was that Browne had visited him at 8.50 pm, ie an hour later than alleged by Browne. This was critical because, if correct, he would have left just in time to catch his aunt returning from work. Rose cross-examined the neighbour at length to which he eventually answered 'I had to use logic with the help of the police to work out what time he called'.

The second issue related to blood found on both the deceased and Browne, both being of type O, the commonest type of blood. Browne's case was that two days before the murder he had cut himself with a razor blade and then had a race with another son of his landlady, Trevor Jones, to see how fast their blood could run down their arms so that they could become blood brothers. This could explain the source of the blood on his clothes. A complaint had been made about the method of testing in the laboratories, because the tests had been started in the absence of the director of the laboratories. The reliability of the forensic evidence was thus put into question.

The case lasted five days and a large number of witnesses were called. In her final speech Rose, having commented on the unreliability of the neighbour's evidence as to timing, said:

> You have not got here a young thug. Before you is a normal boy who comes from a nice family. This case is almost motiveless. It is almost unbelievable that a youth of 17, as he was at the time, should entertain the unnatural desire to rape his own aunt of 50 years of age and murder her.

After retiring for just over two and a half hours, the jury agreed with the defence and returned a verdict of not guilty. Rose had not lost her touch with juries.

19

Temporary Disappointments and Long-Term Achievements

ROSE'S AMBITION IN recent years had been to become a High Court Judge. It was regarded as the pinnacle of a barrister's career and brought with it a knighthood (for men), a pension and security. Likewise it meant no more waiting for briefs to land on one's desk; no more worrying when there was a lull in one's practice; and no more waiting for years to be paid by the Legal Aid Fund. However, there had never been a female High Court Judge before. Rose had hoped it might be her one day, though at only 51 she was still quite young for the office. She had been asked to stand for Parliament and had often been tipped as a future peeress, but it was the High Court Bench to which she really aspired.

In February 1962 Rose became the first woman to be appointed a Commissioner of Assize by the Lord Chancellor. She was to sit in Manchester. This was the first of at least three occasions when she was so appointed to sit in either Liverpool or Manchester. The significance of such appointments was not appreciated by those outside the profession, but it was an important stepping stone to becoming a High Court Judge. Commissioners of Assize try High Court cases and were appointed from time to time to assist High Court Judges with the heavy case load or to try a specific case. They were usually appointed for a period of two to three weeks. They stayed at the judges' lodgings with the High Court Judges and, apart from not wearing red robes, acted and performed as if they were High Court Judges.

In a letter home written on her arrival the first time she was so appointed, Rose described how well she had been looked after during her first stay in lodgings and how the housekeeper had unpacked everything. 'It is all <u>very</u> exciting and tremendously thrilling. I feel less nervous than I did and am quite looking forward to tomorrow' she wrote. She added: 'By the way I am called "Miss Commissioner Heilbron"—I wonder who worked it out!' On her first foray as Commissioner, as with her later appointments, Rose had a varied mix of cases.

On one of the occasions, in April 1967, the *Sunday Telegraph* wrote:

> 'Portia comes to Judgment'. Another woman judge may soon grace the Bench ... earlier this month Miss Rose Heilbron QC sat as Commissioner of Assize in Manchester ... She maintains her femininity as devotedly as her place at the overwhelmingly masculine Bar.

By all accounts she was 'a tremendous success as commissioner' and some of her colleagues wrote hoping that it would lead to a more permanent appointment. The appointments provided a good opportunity to road test a future High Court Judge in the days before the Judicial Studies Board. Rose might have legitimately expected a permanent appointment soon thereafter had she been a man.

A record of only a few of the cases she tried as Commissioner survives. One concerned allowing a 14-year-old girl to use a house for immoral purposes; another concerned theft and assault, in which Rose jailed two men for three years when found guilty of stealing a handbag from a woman, attempting to steal one from another woman, assaulting one woman and attempted robbery with aggravation. She said that women are entitled to walk the streets of Manchester without being attacked and having their handbags snatched. A third concerned the 'Orgy' man whom she sentenced to seven years' imprisonment when he was found guilty of four charges of indecent assault and one of unlawful sexual intercourse with girls of 13 and under. The most substantial case she tried was, however, when she sat in Manchester to hear a fraud case lasting 3–4 weeks involving the Deansgate Mail Order Company.

The family for the previous few years had spent most summer holidays abroad, often in Italy. Ivor Taylor, a junior on the Northern Circuit at the time, had suggested that they join his family at the Lido in Venice in August 1965. With some apprehension, as the Lido was not really Rose and Nat's thing, they agreed. Their apprehension was not misplaced: the spectacle of dogs on the beach wearing collars made of real diamonds was an amusing distraction, but indicative of the wealthy clientele staying on the Lido at the time, far removed from their lifestyle. Nonetheless the holiday had its memorable moments. The family had been to hear 'Tosca' at the Venice Opera House on 18 August 1965 and literally as they walked into St Mark's Square after the opera, the clock struck midnight, ushering in Rose's 51st Birthday.

It was not, however, the incompatibility of many of the sun worshippers which put a dampener on the holiday, but an article in the newspapers which appeared on 13 August 1965. There, on the front page was the announcement that Elizabeth Lane QC was to become the first woman High Court Judge and to sit in the Family Division. She had been made Recorder of Derby in 1961 and was made the first woman County Court Judge (now called Circuit Judge) in September 1962. But she had nothing like the profile of Rose and really only came to public prominence in a judicial role less than three years earlier. Rose was naturally very disappointed and a little surprised.

She did not let her disappointment show to anyone other than her family. She led the tributes at a dinner given by women barristers for which Elizabeth Lane wrote to thank her, saying 'no one has, or ever will, paid me a more handsome tribute than you did in your speech—which I shall always be proud to remember. Thank you so much. Affectionately, Elizabeth'. The following February, Rose appeared before Elizabeth Lane at Liverpool Assizes: the first time a female QC had appeared before a female High Court Judge. Rose had to wait nearly a decade for her turn to come, but there were more 'firsts' to be acquired along the way. There were still only 103 practising women barristers out of a total of 2,073 practising barristers and only three female Queen's Counsel.

It was not the best of summers for Rose. Rose and Nat returned home via Brussels leaving Hilary to spend three weeks in Brussels with the Henrions to improve her conversational French. While Hilary was away Rose fractured her elbow when taking Tandy for a walk in Calderstones Park. On her return Hilary, aged 16, had to be rescued by her parents returning to Manchester airport, as she was not allowed through customs without paying duty on her declared purchases—the problem was that she had spent all her money in Brussels! This no doubt led to a lecture on spending.

CAUSE FOR REFLECTION

The recognition that she was not going to be appointed a High Court Judge in the immediate future gave Rose cause for reflection. By 1966 she was a very senior silk, having been made a Queen's Counsel some 17 years earlier. She had a very large criminal and civil practice, and though the cases became, with time, less newsworthy, there were still plenty of gruesome murder trials and other significant cases. Over the next few years she continued to defend those accused of murder by poisoning, by strangulation, by stabbing and by hitting; those charged with murdering strangers, neighbours and relatives, whether young or old; whether provoked, premeditated or on the spur of the moment; those accused of murder who were quite sane, but wicked, or who were mentally unstable; and those who were innocent. She represented alleged thieves, tricksters, conspirators, fraudsters, bribers, assaulters and defendants accused of every other conceivable crime. Some cases went to the Court of Criminal Appeal. She also continued to prosecute. Criminal cases were mostly funded by legal aid, but some were privately paid.

However, as Rose grew older murder trials lost their allure and she increasingly found more fulfilment in the civil side of her practice. Although famous for her advocacy, she also really loved the law and legal problems and over her career had many cases reported in the Law Reports. Apart from the personal injury and medical negligence cases, she tackled other civil cases and even some divorce cases.

Several of Rose's civil cases went to the Court of Appeal, including a case in 1966 concerning the Factories Acts.[1] In another important case Rose represented an 81-year-old woman, Mrs Gore, who sued the conductor of a bus, Mr Van der Lann, an employee of Liverpool Corporation, for causing her to break her arm when she fell boarding a bus.[2] Mrs Gore had been issued with a free bus pass by Liverpool Corporation. The issue was whether this pass excluded liability for the corporation's servants on the basis that it was no more than a licence which in turn excluded liability. The defendant therefore sought to prevent the action proceeding by way of an injunction. Rose contended on behalf of Mrs Gore that the acceptance by the corporation of her application for a bus pass constituted 'a contract for the conveyance of a passenger in a public service vehicle' which rendered void any exclusion of liability.[3] Rose succeeded and the appeal was dismissed with costs. It was an important case.

Rose continued to enjoy her role as Recorder and lost none of her feminine intuition while so judging. In October 1966, the landlord of

[1] *Kelly v John Dale Ltd* [1965] 1 QB 185.
[2] *Gore v Van der Lann* [1967] 2 QB 31.
[3] Section 151 Road Traffic Act 1960.

the Coach and Horses public house appealed a £10 fine ordered by the magistrates for serving drink to an under aged girl, ie under 18. The 16-year-old girl turned up in court in a working dress and scarf hiding her hair curlers. Rose sent her home to put on make-up, recognising that she had 'dressed down' for the court appearance. There were gasps in court when she returned in full make-up, with her hair piled high on her head and wearing a smart blue blouse and tiny mini skirt, at which point the counsel representing the police acknowledged that he seemed to have no case. Rose commented that 'Women have always deceived, and they always will deceive. A woman's age is a most difficult thing to assess'. The appeal was allowed, Rose suggesting a passport scheme to cut under-age drinking.

Rose, however, began to feel it was time to enhance her London profile and undertake more work in London. Maybe she just wanted a change or maybe she felt that being in Liverpool, unlike other silks, meant that she had been rather sidelined. Nat was now 60 and would soon be retiring and Hilary, aged 17, would soon be leaving school and going to University.

CHAMBERS IN GRAY'S INN

Rose had moved her London chambers to 5 Paper Buildings some time earlier, but it had not worked out very satisfactorily. Even with her reputation, finding alternative chambers to suit her circumstances was not easy, particularly for a woman, and so in the autumn of 1966 Rose approached Gray's Inn to rent premises with a view to setting up her own London chambers. This was, at the time, quite a new proposition for Gray's Inn, which then had few, if any, other sets of chambers and wanted to encourage the process. It was also quite a courageous thing to do at her stage of career, and it was not an insignificant financial burden.

Rose accordingly leased premises on the first floor of 1 Gray's Inn Square on 1 March 1967. The set of rooms overlooked Gray's Inn Square at the front and the delightful gardens, known as the Walks, at the back. They included a magnificent large room with panelling and carving over the large fireplace by Grinling Gibbons, the celebrated seventeenth-century wood carver, whose patron was King Charles II. Rose employed the redoubtable Dorothy Roberts to run the place, although she still retained a clerk in Liverpool. She also employed a lady to clean the rooms, Mrs Hearse. Mrs Hearse lived locally and became a lifelong friend of the family, helping

Rose and Nat well into her eighties and their nineties. Rose spent time and money on decorating and furnishing the chambers. It was a large undertaking and was not up and running until the following year. Rose now had an even larger staff: two in London plus Mrs Simms, two cleaners at Parklands, her clerk, Kay McCall, a full-time gardener and Mrs Shepherd.

HILARY

The new chambers coincided with Hilary's own growing interest in London and the law, having decided herself to become a barrister. She had left school at the end of 1966. She then had a nine-month gap before going to University, having taken the Oxbridge exams that autumn. Rose was not keen on her getting a job, offering to pay her to do odd jobs instead. With hindsight Hilary would have benefitted from travelling and gaining her independence and seeing the world, but gap year adventures were less common in those days. Instead, apart from the period in a solicitors' office, Hilary spent the time at home. However, she did accompany Rose frequently to London, helping her to shop for and furnish the new chambers and went with her on occasions to court.

Hilary also joined Gray's Inn and started eating her dinners which she thoroughly enjoyed and made many friends in London. In July 1967, then aged 18, she was invited to her first Buckingham Palace Garden Party as an unmarried daughter, Rose and Nat being regularly invited to the event. It was an exciting afternoon and Rose bought Hilary a new dress and hat for the occasion.

By now Hilary had also metamorphosised into Hilary Heilbron. At her mother's suggestion, and with her father's approval, on leaving school Hilary changed her surname by Deed Poll from Burstein to Heilbron, keeping Burstein as a middle name. Rose's thinking emanated from a discussion she had had with Baroness Edith Summerskill, whose own daughter, Dr Shirley Summerskill, had done the same thing. Hilary's birth surname was always being mispronounced and misspelt, but more importantly Rose felt that had she been a man, her daughter would have inherited her surname and this would have helped her in her future profession. So why should it make any difference if she was a woman? Whether or not, with hindsight, this was a wise decision it is impossible to say.

In October 1967, Hilary went to Lady Margaret Hall, Oxford University, to read jurisprudence. Rose gave her some short advice: 'do not get pregnant, do not take drugs and watch the traffic'. As has been mentioned, Rose and Nat had always been rather over-protective of their daughter, no doubt having seen life at the coalface in their respective occupations, but it was now time for their daughter to leave the nest. Like any other mother, Rose apparently cried when her daughter left home for the first time. It was the end of Hilary's childhood. Her parents were reluctant to let go and Hilary had to telephone home every night. Oxford with its history, spires and beautiful countryside provided a lovely retreat for Rose and Nat when they visited Hilary each term. Oxford terms were, however, short and there were still long holidays spent in Liverpool. There was the inevitable press comment about 'following in her Mother's footsteps'. Although never specifically encouraged to go into the law, Rose was naturally pleased that her daughter had chosen to become a barrister. She obviously conveyed this to friends. Dame Edith Evans replied to a letter of hers:

> Thank you dear Rose very much for your letter and how delighted you are and rightly so, to have a daughter who is dedicated to what she hopes to choose as her profession, especially these days when so many young people do not know what to decide. Am up to my neck in rehearsals, so please forgive a short note.
>
> Affectionately, Edith.

PREJUDICE STILL PERSISTS

It is astonishing that even in the mid-1960s the old mantra about women advocates still raised its head. Lord Mancroft writing an article entitled 'Men Talking About Women' in *The Times* in August 1966 said:

> Personally I believe in having women in every field of public life ... Naturally some jobs are more suitable than others ... But there are certain natural disadvantages from which women suffer. In theory women barristers have exactly the same opportunities as men, but that is not quite true. Solicitors tend to avoid briefing a feminine barrister unless she is exceptional. And even though they may be absolutely brilliant academically, in court women can often be difficult to hear because their voices are light and high-pitched. Of course there are those who have triumphed like Rose Heilbron, who is a QC and Elizabeth Lane, now a judge; one has overcome her natural liability and the other has a deep, almost masculine voice.

Another disappointment occurred the following year. In early 1968 Rose stood for election as Leader of the Northern Circuit. There had never been a woman leader of any Circuit before and this was new territory. Despite all their professed support, her colleagues on the Circuit chose a man, Richard Forrest QC. Douglas Brown (later a High Court Judge, and a good friend) wrote to Rose informing her of the result in his capacity as returning officer, and commented:

> I can now drop this impartial cloak which my office as 'returning officer' compelled me to wear, and say how sorry I am that the result has gone the way it has. I think the Circuit ought to be thoroughly ashamed of itself. I thought we were progressing a little, but it looks as if we have slipped back.

Rose, as with every step on the legal ladder, had to wait a few years longer for her turn to come.

A BENCHER AT GRAY'S INN

Her colleagues at Gray's Inn were, however, becoming more progressive. Rose always adored Gray's Inn, which had given her her first break in the profession by granting her a scholarship so many years earlier. Nonetheless, she had never been made a Bencher. Benchers are senior members of the Inn elected by other Benchers to sit on high table and be responsible for the governance of the Inn. They come from the ranks of silks and sometimes County Court Judges, usually well in advance of any appointment to the High Court Bench. The Inns of Court also elect Honorary and Royal Benchers. Not every silk is so honoured, but had she been a man, Rose would, given her practice and contribution to the profession, have undoubtedly been made a Bencher many years earlier. She had made contributions to the profession outside her work and had been on the Bar Council, the professional body for the Bar, for several years earlier in her career.

On 14 May 1968, however, the Benchers of Gray's Inn elected Rose as its first woman Bencher. She thus became the first female Bencher of any Inn of Court who had been elected as opposed to automatically preferred on appointment to the High Court Bench, as was the case with Mrs Justice Lane in her Inn. Legal history had been made once more. The following day the then Under-Treasurer of Grays's Inn, effectively the Chief Executive, Os Terry, wrote to Rose:

> I have the honour to inform you that at a Pension held yesterday it was resolved to invite you to the Bench of this Society.

The amount of the Caution Money payable on Call to the Bench is Two Hundred Guineas.

Rose was thrilled. It was long overdue. Her support of Gray's Inn by setting up chambers there and dining at and visiting the Inn more frequently had been rewarded—and justly so. Two weeks later, on 29 May 1968, she was introduced to Pension, the regular meeting of Benchers to deal with Inn business, and accorded 'Voice and Vote'. The Treasurer at the time was Sir Dingle Foot, formerly Solicitor General in Harold Wilson's Labour Government.

Nat and Hilary sent her a telegram: 'Our congratulations, have a great time tonight. Nobody could be happier about it than Hilary and Nat'. Hilary also sent her some flowers with the accompanying note. 'What wonderful news. I'm absolutely thrilled for you. All my dearest love, Hilary'.

Once again, as with most momentous happenings in her life, Rose wrote up the events of the day contemporaneously. It gives a good indication of the frenetic pace of her life at this time. She wrote:

This morning I was off to London on the 12.30 [train]. Kay [McCall, her clerk] brought me 2 black dresses on appro and magically one was ideal. I had no time at all to get anything and I had only returned from Lancaster (Morrison a young man who shot his father after great provocation—Ashworth gave him 4 years—too much).

I am writing this at 2.30 on May 30th because sleep has completely deserted me (on Waldorf [a London hotel] notepaper). Of course I am far too excited after the historical events of last night—to have been the first woman ever admitted to the Bench of Gray's and the first to have been voluntarily chosen as a Bencher [all High Court Judges are automatically made Benchers] was an overwhelming honour, which to me seems the greatest breakthrough of what has hitherto been such a predominantly male preserve.

[She then explained the procedure]. I was admitted and my joy was complete ... A wonderful evening never to be forgotten.

PS. At 6 am. I fell asleep at 4.30 am and woke again at 6 am. I rang for tea and was pleased to find the papers outside the door. The last weeks have been so tremendous that I have caught a touch of Nat's insomnia—I think I need a break but I have 14/16 briefs to read and have to go to Glasgow this weekend to see poor Julia [Nat's sister]. Next weekend is the Labour Lawyers' Dinner and of course we are going to Oxford [where Hilary was studying at the University] ... It looks as though De Gaulle will resign today ... [Dingle] told me the Queen Mum and Prime Minister are coming in Nov.—he wanted me to look after HM and sit near HW [Harold Wilson, the Prime Minister]. It's all going to be marvellous.

There was much amusement as to how to address Rose. Benchers are addressed as Master. Could they call her Mistress of the Bench? It was not thought appropriate—and whose Mistress would she have been!? Rose thus became Master Heilbron. She received many congratulatory letters on her elevation, the dominant theme running through them was that it was long overdue. Sir Elwyn Jones, the then Attorney General, and later Lord Chancellor, wrote: 'At last! Polly and I are delighted. Warmest congratulations'. Geoffrey Lane, later Lord Chief Justice, noted that unlike some High Court Judges, becoming Benchers automatically on appointment, she was not a 'shot gun' Bencher. The Treasurer of Middle Temple in a spirit of amusing rivalry between the Inns, wrote 'How delighted to read that even Gray's has seen the light!' As usual, Rose answered all these letters by hand.

Rose became an assiduous Bencher and regularly attended Pension, the meeting of Benchers to discuss and debate the Inn's affairs and business, and in whom its governance rests. She also frequently attended other functions at Gray's Inn, in particular Guest Nights held each Dining Term, when she could take a guest, and Grand Night, a white tie event held once a year to which famous dignitaries, ambassadors, royalty and others from the law and outside are invited. Over the years she, and later Nat when they moved to live in the Inn, made a number of very good friends among the Benchers of Gray's Inn and it provided a most enjoyable social life for them in London.

As can be seen by Rose's reaction, it was recognition by her professional peers that she found the most rewarding and satisfying of all her professional achievements.

Rose and Hilary in La Baulle 1959

Rose as President of the Liverpool Club of the Soroptimists, 1954

Rose in evening dress

Rose signing a visitors' book

Hilary accompanies her mother as Honorary Colonel, March 1958

Rose as working Silk

Rose - formal but without robes

Rose says formal goodbye to Burnley, 1971

Rose attending event Ambulances for Israel, 1956

Rose giving the prizes away 1960

Rose and Nat playing with Tandy on the
tennis court, Parklands 1962

Parklands 1962

Rose and Nat on holiday outside
St Marks, Venice 1963

Rose outside the Old Bailey before her appearance as
first woman judge there, January 1972

20

Another Landmark Case

HIGH SOCIETY AND A HORSE

ALTHOUGH NOW 53, Rose's public profile remained undimmed, though the intensity of interest in her reduced over the years. There were still articles written in laudatory terms such as the comment that 'the aura of being England's most glamorous woman barrister has always surrounded her' (*Birmingham Post*). She had let her hair go grey, using only a rinse rather than a dye, but she remained a beautiful woman with a lovely skin and looked much younger than her years.

Rose was still invited to talk and continued to draw the crowds at a wide variety of events. These included talks to the Oxford University Jewish Society on the 'Role of the Layman in Law' to an overflowing audience in December 1965; to the London Law Society's Annual Dinner and Dance at Quaglino's Hotel in March 1967; to the National Association of Prison Visitors on the Criminal Justice Bill, sharing a platform with the then Home Secretary, Roy Jenkins.

Rose's prominence in the legal profession at this time was reflected in the invitations she received. She continued to be invited as a guest to interesting functions, such as a dinner given by the High Commissioner for India in honour of the Chief Justice of India in September 1968 and to meet Mrs Richard Nixon, the wife of the Vice-President of the United States, at lunch at the American Embassy in 1958. In 1969 she was invited by the Prime Minister, Harold Wilson, to meet Mrs Golda Meir, the then Prime Minister of Israel, and the following year she was invited by Lady Douglas-Home to a lunch to meet Madame Gromyko, the wife of the then Russian Foreign Minister, sitting between her and the biographer Lady Antonia Fraser. In 1971 she was invited by the President and Council of the Royal Academy of Arts to its Annual Dinner in the presence of the Prime Minister, Edward Heath, who gave the reply on behalf of Her Majesty's Ministers. She also continued to attend a host of other interesting engagement and dinners.

She was presented again to the Queen when Her Majesty visited Burnley in May 1968. In November 1968 she attended her first Grand Night as a Bencher. The guests included Queen Elizabeth, the Queen Mother; the Prime Minister; Harold Wilson; and Jeremy Thorpe, then Leader of the Liberal Party.

Throughout her professional career Rose was constantly asked to give interviews, to write articles for newspapers and women's magazines, to provide photographs, appear on television, give lecture tours and even write a text book. This was most prevalent in the aftermath of her appointment as Recorder, but continued until she retired from the High Court Bench and even afterwards. Rose was particularly disappointed not to have been able to accept an invitation by NBC television to give an interview in 1957. She was not, however, too disappointed to have to decline to appear on a television show as part of a panel in a competition called 'Be Your Own Boss' judging would-be business novices. In 1965 the publishers, George G Harrap wanted to write a chapter on Rose with a photograph of her in a new book entitled 'Women of the Modern World' featuring the likes of Mrs Pandit, Helen Keller and Lady Baden-Powell. All these invitations had to be declined because of the Bar Professional Conduct Rules. She never gave a single interview in her life or commented in public on any of her cases or on any aspect of her career.

Shy and diffident by nature, she had learnt to mingle with celebrities from all walks of life who, to her surprise, were interested in meeting her. Yet, for someone brought up in an entirely different background, these were all exciting encounters and by no means taken for granted. Although by this time Rose was very well known and had met many interesting people, she never lost the excitement engendered by a special invitation. One of her most endearing qualities was an almost child-like thrill at being invited to such gatherings, never expecting such invitations nor feeling, as many people in her position might have done, that she was entitled to them. Nat would always say that she would often hover at the back of the room and he would have to encourage her forward to meet people. Such excitement was almost always accompanied by the female concern of what to wear and many a new outfit was purchased on the pretext of a special invitation.

She was presented to most members of the Royal Family during her life, some on several occasions; she met Prime Ministers, Cabinet Ministers, foreign dignitaries and people from the Arts. Sir John Betjeman, the Poet Laureate, on meeting her at some function enquired where he could buy sheets. At a luncheon party given by Mrs Denis Healy, wife of the then Foreign Secretary, Dame Margot Fonteyn regaled her with fashion tips and how she bought dresses twice a year from Paris. Lord Caernarvon even named a horse after her. 'Rose QC' ran in enough races to deplete the betting resources of the family! This did not stop the stewards on the London to Liverpool trains regularly asking Rose for tips as to the horse's chance of winning!

ROBERT GRAVES AND *SWEET V PARSLEY*

It was, however, another famous poet and man of letters, Robert Graves, whose path crossed with Rose's in 1968 in a case of huge public importance. Stephanie Sweet was a friend of Robert Grave's daughter and had spent summer holidays with the Graves family in Majorca. She was aged 24, an honours graduate from St Anne's College, Oxford and a schoolteacher. She was the tenant of Fries Farm, Watereaton, near Oxford. She let out rooms to student tenants. She still had her own bedroom, but after January 1967 visited the farm only occasionally, having moved to other premises in the city of Oxford.

In June 1967, the police searched the farm and found odds and ends of various drugs including cannabis resin. It was accepted that Miss Sweet had not known that the premises were being used to smoke cannabis resin. She was charged and convicted by the Woodstock magistrates of 'being concerned in the management of premises used for the purpose of smoking cannabis resin' and fined £25. She appealed to the Divisional Court on 22 March 1968. Her appeal was dismissed by a court comprising the Lord Chief Justice and Mr Justice Ashworth and Mr Justice Blain. It was held that the charge was one of strict liability and knowledge and intent were therefore not relevant. On 4 April she was refused leave to appeal to the House of Lords on the ground that the case involved no point of law of general public importance that would justify such a further appeal.

The court had underestimated the reaction to the decision. First to take up her case was Robert Graves. He wrote an article published on the front page of *The Sunday Times* on 14 April 1968. It read:

I have never before in all my long life been confronted with an absolute crime ... In law an absolute crime is one that can be awarded summary punishment, whatever the degree of criminal intent. It does not, in fact, matter whether the criminal knew that his offence, either of commission or omission was a crime. He remains unalterably due for punishment.

The absolute crime in the *Sweet v Parsley* case consisted of 'managing' premises in which an offence had been committed even though admittedly without her knowledge or consent. The offence was the smoking of 'pot' by a group of sub-tenants, and the police approach seems to have been modelled on the habitual abrasive procedure used when charging land-lords with allowing their premises to be used as houses of prostitution ...

One evening last June Stephanie turned up at the farm but found it empty, with the door open. In the hall was a note saying 'Please get in touch at once with the Woodstock police'. She rang them up and they arrived half an hour later headed by a bucolic-looking policeman named Sergeant Parsley. He warned her that he had a search warrant for the farmhouse, on which he had acted, and as a result must ask her to come to the station with him. Here she was informed that she was under arrest, drugs having been found at the farmhouse: to wit cannabis and L.S.D.

After keeping her waiting for three quarters of an hour—she supposes to create the necessary suspense before obtaining a confession—they subjected her to the customary indignities. A tough-looking police-woman marched in, made her strip to the skin, searched her for drugs or needle-marks, all the while whistling through her teeth the same line of 'Westminster Sunset'. Later followed a search of her handbag—and then her cross-examination began ... The whole business lasted for about four hours.

'What a waste' she told us afterwards, 'My lawyer advised me to look as unhappy as possible when appearing before the magistrates. Since, like everyone else, I only had miniskirts in my wardrobe, I fitted myself out with a respectable knee length black and white dress. I even put my hair up, but it didn't work'.

We advised her to appeal which she did. Meanwhile a letter had arrived from the Department of Education and Science to the effect that her con-viction had proved that she was no longer a fit person to teach children, and that if she wished to protest this decision she must visit a psychia-trist and submit his report, as well as providing the most solid references from her university superiors ...

She can do no more, it seems, except try to make the Home Secretary recommend her for the Queen's pardon. Meanwhile Stephanie remains an absolute criminal.

This legal return to the ancient concept of absolute crime is of great interest to anthropologists. In primitive communities, if a man, hunting in the forest, should have the bad luck to see his mother-in-law bathing naked in a lonely pool, this might well be a mortal sin without either excuse or escape. He must die. As a rule, he prefers to starve himself to death in his hut or commit suicide by jumping headfirst from the top of a lofty tree.

The Classical Greek case was Oedipus's murder of his father and marriage to his mother while still ignorant of his parentage. The penalty was banishment and universal abhorrence. Nowadays, I suppose, he would be refused all gainful employment in the United Kingdom and sentenced to 25 years on the Freudian couch.

The article ended with the following poem:

Sweet v Parsley
Whatever Sweet might do was wrong
Even if she did not do it:
Absolute crime is far too strong
For felons not to rue it
So Parsley, armed with the Law's might
Proves abso-bally-lutely right
Her cause is closed in Hell's despite—
No counsel can pursue it.

The newspapers took up her cause too. The leading article in the same *Sunday Times* headed 'Injustice' noted that two issues of equal importance were raised: first the substance of the case and secondly, the effective veto the Divisional Court had on appeals to the House of Lords. There remained at that time no opportunity for the House of Lords, the highest court in the land, to take a decision itself as to whether or not a criminal case on appeal from the Divisional Court was fit for hearing by their Lordships, although it could where civil cases were concerned. The leading article stated:

> The case has serious implications at a time when many more people must be in danger of prosecution on the same grounds as Miss Sweet, and with as little culpability. They should not be branded criminals before the Law Lords have had a chance to make sense out of bad drafting.

Members of the public wrote letters to the newspapers. Emlyn Hooson QC, then a Liberal MP, said that the law on the matter should be reviewed by the Attorney General with a view to introducing an immediate change of law in the House of Commons. A deputation of four Labour MPs arranged to see the Lord Chancellor about the matter and the police set up an inquiry. As one newspaper commented, it conjured up the possibility of Lord Butler, Master of Trinity College, Cambridge, where Prince Charles was then an undergraduate, having to face a criminal charge if dangerous drugs were found in his college. So far as Miss Sweet was concerned, she said: 'I am determined to take this as far as I can. I can't teach in England and I'd find it extremely difficult to get a visa for the US, where I'd planned to go in about a year'.

Robert Graves asked if Rose would take on the case and he wrote to her because he was so incensed at the unfairness and injustice. He lent Miss Sweet the money for the case. The previous lawyers were replaced. Instructed by BM Birnberg and Co, a firm of solicitors frequently instructed by the National Council of Civil Liberties, and leading Ian Brownlie (later Sir Ian Brownlie and a very distinguished international lawyer), the legal team began their fight back. An application was made to the same Divisional Court on 22 April for an extension of time for a renewed application for leave to appeal to the House of Lords and for such leave. Rose explained that there was something new which had not been argued previously: The application on April 4 had been made on the basis that two points of law were involved. They were (i) whether section 5(b) of the Dangerous Drugs Act imposed strict liability creating an absolute offence and (ii) the meaning of 'concerned in the management'. Further authority could be cited on those matters. In addition there was a third point—whether if the section created an absolute offence, there was a defence.

The Divisional Court extended time and adjourned the application until the result of another case in the House of Lords, *Warner v Commissioner of Metropolitan Police*,[1] a case concerning unauthorised possession of drugs, which could have had implications for *Sweet v Parsley*. That case had concerned a man who claimed that he did not know that drugs had been hidden in his van. Lord Parker, the Lord Chief Justice, added: 'I think anybody who has dealt with this case, not least this Court, has great sympathy with this girl—particularly if what we are told is right that she has lost her job'.

Judgment was given in the *Warner* case on 2 May 1968. On 13 May Rose renewed her application for leave, arguing that the *Warner* case had been widely commented upon as being complex and difficult to understand. The Divisional Court certified three

---

[1] *Warner v Commissioner of Metropolitan Police* [1969] 2 AC 256.

points of general public importance and gave leave to appeal. The three questions prepared by the court were:

1. Whether Section 5(b) Dangerous Drugs Act 1965 creates an absolute offence;
2. What, if any, mental element is involved in the offence; and
3. Whether, on the facts found, a reasonable bench of magistrates, properly directing their minds to the law, could have convicted Miss Sweet.

The Hearing in the House of Lords

The case was heard in the House of Lords over five days, beginning on 27 November 1968. Counsel for Parsley was Douglas Draycott QC leading R A Talbot. The court comprised: Lord Reid, then aged 78; Lord Morris of Borth-y-Guest, Lord Pearce, Lord Wilberforce and Lord Diplock. It was a most powerful court. Rose argued many different points of law. Over 60 legal authorities altogether were cited by counsel on both sides to their Lordships. Rose argued that headmasters, hotel keepers, university hostel wardens and even prison governors risked prosecution for drug offences about which they know nothing and that the decision of the Divisional Court threatened the morally innocent. It was very much a test case.

Rose's notes indicate the vast amount of research and work she and her junior had undertaken in preparation for this case. The appeal received wide publicity in the national press. Hilary went to hear some of the argument as this was a topic she herself had been learning at Oxford University and the case had been referred to in lectures that she had attended given by Professor Rupert Cross, the Vinerian Professor of Law. It was really the first time that Rose had been able to discuss legal issues with her daughter. There was an amusing exchange when Lord Reid asked counsel for Parsley to explain what was meant by 'beatnik fraternity', commenting that he had seen pictures of people with rather dirty long hair, but enquiring whether it had any significance beyond that. The response was that they were 'people who have adopted a way of life which included a certain rejection of the standards which ordinary and reasonable people accept' and that long hair was simply a symptom of this. This colloquial description may not have been an entirely correct definition, but this did not stop the words appearing in Lord Reid's speech when he delivered his judgment.

The hard work was worth it. Miss Sweet was vindicated. On 23 January 1969, the House of Lords in a unanimous decision allowed Miss Sweet's appeal.[2] It held that the offence created by section 5(b) of the Dangerous Drugs Act 1965 was not an absolute offence and that Miss Sweet's conviction should be quashed. The words 'used for the purpose' in section 5(b) referred to the purpose of the management and mens rea, ie intent, is an essential ingredient of the offence. It reiterated that mens rea is an essential ingredient of every offence unless some reason can be found for holding that it is not necessary, and the court ought not to hold that an offence is an absolute offence unless it appears that that must have been the intention of Parliament.

Lord Reid described the decision of the Divisional Court as 'an obviously unjust result'. He continued:

> But I think that some amplification is necessary. Our first duty is to consider the words of the Act: if they show a clear intention to create an absolute offence that is an end of the matter. But such cases are very rare. Sometimes the words of the section which creates a particular offence make it clear that mens rea is required in one form or another. Such cases are quite frequent. But in a very large number of cases there is no clear indication either way. In such cases there has for centuries been a presumption that Parliament did not intend to make criminals of persons who were in no way blameworthy in what they did ...

> But when one comes to acts of a truly criminal character, it appears to me that there are at least two other factors which any reasonable legislator would have in mind. In the first place a stigma still attaches to any person convicted of a truly criminal offence, and the more serious or more disgraceful the offence the greater the stigma. So he would have to consider whether, in a case of this gravity, the public interest really requires that an innocent person should be prevented from proving his innocence in order that fewer guilty men may escape and equally important is the fact that fortunately the Press in this country are vigilant to expose injustice and every manifestly unjust conviction made known to the public tends to injure the body politic by undermining public confidence in the justice of the law and of its administration.

> If this section means what the Divisional Court have held that it means, then hundreds of thousands of people who sublet part of their premises or take in lodgers or are concerned in the management of residential premises or institutions are daily incurring a risk of being convicted of a serious offence in circumstances where they are in no way to blame.

---

[2] *Sweet v Parsley* [1970] AC 132.

For the greatest vigilance cannot prevent tenants, lodgers or inmates or guests whom they bring in from smoking cannabis cigarettes in their own rooms. It was suggested in argument that this appellant brought this conviction on herself because it is found as a fact that when the police searched the premises there were people there of the 'beatnik fraternity'. But surely it would be going a very long way to say that persons managing premises of any kind ought to safeguard themselves by refusing accommodation to all who are of slovenly or exotic appearance, or who bring in guests of that kind, and unfortunately drug taking is by no means confined to those of unusual appearance.

Speaking from a rather long experience of membership of both Houses, I assert with confidence that no Parliament within my recollection would have agreed to make an offence of this kind an absolute offence if the matter had been fully explained to it. So, if the court ought only to hold an offence to be an absolute offence where it appears that that must have been the intention of Parliament, offences of this kind are very far removed from those which it is proper to hold to be absolute offences.

Lord Morris of Borth-y-Gest said:

My Lords, it has frequently been affirmed and should unhesitatingly be recognised that it is a cardinal principle of our law that mens rea, an evil intention or a knowledge of the wrongfulness of the act, is in all ordinary cases an essential ingredient of guilt of a criminal offence. It follows from this that there will not be guilt of an offence created by statute unless there is mens rea or unless Parliament has by the statute enacted that guilt may be established in cases where there is no mens rea.

The leader in *The Times* entitled 'The Law Year' commented:

A difference should be recognised between cases of 'lawyers' law' and those dealing with matters directly affecting the lives and interests of large sections of the community on which laymen are as well able to decide as lawyers. On such matters it is not for the courts to proceed on their view of public policy, for that would be to encroach on the province of Parliament.

His self-denying ordinance did not inhibit Lord Reid from joining in the unanimous decision of the House of Lords in the case of Sweet v Parsley, which was in some ways the most important and encouraging judgment issued in the past year.

Rose received a nice thank you letter from Miss Sweet. Some years later on 17 June 1973, Robert Graves wrote to one Elizabeth Bailey: 'Please tell Rose Heilbron that she leads (for me) in the heroine class without danger of demotion'.

21

The Last Years at the Bar

BY 1969 ROSE had her eye fixed firmly on the High Court Bench, but it remained as aspiration and by no means a certainty. London was the centre of the legal universe. The opening of her own chambers in London was part of this strategy. She wanted to do more work in London, but also one suspects she wanted a change professionally. Running a set of chambers brought with it its own difficulties with clerking and staff and obtaining suitable tenants and took up a great deal of her time. It was an unsung accomplishment for a woman to start new chambers from scratch and then be Head of Chambers, particularly in an Inn of Court not then normally associated with chambers, but Rose was used to breaking new ground.

Although Rose did undertake some major cases in London during this period, it did not detract from her practice on the Northern Circuit, nor did it prevent her travelling the country to appear at various Assizes from Leeds to Birmingham to Chester to Nottingham and to Lancaster, to represent clients.

Consistent with her desire to have a more prominent presence in London, and following her election as a Bencher of Gray's Inn, in 1968 Rose had rented a small flat on the third floor of No 1 Verulam Buildings in Gray's Inn. Rose had become fed up with staying in hotels and the Forum Club had long since closed. She still occasionally stayed at the Cowdray Club, where she was a Vice-President and which remained the largest women's club in the country celebrating its 50th anniversary in 1972.

The flat, like chambers the previous year, required a thorough refurbishment and needed furnishing, which task Rose undertook with her usual zeal, in both cases making regular trips to London. Hilary often accompanied her as by then she had become a student member of Gray's Inn and had started eating her dinners. Hilary also loved London. Rose bought some antique furniture and recycled other furniture she already had and made a comfortable second home. She would stay in the flat when she came to London. Hilary lived in it for a few years when she came down from Oxford to read for the Bar and later start practice. Its main disadvantage was the three flights of unforgiving stone steps which had to be climbed to reach it, as there was no lift.

Becoming a Bencher of Gray's Inn added an additional social dimension to Rose's life and gave her more opportunity to meet her colleagues in London and from other Circuits. She also regularly attended a variety of dinners given by the Inn, sitting now on the top table reserved for Benchers, including Guest Nights and Grand Nights set in the magnificent Gray's Inn Hall.

Gray's Inn Hall has always been the centre of the Inn's activity. Gray's Inn itself dates back to the fourteenth century and gained its name from the owner of the land, Sir Reginald de Grey. It was where, together with the other Inns of Court, lawyers lived and worked. The current Hall dates back to the sixteenth century.

History is reflected in its stained glass windows, wood panelled walls, the shields of past Treasurers bearing their coats of arms, the hammer beam roof and the wooden carved screen at the West end of the Hall. Tradition claims that the screen or part of it was made from the wood of a captured Spanish galleon in the Spanish Armada, and that the wood was the gift of Queen Elizabeth I. The Hall was bombed during the Second World War, but the screen was saved, together with some of the stained glass windows and shields.

Rose's new status as a Bencher precipitated invitations by Benchers of other Inns of Court. For example, in November 1970, she was invited as the first woman guest to the Benchers' table in Middle Temple as the guest of Sir Fred Pritchard, a High Court Judge. In 1973 she was the guest of the Treasurer of Lincoln's Inn, Judge Edward Clarke QC, at Grand Day where other guests included Margaret Thatcher and the US Ambassador.

Perhaps most significantly her new position enabled her to be present at the top table to witness Hilary's call to the Bar in July 1971 by the then Treasurer of Gray's Inn, Sir Malcolm Hilberry, a very happy family occasion, Nat watching from the gallery above the screen, together with other relatives of young barristers being called to the Bar.

AS BUSY AS EVER

Rose was never short of work and remained very much in demand. A surviving schedule of her cases for the months of April to July 1970, for instance, indicates that she was in court virtually every day apart from the legal holidays, leaving little time save for the evenings and weekends for preparation. Her murder cases still tended to dominate the headlines, whether it was appearing for a woman charged with murdering her 'Svengali' husband or the man who sent his wife some flowers as a token of his great affection for her and then shot dead her lover. Poison, strangulation, knives, hammers, overdoses and axes employed as the means of death added to the range of cases. Her civil practice likewise flourished during this period. Rose had always kept schedules of damages under various types of injury and she matched this with standard openings to the court so that she could fill in the details. This was time-saving and enabled her to undertake a large caseload.

However, her most notable case legally was a case where she led her good friend Charles Mantell (later Lord Justice Mantell), who recalled that she worked him very hard. The case concerned a boy of 16, and hence a juvenile, who had admitted a charge of attempted rape before the local magistrates. It was subsequently discovered that he had a mental health condition and a propensity to make confessions. The issue was whether the magistrates, as a court of summary jurisdiction, had the power to allow a change of plea from guilty to not guilty. The case went up to the House of Lords, where Rose succeeded.[1] What happened subsequently to the young man is not known.

At the opposite end of the spectrum of Rose's practice was a case about toilets. In November 1971 she appeared for Southport Corporation before the local magistrates. It was charged with obstructing the highway by building a new £8,000 'superloo' in Hill Street, contrary to the 1959 Highways Act. It was alleged that the 'superloo' was unlawful as it was four times the size of the 1891 cabmen's toilets it replaced. No planning permission had been obtained and no notice had been placed upon the site to inform the public of the proposals. The issues revolved around whether there was deemed planning permission to erect the superloo and whether the charge had been brought against the correct defendants. The magistrates, after adjourning, held that they were satisfied that the convenience was proper and convenient and that the Corporation had lawful authority to dig excavations and 'obstruct free passage'. The press had a field day with headlines such as: 'Loo Case Gets

---

[1] *S (an infant) by Parsons (his next friend) v Manchester City Recorder and others* [1971] AC 481 (HL).

Bogged Down'; 'Southport Loo Wins a Straight Flush'; and 'When is a Convenience Convenient?'

In January 1974, Rose was appointed together with an accountant, Stanley David Samwell FCA, as a Department of Trade Inspector under Section 165(b) of the Companies Act 1948 to inquire into Kuehne & Nagel Limited, international freight forwarders. This was another first for women: it was apparently the first time a woman had been appointed an external DTI Inspector. The investigation concerned various malpractices relating to charging by the company for its services perpetrated by managers and employees in the company, many of which were found to have been established.

ROSE SAYS GOODBYE TO BURNLEY

Three events, however, mark out this period of Rose's career at the Bar. The first of these followed the coming into force of the new Courts Act 1971 as a result of which Quarter Sessions were abolished. Recorders were henceforth no longer assigned to particular cities or districts. Instead a Recorder became peripatetic, sitting principally, but not necessarily, in the new Crown Courts on his or her Circuit. Nonetheless, the nature of the work remained the same with a diet of lesser crime from burglary to handling stolen goods to grievous bodily harm. Rose had requested that she be re-appointed to sit in the Greater London area rather than on the Northern Circuit.

Thus Rose's tenure with Burnley came to an end after 15 years. On 17 December 1971, Rose sat at her final Quarter Sessions in Burnley. Tributes were led, on behalf of the Bar, by John Coffey and, on behalf of the solicitors' branch of the legal profession, by Mr Bower. Rose replied expressing her gratitude to the many who had assisted her over the years, commenting on the historical closure of Quarter Sessions at Burnley which had been operating since 1893. She thanked her deputies, Judge Jalland and John Lord, and the Town Clerk and his deputies. There followed a reception and buffet at Towneley Hall during which Rose was presented with a gold brooch and earrings with a design of roses and Nat with a pair of cufflinks with the Burnley logo, which gifts they both treasured until the end of their respective lives. Rose had enjoyed her years at Burnley and Rose and Nat had made many friends. It was, as Rose said in her speech, 'the end of an era', although she still remained a Recorder and was made an Honorary Recorder of Burnley.

SITTING AT THE OLD BAILEY AS A JUDGE

No sooner had she relinquished her association with Burnley Quarter Sessions than her re-appointment as a Recorder under the new system led to her sitting on 4 January 1972 at the Old Bailey as a judge, the first woman to sit as a judge in the very famous criminal court. The publicity it attracted resembled the sort of publicity Rose had received in her early years as a Queen's Counsel with Rose's photograph in hat and coat or in her full-bottomed wig blazoned across the newspaper pages. It even reached the television news. The scene in Court No 7 was amusingly told by Vincent Mulchrone in the *Daily Mail* in an article entitled: 'My Lady of the Old Bailey'.

> With a trace of deep crimson lipstick, and only an occasional pat at her wig, the first woman judge—'My Lady', as they addressed her—took her seat in the Old Bailey yesterday. The seismographs registered nil. The lists in Court No 7 would be heard by 'Miss Recorder Heilbron QC'. And so, without palaver, but with much courtesy and humanity, they were ...
> At 57, the judge is beyond being shocked by words. Her experience of criminals is so deep that her appearance at the Old Bailey should cause little surprise. But the blood and guts that wind up at the Bailey were being presented for the first time to a female judge. The reaction, frankly, is one of masculine curiosity. The facile verdict is that Rose Heilbron has passed another feminine milestone, and the courts will gain ... Hers has been a steady, if determined, climb up the legal ladder ... And she smiled more than most judges do though sometimes her smile rested on the conviction that she was about to be obeyed. 'That's really two questions' she smiled to defence counsel 'Would you like to break it up?' he was much obliged, My Lady, and broke it up. 'I don't suppose' she said at another point, 'that Mr Crow will mind staying a little longer. Probably his day is ruined already ...' She smiled. Mr Crow looked as though he'd take a week off to please her.

The editors went to town. 'My Lady Rose of the Old Bailey' said the *Daily Express*; 'My "Fair" Lady' exclaimed the *Nottingham Evening Post*; 'It's "Yes, My Lady" as Rose Takes Her Seat' commented the *Liverpool Post*; 'Rose ... First Lady of the Old Bailey' echoed the *Daily Mirror*; 'Rose QC Scores Another First' declared *The Sun* and other newspapers followed suit. The news went global from the *Chicago Tribune* to the *South China Morning Post*, to the *Nassau Daily Tribune*, the *Christchurch Star* in New Zealand and many more.

However, it was the *Washington Evening Star*, which in its early edition caused Rose most interest, as for a few hours Rose and Hilary tentatively contemplated the potential damages she might receive for the libel for damage to her reputation. The article commented:

'My Lady' Takes the Bench

A woman judge took the bench at the famous Old Bailey yesterday for the first time in the history of London's central criminal courts.

Miss Rose Heilbron, wearing a barrister's wig and carrying a black hand-bag, presided over court No 7. In her first act, she issued a bench warrant for the arrest of a youth who failed to answer a robbery charge. Lawyers addressed her as 'my lady'.

She is one of 47 lawyers sworn in as criminal judges in the reorganised system of crown courts. She became the first woman criminal in 1956 and the first woman to sit as a commissioner in the old courts of assize. She is 57.

Recognising that it was not the best form of journalism to call a judge a criminal, in the later edition the penultimate sentence was deleted. The managing editor of the newspaper also wrote a letter of apology and all thoughts of riches from libel damages receded!

Rose's sitting at the Old Bailey was more symbolic than any form of professional preferment, as her role remained that of Recorder, but it captured the public imagination. Nonetheless, it prompted a huge number of congratulatory letters from friends, colleagues and acquaintances. Such was the international interest conjured up by a female judge sitting at the very famous Old Bailey that it prompted one Hinkney Marble, a retired Major in the US Air Force, to write from Cincinnati, Ohio to congratulate her. It was the second time he had contacted her, the last being some 25 years earlier when he had sent her a press cutting about her from *Time* magazine. He had first met Rose in 1944 when he, together with three other American officers, had visited a court where she was appearing. Rose, who normally acknowledged the many letters she received from relative strangers more formally, on this occasion wrote:

I well remember meeting you and three other American officers in the High Court when, if my memory serves me right, we were sitting in the Court of Criminal Appeal in the cellars of the building because of air raids.

ROSE APPOINTED LEADER OF THE NORTHERN CIRCUIT

It was, however, the third event, which, though less public, was for Rose professionally and personally the most significant. Following her unsuccessful attempt to be elected Leader of the Northern

Circuit in 1969, Rose said she would not stand for election again and so did not contest the election in 1971 when Godfrey Heilpern QC was elected Leader of the Northern Circuit. On his untimely death in May 1973 Rose was approached to be Leader of the Circuit unopposed, described by one of her colleagues as a 'unanimous election', the first time this had ever happened. It was recognition of the admiration and affection in which Rose was now held by her colleagues on her Circuit. She thus became the first female Leader of a Circuit, for none of the other Circuits had had female leaders. The large number of congratulatory letters she once again received bears consistent witness to the view that the appointment was long overdue.

Leader of a Circuit was, and still is, regarded as the penultimate stepping stone to a High Court judicial career, and it was to prove to be so in Rose's case too, but that was for another year. With the role came added responsibilities and a leadership of a Circuit of approximately 300 barristers, but also traditionally the leading prosecution briefs. She received many letters of congratulation, including one from the then Lord Chancellor, Lord Hailsham and the Lord Chief Justice, Lord Widgery, who wrote 'What a milestone builder you are!'.

Rose loved her Circuit and its camaraderie and its characters. She had, over the years, built up real friendships with her colleagues. The Northern Circuit had a history of great advocates and its fair share of characters. This was the lighter side of the Circuit which Rose enjoyed. Aside, therefore, from its professional significance, becoming Leader of the Circuit, where 34 years earlier Rose had had difficulty even getting a tenancy in chambers and was no doubt viewed warily by her male colleagues, was a personal triumph. It was not just recognition of her professional ability, but also recognition that at last she had been accepted on equal terms, and was admired and liked.

ATTITUDES TO WOMEN

In 1969, 56 women were called to the English Bar, yet of the 2,448 practising barristers only 133 were women. Incredibly, although 20 years had elapsed since her appointment to silk, Rose remained the sole practising female Queen's Counsel at the English Bar. Only two further female Queen's Counsel had been appointed since 1949, namely Dorothy Knight Dix and Elizabeth Lane both becoming

County Court Judges, the latter becoming a High Court Judge in 1965. Moreover, despite Rose's own continued progression up the legal ladder, women generally still found it exceptionally difficult to get started at the Bar, with decisions as to who should be accepted as a tenant in chambers being taken by Heads of Chambers.

The Bar Council set up a committee to look into the role of women at the Bar. All the old shibboleths were still being trotted out such as 'Women only want to fill in time before marriage'; 'They will distract our young men'; and 'It isn't a very feminine thing to do'. However, a shift was beginning to be noticed in the early 1970s. Some chambers started to take on women tenants. They were sometimes described as a statutory woman tenant, although it was not until 1975 that any statute existed against discrimination when the Sex Discrimination Act was passed. A frequent excuse for not taking on a female tenant was the absence of a separate toilet. It was all a far cry from today with proper and fair selection processes, maternity leave and anti-discrimination policies.

Women still had a long way to go and in 1970 Rose, along with other female high achievers, attended the Equal Pay Target Dinner in honour of the Rt Hon Barbara Castle MP given by the Fawcett Society (formerly known as the London Society for Women's Suffrage) at the Dorchester Hotel in London.

Rose's own position was often used as a litmus test by which to judge contemporary attitudes. An article in the *Liverpool Daily Post* in January 1972 entitled 'Prose and Cons' discussed the male feature writers who 'polished their patronising prose' waxing lyrical about Rose's lipstick and even her red and silver ballpoint pen. This was no doubt a reference to Vincent Mulchrone's article in the *Daily Mail*:

> But how does she feel, I wonder, about being sentenced to such slushy sentiment every time she dons her wig? As a female judge she is imprisoned by masculine curiosity. The gossip columnists seem more interested in finding suitable adjectives for her smile at prosecuting counsel—it's enough to strain the quality of anyone's mercy.

> This is, of course, one of the occupational hazards of what is still coyly described in a man's world: 'Whether woman judge, MP, pilot or cleric'.

A similar article appeared in the *Evening Standard* on 4 January 1972:

> 'Another Woman'. The arrival of the first ever woman judge at the Old Bailey this morning was greeted with all the camera-popping ceremonial of the birth of a film star's baby. A woman? Trying murder cases? In a gown and wig? It was as good as man-bites-dog.

The continued grudging amazement with which every instance of female success is received by most men—and many woman—must be absolutely infuriating to those women who consider their abilities and achievements every bit commensurate with a man's.

Rose had lost none of her female following. In another article Elizabethan Staines quotes Rose as saying: 'I defend people not cases', describing her as 'a modest person who shuns personal glory and is as content at the kitchen stove and in the garden as she is in the courtroom. Miss Heilbron is passionately outspoken on the subject of working wives'. She quotes Rose as saying:

> It is wasteful not only to the woman herself but also to the community, that a woman who takes the time and trouble should, possibly on marriage and certainly on the advent of a family, have to relinquish her outside occupation.

HILARY FOLLOWS IN HER MOTHER'S FOOTSTEPS

By the time Hilary became a barrister, the profession had seen women make great strides, but there was still a long way to go. It remained very difficult to secure a pupillage, but Hilary was extremely fortunate in that her mother knew Gordon Slynn (later Lord Slynn) who was then the Treasury Junior, ie did all the junior work for the Government. He usually had two pupils and agreed to take Hilary as one of his pupils without even meeting her, simply because of his friendship with Rose, something unheard of today. Rose, by contrast, had not had any contacts when she began her career, yet until the system became more transparent and fairer, this was how things were done at the Bar. Today there is intense competition for pupillage and all pupils have to go through rigorous interviews and tests with contacts playing no part whatsoever. Hilary did a further pupillage at 1 Brick Court, now Brick Court Chambers, and was then taken on as a tenant to the delight of her parents, a happy association where she remains to this day.

These were commercial chambers. When Rose was a junior at the Bar a woman doing commercial work was a bridge too far. But even in the 1970s and early 1980s it was still very rare to find another woman barrister practising at the Commercial Bar. Hilary remained the only woman tenant in her chambers for over 10 years.

APPOINTMENT AS A HIGH COURT JUDGE

In July 1974, less than a year after she had been made Leader of the Northern Circuit, Rose received a telephone call to ask if she would accept an appointment as a High Court Judge assigned to the Family Division. The appointment was made on the recommendation of the new Lord Chancellor, Lord Elwyn-Jones, who had been appointed after the Labour Party had won the General Election earlier that year. Her assignment to the Family Division was in many ways a waste of her experience, but to appoint a woman to the Queen's Bench Division to try crime and civil cases was, in 1974, still a step too far. Rose had waited a long time for this appointment, but, as she always said, she had learned during her career that she had to be more patient than a man.

Rose was almost 60 and Nat 69. He had retired from general practice when he had reached 65 in 1970 and had taken on a part-time job. Hilary was 25 and had left Liverpool and started her own career at the Bar. Life had moved on. The appointment carried with it a DBE and a pension, the latter being particularly useful, as in those days people had not invested in private pensions as they do today.

Rose accepted with great excitement. The appointment had to remain totally secret until it was announced on 31 July 1974, the last day of the legal term before the Long Vacation. It appeared in *The Times* and other newspapers on 1 August and was also announced on the radio news. The announcement produced a flurry of some 450 letters of congratulation and telegrams, mostly handwritten. Not only did friends, relatives and professional colleagues including solicitors, members of the Bar and of the judiciary write, but so did representatives from a variety of institutions and organisations, legal and otherwise, with which Rose had been associated over the years, including local Liverpool-based and Jewish organisations, magistrates' associations, the Soroptimists and many more. She also received letters from people whom she had perhaps met only once many years back, people she had lost touch with and strangers who had known her late father, thereby providing a kaleidoscope of reminiscences. Mr Cartmell, the lovely gardener then employed at Parklands, even sent her a telegram.

An analysis of the letters shows certain recurring themes. Most commented on the fact that her appointment was long overdue and so well deserved. '[T]he Lord Chancellor has now righted a long-standing injustice' wrote one colleague among many. They referred to her distinguished career. Many referred to the personal 'joy' or true delight of the writer, and the warm affection with which Rose was held by her colleagues at the Bar. The popularity of the appointment featured frequently in the letters, as did the pride of the Circuit and Gray's Inn in her elevation to the Bench, coupled with the sense of loss to the Circuit her appointment created. Many spoke of her personal kindness to them and of the encouragement she had given them when they were young barristers, sometimes referring to cases they had been involved in together. Others spoke of her humility and modesty. Some were quite humorous, but they were, as ever, fulsome in their praise.

Rose replied assiduously to them all. When she had managed to decipher the handwriting she put the name of the sender in the top left hand corner of the letter. Mrs Shepherd then typed out a list in alphabetical order and she ticked them off one by one as she replied. The following extracts from a selection of the letters show not only her range of admirers from all walks of her professional life and from both lawyers and non-lawyers; but they also demonstrate the real affection with which she was clearly held by her friends and colleagues. They portray a contemporaneous picture of her far better than any ex post facto description can.

Henry Lachs, a member of the Northern Circuit and later a Circuit Judge, wrote:

> I think I treasure every case in which you led me: the red bag you gave is battered but proud: it has been a privilege to work so often with you: no client has been denied the full measure of your time and anxious worry over his case.

His Honour Judge Rudolf Lyons wrote:

> I doubt if you appreciate the real respect and affection which both the Bar and the Bench have for you … You are rightly a legend and this crowning of your brilliant career gives us all tremendous pleasure … That you will be successful and that you will prove an adornment to the Bench as you were to the Bar no one has the slightest doubt. I am proud that I can be numbered amongst your friends and grateful for the kindness you have shown me since I came to Liverpool.

George Carman QC, also a Northern Circuit silk and later to become a very fashionable silk in London, wrote:

> I am delighted for you and feel the honour is so well deserved. I do hope you don't miss the arena too much … However, it must be a new and exciting challenge which I am sure you will enjoy.

Let me take this opportunity of thanking you as a younger colleague to whom you have shown such friendship and kindness and help in past years that I feel grateful.

Pat Russell QC, (later Lord Justice Russell), another Northern Circuit silk, wrote:

It seems only a short time ago that I wrote to congratulate you upon your election as leader of the Circuit. That gave me great pleasure—but nothing could compare with my delight at reading the news of your elevation to the High Court Bench a few days ago. Everyone in this part of the world is thrilled and proud. That is the measure of the popularity of the appointment. Many, many congratulations!

Sir Gordon Wilmer, formerly a Lord Justice of Appeal, wrote:

I preserve a lively recollection of calling you within the Bar in 1949 in St George's Hall (or was it in Manchester?). Now, 25 years later, it gives me immense pleasure to see the announcement of your impending, and well deserved, elevation to the High Court Bench. My warmest congratulations to you and all possible good wishes. It is indeed good to read of your thus crowning an already distinguished career at the Bar.

Sir Tasker Watkins VC, a High Court Judge, wrote:

Arthur James wrote to me and stated 'That's it, always the gent making room for a lady'. It is absolutely right of course. It is a privilege to throw down my cloak before you so that you may tread without any discomfort along a path which so many think should have been long before now made available to you.

My congratulations and those of my wife, Eirwen, are most sincere. We are both delighted.

Sir David Croom-Johnson, a High Court Judge, recalled an earlier era:

One thing I'm also sure of—and that is that my father [also a High Court Judge and a supporter of Rose's] would be equally pleased, if he were alive. He always had a great regard for you.

The Right Hon Selwyn Lloyd QC, then Speaker of the House of Commons, said: 'Many congratulations, whether your Ladyship pleases or not! I am delighted'.

Cardinal Heenan, then Archbishop of Westminster, but formerly Archbishop of Liverpool, wrote:

The month started with the splendid news of your elevation to the Bench. I have often wondered why you were not made a judge. In Liverpool we were all proud of you and regarded you as a Portia among advocates.

The honour has been too long delayed but it gives the greatest satisfaction to all your friends.

On the lighter side, prompted by the rarity of a female judge, Mick Maguire QC of the Northern Circuit, encapsulated his congratulations:

Well done that girl! I am happy for you. Love, Mick.

P.S. I do not usually send my love to judges.

Another judge wrote: 'Well done! Glamour and brains on the bench at last'.

Gerald Crowe QC, a silk from the Northern Circuit, wrote from holiday in France:

I managed yesterday to buy an English newspaper which contained a reference to your appointment and at the same time I learnt of President Nixon's resignation. Somehow my faith in justice was restored.

Some joked about whether to call her sister as Judges had hitherto referred to each other as 'My Brother Judge X'.

A busy summer thus ensued. Judicial robes had to be bought, letters of congratulation answered, the DTI Inquiry had to be completed, and adjustments had to be made to home arrangements as Rose would be away from Liverpool a great deal sitting either in London or on Circuit, leaving Nat alone in a large house with only domestic help, including the now elderly Mrs Simms. The time would soon come when the family would sell Parklands and move from Liverpool to London where Hilary had now settled, but Rose first had to get used to her new life.

Rose accordingly became the second woman High Court Judge and the first woman High Court Judge to be appointed straight from the practising Bar. It was no coincidence that of the next seven female High Court Judges that were appointed in the coming years, five hailed from the Northern Circuit, having been influenced by Rose in her early years to begin a career at the Bar. So in the summer of 1974, after 38 years at the Bar, Rose relinquished chambers and exchanged her barrister's wig and gown for her judicial robes. Thus began a new chapter in Rose's career.

22

The Start of Judicial Life

A T 9.30 AM on Tuesday 1 October 1974, Rose took her oath of office and was sworn in as a High Court Judge by the Lord Chancellor, Lord Elwyn-Jones, in his large room in the House of Lords overlooking the River Thames in the presence of Nat and Hilary. She declared:

> I, Rose Heilbron, do swear by Almighty God that I will well and truly serve our Sovereign Lady Queen Elizabeth the Second in the Office of one of the Justices of Her Majesty's High Court of Justice and I will do right to all manner of people after the laws and usages of this Realm without fear or favour affection or ill will.

Hilary had bought her mother a present of a watercolour on her appointment and sent her a card which read:

> To my Darling Mum. A notable and historical accolade to an unprecedented career—so long overdue and so well deserved. Have a Happy Day on this memorable and exciting occasion. My thoughts are with you. Every success and fondest love, Hil xx

It was a proud moment for the family. It was also a time of transformation. A judicial life, at least in the late 1970s and 1980s, was very different from life at the Bar. It had advantages and disadvantages, but Rose had reached the age when she was beginning to tire of the pace of life at the Bar with the constant pressures of running chambers and travelling from Circuit to Circuit. Although she had an established reputation and there was no shortage of work, there were many new younger silks coming up the ranks competing for the same work.

Rose's judicial appointment meant she no longer had to worry about these things. She received a guaranteed income initially of £16,350 per annum, taxed at source, which was inflation proofed, and a pension of half her salary after 15 years on the Bench. This was of great significance as Rose had not put any money into a private pension and, although Nat had a small pension from the National Health Service, they only had modest savings. It would have meant a dramatic drop in lifestyle if the family had had to rely only on Nat's pension. The job also provided security of tenure and Rose could only be removed for misconduct by a motion of both Houses of Parliament.

It was, however, a dramatic change for her, both in lifestyle and the type of work she did. As a High Court Judge her work was based in London. She sat in the Royal Courts of Justice and was assigned a room (Room 32), which backed onto a corridor shared with a few other judges. She was provided with a set of Law Reports and other essential textbooks and assigned a clerk, her first being the delightful Charles Waller, a retired Assistant Chief Constable of Essex. Her clerk would arrange her caseload, type her judgments and generally help in running her judicial life. If anyone wanted to contact the judge about a matter, they first had to go through her clerk. Being a judge could be quite lonely compared with life at the Bar. Inevitably there was a degree of deference accorded to Rose, once a judge, by her former colleagues, particularly those she knew less well.

On her appointment as a High Court Judge Rose relinquished her title as Honorary Recorder of Burnley. She also resigned from some 20 organisations, many women-based, others Jewish organisations and others legal, ostensibly because she was leaving Liverpool, but also in some cases, such as the Society of Labour Lawyers, because she felt that as an impartial judge she should not be associated with any partisan organisation. During her tenure as a judge she also once indicated that she had disenfranchised herself and did not vote. Rose was very aware of her position and probably took it to extremes.

Rose had been brought up in the days when barristers could not speak to the press or advertise or carry visiting cards. Relationships with solicitors were circumscribed, though this did not prevent her having many solicitors as personal friends. On becoming a judge, she rather distanced herself from the solicitors who had instructed her in Liverpool. This was not because she did not feel enormous gratitude for their support, or because she did not enjoy their friendship, often reminiscing warmly about them to the family. It was in part the practical reality of moving away from Liverpool and in part a rather rigid view of what was required of her as a judge and the need not to be seen to be too friendly with solicitors who appeared before her.

Rose had also been brought up in an era of deference and respect and, although she herself was never pompous or demanding of such deference, she retained an instinctive deference herself to the judicial hierarchy. Thus, when asked, for example, to do something by the President of the Family Division, she regarded it as an honour rather than a chore.

TAKING THE JUDICIAL OATH OF OFFICE

1 October 1974 was also the Opening of the Legal Year. After they had been sworn in by the Lord Chancellor, Rose, together with another new High Court Judge appointed at the same time, Mr Justice Oliver (later Lord Oliver), attended the annual service at Westminster Abbey. They then walked at the back of the High Court judicial column given their junior position, as the Judges of all ranks processed from Westminster Abbey to the Houses of Parliament where the annual reception held for those invited to the Opening of the Legal Year took place. Invitees included foreign Heads of Bars and other foreign dignitaries and a selection of members of the Bar as well as the whole judiciary: both High Court and County Court Judges (the latter later called Circuit Judges).

Rose wore full ceremonial regalia—scarlet red robes edged in white ermine which she had had made over the summer and carried white gloves, black cap, and her full-bottomed wig. These robes are worn on special occasions for ceremonial use, with a shorter judicial wig when trying criminal cases and on what are termed 'red letter days', the aetiology of which has never been possible to truly fathom. On other occasions, such as when trying civil cases, High Court Judges wear black robes and the short judicial wig. Sorting out what robes to wear resembled the dilemma of a film star, but without the glamour. In non-criminal courts and appellate courts, non-ceremonial judicial robe wearing has in recent years been simplified and modified, with judicial wigs often not worn or robes dispensed with altogether. However in Rose's time, it was not just choosing the correct robes which was the problem: it was putting them on.

Rose was provided with various detailed instructions as to the sequence of putting on the various pieces of judicial apparel, including diagrams, which Rose then translated into something more intelligible, but equally complicated. Clearly, and not surprisingly, there had been mishaps in the past for one set of instructions recommended that the judge 'carry a few black safety pins for use'. For example, Rose's rendition of the instructions for putting on the Mantle read:

> Clerk holds Mantle open with ermine inside. Put on like cape. Right
> button hole about 12 inches from top end, buttons on to button on Hood

on shoulder (under fur). Judge holds right hand cord and clerk puts other
(Left) buttonhole on button on Hood (under fur). Two red cords threaded
through holes in Hood under point of fur by label. Tie cords under, very
tight inside at neck (double knot) and place inside. Take right hand
ribbon loop on Mantle and button on to same first button on hood. Same
left-hand side. 3 hooks at back (base) of Mantle hooked together.

The robes had not been designed for ladies. Rose in due course
decided to make some alterations to simplify the process including
using press studs.

Aside from sartorial issues, the question of how to address Rose
in Court had to be determined. Rose had always practised under her
maiden name, Heilbron, and that was how she was known in the
legal profession. This required internal consideration in the Lord
Chancellor's Department. It was resolved that:

> Following the precedent which was adopted when Dame Elizabeth Lane
> was appointed a High Court Judge in 1965, Lord Elwyn-Jones thinks it
> appropriate that Miss Heilbron should be known as 'The Honourable
> <u>Mrs</u> Justice Heilbron' in spite of the fact that this is not her married
> name: she will, of course, be addressed and referred to in court as
> 'My Lady' and 'Her Ladyship'.

They had little choice 'Miss Justice' would not bode well for her
future judgments!

Her first day as a fully-fledged High Court Judge was not over.
The assigned judicial Bentley then took her and another judge to
the Royal Courts of Justice where, together with all other High Court
Judges, they attended a judges' meeting in the Lord Chief Justice's
Court. The purpose was to discuss issues of relevance to the judges
including reforms and various practical matters. However, one
suspects that one of the most important issues was the allocation of
Circuits for future legal terms. These were, and still are, allocated
on a combination of seniority and a rota basis, as some cities and
circuits were, and remain, more popular than others, either because
they were nearer to London or the relevant judge's home or because
the accommodation was better. Some Circuits had lodgings at
various centres. For example the Northern Circuit had lodgings at
Manchester, Liverpool, Preston and Lancaster. Winchester Lodgings
was always one of the most popular choices. Rose as a junior judge
came very low down the pecking order in terms of choice. Her first
judicial foray out of London was to Swansea, which turned out to
be far more enjoyable than she had expected.

After the main meeting, as was the practice each legal term, the
various divisions of the High Court then adjourned for individual

meetings of their divisions. Rose accordingly went to the meeting of the Family Court Judges. These meetings tended to be more concerned with issues directly affecting the matters Family Court Judges had to deal with. They provided a forum for an exchange of views on reform, and practical and legal issues. It also provided an opportunity for the Family Court Judges to meet en banc.

Whether it was on 1 October or the next day, Rose sat for the first time as a High Court Judge in the Royal Courts of Justice. The press noted her appointment, but the publicity was more muted than she had been accustomed to receiving in the past. The headlines included: 'M'Lady is a Judge' (the *Evening Standard*); 'Miss Rose Heilbron A Judge' (the *Daily Telegraph*); 'Mrs Justice Mummy' (the *Telegraph*), the last of which caused her daughter endless teasing.

JUDGING IN THE FAMILY DIVISION

On her first day of sitting, as on the days that followed, Rose's work as a Family Court Judge was carried out in private, the titles of the cases often anonymously described by letters. This was because it concerned children and family breakdown, although the rules have since been relaxed. Thus, with a few exceptions, mostly where the case went to the Court of Appeal, her involvement in cases went unknown to the press and public and provided little copy. She had no choice over the work she was given. It was allocated to her, sometimes by the listing office, sometimes by the President of the Family Division. Much of the work she did was harrowing and sometimes the cases could last weeks. Many of the cases were tragic involving fostering or care orders concerning children from disadvantaged homes where the local authority had intervened because the parents were drug addicts or alcoholics and had neglected or abused their children. Others were custody or access battles between divorced parents or warring parents fighting over maintenance or lump sum payments.

As Rose herself explained in the speech she gave on her 80th birthday:

> When I went to the High Court Bench the pace of life changed. In the Family Division we were involved in many truly personal problems and we were at pains to try and overcome the many difficulties, families, and particularly children, faced.

> Sometimes we were able to solve the problems—sometimes they were intractable, but it was a challenge in many respects.

Often children would be represented by the Official Solicitor. He is appointed by order of the court and consents to represent the interests of, and act as guardian ad litem, for an infant and other persons of disability, and he would then be made a party to the ensuing litigation. He often acts in wardship proceedings where it is possible that the interests of the infant may take second place to the evidence and arguments of the adult adversary. The court thus needs the assistance of an experienced and impartial person whose only interest is the child's welfare. The Official Solicitor has other functions too, such as in appropriate cases representing persons committed to prison for contempt of court and applying for their release.

Random extracts from three of her judgments over the years, duly redacted and slightly changed to preserve anonymity, give some flavour of the difficult cases she sometimes had to try. The first case concerned a ward of court 'N', aged 4, who lived with her grandparents, Mr and Mrs Z, because her own parents, Mr and Mrs Y, were unfit. The issue revolved around whether her own parents could have access, which Rose refused:

> N was constantly moved. She had 4 homes—that would not have been so bad, but she was also taken to 4 different hostels—refuges for battered wives—during her intermittent periods with her parents, and she also had many stays of varying duration with Mrs Z. The life this little girl was forced to lead was extremely disruptive and could only result in emotional disturbance and deprivation ... there is no doubt in my mind that there has been unsavoury and corrupting conduct by one or both of these parents ... undoubtedly glue sniffing and possibly sexual misbehaviour has taken place in the home. Drugs have been mentioned, but there is no evidence before me upon which I can make any finding as to that ... There have also been several threats of suicide by Mrs Y ... On one occasion she tried to suffocate G, one of her other children, with a pillow.

The second example concerned a young girl from a professional family who were devoted to her. Sadly the girl was severely mentally handicapped and could do nothing for herself and could not communicate verbally. Her parents had struggled to look after her and coped for several years, but when she was about six years old they were no longer able to cope and had to place her in a residential establishment for handicapped children. They nonetheless saw her frequently. The county council, in whose care she temporarily was, considered that her improvement had been such that she should be placed in a foster home, but the family strongly objected. The family had found another residential home which they felt would suit her best. It is clear from Rose's judgment that she had to hear in great detail and for several days the daily goings-on of this poor child which must have been extremely distressing for all concerned. Rose concluded that the young girl, who was not able to communicate, was not suitable for fostering and that she should be returned to the care of her parents. As she commented:

> There are many reasons that have been given by the doctors, by those concerned with residential homes, by the psychologist ... and by others, which make it plain beyond peradventure that anyone with the history of J and with the unfortunate future that she is going to face, would be quite out of place in a foster home.

Finally, an example of a litigant in person. Rose's judgment began:

> This application, though not, I fear the last, is part of a series of somewhat extraordinary cases. I say at once that the facts are quite unique and exceptional.... I believe I am the eighth or possibly the ninth High Court Judge involved in Mrs Z's affairs and she has already had the services, I understand, of some 17 Counsel and approximately 8 firms of solicitors. One would look in vain for any case approaching the facts and circumstances here.

> The issue which has been at the heart of these proceedings is conduct— conduct again of a strange and sometimes unedifying aspect. As a result of a great deal of unnecessary and repetitious matter introduced by the applicant, this case has covered a massive amount of material and taken an inordinate time to try. I regret this will be therefore a somewhat long judgment.

> It also has a number of unpleasant, and again—I hope—unique features, even in the context of some of the bitterness which matrimonial proceedings seemed to engender. There has been an intensity of feeling by the applicant which has been manifested before and during the hearing and which, I regret, has never abated and probably never will.

Rose would then have to write her judgments, initially at least in longhand, working evenings and weekends and during the legal vacations. Rose only rarely complained about the cases she heard and that was usually because of some particularly trying aspect of it: it was her job, even though some of it must have been very hard to take.

There was, however, one aspect of her work as a Family Court Judge which she really loved and that was adoption cases. In those days when parents wished to adopt children they looked after them on a trial basis, and if all went well, and the social service reports were satisfactory, it was a High Court Judge's task to formalise the adoption. Often the young children came along to court as well and Rose kept a selection of toys in her room for this purpose, taking her wig off and often sitting the young child on her knee, as she would see the family first informally in her room. The joy she saw on the parents' faces when she was able formally to fulfil their dreams of giving them a family was something which understandably gave her great pleasure.

As with the Bar, the time Rose spent in court reflected only a part of the work she did as a judge. Aside from reading the papers for the case and writing her judgments which she did in long-hand or dictated as she could not type, a judge had many other commitments. Judges had to do Section 9 leave applications, as they were called—consider on the papers whether leave should be given to appeal to the Court of Criminal Appeal. Judges' views were sought on contemporary legal issues, both of practice and of reform. Judges also had to attend various judicial meetings and conferences.

Rose continued to receive many letters from the public and young students seeking her advice about life at the Bar. She also received letters from dissatisfied litigants, to which she did not reply. Some weekends she had to be on call as the duty judge in case of emergencies. On one occasion Rose took as a Marshal a young lady barrister, Gillian Temple Day. A Marshal's duties are really those of a social secretary, but the purpose is to give the young barrister an insight into the cases being tried and to learn about the judicial approach from behind the scenes. It was a mutually enjoyable experience and they kept in touch for some time thereafter.

A High Court Judgeship automatically brings with it a knight-hood in the case of a man who becomes a Knight Bachelor and whose wife then becomes Lady. There is no equivalent to Knight Bachelor for ladies and so Rose became a Dame of the British Empire (DBE). However, there was no equivalent spouse's accolade for Nat who remained Dr, a vestigial relic of the inequality of men and women which persists to this day. By a letter dated 16 October 1974, written on 10 Downing Street notepaper, Rose was informed that the Prime Minister had asked the writer to inform her that the Queen had been pleased to approve her appointment as a DBE. On 5 December 1974, Rose was received by the Queen for a private audience lasting about 30 minutes during which she was invested with the Insignia of the Civil Division of the most Excellent Order of the British Empire and henceforth was known as Dame Rose Heilbron.

LIFE ON CIRCUIT

In October 1974, Rose went on Circuit for the first time to Swansea. Her fellow judge was the charming Hugh Griffiths (later Lord Griffiths). As a Family Court Judge Rose's forays on Circuit were limited to three or four times a year. It was less than would have been the case had she been assigned to the Queen's Bench Division. On Circuit Rose would try civil and criminal cases as well as family law cases. Going out on Circuit attracted all the panoply of a previous age. High Court Judges stayed—and still do—in lodgings with a full staff of servants and a butler. These tend to be large old houses in their own grounds, it being thought undesirable that judges, while on Circuit, should mingle with potential litigants. Judges would dress for dinner and would be driven back to the lodgings for lunch. Outriders would accompany the High Court Judge to Court and back and the traffic would be stopped to allow the judges' car to pass, so the journey was relatively swift.

Life in the lodgings was, certainly in Rose's time as a judge, fairly formal, though much would depend on the other judge or judges staying at the lodgings at the same time. Some judges were great fun to be with: others, such as one judge who was teetotal, brought his own crates of apple juice with him, and though charming, may have been less of a laugh. Spouses often accompanied their husbands for at least part of their time on circuit. Nat, after he had fully retired, tended to accompany Rose almost all the time and recalled with some amusement the errands she sent him on, such as buying tights for her to wear. When not doing errands, he would while away the time exploring the town or playing golf.

Going on Circuit not only involved packing enough clothes for 2–3 weeks, a more difficult task for a woman, particularly, for someone like Rose who enjoyed dressing up, but also meant driving up to the relevant city usually on a Sunday and thereby losing part of the weekend. The High Court Judges would attend an annual Service of Thanksgiving at most key Circuit cities, but at different times of the year. There would be a civic procession into and out of the cathedral. Formality dictated that the judges entered the cathedral first and left last. The services were choreographed with precision and the judges were given detailed programmes.

The High Sheriff would welcome the High Court Judges and often sat up on the bench with one of the judges. There were other formal events and ceremonies which required the High Court Judge's presence. For example the High Sheriff of Lancashire used to hang his shield with due ceremony in the presence of a High Court Judge and Lord Derby as Constable of the Castle of Lancaster in June each year. Judges had to attend formal functions when on Circuit: and functions organised by the High Sheriff, by the Bar and the like. The High Sheriff would ask the judges to dinner and Rose frequently returned with a recipe acquired from the wife of a High Sheriff for some new dish to add to her already bulging collection of mostly untried recipes. The judges also gave dinner parties returning hospitality while staying at the lodgings. Fitting in work was not easy.

EQUALITY AT THE JUDGMENT SEAT

If 1974 was the year when Rose was feeling her way and getting her judicial feet, 1975 was the year when her judicial career took off. In April Rose went back to Liverpool in a professional capacity for the first time since she had been appointed a Judge. The family still had their home there, but Rose stayed at the lodgings during the week. It must have felt rather unreal to be sitting on the dais in St George's Hall rather than advocating from the well of the court, but no doubt the welcome she received made it all so much easier.

Rose's first reported case in the Family Division unsurprisingly struck a note for equality, but ironically in favour of the man rather than the woman. The case concerned an application by a husband for financial provision from his wife.[1] Throughout the marriage the family had depended on the wife for financial support. She had financed the children's education at fee-paying schools, purchased the matrimonial home, which was conveyed into the husband's name, purchased a house for the husband's mother and financed the family business which she ran with her husband. The issue revolved around whether the husband was entitled to a sum from the matrimonial home in addition to the transfer of his mother's house. Rose granted the wife's application and declared that she was the beneficial owner of the house, but importantly ordered her to transfer £10,000 to the husband out of the proceeds of sale of the matrimonial home, purchased four years earlier for £16,500.

---

[1] Section 23 and 24 Matrimonial Causes Act 1973.

The case went to the Court of Appeal the following year and was reported in the Law Reports.[2] Rose's judgment was upheld. Scarman LJ said:

I think Heilbron J got it absolutely right when she said in the course of her judgment:

'The factors to be taken into consideration under section 25 [of the Matrimonial Causes Act 1973] are factors relating to both parties but obviously considerations will vary according to whether the party seeking the transfer of property or lump sum is the husband or the wife'.

Of course the court has to take into account the fact that one party is the husband and the other is the wife. It has to take into account much else besides ... In the present case the judge came to the conclusion that the husband needed some capital to enable him to acquire, no doubt with the aid of a mortgage, a house suitable to his station in life and suitable for the accommodation of the three children when they came to stay with him.

He continued:

At the end of the day after a very careful judgment the judge came to a fair and sensible decision, and, speaking for myself, I rejoice that it should be made abundantly plain that husbands and wives come to the judgment seat in matters of money and property upon the basis of complete equality. That complete equality may, and often will, have to give way to the particular circumstances of their married life. It does not follow that because they come to the judgment seat on the basis of complete equality justice requires an equal division of the assets. The proportion of the division is dependent upon the circumstances. The assets have to be divided or financial provision made according to the guidelines set out in section 25. Every case will be different and no case may be decided except upon its particular facts. This is what the judge did in this case and for myself I think she came to a correct and fair decision and I would dismiss the appeal.

It was a ground-breaking decision and is still cited today. Its impact, although wide, did not attract any significant public attention, though the law report in *The Times* exclaimed 'Equality for Wives at the Judgment Seat'.

STERILISATION

In contrast, the case Rose heard in Sheffield which began at the end of July 1975 did hit the headlines. It concerned the sensitive subject of sterilisation of a young girl of 11 who was described as being 'backward' mentally and suffered from epilepsy. An

---

[2] *Calderbank v Calderbank* [1976] Fam 93.

application was made by an educational psychologist and social worker. They were backed by the Council of Civil Liberties. The application was to make the young girl a ward of court because the girl's mother had made moves to have the child sterilised in conjunction with a consultant paediatrician, who had recommended the operation and agreed to perform it. The mother feared her daughter would be seduced as she was mentally handicapped and might give birth to 'an abnormal child'. The case was heard in private and lasted five days. Rose gave a reserved judgment in public on 17 September 1975. The case was reported in the Law Reports anonymously.[3]

In her judgment Rose said:

> I first of all have to decide whether this is an appropriate case in which to exercise the court's wardship jurisdiction. Wardship is a very special and ancient jurisdiction. Its origin was the sovereign's feudal obligation as parens patriae to protect the person and property of his subjects, and particularly those unable to look after themselves, including infants. This obligation, delegated to the Chancellor, passed to the Chancery Court, and in 1970 to this division of the High Court.
>
> The jurisdiction in Wardship is very wide, but there are limitations. It is not in every case that it is appropriate to make a child a ward of court ...
>
> The type of operation proposed is one which involves the deprivation of a basic human right, namely, the right of a woman to reproduce, and, therefore, it would be, if performed on a woman for non-therapeutic reasons and without her consent, a violation of such right ...
>
> This operation could, if necessary, be delayed or prevented if the child were to remain a ward of court ... I think this is the very type of case where this court should 'throw some care around this child' and I propose to continue her wardship which, in my judgement, is appropriate in this case.
>
> In considering this vital matter [of whether to perform the operation], I want to make it clear that I have well in mind the natural feelings of a parent's heart, and though in wardship proceedings parents' rights can be superseded, the court will not do so lightly and only in pursuance of well-known principles laid down over the years. The exercise of the court's jurisdiction is paternal and it must be exercised judiciously, and the judge must act as far as humanly possible, on the evidence, as a wise parent would act ...

[3] *In re D (A Minor) (Wardship: Sterilisation)* [1976] Fam 185.

I cannot believe, and the evidence does not warrant the view, that the decision to carry out an operation of this nature performed for non-therapeutic purposes on a minor can be held to be within the doctor's sole clinical judgement.

It is quite clear that once a child is a ward of court no important step in the life of that child can be taken without the consent of the court, and I cannot conceive of a more important step than that which was proposed in this case.

A review of the whole of the evidence leads me to the conclusion that in the case of a child of 11 years of age, where the evidence shows that her mental and physical condition and attainments have already improved, and where her future prospects are as yet unpredictable, where the evidence also shows that she is unable as yet to understand and appreciate the implications of this operation and could not give a valid or informed consent, and where the likelihood is that in later years she will be able to make her own choice, where, I believe, the frustration and resentment of realising (as she would one day) what had happened could be devastating, an operation of this nature is, in my view, contra-indicated.

For these, and the other reasons to which I have adverted, I have come to the conclusion that this operation is neither medically indicated nor necessary, and that it would not be in D's best interest for it to be performed.

There was no appeal. The mother accepted the judgment with resignation. Rose hit a chord which chimed with public opinion. The case was accorded front page banner headlines: 'Judge Bars No-Baby Op' (Front page of *The Sun*); 'The Right of Every Woman— Judge Rose' (Front page of the *Evening Standard*); 'Judge Bans Bid to Sterilise Girl 11' (Front page *Evening News*); 'Anguish of Loving Mother' (Front page of *The Daily Express*). The *Daily Mail* exclaimed: 'The Humanity of Rose Heilbron'.

> We cannot recall a judgment so firm in its humanity and commonsense as Mrs Justice Heilbron's decision to ban the sterilisation of an 11 year old girl. She did more than uphold the basic right of a woman to have a baby. She upheld the right of every child to be treated as a human being— and not as a suitable case for treatment.

The Times leader article described it as: 'A wise and compassionate decision. Mrs Justice Heilbron's sensitive approach to the case ... should reassure those who feel that a court of law is not the best place to raise delicate issues of this kind'. *The Daily Express*: described it as 'A mother's judgment'. It was believed to be the first time that a court had overruled a doctor's decision supported by the parents over a child's treatment.

23

The Rape Report and More Honours

THE CASE OF *DPP v MORGAN*

SIMULTANEOUSLY WITH TRYING the sterilisation and other cases in her list as well as travelling on Circuit at the end of June 1975 to Stafford, Rose took on another task, as Chairman of an Advisory Group on Rape at the request of the then Home Secretary, Roy Jenkins. Rape has always been an emotive subject with strongly held views on all aspects of it. The establishment of the committee arose out of widespread criticism following a then recent House of Lords decision, coupled with a concerted campaign for reform on rape, led by Jack Ashley MP. Rape is an emotive subject and there was a clamour for reform.

The facts of the case were described by Mr Justice Bridge (later Lord Bridge) in the Court of Appeal as 'somewhat bizarre'. Mr Morgan was a senior NCO in the Royal Air Force. He was 37 years old, his wife 34. They had been married for 13 years and had two sons aged 11 and 12. The marriage had not been happy for some time. It was not disputed that on 15 August 1973 Morgan invited his three co-defendants, who were more junior members of the Royal Air Force, and all complete strangers to him, to his house to have intercourse with his wife, driving them there in his car and providing them with contraceptives.

The three strangers asserted that during the car journey the husband, Morgan, had told them that his wife might put up a show of struggling, but that this would only be a charade stimulating her sexual excitement, as in reality she would welcome intercourse with them. They claimed that, although they were at first incredulous, Morgan had finally persuaded them that he was serious and that their behaviour thereafter was throughout based on their belief that Mrs Morgan was indeed only play-acting. Morgan denied this.

Mrs Morgan's evidence was that she had been awakened from sleep in a bedroom which she shared with her 11-year-old son and that all four accused, including her husband, in part had dragged and in part carried her into another room which contained a double bed. She claimed that she had struggled violently and shouted 'police' several times until a hand was placed over her mouth, that both children had had been awakened, and that thereafter each of the four accused had sexual intercourse with her. As soon as the three strangers left and Morgan had gone to bed, Mrs Morgan drove to the local hospital and complained that she had been raped, her case being that she had done all she could to resist, but that she was throughout held down on the bed by three men while the fourth had intercourse with her.

She was corroborated by the oral and written statements of all four accused which amounted to complete confessions of multiple rapes. However, at their trial all challenged their police statements and asserted that Mrs Morgan was throughout a willing party. Morgan denied that his wife had struggled and asserted that she had evinced pleasure in the treatment to which she was being subjected. Three of the accused were convicted on counts of rape and aiding and abetting rape and another for aiding and abetting rape. Their appeal to the Court of Appeal that the Judge had misdirected the jury was dismissed.

The Court of Appeal however certified the following point of law of general public importance for the House of Lords to consider, namely: 'Whether, in rape, the defendant can properly be convicted notwithstanding that he in fact believed that the woman consented, if such belief was not based on reasonable grounds'.

On 30 April 1975, a majority of the House of Lords, comprising Lord Cross of Chelsea, Lord Hailsham of St Marylebone and Lord Fraser of Tullybelton, answered the question 'No', thereby reversing the Court of Appeal decision. They did not, however, quash the convictions. Instead, they applied the proviso to the Criminal Appeal Act 1968, section 2(1) and concluded that there was no miscarriage of justice on the ground that, even if the Judge had directed the jury differently, the result would have been the same.[1]

The decision was succinctly summarised in the report of the Advisory Group as follows:

> The majority of the House reached the conclusion that a man ought not to be convicted of rape unless the prosecution proved that he 'intended to do what the law forbids, ie have intercourse with a woman without her consent—or being reckless as to whether she consented or not'.

[1] *DPP v Morgan and others* [1976] AC 182.

It inevitably followed from this conclusion that a genuine belief that she had consented must exonerate the accused, because the existence of such a belief was inconsistent with what the prosecution had to prove. This did not mean that the reasonableness of the belief was irrelevant to the outcome of the case or to the practical realities of the trial. Indeed it was emphasised that the more reasonable were the grounds put forward for this belief, the more likely would a jury be to accept its genuineness, and the more unreasonable grounds, the less likely would a jury be to accept that it was true.

In short the House of Lords decided that the reasonableness or otherwise of the belief was one of the factors, but only one, which the jury should take into account in deciding whether the belief was real or genuine. The jury can, and indeed they should, be directed that in considering what the defendant did intend they should take into account and draw all relevant inferences from the totality of the evidence.

Lord Cross in his speech summarised his views by saying that a man who has intercourse with a woman, believing on inadequate grounds that she is consenting to it, though she is not, does not commit rape in ordinary parlance or in law. Lord Hailsham added:

> The only qualification I would make to the direction of the learned judge ... is the refinement ... that if the intention of the accused to have intercourse nolens volens, that is recklessly and not caring whether the victim be a consenting party or not, that is equivalent on ordinary principles to an intent to do the prohibited act without the consent of the victim.

> [In the crime of rape] the prohibited act is and always has been intercourse without the consent of the victim and the mental element is and always has been the intention to commit that act, or the equivalent intention of having intercourse willy-nilly not caring whether the victim consents or not. A failure to prove this involves an acquittal because the intent, an essential ingredient, is lacking. It matters not that it is lacking only because of a belief not based on reasonable grounds.

THE ADVISORY GROUP APPOINTED

The independent Advisory Group which Rose chaired was formally set up in July 1975, although Rose had been asked to chair it earlier. Its other members were Professor Gibbens, Professor of Forensic Psychiatry at London University and a member of the Parole Board; Dr Mia Kellmer Pringle, director of the National Children's Bureau; Professor Brian Simpson, Dean of the Faculty of Law at Kent

University; and Mrs Alison Wright, an economist and researcher. Secretarial and administrative assistance was provided by the Home Office.

No sooner had the Advisory Group been appointed than the clamour for reform escalated following another extraordinary case. A self-confessed rapist of 18, Patrick Moving, who admitted raping two women in their homes after threatening them with a knife, was released from the Old Bailey after receiving a six-month prison sentence suspended for two years. Judge Christmas Humphreys let him free with the surprising comment: 'You are at a difficult age in life and you were overcome by your sexual urges and did something you deeply regret'.

However, it was the *Morgan* case which was intended to be the focus of the Advisory Group's consideration. The terms of reference were:

> To give urgent consideration to the law of rape in the light of recent public concern and to advise the Home Secretary whether early changes in the law are desirable.

The Advisory Group was asked in particular to consider whether to recommend any change in the law as a result of the *Morgan* case, but its terms of reference were wide enough to enable it to advise the Home Secretary of any other amendments which its members thought to be urgent and necessary. Only by passing legislation could the decision be changed, as the House of Lords was the highest court in the land.

The Home Secretary had asked for the report to be in his hands by October at the latest, in time for the next Parliamentary session. It put great pressure on the Advisory Group and added extensively to Rose's workload, effectively wiping out her summer vacation. The time pressures also limited the areas of reform which the committee was able to consider. The meetings were held in London and therefore required Rose travelling, as she still retained her home in Liverpool at this time. The Group met on 20 occasions, sometimes on consecutive days, between 21 July and 1 November 1975. It sought the views of various interested parties and bodies and from foreign jurisdictions. Some 50 individuals and organisations provided written evidence. The committee additionally received written comments from many individual judges, the judiciary as a body, as well as a considerable amount of unsolicited information. It heard oral evidence from Jack Ashley MP, the Criminal Bar Association, the London Metropolitan Police, Dr David Paul and

Lord Hailsham of St Marylebone, one of the majority in Morgan. It considered numerous legal authorities and a variety of statistics. It also considered a draft bill prepared by Lord Hailsham and others drafted by Jack Ashley MP and Petre Crowder MP.

THE RECOMMENDATIONS

The report was sent to the Home Secretary on 14 November 1975. It extended to 35 pages and considered seven main issues. It had been through many drafts, including several re-drafts in Rose's hand, and was subjected to considerable discussion by the committee. It addressed first in detail the decision in Morgan. It concluded that the case had been much misunderstood and was right in principle in requiring the prosecution to establish that the defendant had to have the intention to have sexual intercourse with a woman without her consent or recklessly not caring whether she consented or not. Nonetheless, it recognised that clarification was required and recommended that the ruling on recklessness be brought into statutory form, particularly as this had not been a certified issue before the House of Lords.

Second, it considered that the nature of the belief needed to be restated. It also recommended a new definition of rape emphasising lack of consent rather than violence. Thus it suggested a statutory provision which would:

(i)   declare that (in cases where the question of belief is raised) the issue which the jury have to consider is whether the accused at the time when sexual intercourse took place believed that she was consenting, and

(ii) make it clear that, while there is no requirement of law that such a belief must be based on reasonable grounds, the presence or absence of such grounds is a relevant consideration to which the jury should have regard, in conjunction with all other evidence, in considering whether the accused genuinely had such a belief.

Third, the Advisory Group turned its attention to evidence in rape cases. Having considered the relevant legal authorities, it concluded that in contemporary society there should be some general restriction placed on the open-ended introduction of the complainant's private sexual history. This it suggested should be achieved by direct regulation of the matter rather than by the indirect threat of the introduction of the accused's bad character. There is a general principle in criminal trials that if the defence attacks the character of the prosecution witnesses it risks the defendant having his or her past criminal record drawn to the jury's attention. Such a threat, it was argued, would in any event be of no avail if the accused had no previous record, as is frequently the case in rape trials. In making such a recommendation, the Advisory Group took account of the ordeal suffered by the genuine victim of rape, balancing this against the fairness to the accused. It concluded:

> We think that this improvement in the victim's lot is justifiable, both on humanitarian grounds and on the ground that it will encourage victims to come forward and give evidence which leads to the conviction of the guilty. Secondly, we take the view that the exclusion of irrelevant evidence at the trial will make it easier for the jury to arrive at a true verdict.

The Advisory Group therefore recommended that the trial judge's discretion to permit such evidence would be guided by and based on principles set out in legislation. This should allow the judge to permit cross-examination and to allow evidence in rebuttal dealing with the complainant's previous sexual history with persons other than the accused if the judge was satisfied:

(a) that this evidence relates to behaviour on the part of the complainant which was strikingly similar to her alleged behaviour on the occasion of, or in relation to, events immediately preceding or following, the alleged offence; and

(b) that the degree of relevance of that evidence to issues arising in the trial is such that it would be unfair to the accused to exclude it.

Examples might be where the complainant had had sexual intercourse with the accused previously.

Fourth, it addressed the position of the admissibility of the character of the accused. Consistently with the general law, as set out in the report of the Criminal Law Revision Committee, the Advisory Group distinguished two situations. The first scenario was where the main purpose of the attack on the prosecution witness was directed to the credibility of the complainant or the witnesses for the prosecution. In such a case it concluded that where relevant to the accused's credibility, the accused's character or his previous convictions should be admitted in evidence, consistently with general practice and subject to the discretion of the judge. The second situation was where the attack on the prosecution witness or witnesses was necessary in order to put forward the defence, usually of absence of consent, in which case the character of the accused should not be admitted in evidence.

Fifth, the Advisory Group considered the issue of anonymity of the complainant. It recognised that seeing their names and personal details of their lives revealed in the press was one of the greatest causes of distress to complainants in rape cases. It concluded that it was in the public interest that complainants in rape cases should, in general, be given anonymity in the sense of protection from identification in the press and on radio and television. It recommended that it should only be lifted in exceptional circumstances in order that justice may be done. It suggested that this could be achieved by investing the judge with a discretionary power, upon application in chambers, to remove the restriction, where there were sufficient grounds in the interests of justice for so doing.

Sixth, the Advisory Group considered that juries trying rape cases should have a minimum of four men and four women to keep a balance of the sexes in a crime which peculiarly involved both a man and a woman.

Finally, it addressed the anonymity of the accused. It recognised the argument that it would be unfair that the complainant should be anonymous, even if her complaint was unfounded, and not the accused. Nonetheless it made no recommendation in favour of the anonymity of the accused, indicating that such a radical proposal would have to be concerned with the criminal law generally and not just the offence of rape. It concluded:

> In the first place the present position is that defendants are generally named, even in the case of murder and other most reprehensible crimes; there is no question of the name of the defendant being concealed whatever the circumstances of the case. Even in blackmail cases where the complainant is invariably anonymous it is always the practice for the defendant's name to be disclosed ... and we do not think it desirable to recommend changes in the law of rape which would make it more anomalous than it is at present, without strong justification.

> The reason why we are recommending anonymity for the complainant is not only to protect victims from hurtful publicity for their sake alone, but in order to encourage them to report crimes of rape so as to ensure that rapists do not escape prosecution. Such reasoning cannot apply to the accused. The only reason for giving him anonymity is the argument that he should be treated on an equal basis. We think it erroneous to suppose that the equality should be with her—it should be with other accused personas and an acquittal will give him vindication.

On 20 November 1975, Roy Jenkins wrote to Rose expressing his appreciation of her and her committee's work and indicating that he would study the recommendations carefully. He added:

> The circumstances which gave rise to my decision to appoint an Advisory Group made it necessary for me to ask that the work should be done very quickly. I am particularly grateful for the way in which you have met that requirement despite the considerable personal sacrifice it must have meant during the Vacation—although I am not at all sure that my sentiments will be shared by the Chairman of other committees to whom you have set such a splendid example.

The report was released to the public on 10 December 1975. It received wide publicity and a favourable press overall, though there was some criticism of failing to overrule *Morgan*. The articles summarised the recommendations, but the provisions for anonymity and a ban on cross-examination of the complainant's past sexual history were clearly the most welcome. The *Daily Express* described it as 'A reasonable reform'. *The Times* leader described it as an 'excellent report'. *The Daily Telegraph* leader headlined 'Sense about Rape'. The *Daily Mail* wrote a piece about Rose 'Woman who Led the Inquiry' alongside the main article entitled: 'Tragic Rape Victims: At Last More than Sympathy'. It said: 'Her sympathy and understanding of the human plight have many times been remarked on'.

Jack Ashley MP, whose protestations were largely responsible for the setting up of the committee to report to the Home Secretary, said he was drawing up a private bill based on the report. Mr Robin Corbett, who came second in the ballot, then announced that he would introduce a Private Member's Bill on the subject drafted with Government assistance. The bill had its second reading in February 1976, and went through committee at the end of March 1976. Following further amendments, it received the Royal Assent and reached the statute book on 22 November 1976 as the Sexual Offences (Amendment) Act 1976. The Act provided for a new definition of rape, anonymity for complainants and restrictions on cross-examination of past sexual history of complainants. It added, though not recommended by the Advisory Group, which had considered the issue, a provision for anonymity of defendants. The provision for anonymity of the accused was later repealed by the Criminal Justice Act 1988 so retrospectively agreeing with the recommendations of the Advisory Group.

Unfortunately, the provisions designed to protect women from unnecessary cross-examination of their past sexual experiences were not always strictly observed in court. A television programme about the Thames Valley Police had also highlighted problems with handling complainants in an insensitive way. Five years later, in early 1982 this led to another 'public outcry'. The controversy re-exploded after revelations that a teenage victim of rape had had her award for damages for criminal injuries cut by a third. The then Prime Minister, Margaret Thatcher MP, asked to see Rose. Rose went to 10 Downing Street on 27 January 1982 where she met with the Prime Minister, the Home Secretary and the Lord Chancellor. As the record of the meeting indicates, it was a wide-ranging discussion on the issue and Rose referred to matters which the Advisory Group had discussed and made several suggestions. Rose continued to be kept informed by the Home Office of what was being done and in March of the following year new guidelines were circulated by the Home Office to the police in relation to the more sensitive handling of rape cases.

Rape trials continue to be a source of controversy. For instance, in November 2010, the issue of the anonymity of suspected rapists was being considered for legislation and then dropped. 35 years earlier the Advisory Group had considered this same issue and rejected it.

MORE HONOURS

Professionally 1975 had been a baptism of fire for Rose as a new judge. It had also been a year for recognition of her achievements. On 12 July, she was awarded an Honorary Degree of Doctor of Laws by Liverpool University, where over 40 years earlier she had studied law, getting the First Class degree which had enabled her to begin her journey in the law. The previous evening there had been a dinner in her honour and that of her co-recipients of Honorary Degrees. Later in the year, on 27 September, the Northern Circuit held a dinner in her honour in Lincoln's Inn Hall at which her toast was proposed by David McNeil QC (her successor as Leader of the Northern Circuit and later Mr Justice McNeil). She replied. So many judges and members of the Bar attended, that it caused Sir Fred Pritchard to write the next day: 'Last night was a triumph. As I told you I do not remember a larger attendance at a Circuit Dinner'.

The year ended relatively quietly. Rose received her first invitation to the opening of Parliament on 19 November and the previous week went to Grand Day at Gray's Inn which was attended by the

Prince of Wales, a Bencher of the Inn. Christmas was spent at home in Liverpool. The family holiday was, however, short-lived. On Sunday 28 December Rose left for a two week tour of the Caribbean sponsored by the Foreign Office.

24

Settling into Judicial Life

1 976 BEGAN FOR Rose in the sunshine, some 4,000 miles away from home, but it was no holiday. Her itinerary started on the morning of her arrival in Nassau in the Bahamas, on 29 December 1975, when she called on the British High Commissioner, various Ministers and lawyers. Later in the day she addressed the Bahamas Bar Association on 'The Rule of Law in a Changing Society' and then attended a dinner given by the Chief Justice. The following day she spoke to the Rotary Club on 'The Law and the Family' and attended a dinner given by the Prime Minister and his wife.

On Wednesday 31 December, she flew to Georgetown, Guyana, via Miami, where she stayed with the British High Commissioner. The following day she met the President of Guyana, its Chief Justice and judges and attended an informal supper given by the Chancellor of the Judiciary. On 2 January, she again called on various dignitaries, went to a luncheon and gave another lecture followed by a reception.

On Saturday 3 January, she flew to Trinidad and Tobago where she stayed with the British High Commissioner. She gave two lectures entitled 'The Offence of Rape' and 'Justice and the Family'. She once again attended various functions and met the Governor General, local Government ministers, judges and others.

On 6 January, she visited Port of Spain where the following day she gave another lecture to the Bar Association on 'The Changing Law' and an informal talk to the UK Women's club.

On 8 January, she flew to Barbados, where she was met at the airport by Sir William Douglas and the Acting High Commissioner. She stayed at the Colony Club. She attended many social events in her honour and on the Monday gave another lecture.

On 14 January, she flew to Kingston, Jamaica, once again being met at the airport by the High Commissioner. During her visit she called on the Chief Justice; the Governor General; and the Prime Minister, the Hon Michael Manley MP. She gave a lecture and attended various social events, dinners, and luncheons in her honour. She left for London on Saturday 17 January.

As is apparent, the Foreign Office had scheduled a punishing tour for her with little time for relaxation and sightseeing. She was treated almost as royalty by the local communities and dignitaries wherever she went, was always met at the airport, often by the British High Commissioner, and had cars at her disposal. Nonetheless, it was a very tiring experience, not helped by the fact that half way through she contracted a nasty virus and was quite ill. In all she visited six islands in the Caribbean region, which involved much packing and unpacking of the inevitable large selection of clothes Rose took with her in order to be appropriately dressed on every occasion. Her tour received considerable local publicity and seems to have been a success. Rose too found the tour very interesting and enjoyed meeting so many local people, regaling the family with stories of her experiences on her return.

MOVING TO LONDON

Rose and Nat had decided that Rose's new life as a judge made a move to London inevitable. Nat was now 70 and had retired completely. Rose's work and life, save when she was on Circuit, was London-based. When in London she stayed at the flat in Verulam Buildings. Hilary had by now moved nearby and purchased her own one-bedroomed flat. Nat would visit, but it was difficult to leave a large house unattended for long periods. He did not like living alone in such a big house in an acre of garden which was rather isolated, even though he had Mrs Simms and others looking after him. Rose and Nat wanted to spend more time together and to be nearer to their daughter.

The previous year Rose had engaged estate agents to sell Parklands, but it was not until her return from the Caribbean that she received the first serious offer. Unfortunately the offer fell through and after engaging another firm of estate agents, a purchaser was eventually found in July 1977 at a lower price than they had hoped for. In the week of 5 September 1977, Rose and Nat vacated Parklands and moved to London. They stayed temporarily in the small flat in Verulam Buildings, hoping that a larger flat would soon become vacant in Gray's Inn. Meanwhile Rose put everything in store.

In 1978 a larger flat became available at No 2, Gray's Inn Square and, in December, after it had been refurbished, Rose and Nat moved in. Although it was a large and well-proportioned flat, it was much smaller than Parklands. Rose had wanted to buy a house in London and she had viewed several properties with Hilary, but Nat was against the idea, not least because of the toll commuting would put on Rose. He persuaded her that a flat in Gray's Inn was the solution. Rose still harboured the hope of buying a small week-end place of her own in the country rather than living in rented accommodation all the time, but this never happened. Instead, the excess of furniture in store was stored in the capacious loft space above the flat.

Nat loved living in the flat, but moving from Parklands into which she had put so much effort and energy, was a huge wrench for Rose and she really missed it. It had been her 'baby'. She had built a lovely house in a truly magnificent garden from a plot of land covered in weeds. She loved Parklands, but it was in the wrong city. She particularly missed a garden and, in later years, when Hilary had moved to a house with a garden, she loved to visit and sit in the garden. While Rose made her flat in London most attractive, she always felt it was never really hers, as it was rented from Gray's Inn. It was difficult to translate the modern decor which had inspired her in Parklands to a more traditional flat, although the antiques fitted well. She had to adjust her taste accordingly.

She also had to adjust to life in London. Rose and Nat had left their Liverpool friends behind, but were lucky enough to call on a large circle of friends in London, many based in the Inn. Rose was an assiduous participator in Gray's Inn functions and, accompanied by Nat, would attend most of the social events, particularly the concerts put on by the Inn on Friday evenings. Rose loved talking about the law and its personalities and Gray's Inn provided a medium for this, though that is not to say that she did not enjoy conversation about non-legal matters. On the contrary, she kept abreast of national and international events and enjoyed all things feminine. Living in the flat had the great advantage of being a short walk from the Royal Courts of Justice in the Strand and even nearer to Gray's Inn Hall.

Rose, when she was sitting in London, would usually take the short walk up Chancery Lane to have lunch at Gray's Inn with her fellow Benchers and thus keep in touch with other members of the judiciary and senior members of the Bar. She and Nat enjoyed a busy social life. Rose attended many formal functions, such as the Annual Dinner given by the Lord Mayor for Her Majesty's judges,

Grand Night and Guest Nights at the various Inns of Court, as well as other legal and non-legal events. On one night Rose and Nat were independently guests at a Middle Temple Guest Night.

Nat, for his part, took to London with a vengeance. He became a real tourist, taking himself off to museums and other places of interest and making good use of his Freedom Pass giving him free travel as a senior citizen as he hopped off and on buses. He also took up cooking and became a rather good cook. Rose had always spoilt him in the past by either cooking for him or having a resident cook. She always said that he could not even boil an egg—to which he would retort with one of his oldest jokes that he could boil an egg on the left side! But, always having loved his food and now with time on his hands, he became inspired. He was a bit of a natural, whereas Rose was an avid collector of recipes and would tend to follow a recipe when she cooked, Nat would experiment—and often very successfully. Rose had in recent years become vegetarian in that she did not eat red meat and was not very fond of chicken, but nonetheless it left a large repertoire for Nat's imagination.

Although, therefore, the flat had many advantages, life in London was very different. Rose missed all the domestic help she had had in Liverpool and the use of a personal secretary and found herself doing more domestic chores than she had in the past. However, Nat, as ever, kept her feet on the ground with his sound common sense and good humour and his wealth of stories and sayings.

One of the advantages of becoming a High Court Judge was that after a few years, it was possible to work during part of the legal vacations and take what is termed 'compensatory leave', ie holidays at less busy times of the year. Rose would therefore usually work for two or three weeks in August and she and Nat would take a holiday instead in June when it was less crowded. Without the burden of running a large house, it was easier to lock up the flat and leave. Hilary lived round the corner and could keep an eye on their home if they were away. Each year they would therefore treat themselves to at least one holiday abroad, favouring initially Corfu or the Algarve in Portugal. They also visited Nat's sister, Esta, and her husband, Harry, in Pretoria, South Africa, on several occasions.

PRESIDING JUDGE

Alongside the change in domestic arrangements, Rose's judicial career expanded into new territory. She sat in the Divisional Court of the Family Division, sometimes with the President of the

Family Division, hearing appeals in care and custody cases from Magistrates' Courts. She was invited from time to time to sit in the Court of Appeal, Criminal Division, along with another High Court Judge and a Lord Justice of Appeal as Chairman, hearing criminal appeals from both the Crown Court and the High Court. In 1979 she became the first female judge to sit in the Court of Criminal Appeal. In February 1980, for only the second time in history, the Court of Criminal Appeal sat outside London and held hearings in Manchester. Rose was asked to sit alongside the Lord Chief Justice, Lord Widgery, and Lord Roskill. In March 1979, together with other judges from England and Wales, as well as from other Member States, she visited Luxembourg to learn about European Community Law and how the European Court of Justice worked. The UK had joined the common market in 1973. At the same time she continued to sit regularly in the Family Division and to travel the country as a High Court Judge (Assizes having been abolished by the Courts Act 1971), choosing to return to Liverpool whenever she could, so she and Nat could see their old friends.

Rose was thus delighted when, in 1978, she was made Presiding Judge on the Northern Circuit, achieving yet another 'first' as the first woman Presiding Judge of any Circuit. It was a four-year appointment, initially as Junior Presiding Judge and then as Senior Presiding Judge. It meant that Rose's forays on Circuit would always be to the Northern Circuit. As Presiding Judge her role was to liaise with the Court Administrator and the Lord Chancellor's Office in running the Northern Circuit and the lodgings, the latter surprisingly being quite a troublesome task on occasions. In addition the Presiding Judges acted as a conduit between the Lord Chief Justice and other senior judges and the Circuit on various matters including silk and judicial appointments. Their duties extended to a whole range of issues arising on Circuit, including listing difficulties, Practice Directions and problems that had arisen with cases. They held meetings with other Judges on the Circuit, particularly the Circuit Judges (formerly called County Court Judges). Presiding Judges from all the Circuits attended regular meetings to exchange views on current issues. There was also a pastoral element to the role and Rose would encourage and advise members of the Bar, many of whom wrote to her thanking her for her help and support. All this, of course, added to her already busy workload.

After two years she became the Senior Presiding Judge and Mr Justice Hollings the junior Presiding Judge. The Circuit held a 'Rioja Alta Cenicero Dinner' in their honour on Thursday,

17 January 1982. Cenicero is a wine-making region of Spain. It was not an evening for sobriety. Seven different wines were served followed by brandy.

DEVELOPING A JUDICIAL STYLE

Rose also developed a way of working and writing judgments. As in her days as a barrister she kept copies of Law Reports duly assigned in categories. She had drawn up schedules of the damages awarded in personal injury cases for different types of injuries which her clerk kept updated, as she still tried civil cases when on Circuit. She had drafted pro forma parts of judicial directions on a large number of legal issues eg automatism, provocation, duress and many more for use when trying and summing up criminal cases. She kept a list of useful phrases which she could use in her summing up or judgments. Her large handwriting meant that the judicial notebooks, which the Court Service provided, were soon filled up. Her colour-coding and circling of evidence and Law Reports continued, though it is difficult to fathom whether purple meant good or bad and what the significance of green and red were. It probably meant no more than that those were the colours to hand.

She tended to write out her judgments first in longhand and then ask her clerk to type them. There would often be several re-drafts before any judgment was actually delivered. Charles Waller retired after a couple of years and was replaced by John Leach, who remained her devoted clerk until she retired. In more complex cases, particularly when she was trying criminal cases and had to direct the jury, she would sometimes analyse the evidence in columns. For example in a conspiracy case she used the headings: suppliers or agents, goods, data, costs, documents, person concerned, exhibits, payment. Judgment writing was, and still is, a lengthy process and demanded many hours of work which had to be fitted in around daily court appearances and other commitments. Rose in fact wrote out a document entitled 'Important Judgments'. This described the stages she should go through in drafting a judgment with 17 stages for a judgment containing facts and six stages if it was a legal issue only. Whether she kept precisely to her guidelines in practice is not clear. In those days judges did not take time off to write judgments. Long judgments were written in the vacation, but summings-up to a jury could not wait and required the burning of much midnight oil.

There were occasional press reports of some of the criminal cases she tried, and the odd amusing snippet, but the massive publicity she used to receive was, with one exception towards the end of her judicial career, a thing of the past. The headlines in these days were more to do with the case than with Rose, the Judge: so different from when she had been a young silk. Contemporary examples included: 'Man Attacked his Wife with Garden Fork'; 'Bachelor Fails in Bid to Prove He is the Father'; 'Judge Saves the Crescent'. One amusing piece appeared when she sat at Carlisle in 1980. 'Upon My Oath! M'lud is a Lady' exclaimed the *Evening News* and *Star*. The *Daily Mail* commented:

> She rules with a rod of silk! ... She was the pin-up of the Law Courts in the 1960s, her regular features smiling under her wig as she moved determinedly into the fancy-dress masculine world of English law ... In the North, they like to say that Heilbron rules her courtroom with a rod of silk—smooth and elegant, but very tough.

Rose needed all her talents to deal with her next case.

'MR ASIA'

On the morning of Sunday 14 October 1979, two members of a sub-aqua club were exploring the murky waters of a disused, flooded quarry, known as the Delph, at Eccleston near Chorley in Lancashire, when they made a gruesome discovery. They came upon a handless, mutilated corpse weighted down by means of heavy iron weights. The body was that of Martin Johnstone. The body was so disfigured and butchered that his identity was only ascertained because of the Chinese medallion around his neck. Ironically the inscription on the medallion apparently bore the Chinese characters for 'long life'. Martin Johnstone was 27 at the time of his death. He had been born in New Zealand. He had been a notorious drug dealer operating in the Pan Asia region, particularly, Singapore, New Zealand and Australia, such that he was dubbed 'Mr Asia'. In 1980 the *Auckland Star* alleged that police and taxmen in four countries were hunting assets of about US$50 million in cash and assets from drug deals organised by Martin Johnstone. He had lived the high life and was apparently on the surface an engaging and charming character.

His empire had grown, as had the number of people involved and the tensions within, as individuals started jockeying for position in the hierarchy. Ultimately, it became an international drug organisation or syndicate which spread its tentacles much wider globally to include Australia, the United States and ultimately the United Kingdom. Johnstone became a senior member of this international syndicate. The syndicate operated by using numerous couriers as the means of transporting the drugs from country to country and many millions of dollars were involved.

Johnstone's murder had been orchestrated by another senior member of the syndicate, one Terry Clark, a ruthless operator, who aspired to be its controlling force. He has been variously described as the mastermind or 'Mr Big', but his orders were carried out by others. He was also from New Zealand originally and was 36 years of age. He went under a series of aliases, including the one under which he was ultimately charged for murder, namely Alexander James Sinclaire. He likewise lived the jet-set playboy life and was alleged to have stashed away £25 million in secret bank accounts from his world-wide drug dealing. He had previously been charged and acquitted in Australia of the murder of two other members of the syndicate.

The Trial in Lancaster

Sinclaire and four other members of the syndicate, Andrew Maher, James Smith, Keith William Kirby and Frederick Russell were charged with Johnstone's murder. The case unsurprisingly acquired the epithet: the handless corpse case. All five pleaded not guilty, although Maher and Russell later changed their pleas to guilty. Conspiracy charges were also brought against them and other members of the syndicate in relation to the importation and sup-ply of heroin, which elicited some pleas of guilty from some of the other defendants. The case came on for trial by jury on 5 January 1981. It was held at the Crown Court in the historic Lancaster Castle which had once served as a prison.

Part of the castle dates back to the twelfth century, but the court was built in the Gothic style in the late eighteenth century as part of a substantial modification of the castle. The court had to be modified to cater for so many defendants, to provide room for the number of counsel and to ensure appropriate security arrange-ments. Strict security was provided throughout the trial. Rose, with her enormous experience of the criminal law and criminal cases, was nominated by the Lord Chief Justice to be the trial judge. There were 12 defendants initially arraigned, represented by 23 counsel including 11 silks. In addition the prosecution team comprised two silks and junior members of the Bar from both the Northern Circuit and London.

The prosecution alleged that the motive for the murder was that Johnstone had short-changed the syndicate by failing to account for monies and by cutting or diluting the heroin that was being supplied to another syndicate member. Michael Maguire QC for the prosecution opened the case to the jury by explaining that it was the prosecution's case that:

> On the night of the 20th–21st September 1979, at Sinclaire's flat at 57 Stamford Court, London, Sinclaire made it clear to Maher, who was subordinate to Johnstone in the hierarchy, that Johnstone had to go, and it may well be that it was put in such a way that if Johnson did not go, then Maher himself would have to go, but the intention was and the position was, in the Crown's submission, that it was an order from the syndicate boss, Sinclaire, that Johnston was to be killed. Now, the decision having been made to kill Johnstone, Maher played Judas. It was a cowardly and despicable act. Maher the Judas telephoned Johnstone who was then in Singapore, Maher being in England, and he told Johnstone that he, Maher, had negotiated a drugs deal in Scotland, but that it could not be concluded because the people at the other end of the deal wanted Johnstone's personal attendance ... There was no drugs deal. It was a lie and a charade, but the sort of bait that might bring Johnstone to this country, and indeed Johnstone swallowed the bait and decided to come, and Sinclaire promised to provide Maher with a gun and ammunition.

The case was extremely complex given the international nature of the drugs dealing, involving the peddling of cocaine and heroin through a web of channels and the laundering of the proceeds over many years. There were a large number of people involved in the syndicate, extending far beyond those charged at Lancaster and covering several countries. A huge number of witnesses were called. Some of the defendants, including Sinclaire, did not go into the witness box, choosing instead to make statements from the dock and thereby avoid being cross-examined. There were many legal applications during the hearing made in the absence of the jury and a vast number of legal authorities considered.

The case lasted 121 days. The jury ultimately considered three charges of murder and 13 of drugs conspiracy, some defendants having changed their pleas to guilty on some charges. The jury deliberated for six days. Sinclaire, Billy Kirby and James Smith were found guilty of Johnstone's murder. Three more members of the syndicate were found guilty of drugs offences in addition to two others who had previously pleaded guilty to such charges. Three defendants were acquitted of all charges including Karen Soitch, Sinclaire's young lover and a barrister from New Zealand.

It was, as Rose said during sentencing, 'a most pre-meditated, brutal and chilling murder, carefully organised, well planned, and carried out down to the last gruesome detail'. Rose sentenced Sinclaire to life imprisonment as she did the other defendants guilty of murder. She made a recommendation that Sinclaire and one of his henchmen, Andy Maher, should each serve a minimum of 20 years, while for another she recommended a minimum sentence of 10 years. Sentences were also handed down for the drugs offences. It had been a very costly trial. She made a costs order against Sinclaire for £1 million and made lesser costs orders against some other defendants.

In sentencing Sinclaire, Rose commented:

> You are a ruthless and dangerous man who pursued an evil trade, and you have been convicted of being the mastermind behind this most terrible drug syndicate. You and others peddled misery and death, and that syndicate or some of its members with you at its head, moved to this country and began operations intending to make vast fortunes for its members ...

> It is apparent you had no more time for Johnstone, your erstwhile friend and ex-business associate. He cheated you and other syndicate members. He had to be killed and you organised and ordained that terrible murder. You masterminded it.

It had been a long ordeal for all involved in the case. Rose had effectively decamped to Preston Lodgings where appropriate security could be provided, making the journey to Lancaster each day. She stayed there for the duration, coming home only on occasional weekends. Nat had accompanied her and would sit in court many days listening to the case. The work involved had been enormous. As a judge Rose had to keep on top of the case on a daily basis so that, when the evidence and closing speeches were concluded, she would be ready to analyse and sum up all the evidence in a way the jury could understand and to give any appropriate legal directions.

At the end of the trial Rose was given as a memento of the case, a sketch of the courtroom scene showing the lawyers involved. Unlike her earlier days as a practising barrister, where Rose herself would have been the news, the press now concentrated on the facts of the cases she tried as a judge, the references to Rose being no different from those which would have been made had it been any other male High Court Judge who had been trying the case in question, although there was the occasional exception. That Rose could be accepted as a judge in such an important and difficult case without reference to her being a woman was in itself a great step forward. By all accounts she tried the case well and with the utmost fairness. The only criticism noted of her handling of the case was that she gave too much latitude to the defence which lengthened the trial. Others, however, explained that this was a shrewd move, because it prevented a re-trial which would have been even more costly.

Some of the defendants sought leave to appeal before the Court of Criminal Appeal. Sinclaire and Kirby, who had both pleaded not guilty to murder and were found guilty of murder, appealed against their convictions. Their complaints against Rose's handling of certain issues and her direction to the jury were thrown out as being without merit and they were both refused leave to appeal. Similarly Hinckman was refused leave to appeal against his drugs conspiracy conviction. Two others, who had pleaded guilty to conspiracy charges, had their sentences reduced from 13 to 11 years on the ground that a greater discount should have been given for the fact that they had pleaded guilty. The Court of Appeal also varied the costs order. The issues related to an apparent over-estimate of costs given to the court by the prosecution on which basis Rose had made her order and other legal issues.[1]

The case was of both national and international interest. If anything, the drugs syndicate's operations were more high profile in New Zealand and Australia where other cases, including murder charges, concerning various members of the syndicate and Sinclaire, were pending or had been tried. In 1981 the Australian Government together with three state governments set up a Royal Commission to enquire into drug trafficking and the activities of Sinclaire (also spelt Sinclair aka Clark) and his associates. Books have been written about the syndicate including *Greed* by Richard Hall and *The Mr Asia File* by Pat Booth.

Rose's minimum sentence meant that Sinclaire would be imprisoned until 2001. However, in August 1983, Sinclaire was found dead from a heart attack in Parkhurst prison and with him died the secret location of the £25 million fortune he allegedly had made from drug smuggling.

---

[1] *R v Sinclair and others* [1983] QB 784 (CA).

THIS AND THAT

Rose remained in demand as a speaker and guest. On 24 November 1977, she addressed the 150th Anniversary Dinner of the Printers Charitable Corporation, a Royal Festival Banquet held at the Connaught Rooms in London. The function was attended by 900 guests, including all the press barons of the time and many media figures. Rose proposed the health of the President, the Prince of Wales, and the Prince of Wales responded. Eric Cheadle, Chairman of the Council of the Corporation, read a message from the Queen, Patron of the organisation. Nat and Hilary were also invited and Hilary was presented to the Prince of Wales.

In 1978 Rose was awarded an Honorary LLD at Warwick University, the second of six honorary degrees and fellowships she received in her lifetime. The others doctorates were from Manchester University, Sir John Moore's University and Liverpool University. She was also made an Honorary Fellow of UMIST and of Lady Margaret Hall, Oxford, Hilary's former college.

Rose also acquired—or not—as the case may be—an ancestor. In 1976, John Burrell, the then senior partner of Farrer & Co, the Queen's Solicitors, very kindly wrote to Rose on his retirement to offer her an oil painting left to him by a cousin, which he had mentioned to her some years earlier. The painting was a portrait of Ferdinand Herscher Heilbron who died at the age of 28 in 1631, the age he was painted. He is painted wearing a lovely lace collar. On the index finger of his right hand are two rings and that hand holds two roses. The picture is of no particular value, but it includes a Coat of Arms. John Burrell generously offered the picture to Rose 'in case by any chance the chap was a member of the family!' Whether young Ferdinand, who adorned a wall in Rose's flat, was an ancestor of Rose's has not yet been resolved!

In January 1981, Rose had been elected President of the Association of Lancastrians in London, whose Patron is Her Majesty the Queen, Duke of Lancaster. The Association provided a most enjoyable link with her home county, Lancashire, and she and Nat over the years enjoyed attending their gatherings. Her term of office coincided with the Sinclaire case and Hilary stood in for her at one event attended by over 100 people in May. However, Rose and Nat were able to attend the Annual Dinner and Dance at the Grand Ballroom in the Dorchester Hotel, London later in the year. In her capacity as President, Rose sent a message to the Queen as the Association's Patron, which read:

> The Association of Lancastrians in London assembled at the Dorchester Hotel on the occasion of their seventy-sixth Annual Dinner in humble duty to your Majesty and mindful of your gracious presence as Duke of Lancaster tender to your Majesty unswerving loyalty and warm affection.

Her Majesty the Queen replied on Buckingham Palace headed notepaper on 23 October, the day of the Annual Dinner and Dance thus:

> I warmly thank you and all members of the Association of Lancastrians in London, assembled for your 76th Annual Dinner, for your kind message of loyal greetings. As Duke of Lancaster and Patron of the Association, I received this message with much pleasure and send my best wishes for a very enjoyable evening.

In October 1982, Rose's tenure as Presiding Judge came to an end. She received several effusive thank-you letters, most notably from the Permanent Secretary at the Lord Chancellor's Department, Derek Oulton CB, and the Lord Chief Justice, Geoffrey Lane, with both of whom she had worked closely in that role. Appointment as a Presiding Judge is often an indication that the judge will be elevated to the Court of Appeal when a suitable vacancy arises. There had, at that time, never been a female judge in the Court of Appeal. Earlier in the year Sir John Donaldson had replied to Rose's congratulatory letter to him on his appointment as Master of the Rolls adding: 'you ought to have been in the C.A. long ago and I do hope that it will not be long before you join us'. But it was not to be.

Nonetheless, two other events which had significance for Rose took place in Liverpool during this period. First, chronologically, was the unveiling of her portrait at her Alma Mater, the University of Liverpool, commissioned by the Faculty of Law, followed by a dinner for Rose and Nat given by the Vice Chancellor of the University. The portrait, painted by Charles Oliver, a local artist, shows Rose dressed in her red robes, but without a wig, and stands today in the entrance to the Faculty of Law.

Life's coincidences struck again. Mary, the daughter of the much-loved family gardener, Mr Cartmell, wrote to Nat out of the blue the following year to tell him of the sad news that her father, then a widower, had passed away. She worked as a part-time secretary in the Law Faculty and had seen Rose's portrait, which she liked.

She had apparently been present at the unveiling ceremony and now passed it each day on her way to work. Mary said that her father had always kept a photograph of Rose in pride of place in his bedroom. The letter gives an insight into the loyalty and devotion Rose always engendered in her staff, who often stayed for many years. The previous gardener, Mr Belcher, who had helped design the garden and was described by the family as 'the Professor' for his deep knowledge of plants and trees, had only left because of old age and ill health. His parting had only one advantage, the family was relieved of Rose, who had a loud voice in any event, shouting to the deaf Mr Belcher for all to hear. Mrs Simms worked well into her eighties until the family left Liverpool. Mrs Shepherd on Rose's retirement from the Bench wrote:

> Every time I pass 'Parklands' I look in and think of all the happy and interesting years I spent working there with you. I enjoyed every moment of it and felt quite sad when you moved to London and that era had ended.

The second event was the opening by Her Majesty the Queen of the new Liverpool Law Courts on 2 April 1983. Rose was present and it is believed was presented to the Queen. It was the end of an era, for St George's Hall, the venue of so many of Rose's famous cases, and where Nat had first caught a glimpse of her, ceased to be used as a building to house the courts. Today, its black grime cleaned away, it is a heritage centre and is used for conferences, exhibitions, concerts and other events. Its demise as a court must have caused some nostalgia, not just for Rose, but also for the many others whose career had flourished in the court-rooms in St George's Hall.

On 19 August 1984, Rose turned 70 and celebrated her 70th birthday at a small dinner at Hilary's flat with family. She still looked much younger than her years. She was lucky to have had a wonderful complexion and was keeping her weight within bounds, always a constant battle. Nat had apparently persuaded her not to dye her hair, as he liked it grey. Yet her grey hair, enhanced with some colour, remained thick and shiny and with regular styling was, on Rose, still youthful. In a postcard to wish her Many Happy Returns, Lord Elwyn Jones commented that 'somebody once called that [being 70] the old age of youth'. Although now the age when most people had long retired, Rose still had enormous energy and there were some new horizons yet to conquer.

25

The Final Years before Retirement

ELECTION AS TREASURER OF GRAY'S INN

GRAY'S INN ALWAYS had a special place in Rose's heart. It was therefore a particularly poignant moment in her life when, in the autumn of 1984, she was elected Treasurer of Gray's Inn for the calendar year 1985. She was its first woman Treasurer and the first woman to be Treasurer of any Inn of Court. In the same way as her election a decade earlier as Leader of the Northern Circuit, it was an accolade preferred by her peers and, as such, had a profound significance for Rose personally. Aged now 70, she had just beaten the age limit for holding the office of Treasurer.

The Treasurer is effectively the President of the Inn for one year and addressed by everyone in the Inn as Master Treasurer, whether male or female. Aside from the undoubted prestige such a position bestows, it brings with it a huge burden of work which the Treasurer has to undertake alongside his or her daytime duties. Thus Rose continued in her judicial role as normal.

The Treasurer has many roles. He or she is effectively the Chairman of the Inn for his or her year of office, the Under-Treasurer being the Chief Executive of the Inn. The Under-Treasurer in 1985 was Rear-Admiral Christopher Bevan CB. The Treasurer chairs various meetings and committees of the Inn and presides at Pension addressing the junior Bencher—Master Junior. Pensions are the meetings of Benchers held in legal term time to take important decisions concerning the Inn. The story is told by one of the former members of staff at Gray's Inn, Richard Moore, that Rose needed some training on how to use the wooden gavel which is supposed to descend gently onto a glass block. Rose apparently did this with such gusto at the beginning of dessert one evening, ie when after dinner, coffee and fruit are taken by the Benchers, that Richard Moore was compelled to utter a quiet word in her ear, but to no avail. She did exactly the same the second time, but amazingly the glass survived!

The Treasurer also represents the Inn in relation to matters concerning the profession and attends meetings with representatives of the Bar Council and Treasurers of the other three Inns of Court namely: Lincoln's Inn, Middle Temple and Inner Temple. 1985 was a particularly busy year for the legal profession. First, there was a working party of the Senate, one of the bodies governing the profession to examine entry to the profession. Secondly, there was a committee set up under Lord Rawlinson, a former Attorney General, on the constitution and composition of the Senate. The Chairman of the Bar at the time was, until October 1985, David Calcutt QC and thereafter Robert Alexander QC (later Lord Alexander of Weedon), who was recognised as the leading advocate at the Bar of his generation and in the same chambers as Hilary. Then there were the normal problems which beset the profession which required consideration.

In addition the Treasurer will lunch at the Inn as often as possible, attend all dinners during dining terms, including moots, debates, Guest Nights and Grand Nights. He or she also entertains in his or her official role and invites other judges and lawyers and friends to suppers, concerts and the like. All these events seemed to prompt copious and effusive thank-you letters to Rose for most enjoyable evenings. Dining in dining term time retains certain rituals, each Inn having a variant on the other. In Gray's Inn, apart from the toasting rituals, previously explained, after dinner, the students and barrister members of Hall bang on the tables which prompts the appearance of the chef who walks up to the top table accompanied by a barrage of clapping to be given a glass of port or wine by the Treasurer. Then, before the days of smoking bans in public places, the junior student, which in practice meant the one sitting at the far end of Hall, would ask the Master Treasurer for permission to smoke.

The Treasurer's role includes becoming involved with the students of the Inn and participating at training weekends at Cumberland Lodge in Windsor Park. He or she calls barristers to the Bar on Call Night, saying a few words of encouragement and congratulation, all such talks having to be prepared in advance. He or she is involved in the discipline of students. The Treasurer attends Sunday chapel services at the Gray's Inn Chapel. Rose even dug the first spade of earth on the site of a new building project in the Inn.

The Treasurer also receives many invitations in his or her official capacity and attends Grand Days at the other Inns, formal dinners at the Law Society and other legal and non-legal associations, as well as the normal functions associated with being a High Court Judge, such as the annual dinner for Her Majesty's Judges at the Mansion House. As Treasurer, he or she also has to give many speeches.

In July 1985, the American Bar Association held its annual conference in London. 20,000 American lawyers and their families attended and the pace of social life accelerated for the duration. Arrangements were made at all the Inns to accommodate them for various functions and meetings. Whether it was then or on another occasion, Rose met the first woman US Supreme Court Judge, Justice Sandra Day O'Connor, who is an Honorary Bencher of Gray's Inn and brought her back to the flat for a drink to meet Nat. A special event was the reception followed by dinner at Marlborough House given by Sir Shridath 'Sonny' Ramphal, the Commonwealth Secretary-General, and Mrs Ramphal for Commonwealth and American lawyers to which Nat and Rose were invited. The guests included the former Prime Minister, James Callaghan (later Lord Callaghan).

Many of these functions were formal black tie (tuxedo) events. Unlike a man with one dinner jacket and a few shirts, Rose needed to have a selection of long and short evening dresses. Hilary had found her a dressmaker and thus she was able to have some individually designed eveningwear, a saving of both time and cost. She still enjoyed dressing up for events, time permitting. Nat was, as many husbands learn to be, unusually patient about how long it would take her sometimes to get ready, chastising Hilary once when she suggested some new form of make-up, saying that it would take her mother even longer to get ready.

The year of being Treasurer is normally a very busy year. 1985 was no exception, but Rose thoroughly enjoyed it and addressed it with her usual zeal and enthusiasm. Rose's year of office did produce a few particular highlights. On 15 May 1985, Gray's Inn held a dinner in celebration of the '250th Anniversary of the Appointment of the Metropolitan Bench' in the presence of Her Majesty the Queen and His Royal Highness the Duke of Edinburgh. Rose, as Treasurer, presided and sat on the top table next to the Queen at dinner. It was stated to be the first time that the Queen had been to Gray's Inn and in the letter the following day from her Private Secretary he commented: 'It is unusual for The Queen to come to such a historic place not far from her own home for the first time and you may have noticed how much Her Majesty enjoyed the visit'.

Rose had a further opportunity to dine in the presence of Royalty later in the year. There were two Grand Days at Gray's Inn in Rose's year of office. Guests wore Court dress or evening dress and decorations. Rose took a personal interest in the menus. The Treasurer selects the guests from all walks of life including leading judges, Treasurers of other Inns and Ambassadors. Rose had great fun making up the guest lists and a galaxy of famous people attended. On her first Grand Day, on 9 May 1985, the guests included: Sir John Arnold, the President of the Family Division; Jacques Viot, the French Ambassador; Sir Yeheudi Menuhin, the famous violinist; Sir Simon Townley JP, the Lord Lieutenant of Lancashire; Robert Robinson, the broadcaster; Dame Mary Donaldson, the former Mayor of London; the Treasurer of Middle Temple, John Mills QC; His Excellency The Hon JA Walding, the New Zealand High Commissioner; and Anthony Hopkins, the actor and film star. Other invitees appeared to decline with genuine sadness, but for unavoidable reasons. On one Grand Day Hilary attended with some friends and sat in the well of the Hall with other barristers, sharing the enjoyment of the rituals and drinking out of the Loving Cup declaring before each sip 'To the pious glorious and immortal memory of Good Queen Bess' (Elizabeth I).

The guests at her second Grand Night were equally illustrious and included: Sir John Donaldson, the Master of the Rolls and husband of Mary Donaldson; Sir Alec Guiness, actor and film star; Ludovic Kennedy, the writer; Viscount MacMillan of Ovenden; Mr Kingman Brewster (formerly the American Ambassador to the Court of St James); the Treasurer of Inner Temple, Judge Sir William Stabb QC; Lord Rawlinson; Lord Weidenfeld of Chelsea, the publisher; the Treasurer of Lincoln's Jean-Pierre Warner; and Brigadier Helen Meechie WRAC.

Guest Nights provide an opportunity for members of Gray's Inn, including barristers and students, to return hospitality personally to friends and colleagues. The Treasurer is no exception and Rose invited several guests during her year of office. On one such Guest Night Rose had a hopefully welcome surprise. The late Richard York QC, a Bencher, decided to play a little trick on Rose and enlisted Hilary's support. He announced that he was bringing a guest called Miss Joy Bronfille. In fact this was a pseudonym and Hilary was his guest, still then a junior barrister, and she sat at high table with the Benchers.

Each year Gray's Inn holds a summer garden party on the last Friday in July, known as the Treasurer's Reception, and the Treasurer receives the guests. Rose acquired a new outfit comprising a light blue and white silk dress and jacket and matching hat for the occasion. She invited many personal guests from the profession and a few friends and Hilary also attended with friends, likewise with a new dress.

THE INN EXPRESSES ITS GRATITUDE TO ROSE

Perhaps one of the most poignant moments of the year was when Gray's Inn decided to commission a portrait of Rose to be painted for posterity. It was a great honour, for it happens rarely. The painter ultimately decided upon was the delightful June Mendoza, whose earlier portrait of the Prince of Wales already hung in the Inn. The portrait has been universally acclaimed as a dazzling likeness of Rose dressed in her scarlet judicial robes. It has been variously described as 'magnificent' and 'stunning' and has attracted other superlatives to describe it. June Mendoza got Rose's pose to perfection with her left hand on her hip and her right hand resting on the judicial mantle with the wig on a stand, set against a background of the arches of the Royal Courts of Justice. She even used a little artistic licence to give Rose the narrow waist and slim figure to which she always aspired, but did not always achieve, despite her prolific diets.

Rose would go for sittings to June Mendoza's house in Wimbledon and they became good friends, enjoying each other's company and visiting each other with their husbands socially. In 1987 the portrait was exhibited at the Royal Society of Portrait Painters 93rd Annual exhibition at the Royal Portrait Gallery. The large painting now hangs prominently for posterity in the entrance to the large Pension Room on the first floor of Gray's Inn and has been much admired. Rose obtained from June Mendoza a signed print of the portrait for Hilary which sits on a wall in her study.

All Treasurers and their wives traditionally receive a gift at the end of their tenure. The Treasurer's gift varies, but his wife usually receives a small gold brooch in the shape of a Griffin, the Gray's Inn emblem. A different sort of gift had to be conceived for Rose and a larger version of the spouse's brooch was decided upon.

In addition all Treasurers have a shield displayed in the Inn with their Coat of Arms. The College of Arms discussed the appropriate heraldry directly with Rose, who formally had to petition the Garter King of Arms for the Coat of Arms. It took some time to resolve, because Rose was known professionally under her maiden name and married women generally only bear Arms in conjunction with the Arms of their husband. At the end of August 1988, Mr Dickinson, the Rouge Dragon Pursuivant of the College of Arms, wrote to Rose in these terms:

> The first of two shields is suggested as Arms of Heilbron. The wellhead alludes to the meaning of the name and the cormorant (or liver birds) above is a direct reference to Liverpool. The scales represent your

legal career and judicial position whilst the roses do double duty as Lancastrian symbols and as a play on your name.

I have kept the design of your husband's Arms as simple as possible. The rods of Aesculapius are frequently used in heraldry to denote the medical profession. The inflamed towers are suggestive of the inflamed castles (also on a blue background) which make up the Arms of Dublin.

The shields will be combined to represent your marriage heraldically, your own Arms being placed on a small shield in the centre of your husband's Arms. Your husband's Arms have been designed to take account of this, so that all the elements will remain clearly identifiable when the Heilbron Arms are added.

The coat of arms now hangs in Gray's Inn alongside the arms of all other former Treasurers.

At the first Pension in January 1986, as is the tradition, the Senior Bencher makes a speech thanking the past year's Treasurer for his services. This task fell to Lord Edmund Davies, the former Law Lord. Rose wrote to thank him for his kind words and while what he said at Pension is not recorded, what he wrote in reply to Rose's thank-you letter is:

I have read your letter with very real appreciation and I thank you warmly for it. But I can assure you that I was being purely clinical in my tribute to you at Pension on January 15, for your year as Treasurer was in truth outstanding.

Its historical significance was and will remain important as a milestone on the road to emancipation. There were, however, additional qualities in its texture which were in their way unusual and one of them was unique. Other Treasurers have also been dedicated and hard-working, but your tenure of office occurred at a critical phase of the Inn's history. It is one which calls for unflinching courage in maintaining the supremacy of Pension over all subordinate bodies whose powers are strictly revocable. That courage you steadfastly manifested throughout and, after reflection, I considered it my positive duty as Senior Bencher to draw attention to it.

Gray's Inn will forever be indebted to you, and if only you knew you would know why I pay tribute to you by saying: 'Da, was olda a ffyddlon!'

I should perhaps add that we all appreciate that without Nat's cooperation and support throughout you could never have achieved such a triumph, and he deserves and already possesses our great gratitude.

There were also some more amusing reminiscences. In November 1985, Woodrow Wyatt, former Member of Parliament, journalist and

Rose in judicial robes

Rose attending shield hanging ceremony at Lancaster Castle, 1980

Rose and Nat at Judges' Lodgings

Rose having a fit of the giggles, 1990

Rose as Treasurer of Gray's Inn, 1985

As Treasurer of Gray's Inn calling a student to the bar, 1985

Rose on her 70th birthday

Rose at 79

Rose and Nat on Rose's 80th birthday

The family on Hilary taking silk, 38 years after her mother, 1987

Mother and daughter on Hilary taking silk in 1987

Family gathering on Nat's 85th birthday, 1990

Rose's 80th birthday party at Gray's Inn, with the Lord Chief Justice, Lord Taylor and the Treasurer of Gray's Inn, Sir Iain Glidewell, 1994

author, wrote the second of two autobiographies entitled 'Confessions of an Optimist'. In the book he recounted how in 1939, just married and down from Oxford, he read for his Bar Finals at the Temple just before he joined up for the war and:

> There, fickle in mind, I would gaze speculatively at the beautiful Rose Heilbron, also reading for the Bar. The perfect Portia, she became a judge in 1974. Maybe being sentenced by a beautiful judge is better than being sent down by an ugly one.

The following May Rose was given an Honorary Fellowship by the University of Manchester Institute of Science and Technology (UMIST). The oration delivered by Professor KM Entwistle included this tale, which has a ring of truth about it:

> One can hear Shylock reiterating his opinion of Portia, 'you know the law, your exposition hath been most sound'.

> Her concern for the weighty matters of the law does not cloud her attention to points of detail. On one occasion when she was entering the Judges' Lodgings in Preston, she wished to draw the High Sheriff's attention to dry rot in the skirting boards. High Sheriffs, as part of their outfit, carry swords. So it was that the High Sheriff and the Judge were kneeling on the floor—the High Sheriff testing with his sword the proposition that the wood was rotten, when in walked the butler to announce the service of dinner. The High Sheriff hastily explained what they were about, which earned the sceptical Lancastrian response 'I bet that's what they all say'.

After the excitement of her year as Treasurer, Rose was able to concentrate more exclusively on her role as a Judge. However, in December 1986, history was made once more when Rose sat with Mrs Justice Butler-Sloss (later the first woman President of the Family Division) and Mrs Justice Booth as a Divisional Court, the first all-female Bench.

ABORTION

The penultimate year of Rose's legal career was a memorable one for Rose both professionally and personally. In the middle of February 1987, Rose was asked by Sir Stephen Brown, the President of the Family Division, to deal with a very urgent and high-profile case concerning abortion. Robert Carver, a post graduate student from Magdalen College, Oxford, was attempting to prevent his former girlfriend, with whom he had had a casual relationship, and who was then 21 weeks pregnant, from aborting their child. He was a member of the Oxford University Society for the Protection of the Unborn Child and his case was backed by the pro-life lobby. The legal limit for abortion was 28 weeks. He based his case on the claim that the foetus was capable of being born alive under the terms of the Infant Life Preservation Act 1929 and, that as a father, he had a right over the foetus. The operation had originally been scheduled to take place on 23 February, but the doctors had refused to carry it out pending the decision of the court. The doctors had certified that the abortion should take place for the sake of the health of the female student concerned.

The case was of considerable urgency. The hearing took five days of affidavit evidence and legal submissions with nearly 30 legal authorities being cited. Allan Levy acted as amicus curiae, literally friend of the court, to provide an independent view and assist the court. At the hearing's conclusion Rose, then 72, sat up until 4 am writing her judgment which was about 30 pages long, and delivered it on 23 February, the day originally scheduled for the abortion. She concluded that the applicant was not entitled to an injunction to prevent the abortion either in his own right or on behalf of the foetus.

This controversial and emotive subject attracted huge publicity with banner headlines such as headlines: 'You Are Not Alive' (Front page of the *Daily Mirror*, 24 February); 'Sentenced Not To Be Born' (Front page of the *Evening Standard*, 23 February). The applicant father appealed leading to further headlines such as 'Let My Unborn Baby Live' (Front page of the *Daily Mail*); 'Don't Kill My Baby' (*The Sun*). Rose's picture in her judicial robes was splashed across many newspapers.

The case was unusual for the speed with which it travelled through the hierarchy of the courts. On 24 February, the day after Rose's decision, the case was heard by the Court of Appeal which dismissed the appeal.[1] Five hours later three Law Lords refused leave to appeal. It was in those days one of the quickest legal actions in British judicial history. It reached the House of Lords within 36 hours of Rose's ruling. Abortion always produces strong reactions by people with genuinely held beliefs. This case was no exception and the press coverage and articles and editorials for and against the decision continued for some time. One article describing it as an historic judgment said: 'The real question is not abortion

---

[1] *C v S* [1988] QB 135.

per se, but whether a man has a right to force a woman to have a baby against her will'.

On her retirement, Allan Levy wrote to Rose commenting: 'it was a privilege to be amicus and a small part of the case which has been communicated to many other jurisdictions and will always be a landmark case'.

A SECOND SILK IN THE FAMILY

A few weeks later Hilary learnt that she had been appointed silk aged 38, and 38 years after her mother had achieved that position. She was the twenty-ninth female silk ever appointed and one of the first two female silks appointed who practiced in the Commercial Court. There were still only 25 women practicing silks at the Bar. One morning, a few weeks later, the family, along with other families, attended a ceremony in the House of Lords and Hilary swore an oath to the Lord Chancellor, Lord Hailsham. In the afternoon the new silks appeared in the Lord Chief Justice's Court and other courts where they were called to the Inner Bar. The Lord Chief Justice, Lord Lane, had invited Rose to sit alongside him and Mr Justice Cantley in his court for the ceremony, Nat looking on. Rose uttered these words as her daughter stood up and bowed:

> Miss Hilary Nora Burstein Heilbron, her Majesty having been pleased to appoint you one of her counsel learned in the law, you will take your seat within the Bar accordingly.

> Miss Heilbron, Do you move?

Hilary appropriately bowed again to the court and to her colleagues. It was a poignant family moment.

A POSTSCRIPT

On 2 May 1987, Fenton Bressler, lawyer and criminologist, wrote an article in the *Evening Standard* entitled 'Rosie's Special Appeal'.

> Mrs Justice Heilbron and known at the Bar as 'Rosie' has in her fourteenth year as a Family Division Judge achieved yet another first …

> She has now won the unique accolade of three Appeal Court judges and three Law Lords saying she was correct in her Oxford abortion case judgment—within a bare 36 hours of the precedent-making ruling.

I would have expected nothing less. In fact, to my mind, the disgrace is that Rosie was not one of those Appeal Court Judges.

It is an affront to women that we in England still do not have a woman member of the Court of Appeal; and there could be no finer appointment than this brilliant and popular North Country woman ...

If she were a man, she could have been expected to be appointed a High Court Judge, at the latest by the time she was 50. As it was she had to wait until 1974 until she was 60.

And, perhaps because she was a woman, she was not appointed to the Queen's Bench Division where her vast experience as a criminal practitioner could best have been put to use presiding over major criminal trials. She was shunted into the Family Division.

But Rosie has been a great success there: a handsome Jewish mother with a warmth and a common sense that have made her particularly outstanding in cases dealing with children.

Yet she has been permitted the odd foray back into her old world: in 1981 she presided over Britain's most expensive trial to date ... when the international drug trafficker, Alexander Sinclair was convicted of the grisly murder of an associate ...

Rosie promptly showed she had lost none of her steely mettle from the old criminal days. With more courage than most judges who shy away from giving minimum recommendations when sentencing in murder cases, she said that Sinclair should serve at least 20 years in jail.

We could do with her in the CA.

It was not to be. Although disappointed that she was never promoted to the Court of Appeal and never really understanding why, Rose took it in her stride. She had had a remarkable career and had achieved great things. The Court of Appeal was a step other women would achieve in due course.

26

Retirement

AGED 74, ROSE did not relish the prospect of retirement, but she was resigned to it. Judges appointed in the 1970s, as she was, had to retire at 75 (the age has now been reduced to 70). Nat had for some time been eager for her to retire. He was by then 83, being nine years older than her, and had himself been fully retired for 13 years. He wanted them to be able to spend more time together. She decided, therefore, to retire a year early. As she had not been appointed a High Court Judge until she was 60, she relinquished a little of her pension, as qualification for a full judicial pension would have required 15 years of service on the Bench (today it is 20 years). After nearly 50 years in the law, retirement was going to be a dramatic change to Rose's life.

She retired on 1 November 1988. As is customary for retiring judges there was a valedictory. It was held in Court 22, the court of the President of the Family Division, then Sir Stephen Brown. The court was packed. Nat and Hilary were, of course, present, as were many members of the Northern Circuit and family practitioners. Hilary sat robed in the front row of the court and her father sat in the public gallery. There were several speeches from representatives of the Family Division, solicitors, and the Northern Circuit. Then Hilary rose to speak, something which she had pre-arranged with the President as a surprise for her mother. As her area of practice and law was different from her mother's, she had never before addressed her as a judge. As Hilary rose to speak she noticed tears welling up in her mother's eyes. Perhaps with hindsight she should have warned her, but it was too late and her mother fortunately composed herself. Hilary's address was as follows:

> May it please your Lordship and Ladyship. Although neither a member of the Family Bar nor the Northern Circuit I hope nonetheless that I qualify today to speak from the Bar as a member of the family, your Ladyship's family, in what is for me both a first and last opportunity

to address your Ladyship with a degree of formality and deference which your Ladyship is not normally accustomed to receiving from her daughter at home!

Despite taking some members of the Court by surprise I have, I hope, on this exceptional occasion a reasonable prospect of avoiding a judicial sanction from your Ladyship, and if not I see looking around me the prospect of an instant appeal! It is not for me to add to the warm and wonderful words which I have just listened to with very great pride, but I am most grateful to the President for permitting this filial interruption. It is therefore with the greatest of pleasure that I am able today, in this Court, to add my own good wishes to the many others which your Ladyship has received. I know that my Father joins with me in wishing you a long, happy, fulfilling and enjoyable retirement.

The President responded:

You (Mr Coningsby) have said, and Mr Hytner and Mr Tatham have added their contribution, how she has won the hearts of the Bar, and I believe of the public. She has certainly won the hearts of the Bench and indeed of the Court of Appeal.

Rose, by now, somewhat overcome with emotion, spoke briefly:

I start off by saying that I am nearly—not quite—but nearly speechless, and I am not usually lost for words ... Last but not least to my dear husband and my dear daughter, who gave me quite a shock when she rose to address me. I could not have done any of it without your love and understanding. Thank you all.

GRATITUDE AND ADMIRATION

Later that day Rose held a party for her fellow judges, colleagues and friends in the Law Courts. Her clerk had arranged the most splendid cake, with icing which depicted a woman in red judicial robes. She received many lovely letters and cards on her retirement with reminiscences and flattering comments, saying how much she would be missed and wishing her and Nat well. There are so many to choose from, but the following, from different stages and different perspectives of her career, give a flavour of the esteem and affection in which she was held far better than any narrative.

The Lord Chancellor, The Right Honourable the Lord Mackay of Clashfern, wrote:

Your retirement is an event of importance and a matter of widespread sadness, in which I share. I cannot let it go without thanking you for your many years of service on the Bench.

After nearly 50 years in the law, your record is deeply impressive, bearing in mind your academic achievements and your distinction as one of the first women silks and recorders. As a barrister and as a judge, you have pioneered the way for the many women who will follow you. This alone is an achievement of which you must be proud. Furthermore, you have contributed to the profession as Leader of the Circuit, as Treasurer of your Inn, as Presiding Judge and in many other ways.

You end your career with the admiration and approbation of the whole professional community, and the good wishes of all.

I hope that you and your husband will have a long, active and happy retirement.

The President of the Family Division, Sir Stephen Brown, wrote:

It has been a great privilege to serve in the Division with you … yours has been a remarkable career and we are all very proud of you. You should feel very satisfied having completed the course so magnificently.

Another Judge wrote:

Every now and again a person comes to the Circuit who not only makes a mark in their work and in their progress to elevation to the High Court bench, but who captures the respect and love of the whole Circuit in so doing. There are not so many people of such calibre, but there can be no conceivable argument that you are and always will be one of them.

I have never heard a word about your professionalism and your total fairness in all matters, other than one of praise and that places you in an even smaller category of those who have succeeded in our profession.

What an amazing career you have had.

A solicitor, who used to instruct Rose when at the Bar, and then a Circuit Judge, His Honour Judge Goldstone wrote:

May I write as a Solicitor who instructed you and who learned that a famous Silk could and did care about the problems, mistakes and traumas of ordinary people. You showed to all of us that success did not exclude compassion. I know I learnt a great deal from you and, I believe, so did many others.

You took those qualities on to the bench and they will be sorely missed. It must please you to know that a growing number of lawyers try to follow your example.

The Mayor of Burnley wrote:

You have always been held in special affection here in Burnley where you served us with loyalty and distinction as 'our' Recorder … we have always been very proud and happy about this association. One of the most prominent acknowledgements of this is the new Crown Court which you so kindly opened in 1981.

Sir Desmond Heap, solicitor to the Corporation of London, wrote: 'You have blazed a wonderful trail ... I congratulate you upon it all. Amidst all the pomp and ceremony ... you never ceased ... to look like a woman'.

A letter from Lord Lane, then the Lord Chief Justice, who did not normally deal with family law cases, deserves special mention. It read:

> I'm not in the habit of writing to chaps in the Family Division for reasons which are obvious. You, however, are in a different league, and I can't let the occasion go by without a personal note of thanks (tinged with sadness) for all you have done over the years to help make the wheels (some of which are square) go round more smoothly. Not merely the hard work side of it, even more important, the charismatic aspect has owed much to your benign influence over the years. It's going to be very hard to fill the gap which your departure will leave.
>
> You and that other precocious youngster, Nat, are likely to have many years of active enjoyment left to you. You've both deserved them and you depart with my thanks (and the delightful advantage of my blessing) for all you've done for justice over the years. That sounds pompous— rather in the style of Auntie Marshall, but it's heartfelt for all that. Jan sends her love and so does Geoffrey.

Perhaps the greatest accolade as a judge comes from those to whom he or she dispenses justice. In 2002, Rose received a letter out of the blue from a man in Canada. This one was particularly moving for it is rare for judges to learn what happens as a result of their decisions and sad that Rose was no longer by then able to understand its significance. He wrote:

> Twenty four years ago you did me the greatest service one human being can provide for another, when you awarded me custody of my nine year old son ... I hardly expect you to remember the details; but I want you to know that the instructions you gave me were carefully followed.

He then went on to detail how he had brought up his son and the great successes his son had achieved. He wrote that after attending university in the United States and at Cambridge he had read law and is now a District Attorney in the United States and doing extremely well and himself married. He then commented on Rose's perception of the evidence and how she had believed him against his wife's accusations about him. It ended: 'You may not remember any of this: but please know that you have my eternal gratitude'.

A TIME FOR RETROSPECTION AND REFLECTION

The end of a career is a time for retrospection and reflection. What was the source of Rose's phenomenal success? Undoubtedly she excelled at her job. She established a rapport with juries who were said to have 'hung on her every word', listening intently to her speeches, all the more so because of her fame. She had a particular ability in her final speeches to encapsulate issues in ways a jury could understand. She often brought to them a feminine angle. She was eloquent with a good command of language. She had a facility for finding just the right words or phrase to make her point. She was also an incisive and effective cross-examiner.

Equally, she had the ability to articulate and speak clearly and concisely, with appropriate and occasionally dramatic intonation. She could throw her voice while retaining its pitch so that it carried around the court. These were clearly forensic advantages. She was by all accounts a good tactician and a fighter for her clients, not lacking in courage in standing up to judges. She was also a very good lawyer with a first class brain and argued many a difficult legal point in all the courts of the land. She was thorough in her preparation and mastery of a whole range of areas outside the law from medicine to machinery and from ships to ballistics. None of this came without hard work often late into the night.

Timing and luck undoubtedly played a part. Her career path coincided with a slow progression of women in the professions in the twentieth century. The War gave her a head start when so many male barristers were away, but had she not excelled at what she did she would have lost her practice on their return. Liverpool in particular provided many famous cases.

She never set out to be a pioneer. Yet undoubtedly her success and high profile encouraged other women to become barristers. She broke down barriers making it easier for other women to follow. She was not a strident feminist, but she believed strongly that women should have an equal role in society and had a valuable contribution to make. She was aware that progress was slow, yet remarked on the strides that had already been made and the new opportunities that were opening up.

She never underestimated the importance of the homemaker, yet she recognised the untapped talents and source of work that women provided. Her pleas for equal pay for women and for women to be able to return to work after their children had grown up were examples of her forward-looking approach. She understood the problems facing a working mother. Yet she managed to have a normal home life as wife and mother. Nat provided unyielding support in every way. He did not travel and to that extent she was lucky in having family at home always to be there for her daughter. She undoubtedly had tremendous energy and stamina, a necessary qualification for a working mother, even one with domestic help.

She never gave interviews or posed for photographs. Her good looks and lovely smile no doubt endeared her to the press, as did the novelty of her position. The press photographs of her always seemed to catch her smiling face. She retained her modesty and was diffident by nature, turning down offers for books, articles and interviews even after she retired and was free to do so. In her own career she recognised the quality of patience and accepted that things came later to her because she was a woman, but she got there in the end. Above all she loved her work, the law and enjoyed the legal fraternity and camaraderie which came with it.

ADJUSTMENT TO RETIREMENT

Retirement was therefore a tremendous adjustment for Rose, for the law had not only been her career, but also her life. She could have gone on sitting from time to time as an extra judge, but she decided on a complete break. On retirement she still retained an acute interest in Gray's Inn as a Bencher, though when she reached 72 she could no longer attend Pension, the Inn's meetings, but she still regularly attended Guest and Grand Nights and the Inn's social activities with Nat. Having a daughter at the Bar was another way of keeping in touch, but it was not the same. She missed being part of it.

Rose always loved discussing the law and legal issues and she found in Hilary a ready sounding board. But once such discussions became abstract and she had moved away from the daily hurly-burly, they had less meaning. After they had moved to London in the mid-1970s Hilary saw her parents regularly, often going to supper to their flat at the weekend or inviting them to her flat and, later her house, where sometimes they would stay overnight. Occasionally the family still managed to have holidays together. But Hilary had her own life. In later years, and particularly after retirement, Rose, by now getting older and without any secretarial help, would rely on Hilary more. She would regularly compile a list of questions on which to ask Hilary's advice, ranging from whether she should accept an invitation or how she should reply to a letter or just whether she should buy a new dishwasher. Sometimes Hilary would help her draft speeches and do a little typing for her.

The flat at 2 Gray's Inn Square, whilst comfortable, exceptionally conveniently situated and relatively spacious, being rented from the Inn and without a private garden, was not a home to Rose in the way Parklands had been. When, after retirement, Rose was spending much more of her time at home, she felt the absence of a house and garden she owned more acutely than when she had been working. Nonetheless she redecorated and partly refurbished the flat in 1995. She did find some of the domesticity of life, when unrelieved by legal work, rather dull, particularly since by this time she had less domestic help than she had had in earlier periods of her life.

She was, however, getting older, and could not do as much as she had before. Hilary's attempts to try to persuade her to learn how to use a computer fell on deaf ears. Nonetheless, Rose and Nat seemed to while away their days happily enough, watching television— she was a great fan of the 1980s hits 'Dallas' and 'Dynasty', doing errands and correspondence, shopping for food which Nat loved and, after nearly 60 years of marriage Rose was resigned to, visiting friends and Hilary, enjoying other social activities and having nice holidays, initially abroad and later in England. They did a little entertaining either in the flat, but more often at the Garrick Club, where Nat was a member and which they both enjoyed.

In addition Nat was always there with his jokes. He would leave dotted around the flat funny little notes for Rose to find unexpectedly which made her laugh, often signing with a fake name such as Hannibal, Sebastian or Pedro, but in his unmistakable handwriting. Rose kept most of them, as she did all his letters. They show the deep love they had for each other throughout their marriage and as Rose once said towards the end of her days, 'old love' is special. She also got used to being told irritatingly when she dropped something that it was 'on the floor' or when Nat was feeling below par that 'he would not fight a tiger'.

It is, however, a wonder that she could read his notes as Nat, like many doctors, had notoriously illegible handwriting, such that in 1963 he received this letter from HM Inspector of Taxes who had clearly had a sense of humour:

> I have received the enclosed medical certificate from a Mr X, who is a member of staff of this Income Tax District. That much I was able to decide by reference to the handwriting on the envelope in which the certificate was forwarded.

From what Mr X is suffering I am not quite clear but I suspect the word on the certificate is 'Chill'. It could not be 'Mitral Valvotomy', otherwise there would be more squiggles on the certificate.

I am sorry to trouble you, but I have to report to Somerset House the precise nature of Mr X's illness and the Board's doctor would not stand for a facsimile of the outline on the certificate unless, of course, this particular marking is a code sign between members of the medical profession.

Yours sincerely (and long suffering)

H.M. Inspector of Taxes.

Having worked all her life, Rose did not really have a hobby other than her family and her home and the hobbies of her youth were no longer practical. She did not have many professional female friends, as there were few of her generation who were working women. Her female friends were largely the wives of colleagues or of Nat's friends. Nat, on the other hand, always had his sport, if no longer to play, at least to watch. He continued going to the MCC to watch cricket and the test matches until his nineties and thereafter watched it all on television. After the onset of Rose's illness and later death, his keen interest in sport and the ability with Sky television to watch all forms of sport at any time of the year from all around the world was his lifeline.

After retirement Rose was still feted at events and invited to grand occasions. For instance she was a guest at several Grand Nights of other Inns. On 10 May 1990, Lord Justice Parker, then Treasurer, invited her to Lincoln's Inn Grand Day. Other guests included: Princess Margaret, Sir Geoffrey Howe, the Duke and Duchess of Grafton, Dame Ninette de Valois, Lord Alexander and Lord Slynn. On 22 November 1994, Sir Christopher Slade invited her again to Grand Day at Lincoln's Inn. She attended the celebration dinners given in honour of Hartley Shawcross's 90th birthday given by JP Morgan where she had pride of place sitting next to him, and she also attended the House Dinner held for him at Gray's Inn.

She still received invitations to give interviews about herself or her cases and was asked more than once to appear on Desert Island Discs, but declined.

On 18 May 1989 the Circuit gave her a retirement dinner. She replied to the toast, and reminisced:

People so easily forget that practice, except for a very few, was hard work and no sinecure materially. Yet we were dedicated and devoted to our profession despite the poor remuneration, the lack of Legal Aid and even in forma Paupers Cases.

The injustices were so great that Legal Aid had to come to the assistance of the public. But the scheme had its ups and downs—recently more of the latter. In those far off days it could be a real struggle to get started and even more so for women.

ROSE'S 80TH BIRTHDAY

On 19 August 1994, Rose celebrated her 80th birthday quietly with Nat and Hilary. Hilary had wanted to throw a large party for her, but she resisted. Ultimately the matter was taken out of both mother and daughter's hands when, at the instigation of Dick Stone, a fellow Bencher and his wife Sue, and the then Treasurer of Gray's Inn, Sir Iain Glidewell, Gray's Inn gave her a House Dinner. It is an honour bestowed only rarely, the previous one being for Lord Shawcross's 90th Birthday in 1992. Instead, as her birthday present, Hilary had made for her a glamorous long couture evening gown to wear for the occasion.

The dinner, which took place on 28 October 1994, was over-subscribed. It was a very happy and memorable occasion filled with friends, colleagues and the elite of the legal world: the then Lord Chief Justice, Lord Taylor; the previous Lord Chief Justice, Lord Lane; and the Master of the Rolls, Lord Bingham (later Lord Chief Justice and Senior Law Lord) among the many dignitaries. The Treasurer and Rose both gave speeches. In her speech Rose awakened some of the more junior invitees to the difficulties she had had in her early years at the Bar and making them roar with laughter at some of her jokes and reminiscences. She added:

> This is a very emotional occasion for me and I cannot begin to express my deep gratitude to Iain, Richard and Susan and many others for all their trouble and hard work in producing this magnificent celebration. Never in my wildest dreams did I expect to see so many of my friends, some of whom have travelled a great distance to be here to honour me. I am quite overwhelmed.

She also received many wonderful letters from both old friends and colleagues, including those living abroad, who were unable to attend the celebration. Hartley Shawcross wrote:

> I find it difficult to believe that so many years have passed since we first met ... This makes me all the more anxious to send you my best wishes for very many more happy returns of the day.

The Hon Dame Roma Mitchell AC DBE, Governor of South Australia, and the first Australian woman judge in 1965, wrote:

> May I join with your many admirers in congratulating you upon the attainment of your 80th birthday on 19th August 1994 (ten months after mine!). I well remember my elation when you became Queen's Counsel in 1949, then a remarkable achievement for a woman. The celebratory dinner on 28th October will be a great tribute to you not only as a Bencher but also as a trailblazer for women in the law.

The following year brought Rose particular personal pleasure when Hilary was herself elected a Bencher of Gray's Inn and she watched her accorded 'Voice and Vote' at Pension, making them the first mother and daughter Benchers of the Inn.

Had she been alive, Rose would also have been thrilled and deeply honoured to have known that, in June 2012, Gray's Inn named after her the ground floor room which is situated under the archway between South Square and Gray's Inn Square, calling it the 'The Rose Heilbron Room'. It is used as a modern IT equipped conference room. Above all it is a further recognition of the affection with which she was held in Gray's Inn and of her status in the legal profession.

ILLNESS STRIKES

Little was anyone to know at the time, but Rose's 80th Birthday party was in reality to be one of her last major appearances on the legal stage. Illness strikes unexpectedly and is no respecter of convenience. Rose had been fortunate in that she had had 80 years of remarkably good health, but her twilight years were blighted by illness. In her early eighties she started to exhibit the first symptoms and signs that something was not quite right and her behaviour was at times marginally odd, which was most unlike her. Nat had noticed it, and being a doctor clearly recognised the symptoms. Not having witnessed dementia before, Hilary rather shrugged her shoulders, as there was not much that could be done, for in all other respects she led a normal life. Even with the benefit of hindsight it was probably better that Rose had the extra years of relative normality than being at the hands of doctors. Nat was the one who suffered most as he had to live with it.

In 1997 Hilary had decided to renovate and extend her house: a major project estimated to last six months with the inevitable dust and mess. Midway through the building works Rose's symptoms worsened and Hilary called for the doctor. Things came to a climax and Rose was admitted to hospital and then, as she had temporarily become unable to walk, to a nursing home for a few months. Nat moved in with Hilary and the builders for three months, probably no bad thing as it was a distraction, even if heartily difficult for a 92-year-old, as he then was, to live in a limited number of dusty rooms surrounded by packing cases, builders' mess and props holding up walls.

After a few months Rose was able to return to her flat where she was cared for by a stream of different carers and by Nat and Hilary, but she had several further admissions to hospital with a broken femur and various infections. Eventually, in July 2000, looking after her in the flat became impractical as her illness was degenerative and although it was something Hilary had vowed she would never do, there was no option with a 95-year-old father but to move her permanently to a nursing home accessible both to the flat where Nat lived and to Hilary's home. The family provided a daily personal one-to-one carer for her in addition to the regular nursing staff to ensure that she had the best possible care. She never returned to her home: it was thought it would be too upsetting, but as the nursing home was near to where Hilary lived, for the first few years she was able to spend days out at her house.

Rose did not suffer from classic Alzheimer's, although no one really knows. She was said to have a form of vascular dementia, ie parts of the brain just died following a series of small strokes. The diagnosis was largely irrelevant as the symptoms exhibited by both causes are very similar. The consequence was a gradual and progressive deterioration of her brain on its long journey into oblivion. With it came the accelerating loss of the ability to communicate in any normal sense and a slow physical degeneration. The thing that always haunts the relatives of a sufferer, as it did Rose's family, is what she really knew or felt and whether and what insight, if any, she had into her condition, particularly in the earlier stages of her condition when at times she was clearly frustrated and did have lucid periods. She recognised Nat and Hilary almost to the end and, even at the end, Hilary sensed she knew who she was—maybe the maternal instinct overcomes all. Fortunately, she was never in any physical pain. She retained her beauty throughout her illness, looking much younger than her years, always seemingly enjoying having her hair done or lipstick put on her. She was ill altogether for over eight years.

In one respect she was lucky. Nat, who after all was considerably older than her, was fit enough to visit her regularly, which he did unfailingly and lovingly, initially daily and later twice a week right until the end in his 100th year. It was a very sad and difficult period for him—he had lost his lifelong companion in any meaningful sense and yet she was there physically. Hilary was also a very regular visitor and tried to do her best for her. She too had lost her mother and saw only the physical shell of what had once been a wonderfully warm and vital personality with a first class brain. The roles had been reversed and in reality Rose was now the child, increasingly dependent on others for her needs. It is a reflection on the ephemeral nature of fame that, although she was hugely famous in her time, in the end the only people who really mattered were her husband and daughter. It is hoped that in some way in those later years she recognised their love for her and it was a comfort to her.

She lived long enough for Nat to celebrate his 100th birthday on 25 July 2005 and for them to celebrate their diamond wedding on 9 August 2005, receiving two cards from the Queen, neither of which events sadly registered with her. She died peacefully, aged 91, in the afternoon of 8 December 2005, Nat and Hilary at her bedside.

AFTER ROSE'S DEATH

Even after her death the last vestiges of early discrimination remained, a telling reminder, if one was needed, of what she had had to endure. Since the Judicial Pensions Acts of 1959 as amended in 1981, all surviving spouses of High Court Judges have been entitled to a widow's pension, which represented a percentage of a judge's pension. When the legislation was introduced there had been no female High Court Judge. The position was rectified by the Courts and Legal Services Act 1990 and the judicial pension of the High Court Judge was extended to widowers. However, Rose was appointed in 1974 and retired in 1988. The other two female High Court Judges had survived their husbands, but Rose pre-deceased her husband. Despite attempts by Hilary to get a modest ex gratia payment for her father as, then aged 100, it was unlikely either to create a precedent or be very costly, the powers that be would not agree. Thus Rose remains in history the only High Court Judge who, since judicial pensions were introduced, has not been able to provide a pension for her surviving spouse through no fault of her own, other than being a woman.

Three months later, on 20 March 2006, Gray's Inn held a Memorial Service for her at the Temple Church. Rabbi Weiner of the West London Synagogue, the Synagogue of which both Rose and Nat were members, officiated together with the Master of the Temple Church, Robin Griffith Jones and the Rev Roger Holloway, the Preacher from Gray's Inn. Nat was initially against the idea, but in the end came round and hopefully found it comforting. It was well attended, given that by then so many of Rose's contemporaries had passed away, and had lovely music. Sir Charles Mantell, an old friend of the family, and Sir Alan Ward, the then Treasurer of Gray's Inn, gave readings. Hilary gave a personal address and Sir Christopher Rose, another very close friend, gave the other address. Hilary concluded as follows:

> And so to her legacy. I would like to think that just as she inspired me to come to the Bar, her success has been an inspiration to other women to follow in her legal path. What was so unusual 50 years ago is now commonplace. She was indeed a woman before her time. And despite the fact that she would be the last person to take any credit for it, she did indeed blaze a trail for women in the law ...

> We, her family, her friends and colleagues have all been enriched by having known her. To adapt Shakespeare: she was not a Rose by any other name: she was that Rose. She was indeed a remarkable person: barrister, judge, colleague, friend, wife and mother in all of which roles she excelled. May she live on in our memory.

Epilogue

WRITING MY MOTHER'S biography has been for me an amazing journey, providing a reminder of what she achieved and the way she did it, blazing a trail as she went. But above all, it has been a reminder of her as a mother and of her love and guidance, for to me she was always 'Mum'—my Mother and professional mentor and inspiration. In so doing I have tried, though I am sure not always successfully, to engender some detachment from the subject and not to put her on a pedestal.

I have also tried to portray her not just as a barrister, but also in her role as a wife and mother with insights into her daily home life. My Mother was not perfect, as she would have been the first to admit, otherwise she would have been a much less interesting person. However, it remains incontrovertible that amongst the many thousands of pages of print from newspapers, letters and other sources that I have read, I have only ever seen her described in glowing terms. It is true that the press were less critical 60 years ago, but her career spanned many decades and it was always the same flattering and favourable coverage, as can be seen by the reader.

Undoubtedly her success and uncritical fame must have caused some jealousy at times. Some of her colleagues may have considered her less good a lawyer or advocate than they were, justifiably or otherwise, but in the end she won them all over.

My Father outlived my Mother by four and a half years, passing away on 23 June 2010, one month short of his 105th birthday. He had lost his companion in any real sense many years earlier when my Mother took ill. He missed her dreadfully. He had many interests and friends and loved his family, but from that first glance across a cavernous court-room in St George's Hall, my Mother had been the centre of his life and it was a love story that lasted over 60 years.

Nonetheless, he retained his zest for life and kept his mental abilities until the end. Unlike my Mother, he was aware that I was writing her biography and was pleased I was doing so, regularly providing me with anecdotes from his phenomenal memory. He had lived through it all. My Mother justifiably described him as her tower of strength. He had fulfilled the role of male consort impeccably at a time when it was unusual to have a career wife, let alone one as successful as my Mother. He was very popular in his own right and much respected and admired. Even in his second century he always had time for everyone making them laugh with one of his many jokes. He would have been so touched that Gray's Inn lowered the flag to half-mast on his death, although unlike my Mother, he had no direct association with the law.

There was one recollection of which my Father was particularly proud and he repeated it to me many times. He wanted me to put it in her biography as it in a sense epitomized my Mother's struggles and her qualities, and so I do. It occurred at a dinner towards the end of her judicial career, where she was to give a speech to the Northern Circuit, the Circuit where she had appeared as a barrister all her working life and later, less frequently, as a judge.

Chatting before the dinner to the late Lord Justice Russell, a good friend, my Father commented: 'Rose is a bit concerned about what to say in her speech—she hopes it will be alright', to which Pat Russell responded: 'Nat, it does not matter what she says—they all love her here'. It is a fitting epitaph for a remarkable woman, my Mother.

Index

Please note that references to RH refer to Rose Heilbron